Citizens into Dishonored Felons

Studies in German History
Published in Association with the German Historical Institute, Washington, DC

General Editor:
Simone Lässig, Director of the German Historical Institute, Washington, DC, with the assistance of **Patricia C. Sutcliffe**, Editor, German Historical Institute

Recent volumes:

Volume 28
Citizens into Dishonored Felons: Felony Disenfranchisement, Honor, and Rehabilitation in Germany, 1806–1933
Timon de Groot

Volume 27
Brewing Socialism: Coffee, East Germans, and Twentieth-Century Globalization
Andrew Kloiber

Volume 26
End Game: The 1989 Revolution in East Germany
Ilko-Sascha Kowalczuk

Volume 25
Germany on Their Minds: German Jewish Refugees in the United States and Their Relationships with Germany, 1938–1988
Anne C. Schenderlein

Volume 24
The World of Children: Foreign Cultures in Nineteenth-Century German Education and Entertainment
Edited by Simone Lässig and Andreas Weiß

Volume 23
Gustav Stresemann: The Crossover Artist
Karl Heinrich Pohl

Volume 22
Explorations and Entanglements: Germans in Pacific Worlds from the Early Modern Period to World War I
Edited by Hartmut Berghoff, Frank Biess, and Ulrike Strasser

Volume 21
The Ethics of Seeing: Photography and Twentieth-Century German History
Edited by Jennifer Evans, Paul Betts, and Stefan-Ludwig Hoffmann

Volume 20
The Second Generation: Émigrés from Nazi Germany as Historians
Edited by Andreas W. Daum, Hartmut Lehmann, and James J. Sheehan

Volume 19
Fellow Tribesmen: The Image of Native Amerians, National Identity, and Nazi Ideology in Germany
Frank Usbeck

Volume 18
The Respectable Career of Fritz K: The Making and Remaking of a Provincial Nazi Leader
Hartmut Berghoff and Cornelia Rauh

For a full volume listing, please see the series page on our website:
http://berghahnbooks.com/series/studies-in-german-history

Citizens into Dishonored Felons

Felony Disenfranchisement, Honor, and Rehabilitation in Germany, 1806–1933

Timon de Groot

First published in 2023 by
Berghahn Books
www.berghahnbooks.com

© 2023, 2026 by Timon de Groot
First paperback edition published in 2026

All rights reserved. Except for the quotation of short passages
for the purposes of criticism and review, no part of this book
may be reproduced in any form or by any means, electronic or
mechanical, including photocopying, recording, or any information
storage and retrieval system now known or to be invented,
without written permission of the publisher.

Library of Congress Cataloging-in-Publication Data

Names: De Groot, Timon, author.
Title: Citizens into dishonored felons : felony disenfranchisement, honor, and rehabilitation in Germany, 1806–1933 / Timon de Groot.
Description: First edition. | New York : Berghahn Books, 2023. | Series: Studies in German history ; Volume 28 | Includes bibliographical references and index.
Identifiers: LCCN 2022054605 (print) | LCCN 2022054606 (ebook) | ISBN 9781800739581 (hardback) | ISBN 9781805391128 (open access ebook)
Subjects: LCSH: Ex-convicts—Suffrage—Germany. | Felon disenfranchisement—Germany. | Germany—Politics and government—1789–1900. | Germany—Politics and government—1871–1933.
Classification: LCC JN3809 .D35 2023 (print) | LCC JN3809 (ebook) | DDC 364.8094309/034—dc23/eng/20230118
LC record available at https://lccn.loc.gov/2022054605
LC ebook record available at https://lccn.loc.gov/2022054606

British Library Cataloguing in Publication Data
A catalogue record for this book is available from the British Library

EU GPSR Authorized Representative
LOGOS EUROPE, 9 rue Nicolas Poussin, 17000, LA ROCHELLE, France
Email: Contact@logoseurope.eu

ISBN 978-1-80073-958-1 hardback
ISBN 978-1-83695-386-9 paperback
ISBN 978-1-80073-959-8 epub
ISBN 978-1-80539-112-8 web pdf

https://doi.org/10.3167/9781800739581

The electronic open access publication of *Citizens into Dishonored Felons: Felony Disenfranchisement, Honor, and Rehabilitation in Germany, 1806–1933* has been made available under a CC BY-NC-ND 4.0 license with support from the German Historical Institute Washington.

This work is published subject to a Creative Commons Attribution Noncommercial No Derivatives 4.0 License. The terms of the license can be found at http://creativecommons.org/licenses/by-nc-nd/4.0/. For uses beyond those covered in the license contact Berghahn Books.

Contents

List of Figures	vi
Acknowledgments	viii
List of Abbreviations	x
Introduction	1
Chapter 1. "Rights of Citizenship Are Conditional Rights": Disenfranchisement, Honor, and Trust in the Criminal Codes before German Unification	19
Chapter 2. Institutions of Honor: A Leveling Society Seeking to Protect Its Institutions	48
Chapter 3. Political Offenders vs. Common Criminals: Challenging the Distinction	82
Chapter 4. "The Chain of Dishonor": Petitioning for Rehabilitation in Imperial Germany	125
Chapter 5. "The Blessing of the War": World War I as a Chance for Rehabilitation	153
Chapter 6. "Your Honor Is Not My Honor": Disenfranchisement and Rehabilitation as a Political Battleground from the War to the End of the Weimar Republic	172
Conclusion	206
Bibliography	213
Index	234

Figures

0.1. Cartoon by August Roeseler. Image reads in slang: "Don't be so proud, Scheck! Back then I done lost my rights 'cause I set a couple little things on fire, but in a year we'll be equal same as ever!" August Roeseler, "After the animal show," *Fliegende Blätter* 127 (1907): 84. Courtesy Heidelberg University Library.   4

0.2. Cartoon by Adolf Oberländer. Image reads in slang: "At first they sentenced me to four months in prison and three years without my civil privileges. After I appealed, they withdrew the loss of civil privileges. I would rather have them withdraw the four months; what am I supposed to do with civil privileges?!" Adolf Oberländer, "Superfluous mercy," *Fliegende Blätter* 68 (1878): 192. Courtesy KB, national library.   5

2.1. Cartoon by Eduard Thöny. Image reads: "So you've lost your honor for three years, do you know what that means? – No – For example, you are not allowed to exercise the right to vote – (in slang) Alas, I shall become a Prussian." Eduard Thöny, "Harte Strafe" (Harsh Punishment), *Simplicissimus* 13, no. 2 (1908): 23. Courtesy Klassik Stiftung Weimar.   63

2.2. Cartoonist Thomas Theodor Heine mocking the reverence for people working in public service: "Can you please tell the way to the Grimmaische Strasse?" – (in slang) "You, listen, a decent man keeps his hat in his hand when he's talking to a royal official." Thomas Theodor Heine, "Durchs dunkelste Deutschland 9: der Beamte," *Simplicissimus* 6, no. 42 (1901): 329. Courtesy Klassik Stiftung Weimar.   68

3.1. Sentences of disenfranchisement divided by criminal offense, 1882–1914. Source: *Statistik des deutschen Reichs, 1882–1914*. © Timon de Groot.   85

3.2. Annual number of perjury sentences, 1882–1914. Source: *Statistik des deutschen Reichs, 1882–1914*. © Timon de Groot.   86

3.3. Annual number of disenfranchisement sentences compared to penitentiary (*Zuchthaus*) sentences, 1882–1914. Source: *Statistik des deutschen Reichs, 1882–1914*. © Timon de Groot.   89

3.4. The trial of high treason against Joseph Breuder and accomplices before the supreme court in Leipzig in 1881. Fritz Waibler, "Der Socialisten-Hochverrathsproceß vor dem Reichsgericht in Leipzig," *Illustrirte Zeitung*, 29 October 1881. 96

3.5. Mockery of judges considering membership of the Social Democratic Party as an aggravating circumstance. A lawyer pleads: "Even if the crime of robbery and murder, which my client carried out, may be so despicable, I still plead for mitigating circumstances – the accused is namely not a Social Democrat." Hans Gabriel Jentzsch, *Wahre Jacob*, 1 August 1899. Courtesy Klassik Stiftung Weimar. 107

3.6. The Penitentiary Bill was meant to protect the people who are "willing to work" by severely punishing people who blocked their access to work. An anonymous Cartoonist depicts the Penitentiary Bill here as a malfunctioning scarecrow, scaring away the wrong things. Anonymous, *Wahre Jacob*, 17 January, 1899. Courtesy Klassik Stiftung Weimar. 112

4.1. Cartoonist Thomas Theodor Heine mocks German officials' preoccupation with a criminal record. "Throw him out, the guy was in prison once," a police officer says about an individual who is about to enter heaven. Thomas Theodor Heine, "Zur Fürsorge für entlassene Sträflinge," *Simplicissimus* 11, no. 41 (1906): 658. Courtesy Klassik Stiftung Weimar. 133

6.1. Cartoonist Thomas Theodor Heine depicts the political fellow traveler as a chameleon crawling out of a dilapidated house: "Which way is the wind blowing today?" Thomas Theodor Heine, "Der Mitläufer," *Simplicissimus* 24, no. 9 (1919): 117. Courtesy Klassik Stiftung Weimar. 182

6.2. Cartoonist Thomas Theodor Heine deliberately deprives the political assassin of the status as an "honorable" political offender by depicting him as a sneaky robber after the murder of Walther Rathenau. Thomas Theodor Heine, "Der politische Mord," *Simplicissimus* 27, no. 16 (1922): 229. Courtesy Klassik Stiftung Weimar. 197

Acknowledgments

This book is the result of a research project that I conducted at the Max Planck Institute for Human Development in Berlin between 2014 and 2018. Parts of chapter 4 draw on an article that was already published in the journal *German History* in 2021 ("The Criminal Registry in the German Empire: The 'Cult of Previous Convictions' and the Offender's Right to Be Forgotten," *German History* 39, no. 3 [2021]).

I first wish to thank Ute Frevert and Birgit Aschmann for hosting me in Berlin. Their feedback on my research and our substantive talks about honor in German history have been very helpful and inspiring. Furthermore, I drew much inspiration from participating in both their research colloquia at the Humboldt-Universität and at the Centre for the History of Emotions at the Max Planck Institute for Human Development. I also wish to thank the members of the research group "Moral Economies of Modern Societies," who have all been great company during my research for this book. I specifically want to mention Thomas Rohringer and Paul Franke, who made important critical comments on the first drafts of the chapters. In addition, my research benefitted much from intellectually stimulating discussions with the members of the "Law and Emotions" reading group in Berlin (Gian Marco Vidor, Laura Kounine, Pavel Vasilyev, Daphne Rozenblatt, Stephen Cummins, and Sandra Schnädelbach).

In 2016, I participated in two research seminars, one in Frankfurt/Oder and one at the German Historical Institute Washington, which helped me sharpen my thoughts. Both were invaluable experiences. I would like to thank the organizers of these seminars: Thom Wolfe, Timm Beichelt, Anna von der Goltz, and Richard Wetzell for hosting them, and all the other participants for their inspirational contributions. During my research, I also spent a semester as a visiting researcher at the University of California at Berkeley. I am grateful to Rebecca McLennan for hosting me and for the meetings we had to discuss my project. In addition, I wish to express my gratitude to Richard Wetzell, Christoph Nübel, Sylvia Kesper-Biermann, Rebekka Habermas, and James Whitman for making time to discuss my work.

I would like to thank Adam Bresnahan, Sharon Park, and Hans Blanken for their comments on the earliest drafts of this work, and Monika Freier for helping me settle in Berlin and for helping with other practical matters. Most of all, I would like to thank my editor at the German Historical Institute, Patricia C. Sutcliffe, for her support in publishing the book and her precise editorial comments. Unfortunately, publishing the book took longer than I had hoped—partly due to the Covid pandemic—but I am glad that her support did not diminish over time.

As mentioned, most of the research for the book was done in Berlin between 2014 and 2018. I sometimes imagined that studying history in Berlin in this era must be like studying philosophy in Athens in 330 BCE. With its three universities, the several academic institutes dedicated to the study of history, and its abundance of museums and archives, one can really immerse oneself in history here. The fact that I could share this experience with Marlijn Meijer makes me all the more grateful.

Abbreviations

AKK	Archiv für Kriminalanthropologie und Kriminalistik
BA-BL	Bundesarchiv Berlin-Lichterfelde
BfG	*Blätter für Gefängniskunde*
BLHA	Brandenburgisches Landeshauptarchiv
DJZ	*Deutsche Juristen-Zeitung*
GAS	Goltdammer Archiv für Strafrecht
GStA PK	Geheimes Staatsarchiv Preußischer Kulturbesitz
IKV	Internationale Kriminalistische Vereinigung
LAV BW, S	Landesarchiv Baden Württemberg, Hauptstaatsarchiv Stuttgart
LAV NRW, R	Landesarchiv Nordrhein-Westfalen, Abteilung Rheinland
MKS	*Monatsschrift für Kriminalpsychologie und Strafrechtsreform*
MSPD	Majority Social Democratic Party of Germany (*Mehrheitssozialdemokratische Partei Deutschlands*)
PJ	*Preußische Jahrbücher*
RStGB	*Reichsstrafgesetzbuch*
SPD	Social Democratic Party of Germany (*Sozialdemokratische Partei Deutschlands*)
USPD	Independent Social Democratic Party of Germany (*Unabhängige Sozialdemokratische Partei Deutschlands*)
ZStW	*Zeitschrift für die gesamte Strafrechtswissenschaft*

Introduction

In 1941, the special court in Berlin convicted several Jewish people of illegal trade using ration cards. They each got different sentences, some of which included the death penalty, and in most cases the sentence also included the deprivation of their civil privileges. Many Germans were astonished by these sentences. Jewish citizens had, after all, already long been deprived of most of their rights.[1] Word of people's astonishment about these disenfranchisement punishments reached the Ministry of Justice, where an internal discussion then unfolded.[2] In response to the consternation, Heinrich Himmler, in his function as Reich Commissioner for the Consolidation of German Nationhood, ordered that these sentences not be handed down to Jewish people for the simple reason that they did not have these rights to begin with, so they could not be deprived of them.

Himmler's decision was in line with the directives of the Polenstrafrechtsverordnung, a penal policy introduced for subjects of the Nazi empire living in the eastern occupied territories who were not on the so-called Deutsche Volksliste.[3] The Polenstrafrechtsverordnung denied the possibility of disenfranchising subjects who had already been stripped of most of their civil rights. According to Himmler, the same principle should have applied to the verdicts of the judges in Berlin.[4] Yet Himmler's orders were not accepted without critique from legal experts at the Ministry of Justice, some of whom noted that the German penal code prescribed the withdrawal of a felon's civil privileges in numerous cases and that judges could not willingly neglect these legal prescriptions. They also noted that these prescriptions applied not only to people with German citizenship rights but to every person residing on German soil. It was territory that determined the law's jurisdiction and not the status of the subjects; consequently, the punishment should be applied even to travelers temporarily staying on German territory.

What was it about these verdicts that upset Himmler so much? In essence, he was disturbed not by the verdicts themselves but rather by the wording of the official name of the privileges they revoked. In German, they were called one's

---

Notes from this chapter begin on page 14.

"civil rights of honor" (*die bürgerlichen Ehrenrechte*). The notion of honor was indeed intimately connected with the punishment of disenfranchisement; this punishment was in fact more colloquially known as an "honor punishment" (*Ehrenstrafe*).[5] When newspapers reported on this punishment being carried out, they commonly used the phrase "loss of honor" (*Ehrverlust*). This terminology had its origins in legal thought of the early nineteenth century in which citizenship, crime, and honor were crucially connected. Himmler thus believed that stripping Jewish people of their "honor" basically implied that they were entitled to a certain kind of "honor" to begin with.

Himmler urged judges to avoid these verdicts at all costs.[6] He could not accept the idea that Jewish people without a criminal record were entitled to respect and were supposed to be viewed as "honorable." In the end, the Minister of Justice, Franz Schlegelberger, came up with a compromise: all verdicts that included §34 (the section that regulated the deprivation of civil privileges) and applied to Jewish people (or others not on the German *Volksliste*) should thenceforth omit the phrases "loss of honor" and "deprived of their civil privileges." In other words, judges had to state that §34 applied to these offenders without mentioning the contents of this paragraph. In this way, the Nazi authorities could uphold the fiction of abiding by a rule of law while avoiding the implication that Jewish people were entitled to a certain "honor." Officials of the Ministry of Justice were satisfied with this compromise.

Felony Disenfranchisement in German Society

Even if this was a trivial moment in the persecution of Jewish citizens in Nazi Germany (since the legal status of Jewish citizens had already been decimated), the internal discussion in the Ministry of Justice in 1941 illustrates the peculiar connection between the punishment of disenfranchisement and the notion of honor in German legal thought. This book is about the history of that punishment and its significance in German society in the long nineteenth century. It aims to explain the rationale behind the punishment and show how it functioned satisfactorily—in the eyes of the authorities—during the era of the German Empire (1871–1918) before it became heavily politicized in the time of the Weimar Republic (1918–33).

Felony disenfranchisement (*die Aberkennung der bürgerlichen Ehrenrechte*) emerged in several of the newly introduced German penal codes in the early nineteenth century, roughly in the period between the dissolution of the Holy Roman Empire in 1806 and the end of the so-called *Vormärz* period in 1848. Eventually it was codified in §34 of the 1871 Reich Penal Code of the German Empire.[7] The punishment was handed down to all sorts of offenders up to 1969, when it was abolished from the law. During the time of the German Empire, criminal courts deprived, on average, about fifteen thousand German citizens of their civil privileges annually. Surely, however, the significance of this punishment lay not in the number of sentences in which it was handed down. Compared to the death penalty, it was meted out very frequently, but it was added to only 5 percent of all prison and penitentiary sentences, making it a marginal punishment compared to incarceration.[8]

There are many ways to look at the significance of a punishment. One way is to look at its emotional impact. However, one segment of German society clearly believed that felony disenfranchisement had no emotional impact on German citizens at all. Satirists of the German Empire, for instance, often lampooned the indifference convicted felons felt toward this punishment and the apathy with which the lower classes regarded their civil privileges. For example, in 1897, during the heyday of bicycle mania, a reporter for the satirical magazine *Kladderadatsch* jokingly wrote that the Reichstag was contemplating the introduction of a law that would prohibit disenfranchised felons from riding a bicycle. After all, the author argued, this would increase the emotional impact of the punishment as riding a bicycle was something that all members of society genuinely enjoyed (whereas they did not care about their voting rights).[9] Furthermore, class perceptions often played a role in such humor. The satirical magazine *Fliegende Blätter* regularly published cartoons mocking people from lower economic classes who were deprived of their civil privileges. One cartoon from 1907 depicted a farmer standing next to his award-winning ox with the caption: "Don't be so proud, Scheck! Back then I done lost my rights 'cause I set a couple little things on fire, but in a year we'll be equal same as ever!" (see Figure 0.1). In this case, farmers deprived of their privileges were the object of ridicule; in other cases, vagrants were mocked in cartoons with similar captions (see Figure 0.2). In yet another cartoon, a judge reads a sentence to a defendant, who answers: "no problem—I wasn't planning on voting next time around anyways!"[10]

Even though these satirists mocked the ineffectiveness of this punishment, their cartoons represented its significance in political discourse. These jokes asserted that some members of German society were indifferent to their civil privileges, enabling the authors to address fundamental issues about social stratification and civil morality. In other words, authors instrumentalized the critique of the ineffectiveness of a punishment to address broader class issues in German society.

Legal scholars also criticized felony disenfranchisement's ineffectiveness. The most important of these critics was Otto Mittelstädt, a trained legal scholar who held many important positions in the Prussian bureaucracy and wrote some influential commentaries on the German legal system.[11] In 1879, when he was a judge in Hamburg, he published a book titled *Gegen die Freiheitsstrafen*, in which he revealed himself to be one of the most vehement critics of the German penal system. He believed that punishments should primarily be about deterrence and should therefore principally strive to bring humiliation and disgrace (*Schmach*

Figure 0.1. Cartoon by August Roeseler. Image reads in slang: "Don't be so proud, Scheck! Back then I done lost my rights 'cause I set a couple little things on fire, but in a year we'll be equal same as ever!" August Roeseler, "After the animal show," *Fliegende Blätter* 127 (1907): 84. Courtesy Heidelberg University Library.

und Schande) upon offenders.[12] The modern penal system, he argued, utterly failed in its mission to deliver the message that crimes are impermissible acts that constitute a moral harm.

Depriving offenders of their civil privileges was one example of an ineffective punishment for Mittelstädt. Disenfranchisement did not humiliate and disgrace offenders as much as he thought it should. Even though its whole purpose was

Figure 0.2. Cartoon by Adolf Oberländer. Image reads in slang: "At first they sentenced me to four months in prison and three years without my civil privileges. After I appealed, they withdrew the loss of civil privileges. I would rather have them withdraw the four months; what am I supposed to do with civil privileges?!" Adolf Oberländer, "Superfluous mercy," *Fliegende Blätter* 68 (1878): 192. Courtesy KB, national library.

to damage offenders' "sense of honor" (*Ehrgefühle*), he argued that offenders did not genuinely experience the shame of the punishment.[13] These words resonate with American legal scholar James Q. Whitman's definition of penal degradation: the "treatment of others that makes them feel inferior, lessened, lowered."[14] In other words, a punishment was supposed to have a crucial emotional effect, but Mittelstädt believed this effect was seriously lacking.

Even though some felons seemed indifferent to the punishment, as Mittelstädt observed, his claim about the emotional impact of felony disenfranchisement ought not be overgeneralized. Mittelstädt wished to reintroduce corporal punishment in the German penal system, so he contrasted the apathy surrounding disenfranchisement with the actual pain people felt as a result of corporal punishment. Even so, the emotional impact that disenfranchisement had on citizens might have been more diverse and nuanced than Mittelstädt and other critics believed. Therefore, in this book, I aim to address the emotional impact of the punishment once again, going beyond people's mere interest or disinterest in the civil privileges suspended by this punishment. In fact, I will show that German people interacted with this punishment in multifaceted ways, with authorities utilizing it as an instrument for reinforcing societal hierarchies, while others used it to fight for reforms.

By focusing on German citizens' emotional attachment to this punishment, I aim to shed light on what it meant to them to be German citizens and what constituted "civil morality." Following the American moral philosopher Martha Nussbaum, I view emotions as "judgements of value and importance," judgments reflecting the core beliefs of moral agents.[15] The emotional experience of people affected by the penal system thus informs us about their broader moral beliefs, what they believed constituted a good life as a citizen, and how much their ideas of civil morality converged around the notion of honor.[16] Importantly, I thus not only engage with the emotions of those who were punished but also with the emotions of the broader German public, for instance, in reacting to a public verdict. This is fundamental to fully assessing the impact of punishment on society.

The Uncontested Existence of Felony Disenfranchisement

Many scholars of the history of criminal policy have emphasized the disciplining aspect of legal punishment. One representative of this approach is the famous French historian Michel Foucault, who argued that the type of power exercised in prisons played a part in the way modern subjects were formed through a process of disciplining bodies and normalizing deviance. Foucault's theory views punishment as one of many ways in which power is exercised and embodied in modern societies.[17] In addition, criminal justice is often connected with welfare policy in modern societies. For example, British criminologist David Garland speaks in this context of the penal-welfare complex—a historical entanglement between welfare programs and penal measures; in modern penal regimes, in fact, the act of punishing is not much different from educating or curing individuals.[18]

Recent scholarship on Germany's history of crime and justice has also explored the contributions of criminal justice to welfare policies, education, and medical treatment. German historian Desirée Schauz, for instance, studied the growing influence of welfare organizations in German prison facilities and argued that these organizations set up welfare programs based on individuals' need for resocialization, among other things, through work distribution. The implementation of these programs was often accompanied by conflict, and the results were often disappointing as there was a high rate of recidivism. Schauz regards this development as evidence that punishment was increasingly considered a form of applied social knowledge.[19] Describing similar developments in the German penal system, American historian Warren Rosenblum even argues that the emergence of welfare assistance in courts in the Weimar Republic—despite the controversy surrounding its practical application—demonstrates that there was a consensus among penal experts in favor of a "social approach" to criminal justice.[20] Many other scholars of German criminal justice, furthermore, point out the important influence of medical doctors in the German penal system and the spread of the idea that criminality could be cured like a mental illness, which predominantly arose in the second half of the nineteenth century and the first half of the twentieth.[21]

Notwithstanding the crucial insights these authors have had into the educational and disciplinary aspects of modern penal regimes, nineteenth-century observers regarded disenfranchisement as important on account of its symbolic function. According to them, the significance of the punishment lay not only in its emotional impact on the person being punished but also in its emotional expressiveness for the governing body inflicting it. The punishment was designed by nineteenth-century lawmakers both to penalize wrongdoers and to safeguard the honor that came with German citizenship. Felony disenfranchisement was thus essential to sustaining a moral order in society since it helped demarcate the boundary between permissible offenses that did not affect the honor of citizenship and morally reprehensible crimes that offended against the "honorable trust" bestowed on citizens.

This resonates with the ideas put forward by the famous French sociologist Émile Durkheim, who wrote in his 1893 key work *The Division of Labor in Society* that "punishment is above all intended to have its effect upon honest people ... [I]t serves to heal the wounds inflicted upon the collective sentiments."[22] Punishment, he argued, "consists of a passionate reaction graduated in intensity, which society exerts through the mediation of an organized body over those of its members who have violated certain rules of conduct."[23] Moreover, in Durkheim's theory, punishment had a communicative function, sending a message to all members of society: it was "a sign indicating that that the sentiments of the collectivity are still unchanged."[24] By inflicting a punishment, the governing authorities attempted to reinforce the collective morality by giving voice to the collective sentiments about the wrongfulness of a certain act. The ritualistic execution of punishment was therefore central to his theory as it helped to create social cohesion within a community. Indeed, many nineteenth-century German advocates of felony disenfranchisement thereby indirectly and unwittingly supported Durkheim's view that punishment had such a communicative function by which it reflected the moral order a society tried to uphold.[25]

Durkheim crucially argued that the authority of a governing body to execute a punishment stemmed not from the actual harm a crime did to a society but from the "common consciousness" of a society being offended. Underlying this theory was the idea that there was something like a "common consciousness": a certain consensus within a society about the moral categories that could be offended. In other words, when applied to the case of felony disenfranchisement, there had to be some agreement about circumstances that would justify a felon's disenfranchisement. As I argue in this book, however, social agreement about the execution of this punishment was frequently lacking; defendants, courtroom observers, and politicians often heavily criticized or protested verdicts. Such conflict about verdicts undermined Durkheim's theory about the "collectivity" sanctioning its members. In reality, it is not "society" that punishes but specific authoritative figures who impose punishments on specific people, with a great deal of dissent among both subjects and observers of these punishments.[26] This was without a doubt also the case in Imperial Germany.

Still, the idea of social consensus converging around this punishment should not be dispensed with completely. Protests against felony disenfranchisement often had one thing in common: they were based on the belief that the punishment had an emotional impact on more people than just the person being punished. Indeed, commentators believed that it "functioned" by reinforcing hierarchical relations in German society and reasserting concepts of "honorable" and "dishonorable" actions. However, this did not mean that every disenfranchisement was a way for the authorities "to give voice" to collective sentiments. Rather, given the emotional power of disenfranchisement, one could say that the authorities frequently instrumentalized the idea that punishment stemmed from certain collective beliefs by disenfranchising certain offenders. In this way, they hoped to manipulate collective sentiments about certain people and certain crimes.

People constantly tried to renegotiate the conditions under which felony disenfranchisement should be imposed and actively debated what constituted "honorable" conduct. Even so, people did not consider the punishment redundant but rather believed that disenfranchisement was a vital component of Germany's penal system. That is, there was at least consensus that felony disenfranchisement added value to the German penal system. If people truly believed that it was a superfluous punishment, there would not have been so much resistance to it being carried out in specific cases, and verdicts to punish people with disenfranchisement would not have sparked that much controversy. In fact, in the German Empire there was almost no protest about the simple existence of this punishment, there was only occasional protest when it was handed down to specific people in specific cases (as discussed in chapter 3). Although this changed after World War I, when it became too deeply politicized, before that time it was an immutable aspect of German criminal policy that could be instrumentalized and incorporated in the reform agendas of politicians, criminal justice experts, and other members of civil society.

Historicizing the Notion of Honor

As noted before, the emotional impact of felony disenfranchisement derived from its intimate association with the notion of honor. Thus, it is not surprising that many historians interpret this punishment as a relic of early modern or even medieval European criminal policy.[27] In some ways, this interpretation is understandable since it was common practice in feudal society and in the European *Ancien Régime* to exclude certain people from guilds, to bar them from practicing certain crafts, and to banish and brand them as "*unehrliche Leute*" (dishonest people).[28] Such people, one could argue, constituted an early class of precarious workers.[29] Accordingly, Franz von Liszt, in the 1932 edition of his *Lehrbuch des deutschen Strafrechts* (one of the most influential German textbooks on criminal justice of the nineteenth century), unambiguously placed felony disenfranchisement in the medieval tradition and dismissed it as "a doomed, final remnant of the medieval penal arsenal."[30]

The characterization of felony disenfranchisement as archaic broadly supports the thesis of James Q. Whitman, who has done some of the most compelling work on the importance of honor in the history of punishment in the nineteenth century. In his view, the "mild" treatment of offenders in the modern criminal justice system in Germany can only be explained as the result of a process of "leveling up." Over the course of time, he argues, "regular" offenders came to be treated like the privileged, "honorable" offenders and were entitled to the same "honor" as the aristocrats, while all degrading elements were abolished from penal law.[31]

Even so, one can dispute whether the notion of honor in late nineteenth-century penal policy really had the same meaning as it did in the early modern era. The notion of honor, after all, was complex, not only because it entailed a description of the "objective" qualities of a person (that is, one's rights, privileges, and membership in certain groups), but also because it contained a crucial subjective dimension. As German sociologist Georg Simmel famously observed in his *Soziologie*, honor forges a strong connection between the objective categories of membership and privileges and personal beliefs about moral value and entitlement.[32] Furthermore, honor is a kind of "symbolic capital," as described in the theory of Pierre Bourdieu: something that people constantly need to reproduce and utilize through their bodily postures and stances.[33]

Historians have thus noted how an appeal to one's honor was an important motivator for action. German historian Birgit Aschmann, for instance, showed in her study of the three wars between Prussia and France that appeals to the honor of the national leaders of both states influenced their decision to go to war.[34] The subjective dimension of honor also changes over time.[35] The historicity of the notion of honor is illustrated by its use in the context of dueling. For instance, it is well known that the German bourgeoisie adopted the aristocratic practice of dueling, which its members had not previously been entitled to, from 1848 onwards. Some historians have claimed that this adoption was proof of the militarization of German society and an expression of the premodern beliefs about honor that German imperial subjects held, in particular, members of the bourgeoisie. Yet, as German historian Ute Frevert has argued, the bourgeois culture of dueling was more an expression of the modern bourgeois values of masculinity, individualism, anti-materialism, and self-restraint, and thus helped to constitute the liberal identity of the German bourgeoisie.[36] These observations confirm that just because bourgeois citizens had a notion of honor did not necessarily mean that they had an early modern mindset.[37]

A German Trajectory

In fact, most nineteenth-century legal experts did not associate felony disenfranchisement with early modern criminal law. On the contrary, they generally justified the punishment as serving the aims of an entirely modern penal system. It is therefore interesting to note that in the original 1880 version of the above-mentioned textbook, Franz von Liszt listed four legal goods (*Rechtsgüter*) that punishments in modern societies could potentially restrict or destroy: life, liberty, property, and honor.[38] Furthermore, depriving people of their privileges, Liszt argued, was a punishment perfectly suited to damaging a citizen's honor. Honor, in this context, was intimately connected to citizenship, which really distinguished this punishment from the early modern punishments of banishment and branding. Unlike those punishments, disenfranchisement was not supposed to affect criminals' commercial affairs and their place, for instance, in the job market but only their legal status in relation to the state. It commonly deprived an offender of the rights to join the army, to vote, to sign important legal documents, and to testify in court. This concept was made explicit in a 1909 draft for a reformed penal code for the German Empire: "The honor punishments should leave the private rights and social position of the convicted untouched and should only affect the guilty person's public rights."[39]

The difference between the older and modern "honor punishments" can thus be traced back to two important shifts that took place over the course of the eighteenth and nineteenth centuries: the emancipation of the free market from guilds and corporations, and the expansion of state bureaucracy and its growing monopoly on all kinds of penalization. In other words, whereas corporate institutions used to sanction their members, they lost this right as punishment gradually became the primary prerogative of the state.[40] Thus, there were two modern aspects of felony disenfranchisement: it was egalitarian, in that it was imposed on people based solely on the nature of their crime, unlike the penal system of the *Ancien Régime*, in which status differences often determined a punishment's harshness;[41] and it was connected to the emerging ideas of citizenship in the German states. The logic of the connection with state citizenship worked in two ways. First, the punishment ensured that people deemed "morally unworthy" were excluded from civil privileges so that the "honor" of citizenship remained protected from their negative influence. Second, all defendants who were not officially stripped of their privileges were entitled to a certain "honor." In this way, the punishment became intrinsic to "the age of citizenship."[42]

Disenfranchisement was not unique to German law. Compared to other countries with similar punishments, however, Germany did pursue a unique trajectory. It is safe to say that this punishment was an import from the French legal system. The punishment known as *dégradation civique*, which entailed the withdrawal of one's political rights (*droits politiques*), was first introduced in the First French Republic and mainly targeted the enemies of the revolution.[43] This political aspect was lost on German lawmakers, though. As in the legal reforms under Napoleon, the German codes reserved disenfranchisement for crimes with an explicitly apolitical character in the eyes of the legislative power. Time and time again, this apolitical character was defended as one of the core characteristics of this punishment in Germany.

In addition to the French *Code Pénal*, disenfranchisement is also known in the common-law tradition. In fact, it became—and still is—an important part of American penal law. As American historian Pippa Holloway argues, this punishment had the function (as it had in Germany) of safeguarding respect for citizenship as "suffrage by degraded individuals would undermine the dignity of their [i.e., other citizens'] own citizenship."[44] Nevertheless, in the United States, the punishment was increasingly instrumentalized, especially during Reconstruction, to disenfranchise a specific part of the American population.[45] This happened above all in the South and was directed against former slaves. Such racial profiling in the execution of this punishment was not common in Germany. In fact, the example at the start of this Introduction illustrated the opposite: people in Nazi Germany were excluded from this punishment on racial grounds. These two ways of instrumentalizing felony disenfranchisement demonstrate a crucial difference between two twentieth-century racial states. Whereas the American state aimed to make a certain group into second-class citizens by disenfranchising them, the Nazi state aimed to denaturalize a group by depriving them of their citizenship status altogether. In short, one can say that the German punishment of disenfranchisement differed from the French version in its apolitical pretension, and it differed from the American version in its egalitarian pretension, whereby all citizens were equally subjected to the punishment—provided they were citizens.

The Structure of the Book

In this book, I describe the history of the punishment of disenfranchisement from multiple perspectives. To do so, it was necessary for me to consult various kinds of sources and media. Governmental statutes and laws, bureaucratic decrees, important verdicts, transcripts from trials, newspaper articles, and academic treatises are all included in this study. I began my research in the archives of justice ministries of the German Empire and the Prussian state, which are stored at the Bundesarchiv in Berlin and the Geheimes Staatsarchiv Preussischer Kulturbesitz in Berlin. In addition, the files of the local administrations of Aachen and Düsseldorf in the Landesarchiv Nordrhein-Westfalen yielded important insights. From there, I continued to analyze the intellectual debates in the most important academic journals of the time, important verdicts, political debates in the Reichstag, and broader media discussions in Imperial Germany.

Alongside the more "traditional" sources, I studied several petitions written by people who had been deprived of their rights and wanted them restored. I did this to include offenders' "voices," particularly since, as many scholars have noted, these are often ignored in the history of crime and justice. German historian Philipp Müller pointedly called this the "*longue durée* of silence."[46] For this book, this research into offenders' voices was not an end in itself but allowed me to better grasp the dialectics of inclusion and exclusion pertaining to citizenship, as well as the emotional impact of the punishment. These voices also provide concrete evidence of the ways in which convicts reflected on their crimes and punishments. I will compare several individual cases of German citizens who sought to have their rights restored and analyze the discursive resources they used in their petitions. This will render a fuller picture of the experience of citizenship in the German Empire and how various conceptions of citizenship related to perceptions of the moral permissibility of particular offenses.[47]

In presenting the different roles punishment played in German society, I engage in this book with many issues discussed in Warren Rosenblum's book *Beyond the Prison Gates* and Desirée Schauz's *Strafen als moralische Besserung*. For example, the book addresses prejudices against discharged prisoners in the German Empire and welfare workers' efforts to help reintegrate them into society. However, I am less concerned here with the "irresistible reform wave" that made its way through the German criminal justice system and led, in the end, to the system of welfare assistance for ex-convicts in the Weimar Republic. Whereas Rosenblum and Schauz emphasized the execution of punishment—the disciplinary techniques applied inside prison facilities and social programs that were implemented to assist (ex-)convicts—I argue that the legal categories and the content of verdicts also mattered. The sentence itself affected people, irrespective of what penal officers and welfare workers had to say about it.[48] In this book, I therefore focus more on the history of ideas about citizenship, honor, and trust in the long nineteenth century.[49] The book ultimately seeks to understand what stripping offenders of their "honor" tells us about the relationship between citizens and the law. It prioritizes the perspectives of offenders who sought to have their rights restored—in many cases without the assistance of welfare workers, but always in direct contact with judicial authorities.

This book also builds on many excellent historical studies on the emergence of the science of criminology in the German Empire that focus on the discursive strategies employed in this field in constructing the notion of "the criminal." These studies elucidate the shifts that took place in the nineteenth century: from an emphasis on depraved people who willfully neglected their moral duties to an emphasis on "degenerates" who became "criminals" due to socioeconomic or biological factors. Although these insights provide important context for my study, felony disenfranchisement often proved challenging to scholars of legal studies and criminology. This is because the decision to impose the punishment of disenfranchisement was frequently based not on the offenders' reform potential—that is, whether they were "corrigible"—but on the seriousness of the offenses.[50] However, as I will show, these two ways of characterizing offenders were not always seen as conflicting with each other. In fact, when contemporary criminological works increasingly highlighted the reform potential of offenders, scholars began to explicitly contemplate whether these categories could coexist with the punishment of disenfranchisement and the underlying distinction between "honorable" and "dishonorable" behavior. Social theories of criminal justice thus stood in a complicated relationship to felony disenfranchisement. For a long time, scholars believed that the punishment might be compatible with their "modern" theory. This demonstrates how ingrained the punishment was for nineteenth-century scholars but also that the punishment could be carried out and instrumentalized in several ways.

The book is divided into six chapters. The first chapter, which deals with the time before 1871 (the year the Reich Penal Code was implemented), discusses the intellectual and political origins of the punishment of disenfranchisement. It engages with the ideas of prominent legal thinkers and philosophers from several of the German states and looks at the general intellectual justification of the punishment of disenfranchisement from the time of the Napoleonic Wars onwards. Central to the chapter are the way that notions of honor and trust were connected to disenfranchisement and how the idea of "civil honor" became the hegemonic understanding of honor.

The second chapter seeks to place the punishment of disenfranchisement in the more explicit context of the introduction of the Reich Penal Code and other legislation of Imperial Germany. It specifically looks at the interests of social groups in the codification of disenfranchisement and subsequent debates about how it should function. To do this, it analyzes why legislators and other authorities felt it was important to exclude disenfranchised felons from certain institutions and explains how some later appeals were intended to advocate more egalitarian membership in these institutions.

Whereas chapter 2 discusses the exclusionary effects of disenfranchisement and legislators' justifications for this, chapter 3 looks at the actual sentencing. Sentencing criminals to disenfranchisement was essentially a performative act that transformed citizens into dishonored felons. Chapter 3 therefore seeks to explain the political significance of these sentences by showing how the authorities utilized them to determine who could be viewed as a "political" agent. Chapter 4 then focuses on the individual experiences of disenfranchised felons. Against the background of the notions of stigma, passing, and rehabilitation, the chapter analyzes petitions by people who wanted their rights restored, examining their motivations by considering the ways in which disenfranchisement affected them. This chapter truly makes the case that the punishment was more than a relic from premodern times.

The final two chapters seek to uncover why felony disenfranchisement fell out of favor and was ultimately abolished from the penal code in the early German Federal Republic. Chapter 5 discusses the period of World War I and highlights how ex-convicts' petitions gradually became more political and how authorities, under pressure as a result of the war-time economy, started letting "dishonored" ex-offenders join the army, thereby abandoning a cherished principle. The final chapter gives an overview of some uses of the punishment in the Weimar Republic and describes major controversies such uses of the punishment engendered among politicians and legal scholars, which finally prompted them to believe that the punishment was too easily misused and should thus no longer be a part of penal law. The political use of felony disenfranchisement became clearest during the Nazi era. However, as the final two chapters make clear, it was not only the politicization of the punishment but also the failure of those on whom it had been imposed to internalize ideas of "dishonor" that made it controversial. This ultimately enabled people sentenced with disenfranchisement to band together and protest their sentences rather than simply "atone" for their crimes.

Notes

1. This effectively started with the Civil Service Law of 1933 and reached its peak with the Reich Citizens Act as part of the Nuremberg Laws in 1935. See Dieter Gosewinkel, *Einbürgern und Ausschließen: Die Nationalisierung der Staatsangehörigkeit vom deutschen Bund bis zur Bundesrepublik Deutschland* (Göttingen: Vandenhoeck & Ruprecht, 2001), 380–93.
2. This exchange is preserved in the files of the Ministry of Propaganda: BA-BL, R 55/1423.
3. See Diemut Majer, *"Fremdvölkische" im Dritten Reich: Ein Beitrag zur nationalsozialistischen Rechtssetzung und Rechtspraxis in Verwaltung und Justiz unter besonderer Berücksichtigung der eingegliederten Ostgebiete und des Generalgouvernements* (Boppard am Rhein: Boldt, 1981), 744–59.
4. This thought was also explicitly endorsed by the man who drafted this policy, State Secretary Roland Freisler, in a series of articles for the official legal journal of the National Socialist regime: Roland Freisler, "Das Deutsche Polenstrafrecht," *Deutsche Justiz* 103 (1941): 1139–42; *Deutsche Justiz* 104 (1942): 25–33, 41–46. He remarked that the deprivation of people's civil privileges was not included as a punishment since they did not possess these privileges to begin with (31).
5. Consider also the titles of the following treatises on the topic: Oswald Marcuse, *Die Ehrenstrafe. Eine rechtsvergleichende Darstellung nebst Kritik unter besonderer Berücksichtigung des*

geltenden Deutschen Strafrechts (Breslau: Schletter, 1899); Hermann-Victor Kießlich, *Die Ehrenstrafen* (Berlin: Siemenroth, 1911); Friedrich Behrendt, *Die Ehrenstrafen und ihre Weiterbildung* (Heidelberg: Rößler & Herbert, 1914); Irene Fuchs, *Die Ehrenstrafen der Vergangenheit und Gegenwart* (Cologne: Studentenburse, 1929); Emil Kühne, *Die Ehrenstrafen* (Würzburg: Triltsch, 1931).

5. Franz von Liszt, *Lehrbuch des deutschen Strafrechts*, 10th edn. (Berlin: De Gruyter, 1900), 253.
6. BA-BL, R 55/1423, message of Heinrich Himmler, 22 January 1942.
7. The research in this book is limited to punishments codified in the official Reich Penal Code. It is important to note that the German Empire was a legally pluralistic society with several "honor courts," each of which also had the power to punish people, and the Military Penal Code was especially important. Nevertheless, the punishments meted out by these special "honor courts" will not be taken into consideration here. A good account of the multinormative consequences of these honor courts is provided in Peter Collin, "Ehrengerichtliche Rechtsprechung im Kaiserreich und der Weimarer Republik. Multinormativität in einer mononormativen Rechtsordnung?," *Rechtsgeschichte—Legal History* 25 (2017): 138–50. On the honor courts of medical professionals, see Andreas-Holger Maehle, *Doctors, Honour and the Law: Medical Ethics in Imperial Germany* (Basingstoke: Palgrave Macmillan, 2009). On the honor courts of reserve army officers, see Hartmut John, *Das Reserveoffizierkorps im deutschen Kaiserreich 1890–1914* (Frankfurt a.M.: Campus, 1981), 368–430.
8. See the discussion of crime statistics in chapter 3.
9. *Kladderadatsch* 50.47 (21 November 1897), 190.
10. *Fliegende Blätter* 114 (1901), 92.
11. Hans Hattenhauer, "Justizkarriere durch die Provinzen. Das Beispiel Otto Mittelstädt," in *Preußen in der Provinz*, ed. Peter Nitschke, 35–62 (Frankfurt a.M.: Peter Lang, 1991).
12. Otto Mittelstädt, *Gegen die Freiheitsstrafen. Ein Beitrag zur Kritik des heutigen Strafensystems* (Leipzig: Hirzel, 1879), 84.
13. Ibid. As an alternative, he advocated "modern" forms of public punishment, like pinning an offender's name and picture to a pillory. He believed that this would have a greater deterring effect, which, according to his theory, would make it a more adequate form of punishment.
14. James Q. Whitman, *Harsh Justice: Criminal Punishment and the Widening Divide between America and Europe* (Oxford: Oxford University Press, 2005), 20.
15. Martha C. Nussbaum, *Upheavals of Thought: The Intelligence of Emotions* (Cambridge: Cambridge University Press, 2001). See specifically the discussion on pages 49–56. The connection between emotions and moral values also forms a central part of Hans Joas's theory of the genesis of values: Hans Joas, *The Genesis of Values* (Chicago: University of Chicago Press, 2000). Even though analyzing the emotional significance of punishment inevitably draws our attention to conceptions of "the self," it is good to keep in mind that the values these emotions express can (or must) be shared. Evidently, people also deal with norms and expectations about emotional expression, which is a central aspect in Barbara Rosenwein's concept of "emotional communities." See the introduction to Barbara H. Rosenwein, *Generations of Feeling: A History of Emotions, 600–1700* (Cambridge: Cambridge University Press, 2016). I will also address conflicts over the question of whether the expression of certain emotions is justified in the context of punishment and rehabilitation, but in general I will analyze these questions in light of how these expectations reflected a person's attachment to a certain moral code.
16. This is particularly interesting in the context of the German Empire as the question of common citizens' adherence to the general category of citizenship in the German *Obrigkeitsstaat* is still a pressing issue. See Sven Oliver Müller and Cornelius Torp, *Das deutsche Kaiserreich in der Kontroverse* (Göttingen: Vandenhoeck & Ruprecht, 2009), specifically James Retallack's chapter, "Obrigkeitsstaat und politischer Massenmarkt," 121–35.
17. Michel Foucault, *Surveiller et punir. Naissance de la prison* (Paris: Gallimard, 1975).

18. See David Garland, *Punishment and Welfare: A History of Penal Strategies* (London: Gower, 1985), 131–57. A similar view of the entanglement of welfare policy with penal elements and ideas about natural selection is central to Detlev Peukert's analysis of welfare policies in the German Empire and the Weimar Republic; see Detlev Peukert, *Grenzen der Sozialdisziplinierung. Aufstieg und Krise der deutschen Jugendfürsorge von 1878 bis 1932* (Cologne: Bund-Verlag, 1986); idem, *Die Weimarer Republik. Krisenjahre der klassischen Moderne* (Frankfurt a.M: Suhrkamp, 1987), 132–48.
19. Désirée Schauz, *Strafen als moralische Besserung: Eine Geschichte der Straffälligenfürsorge 1777–1933* (Munich: Oldenbourg. 2008).
20. Warren Rosenblum, *Beyond the Prison Gates: Punishment and Welfare in Germany, 1850–1933* (Chapel Hill: University of North Carolina Press, 2008); idem, "Welfare and Justice," in *Crime and Criminal Justice in Modern Germany*, ed. Richard F. Wetzell, 158–81 (New York: Berghahn Books, 2014).
21. Richard F. Wetzell, *Inventing the Criminal: A History of German Criminology, 1880–1945* (Chapel Hill: University of North Carolina Press, 2000).
22. Émile Durkheim, *The Division of Labour in Society*, trans. W. D. Halls (London: Macmillan, 1984), 63.
23. Ibid., 52.
24. Ibid., 63.
25. Cf. David Garland, *Punishment and Modern Society: A Study in Social Theory* (Oxford: Clarendon, 1990), 23–47.
26. See Garland's criticism of Durkheim: David Garland, "Sociological Perspectives on Punishment," *Crime and Justice*, no. 14 (1991): 115–65.
27. Many scholars present felony disenfranchisement as a remnant of earlier punishments. See, for example, Mareike Fröhling, *Der moderne Pranger. Von den Ehrenstrafen des Mittelalters bis zur Prangerwirkung der medialen Berichterstattung im heutigen Strafverfahren* (Marburg: Tectum Verlag, 2014). It is also discussed as such in Albert Esser, *Die Ehrenstrafe* (Stuttgart: Kohlhammer, 1956). Consider, too, the title of this book: Ludgera Vogt and Arnold Zingerle, *Ehre. Archaische Momente in der Moderne* (Frankfurt a.M.: Suhrkamp, 1994). Otherwise, this punishment is seldom mentioned in historical research on crime and criminal justice in Imperial Germany. The available examples do not attribute much importance to it: Alexandra Ortmann, *Machtvolle Verhandlungen. zur Kulturgeschichte der deutschen Strafjustiz 1879–1924* (Göttingen: Vandenhoeck & Ruprecht, 2014), 202; Rosenblum, *Beyond the Prison Gates*, 132–33. An exception is Sylvia Kesper-Biermann, *Einheit und Recht. Strafgesetzgebung und Kriminalrechtsexperten in Deutschland vom Beginn des 19. Jahrhunderts bis zum Reichsstrafgesetzbuch von 1871* (Frankfurt a.M.: Klostermann, 2009). Kesper-Biermann's study focuses on the development of German legislation, whereas the present study also aims to examine how the punishment was carried out.
28. Karl Härter, "Security and 'Gute Policey' in Early Modern Europe: Concepts, Laws, and Instruments," *Historical Social Research* 35, no. 4 (2010): 41–65. See also Richard van Dülmen, *Der ehrlose Mensch. Unehrlichkeit und soziale Ausgrenzung in der frühen Neuzeit* (Cologne: Böhlau, 1999).
29. Marcel van der Linden, "San Precario: A New Inspiration for Labor Historians," *Labor: Studies in Working-Class History of the Americas* 10, no. 1 (2014): 9–21, 13.
30. Franz von Liszt, *Lehrbuch des Deutschen Strafrechts*, ed. Eberhard Schmidt, 26th edn. (Berlin: de Gruyter, 1932), 398. This phrase was not found in one of the earlier versions of the textbook.
31. Whitman, *Harsh Justice*, 9–12.
32. Georg Simmel, *Soziologie. Untersuchungen über die Formen der Vergesellschaftung* (Leipzig: Duncker & Humblot, 1908), 600–3.

33. Pierre Bourdieu, *Outline of a Theory of Practice*, trans. Richard Nice (Cambridge: Cambridge University Press, 1977), 10–30.
34. Birgit Aschmann, "Ehre—Das verletzte Gefühl als Grund für den Krieg," in *Gefühl und Kalkül—Der Einfluss von Emotionen auf die Politik des 19. und 20. Jahrhunderts*, 151–74 (Stuttgart: Steiner, 2005).
35. See Friedrich Zunkel, "Ehre, Reputation," in *Geschichtliche Grundbegriffe. Historisches Lexikon zur politisch-sozialen Sprache in Deutschland*, ed. Otto Brunner, Werner Conze, and Reinhart Koselleck, vol. 2 (Stuttgart: Klett-Cotta, 1975), 1–63; Ute Frevert, "Ehre—Männlich/Weiblich. Zu einem Identitätsbegriff des 19. Jahrhunderts," *Tel Aviver Jahrbuch für deutsche Geschichte* 21 (1992): 21–68; Martin Dinges, "Die Ehre als Thema der historischen Anthropologie. Bemerkungen zu Wissenschaftsgeschichte und zur Konzeptualisierung," in *Verletzte Ehre. Ehrkonflikte in Gesellschaften des Mittelalters und der Frühen Neuzeit*, ed. Klaus Schreiner and Gerd Schwerhoff, 29–62 (Cologne: Böhlau, 1995); Birgit Aschmann, *Preußens Ruhm und Deutschlands Ehre. Zum nationalen Ehrdiskurs im Vorfeld der preußisch-französischen Kriege des 19. Jahrhunderts* (Munich: Oldenbourg, 2013); Ann Goldberg, *Honor, Politics, and the Law in Imperial Germany, 1871–1914* (Cambridge: Cambridge University Press, 2010).
36. Ute Frevert, *Men of Honour: A Social and Cultural History of the Duel* (Cambridge: Polity Press, 1995).
37. A prominent defense of the thesis of the "feudalization of the bourgeoisie" is found in another study of the duel: Kevin McAleer, *Dueling: The Cult of Honor in Fin-de-Siècle Germany* (Princeton, NJ: Princeton University Press, 1994). For another rebuttal of the feudalization theory, see David Blackbourn, *The Long Nineteenth Century: A History of Germany, 1780–1918* (Oxford: Oxford University Press, 1998), 367.
38. Franz von Liszt, *Lehrbuch des deutschen Strafrechts*, 10th edn. (Berlin: De Gruyter, 1900), 253. Consider also Josef Kraus, *Das Rechtsgut der Ehre vom kulturgeschichtlichen und legislativpolitischen Standpunkte dargestellt* (Vienna: Manz, 1905), 34.
39. *Vorentwurf zu einem deutschen Strafgesetzbuch* (Berlin: Guttentag, 1909), 162.
40. This, of course, is a typical model depiction of the relation between the rise of state bureaucracy and the deregulation of the market, which developed differently in different countries in Europe. See Lutz Raphael, *Recht und Ordnung. Herrschaft durch Verwaltung im 19. Jahrhundert* (Frankfurt a.M.: Fischer, 2000), 41–75. For the German states more specifically, see Bernd Wunder, *Geschichte der Bürokratie in Deutschland* (Frankfurt a.M., 1986), 21–23. The idea of the "punitive state" emerging simultaneously with the creation of the liberal market is inspired by the works of Loïc Wacquant and Bernard Harcourt, who focus mostly on France and the United States; Germany was different in many respects. Nonetheless, the deregulation of the market also played an important ideological role in the modern justification of the punitive powers of the state in Germany. See Bernard E. Harcourt, *The Illusion of Free Markets: Punishment and the Myth of Natural Order* (Cambridge, MA: Harvard University Press, 2012); Loïc Wacquant, *Punishing the Poor: The Neoliberal Government of Social Insecurity* (Durham, NC: Duke University Press, 2009).
41. *Allgemeines Landrecht für die Preußischen Staaten* from 1794 was a case in point as it made clear distinctions between the norms that were applied to the noble estate and to members of the other estates.
42. The famous Dutch statesman Johan Rudolf Thorbecke used this term in an 1844 lecture on this topic: "Over het hedendaagsche staatsburgerschap," in *Historische schetsen*, 84–96 (1872). As his biographer pointed out, Thorbecke's thinking was firmly rooted in German philosophy and legal thought: Jan Drentje, *Thorbecke: een filosoof in de politiek* (Amsterdam: Boom, 2004).
43. Anne Simonin, *Le déshonneur dans la république. Une histoire de l'indignité 1791–1958* (Paris: Grasset, 2008), 52.
44. Pippa Holloway, *Living in Infamy: Felony Disenfranchisement and the History of American Citizenship* (Oxford: Oxford University Press, 2014), 15.

45. Not much has changed since then. As Jeff Manza and Christopher Uggen argued, if disenfranchised felons had been allowed to vote, the electoral outcomes of the 2000 presidential election would likely have been different: Jeff Manza and Christopher Uggen, *Locked Out: Felony Disenfranchisement and American Democracy* (Oxford: Oxford University Press, 2006), 192.
46. Philipp Müller, "'But We Will Always Have to Individualise'. Police Supervision of Released Prisoners, Its 'Crisis' and Reform in Prussia (1880–1914)," *Crime, Histoire & Sociétés / Crime, History & Societies* 14, no. 2 (2010): 55–84. See Rebekka Habermas, "Von Anselm von Feuerbach zu Jack the Ripper," *Rechtsgeschichte—Legal History* 3 (2003): 128–63.
47. One of my key assumptions in this book is that petitions can be interpreted as ego-documents that provide essential information about the subjective experience of historical agents, even if they were written with a specific purpose in mind. See Otto Ulbicht, "Supplikationen als Ego-Dokumente. Bittschriften von Leibeigenen aus der ersten Hälfte des 17. Jahrhunderts als Beispiel," in *Ego-Dokumente. Annäherung an den Menschen in der Geschichte*, ed. Winfried Schulze, 149–74 (Berlin: Akad.-Verl., 1996). Like any text, petitions have multiple layers and contain traces of the subjective experience of the ex-offenders who wrote them. To help examine these layers, I was inspired by the method of "responsive reading," which has been applied mostly to early modern history by historians like Ulinka Rublack: Ulinka Rublack, "Interior States and Sexuality in Early Modern Germany," in *After the History of Sexuality: German Genealogies with and beyond Foucault*, ed. Scott Spector, Helmut Puff, and Dagmar Herzog, 43–62 (New York: Berghahn Books, 2012). The basic idea is to repeatedly read through a statement to identify the different features of the account the author gives of herself. Particularly important are the "voice of the 'I' speaking" and the ways petitioners speak about relationships and how they "experience themselves in the relational landscape of human life"; ibid., 55.
48. In their comprehensive studies of imprisonment in German history, Desiree Schauz and Thomas Nutz both explicitly acknowledge that the development of legislation is not their central concern. They point out that the absence of a Code of Prison Administration meant that it was largely welfare organizations and penal experts that determined how punishments were carried out in the nineteenth century. Legal scholarship and penal policy are separate universes, one could argue. See Thomas Nutz, "Strafrechtsphilosophie und Gefängniskunde. Strategien diskursiver Legitimierung in der ersten Hälfte des 19. Jahrhunderts," *Zeitschrift für neuere Rechtsgeschichte* 22 (2000): 95–110. Notwithstanding this important insight, an important aim of this book is to show that penal law ultimately played an important role in how crimes were evaluated in debates about what just punishments for them could be.
49. Rosenblum, *Beyond the Prison Gates*, 2. In this study, the author only briefly mentions the laws on felony disenfranchisement in the chapter on World War I (132–33). Curiously, he writes that these regulations were laid down in §44 of the Reich Penal Code, but, in reality, it was §34. Presumably Rosenblum was referring to §44 of the *Vorentwurf zu einem deutschen Strafgesetzbuch* of 1909, but this proposal was never ratified as law.
50. Studies on the history of criminology focus on how the notion of "the criminal" was constructed within the discipline. These studies shed light on the shift that took place in the nineteenth century from an emphasis on depraved people who willfully neglected their moral duties to an emphasis on "degenerates" who became "criminals" due to socioeconomic or biological factors. Most important in this regard is Wetzell, *Inventing the Criminal*; Peter Becker, *Verderbnis und Entartung. Eine Geschichte der Kriminologie des 19. Jahrhunderts als Diskurs und Praxis* (Göttingen: Vandenhoeck & Ruprecht, 2002); Christian Müller, *Verbrechensbekämpfung im Anstaltsstaat. Psychiatrie, Kriminologie und Strafrechtsreform in Deutschland 1871–1933* (Göttingen: Vandenhoeck & Ruprecht, 2004); Marie-Christine Leps, *Apprehending the Criminal: The Production of Deviance in Nineteenth-Century Discourse* (Durham, NC: Duke University Press, 1992).

Chapter 1

"Rights of Citizenship Are Conditional Rights"
Disenfranchisement, Honor, and Trust in the Criminal Codes before German Unification

In 1866, shortly after the end of the Austro-Prussian War, a number of people who resided in the Duchy of Nassau and the Free City of Frankfurt (both annexed by the Kingdom of Prussia after the war) appealed to the Prussian king to have sentences handed down by local courts reversed.[1] One of them was a crop farmer named Johannes Wagner from Weiperfelden, a village in the territories of the Duchy of Nassau. For years, Wagner had functioned as the head (*Gemeindevorsteher*) of his local community. However, he had also served time in the penitentiary (*Zuchthaus*) as he had been found guilty of forging official documents (*Urkundenfälschung*) on multiple occasions. In addition to time behind bars, his sentence included the lifelong suspension of his political rights, which implied that he was no longer eligible to hold public office. Nonetheless, after his release from the penitentiary, he had served as the head of his community for years without any objections.

This situation changed when representatives of the Duke of Nassau in Usingen found out about Wagner's conviction. The central government had apparently not been aware of it previously, and, upon its discovery, Wagner was immediately removed from office and denied the further exercise of his function. After the annexation of Nassau by Prussian forces, though, Wagner quickly sent a request to the Prussian king to have his sentence reversed so that he could once again take up his office in his local community.[2] What is interesting about Wagner's case is that the deprivation of his rights (imposed on him by a local court) was only enforced after the state government of Nassau interfered in the affairs of this rural community. Before that time, his local community seemed uninterested in his criminal past.

Notes from this chapter begin on page 41.

Johannes Wagner's story, therefore, offers an insight into the complex relationships that existed in the German states between legal punishments, the right to political participation, state power, and local politics. This chapter investigates why states in the early nineteenth century had a strong interest in enforcing the suspension of civil privileges for people like Wagner, as well as what the purpose of this type of punishment was. The suspension of rights as punishment played a crucial—yet often overlooked—role in the history of the German states' formation. In fact, the provisional character of citizens' rights to political participation was a quintessential element of states' efforts to create a moral order among their citizens, which, in turn, was supposed to safeguard the institutions through citizens' exercise of their civil privileges.

Civil Privileges as Provisional

According to the Prussian Penal Code of 1851 (which was still in effect in 1866), felons had to forfeit several of their rights to public participation after their release from prison. This measure, designed to turn felons into second-class citizens, was an important element of the penal system of the German states before unification. The specific rights listed in the code included, among others, the right to wear the state's cockade, the right to join the army, the right to hold public office, the right to vote or be elected to positions pertaining to public affairs, the right to be a witness for notarial records, and the right to be the guardian or custodian of a child.[3] Together, these rights belonged to a special category: the "civil privileges" (*bürgerliche Ehrenrechte*).[4] All German states had criminal codes with similar regulations enabling judges to strip offenders of their civil privileges.

It is important to note, in relation to the context of these codes, that political citizenship was never associated with a stable set of privileges in the first half of the nineteenth century. The regulations on the distribution of privileges of citizenship varied greatly across the various European legal regimes, and the different German-speaking states did not have a uniform notion of the rights of political citizenship in the first half of the nineteenth century.[5] The privileges enumerated in the Prussian Penal Code of 1851, for example, were only gradually introduced during the period of the Restoration. Nonetheless, a common characteristic of nearly all the codes regulating the distribution of these privileges was an emphasis on their provisional character.

The provisionality of civil privileges first emerged, as Andreas Fahrmeir argues, in the regulations of the First French Republic (1792–1804). This code generated a body of "respectable and independent adult men" with the privilege of participating in the political affairs of the republic.[6] This body of men was first and foremost defined by their privileges: their rights to political participation. It might be tempting to focus on the notions of "independent" or "adult" in this description of political citizenship, but equally important is the notion of "respectable." The inclusion of this term, after all, indicates most clearly that the rights to political participation were essentially granted on provisional grounds; political citizenship was dependent on one's respectable reputation. Hence, the French regulations on political citizenship included the provision that one could lose these rights "by forfeiting one's honor through a criminal conviction or temporarily through servitude or bankruptcy."[7] Felony disenfranchisement therefore characterized much of the politics of both the First French Republic and the Restoration monarchy.[8]

In many European states, political rights were gradually expanded to include a larger class of citizens, particularly in the German-speaking world, where changes tended to derive from reform from above rather than revolution from below.[9] The most important differences in the historical development of regulations between France and the German states in the period of the *Vormärz*, however, was that the German debates strongly emphasized citizens' rights to participate in the political life of the local community, the so-called *Gemeinde*. This contrasted sharply with the more state-oriented regulations in France.[10] For instance, citizenship in Prussia was heavily influenced by the idea of "local autonomy," which was endorsed in the important Stein-Hardenberg Reforms of the first decade of the nineteenth century and the introduction of the Municipal Ordinance in 1808. This ordinance, designed by Baron Karl vom und zum Stein, reformed traditional citizens' law (*Bürgerrecht*) and was intended to strengthen the autonomous administration (*Selbstverwaltung*) of local communities by giving male residents of towns (who had a certain amount of property at their disposal) the right to political participation (*Teilnahme*). As German historian Reinhart Koselleck argues, the ultimate aim of this policy was to create a "local rule of the common man."[11]

Yet the notion of civil privileges (*bürgerliche Ehrenrechte*) was not included in Stein's Municipal Ordinance. The notion of Bürgerrecht discussed in the ordinance mostly concerned the wealthy inhabitants of cities, but this was not yet civil privileges as they later came to be defined. The Bürgerrecht was rather an expansion of the liberties that inhabitants of cities had been granted ever since the Middle Ages.[12] In fact, the rights of state citizens (*Staatsbürger*) in the nineteenth century emerged out of a combination of the municipal rights granted to inhabitants of the cities and the rights to participation in state affairs.[13] After all, the state reforms in the German states from the onset of the modern era (the so-called *Sattelzeit*), especially the reforms in the German client states of the French Empire in the Confederation of the Rhine from 1806 onwards, mainly aimed to expand a large bureaucratic system of government.

For instance, during this period, public officials were increasingly appointed on the basis of their individual competence (the *Leistungsprinzip*) instead of their hereditary privileges.[14] They started functioning as servants of the state (*Staatsdiener*) rather than as servants of princes (*Fürstendiener*), as Max Weber distinguished the two kinds of civil servants, and for the first time people who were not members of the traditional aristocracy became eligible to hold public office.[15] In this sense, a new class of privileged citizens emerged in these states.[16]

Alongside the privileges of participation in government (either as a civil servant or as a representative), yet another civil privilege was fundamental to the discussion of felony disenfranchisement: the right to join the army. In 1807, Prussia created a national army for the first time; modeled on the French revolutionary armies (the Jacobin model), it was comprised of national citizens.[17] From that period onwards, most German states introduced conscription for their own citizens; most soldiers had previously still been recruited from foreign nations.[18] The right (and the duty) to join the army—together with the right to wear the state cockade—thus became one of the central privileges of state citizenship. Nearly all young male citizens were required to join the army, though they were carefully inspected before they enlisted.[19] This, too, demonstrates how civil privileges were not just an expansion of the privileges that inhabitants of the German cities enjoyed but a combination of the rights granted to the wealthy citizens in towns (such as election rights) and other privileges that concerned participation in the (nation-)state. All in all, these privileges granted a large set of men something quite new: "state citizenship" (*Staatsbürgerschaft*).[20]

In the nineteenth century, however, none of these civil privileges were listed in a bill of rights or in any of the German constitutions.[21] As mentioned above, Stein's Municipal Ordinance included regulations about privileges for landowning men who resided in Prussian towns, but these were not yet civil privileges proper. The contents of the civil privileges were also left unmentioned in the 1850 Prussian Constitution and in the revised Prussian municipal ordinances. Hence, it is crucial to note where these civil privileges were commonly defined, namely, in the penal codes, as in the case of both the 1851 Prussian Penal Code and the 1855 Saxon Penal Code.[22] There is no better evidence that, in the minds of the German authorities, the question of civil privileges was intimately connected with the topic of crime and punishment. Every legal codification of citizenship rights was in one way or another combined with a discussion of the criminal acts that might cause someone to lose these rights: a clear sign that these civil privileges were essentially understood as provisional.

Indeed, according to most natural law accounts of the notion of privilege, the fact that rights could be suspended was one of the key aspects of the definition of privilege.[23] "Citizenship right is a conditional right," the prominent legal scholar Karl Salomo Zachariae argued, for instance, in his influential *Vierzig Bücher vom Staate* of 1842: "he who enjoys a right only conditionally loses this right as soon as the condition on which the right is based ceases to exist."[24] Of course, there was a certain paradox in the fact that most of the privileges of state citizenship were also duties—something Zachariae also pointed out.[25] Another paradox was that all people—men and women—could be disenfranchised since the penal law applied to all subjects. The influential Wilhelmine legal scholar Karl Binding considered this a contradictory element of the policy of disenfranchisement when he wrote about it in his legal textbook.[26] However, one could argue that this element—the punishment also being handed down to subjects who were not in possession of these privileges—supports the idea that the punishment had a larger aim. Beyond stripping people of their privileges, it was also designed to have a greater emotional impact on the punished subjects and on the society that administered it.

Nonetheless, the character of these rights as privileges dominated most of the discussions of state citizenship in this period. It is striking to see how closely the topic of crime and punishment was related to the discussion of the nature of civil privileges—much more than it was in the twentieth century, when civil rights increasingly came to be understood as unconditional.

The Broken Trust Argument

In the legal configuration of the German states of the Restoration and *Vormärz* (1813–48), there was an intimate connection between civil privileges and penal law, but the logical nexus between criminal offenses and the revocation of civil privileges is perhaps puzzling to present-day observers: why were people deprived of their rights to vote and join the army if they were guilty of a criminal offense? This connection was particularly difficult to justify from the perspective of the penal theory of retribution: what was proportional about stripping a person's right to join the army if he committed perjury? Such questions demanded a more thorough philosophical grounding of the stripping of civil privileges that described the damage of crimes like perjury, robbery, and usury in more abstract, state-related terms.

Lacking clear statistics about the people whose civil privileges were revoked, it is best to look at why people believed felony disenfranchisement was crucial to the penal systems of the German states. In this context, it is problematic that few legal scholars felt the need to justify its existence; felony disenfranchisement was apparently rather uncontested in German penal policy. One Hessian judge, Friedrich Noellner, however, did critique felony disenfranchisement, and in the foreword to his book on this punishment, he called it one of the most neglected topics in German academia precisely because it seemed so self-evident to many legal scholars that serious offenders were deprived of the right to participate in political life.[27]

During the 1830s and 1840s, a small but increasing number of scholars, like Noellner, began suggesting that disenfranchisement should be implemented differently, or even abolished. The overarching aim of these scholars was to highlight the "moral reform" of offenders.[28] Noellner's argument, for instance, was that disenfranchisement implied ex-convicts were still morally condemnable after they were discharged from prison, so their disenfranchisement sabotaged their process of moral reform.[29] Nevertheless, most such criticism fell on deaf ears where the German authorities were concerned.[30] In fact, after the revolutions of 1848–49, legal scholars increasingly emphasized the fundamental importance of elements in the penal system that dishonored the criminals.[31]

Only after such critics suggested that the policy of disenfranchisement required serious readjustment did some scholars feel the need to remind the German scholarly community of why the punishment existed in the first place. Before 1848, there was one author who made significant contributions to this debate and defended the policy of felony disenfranchisement in its most extreme forms: Adolf (sometimes spelled Adolph) von Wick, an auditor serving in the judicial government of the Duchy of Mecklenburg, who was occupied with penitentiary reforms in the municipality of Bützow.[32] Wick wrote an exhaustive account of the policy of felony disenfranchisement titled *Über Ehrenstrafen und Ehrenfolgen der Verbrechen und Strafen*, which he published anonymously in 1846. In it, he tried to justify this punishment for a certain class of offenders and unambiguously defended it as having an important function in modern society.

Wick published his treatise when several authors were beginning to criticize aspects of this punishment. Not surprisingly, the debates regarding its purpose went hand in hand with debates on the distribution of civil privileges. For instance, when law professor Carl Hepp, an influential commentator of the penal code of Württemberg, started agitating against the "wretched condition" of the penal system in the 1840s, he complained about both the confusion surrounding what political citizenship entailed exactly and the need to define the grounds for suspending civil privileges more clearly. In his view, these problems were intimately connected because political citizenship entailed more privileges than it had previously. By then, for instance, it also included the right to be member of a jury, or, in some cases, the right to take up arms as part of a civilian militia (a right granted to the citizens of Württemberg in 1848).[33]

In Wick's treatise defending the punishment, one notion clearly stands out: trust. It played a crucial role in Wick's entire understanding of civil privileges as provisional and accounted for the theoretical connection between criminal behavior and felony disenfranchisement. Civil privileges were granted to certain residents of the German states, he argued, as a token of the trust these states had put in them; consequently, the bestowal of these privileges had to be understood as nothing short of an "honor." Clearly, in his account, the notions of honor and trust were closely intertwined: "all honor and respect are in their deepest foundations based on trust."[34] Or elsewhere:

> Honor is trust in man and common honor or, more correctly, civil honor is the form of civil trust that develops a society of men. Every people and every estate is permeated

by a common spirit, and this spirit is accompanied by a common trust in which each individual participates without having to prove his worthiness.[35]

In other words, Wick characterized civil privileges as something a sovereign awarded citizens not on the basis of some accomplishment but as a benevolent (albeit provisional) gesture. This meant that the citizens' relationship to the state was neither one of complete submission nor one of unconditional entitlement. Rather, the state put its trust in its citizens by granting them the privilege to participate in its administration and elections, or to join its army.

Wick was not unique in drawing this connection between citizenship and trust. In fact, many authors emphasized the crucial importance of trust for the exercise of citizens' civil privileges.[36] Likewise, political commentators in the German states frequently made the connection between trust and civil participation before unification. A clear example of this is the definition of citizenship (*Staatsbürgerschaft*) that Julius Merkel, the burgomaster of the Saxon town of Zwenkau, gave in 1863: citizenship was "the honorable trust" (*das ehrende Vertrauen*) the state places in citizens and subjects by letting them participate in public affairs.[37]

The difference between this way of thinking about political trust and that of current political theory is significant. Nowadays, the question is often approached from the perspective of citizens trusting their government with the discretionary powers they grant it.[38] Early nineteenth-century German debates about political citizenship, however, emphasized that the state (however unclear the definition of that concept was) put its trust in its subjects—especially when "common" citizens got the right to participate in several aspects of public decision-making. Evidently, this theory fit well with the model of constitutional monarchy dominant at the time. It was, in the end, the monarchs who bestowed privileges on their citizens.[39]

In debates on the expansion of civil and political rights from the late eighteenth century to the period of German unification, the notion of public trust figured prominently in citizens' demands for more rights to political participation. The Prussian statesman Johann Gottfried Frey, for instance, argued in 1808 that it was impossible to have a good political administration without "mutual trust and reciprocal respect" between the state and its citizens.[40] Furthermore, during the revolution of 1848, the notion of the "trust state" (*Vertrauensstaat*) was actively deployed by citizens demanding more political rights.[41] Hence, in both cases, the notion of trust was not used to strengthen the discretionary power of the government but to demand more political rights for its citizens.

Civil privileges were thus commonly seen as privileges awarded on the basis of a relation of trust between citizens and the state. In turn, this meant that the principal justification for revoking these privileges for criminals was the idea that they were being punished for breaking the trust upon which their citizenship status was based. Wick's depiction of the relation of trust was thus infused with arguments that were common in contract theories of government, namely, that trust was an essential resource for the functioning of the contract. Nonetheless, he added the extra dimension of "honor" to secure this connection. In other words, felony disenfranchisement restored the foundation of trust on which the political community was based by excluding persons who had offended against these terms.[42]

Dishonorable Crimes: Perjury as a Prime Example

Wick gave considerable weight to the question of which offenders should be subjected to felony disenfranchisement. He concluded that it should be specifically reserved for people who had committed offenses against the public trust.[43] It is important to keep in mind that Wick intended for his theory to serve as a comprehensive account of the existing laws in the several German states, suggesting that his ideas could also be traced back to many of the actual laws. To mention one example, the text accompanying the Municipal Ordinance of the Kingdom of Saxony from 1837 stated that people who committed a "disgraceful crime were to be denied all public trust."[44] In short, Wick was not defending a merely abstract utopian idea but a theory based on his understanding of the laws.

One defining aspect of Wick's theory was that he conceived only of some criminal offenses as breaches of trust. As the text of the Saxon law showed, there was a special category of so-called disgraceful crimes, which felony disenfranchisement specifically targeted. In Wick's account, for instance, excessive violence or crimes of passion committed in public were not seen as offenses against public trust: "He who inflicts bodily harm on his enemy by open violence is not generally considered dishonored; but if he does it insidiously, he is committing a dishonorable act."[45]

So, what *was* an offense against public trust? For Wick, the offender's intention (or, more precisely, disposition) was the ultimate criterion for determining whether a crime also offended against public trust, so the distinction could not be made on the basis of the act alone. Although punishable, violent behavior resulting from genuine passion was not in itself an offense against public trust, but if the action also brought some kind of private advantage to the perpetrator, this would testify to a so-called dishonorable disposition (*ehrlose Gesinnung*).[46] Again, this was not just Wick's opinion; the concept of "dishonorable disposition" was included in most German penal codes.[47]

This notion of disposition (*Gesinnung*) is crucial to understanding the system of criminal justice in nineteenth-century Germany. Although it was also often used to refer to one's general political worldview and membership in a political association, the concept was especially fundamental to the moral-philosophical discourse that determined most of the ideas on the origins of criminal behavior for a good part of the nineteenth century.[48] This discourse helped shape the dominant image of "the criminal" in scholarly works on criminal policy from the early nineteenth century. According to historian Peter Becker, the general image of the criminal at that time was that of a bourgeois man who voluntarily chose a life of crime.[49] "The criminal" refused to obey the maxims of action dictated by good conscience, thus indicating that he had an "evil disposition." Within this framework, a criminal career was essentially seen as a self-imposed destiny as the criminal presented the diametric opposite of the model citizen who listened to the voice of his conscience and was bestowed with an "honorable" disposition.[50]

In his study of early nineteenth-century criminologists, Becker discussed the notion of crime as an overarching category and made little distinction between different crimes.[51] For Wick, however, there were three types of offenses that had to be understood as breaches of public trust by definition and therefore unconditionally testified to a dishonorable disposition. Wick believed this principle should be upheld regardless of one's social rank. Thus, in his view, people belonging to the aristocracy or the educated classes (*die gebildete Stände*) should also be subject to felony disenfranchisement if found guilty of committing any of these offenses.[52] His analysis highlighted all offenses that included any form of deceit: "It is natural, then, that nothing so much opposes honor as that which undoes faithfulness and trust, namely, deceit."[53] This category included swindle, forgery, and counterfeiting, but the key offense in this category was perjury: a breach of the oath that was crucial to many public affairs. The oath, after all, was the clearest sign of the trust that the state put in its citizens, so perjury was conceived as the ultimate breaking of this trust. As Wick put it, every act of perjury presupposed a "total depravity of disposition" (*totale Verworfenheit der Gesinnung*).[54]

For this reason, a more detailed examination of the function of the laws on perjury in the conceptual relation between states and their citizens is enlightening. In fact, it is very likely that the centrality of "public trust" in Wick's theory of felony disenfranchisement derived from debates on punishments for committing perjury, which had occupied the minds of many legal scholars in the German states since the mid-eighteenth century.

For most of European legal history, perjury was understood as an offense against God and was treated in roughly the same way as blasphemy.[55] For example, a definition of the act of perjury as a religious offense can be found in the *Constitutio Criminalis Theresiana* (henceforth *Theresiana*), the criminal code for the territories of Austria and Bohemia that the Habsburg monarch Maria Theresia introduced in 1769: "Perjury is when one knowingly and with deceptive intent takes God as witness of an untrue statement."[56] This code further described offenses against God as the worst kind one could commit.[57] For many nineteenth-century legal scholars, this definition served as the primary example of false testimony in the early modern period.[58]

However, over the course of the eighteenth century, the conception of perjury underwent a fundamental shift in Western Europe. The conception of perjury as a religious offense was seriously challenged under the influence of the Enlightenment. Many influential Enlightenment thinkers argued that perjury should no longer be understood as an offense against God but should rather be understood either as an offense of people against other citizens (a civil offense) or as an offense against the state in general (a public offense). For instance, in their prize-winning essay, Enlightenment scholars Hans Ernst von Globig and Johann Georg Huster described the witnesses' breach of their duty to tell the truth as "the greatest injury to public fidelity and trust." Considering it an egregious offense, they believed that it deserved a very harsh punishment.[59] Many authors subsequently took up the phrase "public fidelity und trust" (*öffentliche Treue und Glauben*) as the primary good damaged by the act of perjury.

Enlightenment thinkers like von Globig and Huster thus redefined what had previously been viewed as acts concerning the relation between men and God as acts concerning the relation between the state and its citizens. This was not only part of the general turn away from the influence of religion in criminal law; more importantly, it was also part of the complete redefinition of the relation between people and the state envisioned by these Enlightenment thinkers.

The influence of Enlightenment ideas on legislation concerning perjury can be seen in what happened with the *Theresiana*. Although the *Theresiana* succeeded in unifying the Austrian system of criminal justice, it also elicited a great deal of controversy. It was widely perceived as a reactionary move against the spirit of Enlightenment in Europe, with its descriptions of the proper use of torture being regarded as particularly regressive. The code did not last long: the *Theresiana* was only in effect in Austria for seventeen years; it was replaced by the code of Emperor Josef II in 1787. This code, which quickly gained a reputation for being very progressive, took a completely different approach to the question of perjury. According to the so-called *Josephina*, one could speak of perjury when a person deceived another person "with base intention in order to damage or infringe upon the other's property, honor, freedom or rights."[60] It is no coincidence that this change occurred under Josef II's reign—he also introduced the most drastic bureaucratic reforms of the era.[61] Although perjury was not defined as a public offense per se, the *Josephina* broke completely with the traditional idea that perjury was an offense against God. Hence, Liszt, in his 1876 academic treatise on the history of the legal concept of perjury, argued that it was hard to find a more dramatic change in criminal law (or even in central European culture, in general) than the shift from the *Theresiana* to the *Josephina*, particularly in this respect.[62]

The two interpretations of perjury as a civil offense and a public offense co-existed for a long time. But, in the end, the idea that perjury was a public offense gained greater currency in German legal scholarship. The most important contribution to the debate in Germany came from the Heidelberg professor of law Carl

Joseph Anton Mittermaier, who believed that perjury was undoubtedly a crime directed against the state and, thus, belonged to the category of crimes against "public fidelity and trust." Mittermaier, in fact, placed perjury on the same conceptual level as counterfeiting: "The state, which bases its most important claims on statements under oath and on money, loses the most important means standing at the foundation of its trustworthiness."[63] Consequently, Mittermaier cast public trust as the primary foundation of the state, with money and the oath of its citizens being the two principal symbols of this trust. In essence, forging money or breaking an oath endangered the very foundations of the state.

Mittermaier's position became the dominant opinion in legal literature toward the middle of the nineteenth century. In his lengthy book on all crimes contained in the German penal codes, Carl Hepp, mentioned above, listed crimes against public trust as one of the six major categories of criminal offenses.[64] Furthermore, the influence of scholars like Mittermaier led other German states to quickly follow the *Josephina* and drop the religious description of the act of perjury in favor of describing it as an offense against public trust. The most telling example of this can be found in a criminal code drafted for the Kingdom of Bavaria in 1828:

> Violating such a sign (namely, of the truth) is no longer simple deception limited to a particular case. Rather, it undermines all possible statements that are dependent upon the trustworthiness of the perjurer. Indeed, they do violence to the believability of the oath in general because a demeaned instrument loses its value in all arenas.[65]

This definition also clarifies why people believed depriving perjurers of their civil privileges seemed commensurate with their crimes: perjurers had offended against the general trust of their political community. This belief was also included in several modern German penal codes, which clearly distinguished this offense from other criminal offenses, for example, against property. Ultimately the offense was included in the Reich Penal Code as one of the offenses against "public order."[66] The type of punishment reserved for it (disenfranchisement) was additionally meant to stigmatize offenders as people who had disrespected the moral order of the state.

Other Dishonorable Offenses: Profit-Seeking Crimes

The example of perjury is particularly informative since it clearly demonstrates the legal rephrasing of the definition to fit the "broken trust" theory of criminal offenses that Wick emphatically supported.[67] It is, nonetheless, important to consider that perjury was not the only offense categorized as an offense against public trust. As mentioned above, Wick grouped it together with other forms of deceit like swindle, forgery, and counterfeiting, yet he saw these crimes only as the first category of offenses testifying to a dishonorable disposition by definition. The second group he mentioned were offenses directed against property, primarily theft.

The inclusion of crimes against property was based on the idea that property rights were an essential component of the social contract. For Wick, it was self-evident that property and trust were two sides of the same coin. He argued that property was the basis of all contracts in society and that people had to trust one another to know what belonged to whom.[68] Consequently, Wick made no exception for people who appropriated things that did not belong to them out of poverty or misery, claiming that theft and robbery were categorically offenses against public trust. Indeed, public perceptions of robbery underwent a significant shift after the seventeenth century. As historian Peter Spierenburg argues, "taking pride in not being considered a thief was the earliest manifestation of a new masculinity."[69] Spierenburg explains this change by pointing out that "economic solidity" had become a primary source of honor for men. In other words, honor increasingly came to be associated with property ownership. Indeed, many historical works on the rise of modern penal regimes point to the growing preoccupation of the middle classes with property crimes during the eighteenth century.[70] Historian Rebekka Habermas also demonstrates that in nineteenth-century Germany, litigants in robbery trials were ultimately more concerned with honor than with anything else.[71] This illustrates that robbery was constructed as the ultimate example of a transgression against the norms of respectable citizenship.

Interestingly, though, Wick did not generally distinguish between robbery (*Raub*) and theft (*Diebstahl*) but regarded both simply as forms of disrespect against the sanctity of private property. In this respect, Wick's words echoed the regulations of most of the penal codes of his time. But other thinkers had different opinions. A few decades earlier, the influential proponent of German Idealism, Johann Gottlieb Fichte, for example, distinguished theft and robbery in his political philosophy in terms of their honorableness: one was dishonorable and the other was not. Someone who appropriated something in secret, Fichte argued, committed theft, whereas someone who openly (and often violently) appropriated something committed robbery; the secrecy of theft abused people's trust, making theft dishonorable, while the openness of robbery prevented such abuse of trust, so it was not inherently dishonorable: "Robbing is vigorous; it counteracts open violence with a force that never trusts; theft is cowardly; it uses the trust of the other to hurt him."[72] Fichte's distinction, however, was relatively old-fashioned; most penal codes from the first half of the nineteenth century differentiated between the two crimes on the basis of the degree of violence involved rather than the degree of secrecy. Nonetheless, it is interesting to see how the notion of trust figured prominently in Fichte's account of penalties for crimes against property. Furthermore, the notion that certain crimes were more dishonorable because they abused someone's trust remained a vivid element of legal thought in nineteenth-century Germany.

The last category in Wick's account of crimes that unconditionally testified to a dishonorable disposition were all offenses with a profit motive. It was a rather complicated category since Wick clearly did not believe that all forms of financial benefit were indicative of a dishonorable disposition. He thus made a distinction between the notion of "acquisition" (*Erwerb*) as the compensation an individual received in exchange for labor or goods and the notion of "profit" (*Profit* or *Gewinn*), which he defined as any gain at the cost of others.[73] The most central of profit-motivated offenses was usury. Nonetheless, Wick was also suspicious of "normal" acts of acquisition. In modern society, he argued, acquisition often degenerated into profit, which is why he considered crimes with the aim of profit-seeking quite characteristic of modern society, rendering efforts to combat usury and curb all forms of excessive acquisition the modern state's primary pursuits.[74]

The most important part of Wick's elaborations on dishonorable crimes was this notion of the pursuit of profit (*Gewinnsucht*). Wick used it to identify which offenders should ideally be punished with felony disenfranchisement, and it is no coincidence that his ideas were in line with most penal codes of the German states. Many German penal codes used this concept as a measuring stick for determining whether a crime was dishonorable or not. Beyond this, Wick thought that the condemnation of a pursuit of profit was important for maintaining the estate-based social order. In his view, someone who acted in pursuit of profit moved away from their traditional place in society.[75] The nobility and civil servants should not engage in commerce, he argued, and craftsmen were not supposed to exercise crafts other than their own. People only left their position in society to pursue profit, according to Wick, and such profit-seeking behavior fundamentally disrupted the social order. After all, there was "no profit estate," he emphasized.[76] Thus, Wick believed that felony disenfranchisement and its condemnation of profit-motivated action clearly contributed to maintaining a certain kind of moral economy in German society.

The survey of offenses that Wick considered dishonorable by definition raises the question of whether he also believed that some offenses were not dishonorable by definition. Fichte's abovementioned comments on the distinctions between robbery and theft, in fact, already suggest an answer as the underlying distinction between the secrecy and openness of an offense determined whether it was dishonorable. According to this theory, the paradigmatic example of an overt offense was the political offense: the political offender openly protested against the government and made no secret of his convictions. There was nothing clandestine about political crimes as they were considered clear acts of conscience.[77] As a result, many people argued that political offenders need not display a sense of remorse for their actions. This was a point the liberal professor Karl Biedermann strongly emphasized when he covered the trial of the conspirators of a Polish uprising in 1847, the so-called *Polenprozess*, which was one of the first political trials on such a large scale in the state of Prussia: "Everybody knows that political crimes do not necessarily require a dishonorable disposition to be carried out; one cannot therefore assume that political offenders will always redeem their offenses with expressions of remorse."[78] Indeed, political offenses were the most important crimes omitted from Wick's set of dishonorable crimes. Like Fichte and many others, Wick also seems to have believed that political crimes were not dishonorable, consistently discussing them alongside dueling, another crime typically motivated by a supposedly honorable disposition.

The list of offenses not deemed dishonorable crimes very frequently coincided with a certain class privilege as upper-class citizens were seldom subject to felony disenfranchisement. Some of the penal codes of the early nineteenth century even explicitly excluded the "educated classes" from felony disenfranchisement.[79] Accordingly, these regulations expressed a certain prejudice that people from these classes were not capable of committing dishonorable offenses. In practice, an "honorable disposition" could signify both a privileged class position as well as an individual moral disposition in the penal codes.[80] Wick made no clear distinction between an individual's disposition and class privilege since it would otherwise have made no sense for him to describe citizenship as a privilege. One had to maintain traditional ideas about estate privilege for the broken trust argument to work. In the end, this was also the criticism he raised against critics of felony disenfranchisement: they failed to understand that citizenship and the privileges it entailed were a form of estate honor (*Bürgerehre*): "The modern notion of honor is in essence estate honor."[81] Hence, by focusing on the fact that citizenship (*Staatsbürgerschaft*) was an estate privilege, Wick managed to combine modern ideas about government and trust with traditional, feudalistic ones.

Sustaining a Moral Order

Wick's defense of felony disenfranchisement as a sensible form of punishment highlighted its key features. By repeating that the perjurer, above all, deserved to have his civil privileges revoked, for instance, he distinguished the citizens who abused the trust bestowed upon them from professional robbers (*Gauner*), the malicious bane of bourgeois society.[82] Clearly, felony disenfranchisement primarily aimed to punish those who had enjoyed these privileges and failed to respect them: being barring from taking up a public office, wearing the state cockade, or signing legal documents would obviously be irrelevant to people who did not enjoy these privileges in the first place.

The function of felony disenfranchisement was undeniably communicative:[83] it symbolically differentiated between dishonored and respectable citizens. In the eyes of many, this distinction was crucial for maintaining the positive image and respectability of the privileges of citizenship. As a result, the counterpart of the broken trust argument was that citizens had a duty to respect their civil privileges. If law-abiding citizens shared the same privileges as dishonest people, the value of these privileges would be undermined, many claimed. The influential German criminal law scholar Gallus Aloys Kleinschrod, for example, wrote in 1799: "The honest, law-abiding citizen cannot have respect for his own honor and that of others if he sees that serious criminals enjoy the same privileges as he himself."[84] This argument came up again and again in various formulations when penal codes were discussed in the several German states. During the debates about the introduction of a penal code for the Kingdom of Hanover, for instance, Hanoverian politician Johann Carl Bertram Stüve remarked: "The degree to which one leaves the honor of the criminal unscathed is the same degree to which one diminishes the honor of law-abiding citizens."[85] Thus, Stüve, too, presented felony disenfranchisement as a symbol of the moral order of society.

This idea of punishment as a communicative practice fits well with Émile Durkheim's ideas about punishment as a "reaction of passionate feeling."[86] For Durkheim, as he explained in his theory, punishment was not a utilitarian or goal-driven exercise for combatting particular crimes but a way of upholding the moral order of society as a whole. This is also why Durkheim felt that punishment had a "sacred" element to it: "acts that it punishes always appear as attacks upon something which is transcendent."[87] In the French context, historian Anne Simonin therefore used the term *éthocratie* to describe the application of these kinds of punishments.[88] The concept of dishonored citizens served to maintain the fiction of society having a well-defined order. After all, a society that believed itself free of crime "would fall into chaos bereft of the signs of its own existence as an authoritative order."[89] This explains why this punishment was not introduced to penalize people who did not have any civil rights in the German context: it explicitly served to reinforce the moral order for citizens of the German states.

Wick defended this communicative function of the punishment, and other eminent scholars shared this view, as evidenced by this remark from the influential conservative Prussian scholar Julius Friedrich Stahl:

> Losing the respect of others and one's respectable position in society is the worst punishment for a crime committed. Even if this respect is something internal, something that the state has no power over, the simple act of making the crime public and carrying out the punishment diminishes the criminal's respectability. However, taking away certain rights, which diminishes not only the criminal's respectability but also his legal possibilities, does lie within the sphere of the state's power.[90]

Nevertheless, this moral function of the punishment of depriving offenders of their civil privileges may have had little impact on many offenders who were likely indifferent to the consequences. In fact, Wick and many other legal scholars acknowledged this. Why would people of the lower classes care about their honor, especially if they did not even enjoy these civil privileges? Consequently, class perceptions were quite significant in the evaluation of the effects of felony disenfranchisement.

Of course, as mentioned, punishment in Durkheim's theory serves not just to correct certain wrongdoers but to reinforce the cohesion of society. Nonetheless, Wick also clearly had in mind a notion of which people should be most affected by the punishment. Wick's focus on offenses like perjury and forgery made it clear that he primarily had people who abused civil privileges for their own ends in mind. Given that this legal punishment marked offenders as essentially untrustworthy, it had a very direct and sometimes severe effect on members of specific classes of society, such as civil servants. This is also the reason legal scholars who found felony disenfranchisement too severe argued against it by referring to stories such as that of Johannes Wagner about people who held a public position but were exposed as "dishonored" offenders.[91]

Civil servants were people who had actively enjoyed civil privileges before they were sentenced. Of course, civil servants also enjoyed special protection from criminal law, meaning that the exercise of their profession was often safeguarded from criminal investigation, but only to a limited extent. If they undermined the trust of their position, their sentences were as harsh as those of other citizens.[92] Certain lower civil servants (including the *Subalternbeamten* and *Unterbeamten*), especially postal employees, were deprived of their civil privileges much more frequently if they seriously broke the trust endowed in them. After all, they were entrusted with important official documents, so a breach of this trust was severely penalized.

Apart from lower civil servants like postal employees, however, Wick argued that this punishment particularly impacted members of the so-called serving classes (*die dienende Classe*), better known as the class of the *Gesinde*.[93] In fact, he argued that felony disenfranchisement affected them the most severely, and in great numbers. The notion of the serving classes was rather vague, particularly in the first half of the nineteenth century when German society (Prussian society, above all) was in the midst of a great transition—especially concerning the place of "the family" in state affairs. This was because during the *Sattelzeit*, before the bureaucratic reforms, Prussian politics made no clear distinction between state and family affairs. Toward the end of the eighteenth century, however, family affairs were gradually transferred to the private domain, with considerable consequences for the serving classes.[94] In particular, this meant that the number of household servants grew while the number of more highly educated servants who took care of education and administration decreased. Nonetheless, at the beginning of the nineteenth century, the concept of *Gesinde* still included both less and more highly educated servants.

The criminal offenses of servants often had a special status in the penal codes. As with civil servants, they were seen as standing in a special relationship of loyalty to their masters (*Treueverhältniss*). This automatically rendered many of their offenses special ones, which meant that they often faced more severe punishment compared to other people for the same crimes (especially theft). Nonetheless, there was some ambivalence concerning servants' status in the penal codes: in certain instances, servants' offenses resulted in milder punishments since minor offenses were still considered to fall under the remit of the master's disciplinary powers (*Züchtigungsrecht*). Criminal law, after all, had only recently begun to apply to "family matters."[95]

As there is no meaningful data about the number of servants incarcerated in the Restoration and *Vormärz* period, it is hard to assess the accuracy of Wick's assertion that felony disenfranchisement affected this class in great numbers. Even so, some prison wardens made similar observations. For instance, Friedrich Wick, the warden of the penitentiary in Bützow (it is unclear whether he was directly related to Adolf Wick), pointed out that one-third of his inmates were from the serving classes.[96] Among the female population, this percentage was probably even higher. In 1844, 80 percent of the women incarcerated in the Saxon prison of Hubertusburg, for example, were former servants.[97] During the first half of the nineteenth century, public outrage about the decay of morality and loyalty among the "serving classes" also stimulated the discussion about the sanctioning of servants. Many believed that servants were less trustworthy and loyal than they had been in former times. Numerous essay contests about how to combat this problem underscored how important this question was perceived to be.[98]

Felony disenfranchisement as a form of punishment seriously affected the serving classes because they depended on certificates of good conduct for employment. Codified in the 1794 General State Laws for the Prussian States (Allgemeines Landrecht für die Preußischen Staaten), these certificates became even more important when the so-called *Gesindebücher* were introduced in 1846. From then on, servants had to register all their penalties in a journal that they were to carry with them.[99] Hence, the problem was not that they were so attached to their civil privileges (in fact, they often did not have them) but that such punishments undermined their future employment prospects. Thus, contrary to Wick's argument, one cannot deny that the punishment had a deterrent effect because most needed to be increasingly flexible and mobile for their employment and could not afford to have such penalties listed in their journals.[100]

Restoring Rights: Possibilities for Rehabilitation

As one of the staunchest supporters of the punishment of felony disfranchisement, Wick was also firm about how long it should last. He argued that disenfranchisement should always be for life: "It is essential to honor as a common trust that its consequences on the criminal are indelible."¹⁰¹ In most German penal codes, this was indeed the case, but regulations varied from state to state. Wick's view was rooted in his belief that felony disenfranchisement truly constituted a loss of honor, which was not just a bureaucratic label but something that sprouted from the judgment of the people. In fact, in his mind, there was no conceptual difference between infamy before the law and infamy before the court of public opinion. Thus, his radical conclusion was that no judge or other public authority should be allowed to decide that someone's honor had been restored; this power belonged solely to the "jurisdiction" of public opinion:

> If by public opinion one understands the pure, original voice of the people that speaks in our customs and institutions and their historical development, then one can correctly say that this *vox populi* exerts the highest judgment over right and wrong, honor and dishonor.¹⁰²

Before further discussing the possibilities for rehabilitation, it is perhaps important to point out certain differences between the Prussian and Saxon codes as they each expressed different views of who determined a person's unworthiness for office. The Saxon penal code of 1856 automatically imposed felony disenfranchisement after any penitentiary sentence but left open felons' worthiness to hold public office. In Prussia, unworthiness to hold office was a *de jure* consequence of the law. Nonetheless, people could be restricted in exercising their civil privileges in a different way in Saxony. This was in fact covered by the Saxon Municipal Ordinance: an addendum from 1837 stipulated that the Municipal Council had the final decision concerning whether an offender would be denied the right to exercise civil privileges.¹⁰³ In this sense, the decision was much more of a communal affair than in Prussia, where it was made by a single judge.¹⁰⁴ This shows the difference in the ways this punishment could be approached and how jurists believed it was connected to the moral beliefs of the people.

Wick's arguments regarding the possibility of rehabilitation echoed certain phrases from guidelines distributed by the Prussian state, particularly concerning the question of returning a person's right to wear the state cockade. Prussian Minister of the Interior Otto Theodor von Manteuffel clarified an important condition for a citizen to regain his right to wear the state cockade in an 1845 circular: "The person seeking restoration of rights has fully recovered the respect and trust of his fellow citizens."¹⁰⁵ This formulation helped Wick argue that there was no room for rehabilitation in the law since it was impossible for a judge to decide if somebody had indeed recovered the respect and trust of his fellow citizens.

In this regard, Wick's beliefs nonetheless deviated from the penal practices of many German states, where the rehabilitation of rights was often possible for people who were severely affected by their disenfranchisement. In fact, the notion of rehabilitation was as prominent in discussions about felony disenfranchisement as was the notion of honor. In the 1865 edition of Carl Theodor Welcker and Carl von Rotteck's *Staatslexicon*, lawyer Karl Buchner defined the notion of rehabilitation as "The cancellation of all legal incapacities resulting from a sentence."[106] Buchner's entry was largely dedicated to the topic of felony disenfranchisement. As this punishment was the primary legal hindrance resulting from criminal convictions (next to police supervision) in the German penal codes, Buchner viewed rehabilitation and felony disenfranchisement as two essentially related notions.

In the end, the main question concerning rehabilitation was who should be responsible for making the decision? The answer to this question was clear: it could only be given as a pardon from the head of the state and was, thus, a form of *landesherrliche Gnade*, or mercy on the part of the sovereign. Such mercy intimately connected rehabilitation to monarchical rule, which reinforced the notion that the rights of public participation were truly privileges, that is, something the head of state determined. There was also the question of the criteria for determining whether someone was eligible to have his rights restored in the first place. Monarchs delegated this decision to a state bureaucracy, as is clear from the guidelines of the Prussian state codifying a procedure for the restoration of the right to wear the state cockade. An 1822 decree stated that anyone within Prussian jurisdiction was permitted to petition to restore this right. The only requirement was that the petitioner append to his letter of petition a certificate of good conduct during his time in the penitentiary.[107] The local police commissioner would collect all the information about the petitioner and was expected to report his findings to the Ministry of the Interior and the Ministry of Justice, both of which subsequently advised the monarch. In other words, although the restoration of the privileges was a form of monarchical grace, it was organized on the principles of the bureaucratic state.

Wick repeated his arguments against the possibility of rehabilitation in an 1851 article for the *Archiv des Criminalrechts* and ended up in a debate with the Privy Councilor of Karlsruhe, Wilhelm von Brauer.[108] Brauer's opinion was the opposite of Wick's. He advocated that it was the judge's duty to decide whether an offender had improved his conduct. This meant that Brauer also opposed rehabilitation as a form of sovereign mercy and saw it rather as a part of bureaucratic governance. Brauer believed that local authorities played an important role in determining whether one's conduct had improved. The judge, he argued, had to rely on the reports of pastors and local authorities to make his decision.[109] In fact, this was already common practice in some German states. In the Kingdom of Württemberg, for instance, offenders had been able to petition the judge for the restoration of their civil privileges since 1849.[110]

In fact, many of the penal codes implemented after Wick had published his treatise in 1845 also introduced the deprivation of civil privileges for a limited period of time (for instance, in the 1851 Prussian code it was limited to a maximum of ten years), together with the possibility of rehabilitation. This gave Wick occasion to republish his book in 1853: he wished to remind the German public that this form of punishment was a genuine expression of German public opinion, underscoring the morally reprehensible character of certain crimes, and that the current laws failed to take this seriously.

"Civil Honor Rests on Irreproachableness"

The concept of honor, in combination with the notion of trust, was the central term around which the entire policy of felony disenfranchisement revolved. Whoever violated the general trust that stood at the foundations of the political community was dishonored from that moment on. Conceptually speaking, this also meant that the notions of honor and trust were no longer seen as purely individual qualities. Rather, they took on more abstract definitions around the turn of the nineteenth century.[111] German historian Ute Frevert has shown that the verb "trust" gradually came to be used as an independent noun and that the concept also became invested with emotional values during this period.[112] Indeed, one of the most influential texts on criminal law from the first half of the nineteenth century, Konrad Franz Roßhirt's *Geschichte und System des deutschen Strafrechts*, defined public trust as a "common sentiment."[113]

The emergence of another concept in legal discourse was crucial in this respect, too: the notion of *Rechtsgut*, from the two German words *Recht* and *Gut*, meaning a legal good.[114] Historical inquiry into the origins of the term has shown that the concept of *Rechtsgut* was developed by nineteenth-century legal scholar Johann Michael Franz Birnbaum, who introduced the term to criticize the idea (defended by the famous Enlightenment legal scholar Anselm Feuerbach and others) that criminal offenses should be defined as violations of other people's rights. Birnbaum argued that penal law was supposed to be about more than just the protection of people's individual rights; it was about the protection of certain goods that make society function: legal goods.[115] The term *Rechtsgut* was therefore meant to encompass more than just a person's individual rights—it was really a good that circulated in society. As a result, honor and trust were quintessentially seen as goods that were more abstract than individual rights that could be damaged by criminal acts. Indeed, the introduction of such categories as transcendent individual rights and feelings resonates with Durkheim's statement that punishment "continues always to bear a stamp of religiosity."[116]

This indicated that part of the state-building process of the nineteenth century involved German states' effort to transform "civil honor" (*staatsbürgerliche Ehre*) into the hegemonic understanding of honor and to have it coexist with other notions of honor. One could encounter this idea—that several interpretations of the notion of honor coexisted but that one was hegemonic—in important Wilhelmine legal commentaries that discussed what kind of "honor" disenfranchisement actually targeted. There were a few alternative voices, such as that of the liberal Prussian journalist Ernst Rethwisch, who argued that there was just one kind of honor and that disenfranchisement targeted this "general human honor": "whenever someone denies another person the capacity to develop those virtues that are shared in essence by all . . . injury is done to human honor."[117] However, the influential Wilhelmine legal scholar Otto von Gierke held a more common understanding of this specific kind of honor, placing it in a hierarchy extending from general human honor to the specific individual honor awarded to people through decorations and promotions. "Honor as a citizen" stood above general human honor and below "special" honor, which was the honor of belonging to a certain group, like the army or a private guild.[118]

Of course, this layered definition of the notion of honor coexisted with the gendered concept of honor. For instance, in Johann Caspar Bluntschli's 1858 *Staats-Wörterbuch*, the Bavarian lawyer and Germanist Konrad von Maurer argued: "When thinking of the high honor of the respectable lady, most weight is given to sexual chastity."[119] Yet, this "high honor" was also supposed to be distinguished from the "regular" honor of man and woman, which, in his mind, consisted in respect for their life and property.

In this way, the notion of "civil honor" became part of the moral vocabulary of citizenship and a powerful rhetorical device for exalting the ideal citizen. "Civil honor rests on irreproachableness by virtue of which someone is given full trust within a state," a commentator noted in 1851.[120] Honor thus became highly associated with the question of whether someone was a law-abiding, "irreproachable" (*unbescholten*) citizen, something the historian Friedrich Zunkel called the "civil equation of positive law and honor."[121] However, this use of the notion of honor and the attempt to make it the hegemonic understanding of honor also sparked much controversy. Intellectuals of the German Empire vehemently debated the differentiated definition of honor, often leading to outcries about the "confusion in honor concepts."[122] To put it another way, honor was a "fluid" concept.[123]

This meant that not all members of German society equated being honorable with being a law-abiding citizen; this was especially true of those who claimed that the law should have no say in determining their honor. For instance, German aristocrats and bourgeois individuals often regarded their honor as an expression of their unique individuality, contrasting it with the "boring" uniformity of the modern state. In fact, they frequently defended their personal honor in unlawful duels, thereby protesting "against everything they disliked about civil society."[124] Hence, upper-middle-class individuals commonly defined their honor in opposition to the development of the ubiquitous state and the idea that citizenship itself conferred "honor." The Prussian aristocrat Herrmann von Gauvain, who fiercely defended dueling in an essay for the *Berliner Revue* in 1865, argued that the progressivist and liberal creed in which every individual was subsumed under the category of citizenship was diametrically opposed to the "Germanic" honor that belonged to the unique individual.¹²⁵ In other words, the uniformity that modern ideas of citizenship engendered destroyed the "personal independence for which honor is willing to fight," as German philosopher Georg Wilhelm Friedrich Hegel once put it.¹²⁶

One must bear this idea of honor in mind when considering the remarks of one of the earliest critics of felony disenfranchisement, Wilhelm von Humboldt. In his reflections on penal law in his 1792 book *Ideen zu einem Versuch, die Gränzen der Wirksamkeit des Staats zu bestimmen*, Humboldt argued—before it was even introduced in German penal codes—that the idea of depriving someone of honor as a punishment should be completely rejected. It was not the harshness of the punishment that drove his view, as many later critics would claim, but rather his understanding that "real honor" could not be subjected to state power: "the honor of a man, his fellow citizens' good opinion of him, is in no way something that the state has the power to affect."¹²⁷ The idea that the state could damage or protect one's honor thus fundamentally contradicted the personal beliefs of many "honorable" members of German higher classes, such as Humboldt's. Resistance to this idea would long endure. German chancellor Otto von Bismarck, for example, famously stated before the Reichstag in 1881: "My honor lies in no one's hand but my own, and it is not something that others can lavish on me."¹²⁸

The discrepancy between both Humboldt's and Bismarck's statements and the hegemony of the state concept of honor partially derived from the "dual" nature of their elitist notion of honor. In much of the literature on the topic of honor—especially in the literature from the nineteenth century—one encountered the distinction between "internal" and "external" honor.¹²⁹ This distinction sought to capture the difference between honor as the mere "external" recognition of one's value and honor as an "internal" subjective entitlement and sense of worth. In many respects, this individual and subjective element of the notion of honor contradicted the idea that the laws could regulate who was considered honorable. After all, according to this understanding, the individual was considered the measure of his or her own honor. On these grounds, the dueling German bourgeoisie emphatically distanced themselves from civil honor laws that regulated the distribution of honor and adhered instead to its own "code of honor."¹³⁰

Despite the strong opposition of the higher classes in the German states to equating honor with citizenship, the rise of the notion of *staatsbürgerliche Ehre* was inexorable. Irreproachableness (*Unbescholtenheit*) came to be a symbol of the Prussian politics of citizenship, with this notion coming up occasionally in regulations on the exercise of political rights. Whenever people criticized the dominance of the model of national citizenship over traditional aristocratic privileges, irreproachableness always played a central role.¹³¹ The penal law of the state and the local administrators of criminal justice thus gradually became the sole authorities in questions of honor and dishonor. All of this has to be seen as part of a broader attempt to make people primarily subjects of the state and to make the state the only arbiter in these questions.

Notes

1. GStA PK, I. HA Rep. 77 tit 1001, no. 8.
2. GStA PK, I. HA Rep. 77 tit 1001, no. 8, letter from 19 July 1867.
3. *Strafgesetzbuch für die Preußischen Staaten* (Berlin 1851), §12.
4. The different German states had different names for these privileges. In Saxony, for example, they were called "political privileges" (*politische Ehrenrechte*). Prussian *bürgerliche Ehrenrechte*, however, were taken over in the Reich Penal Code. The content of these privileges is not easily covered by the notion of "political rights" or "civil rights," as T. H. Marshall famously defined them (T. H. Marshall, "Citizenship and Social Class," in *Sociology at the Crossroads and Other Essays*, ed. T. H. Marshall, 67–127 [London: Heinemann, 1963]). For this reason, I use the notion of civil privileges rather than civil rights.
5. Andreas Fahrmeir, "Nineteenth-Century German Citizenships: A Reconsideration," *Historical Journal* 40, no. 33 (1997): 721–52.
6. Andreas Fahrmeir, *Citizenship: The Rise and Fall of a Modern Concept* (New Haven, CT: Yale University Press, 2007), 227–32.
7. Fahrmeir, *Citizenship*, 40.
8. Cf. Anne Simonin, *Le déshonneur dans la république. Une histoire de l'indignité 1791–1958* (Paris: Grasset, 2008).
9. The historical debate on the question of citizenship is often characterized by a strong interest in the questions of belonging, inclusion, and exclusion. This interest started with Rogers Brubaker's comparative study of the French and German regulations on citizenship, *Citizenship and Nationhood in France and Germany* (Cambridge, MA: Harvard University Press, 1992). In relation to nineteenth-century Germany, these themes have mostly been taken up by historians Andreas Fahrmeir and Dieter Gosewinkel, whose primary focus is on the laws regulating the acquisition of citizenship status. The German notion used in this context is often that of *Staatsangehörigkeit*—citizenship, nationality—literally, belonging to a state. Nonetheless, I prefer to look into the question of the privileges that state citizenship entailed. Whenever I use the word "citizenship," therefore, I mean the notion of *Staatsbürgerschaft* rather than *Staatsangehörigkeit*. Cf. Dieter Gosewinkel, "Staatsbürgerschaft und Staatsangehörigkeit," *Geschichte und Gesellschaft* 21, no. 4 (1995): 533–56; Andreas Fahrmeir, *Citizens and Aliens: Foreigners and the Law in Britain and the German States, 1789–1870* (New York: Berghahn Books, 2000); Dieter Gosewinkel, *Einbürgern und Ausschliessen: Die Nationalisierung der Staatsangehörigkeit vom Deutschen Bund bis zur Bundesrepublik Deutschland* (Göttingen: Vandenhoeck & Ruprecht, 2001); idem, *Schutz und Freiheit? Staatsbürgerschaft in Europa im 20. und 21. Jahrhundert* (Berlin: Suhrkamp, 2016); Eli Nathans, *The Politics of Citizenship in Germany. Ethnicity, Utility and Nationalism* (Oxford: Berg, 2004).
10. Fahrmeir, *Citizenship*, 28–29.
11. Reinhart Koselleck, *Preußen zwischen Reform und Revolution. Allgemeines Landrecht, Verwaltung und soziale Bewegung von 1791 bis 1848* (Stuttgart: Klett, 1967), 571. Nonetheless, the traditional nobility still had a powerful position in the municipal governments after Stein's reforms

and during the *Vormärz* period. Cf. Bernd Wunder, *Geschichte der Bürokratie in Deutschland* (Frankfurt a.M., 1986), 25–26.

12. Emil Siegert, *Die im Vollbürgerthum enthaltenen bürgerlichen Ehrenrechte nach deutschem Reichsrecht* (Greifswald: F. W. Kunike, 1895), 12–13; Franz von Holtzendorff and Felix Stoerk, "Das deutsche Verfassungsrecht," in *Encyklopädie der Rechtswissenschaft in systematischer und alphabetischer Bearbeitung*, ed. Franz von Holtzendorff, 5th edn., 1041–153 (Leipzig, 1890), 1084.
13. Gérard Noriel, "Der Staatsbürger," in *Der Mensch des 19. Jahrhunderts*, ed. Heinz-Gerhard Haupt and Ute Frevert, 201–27 (Essen: Campus, 2004), 204.
14. Bernd Wunder, "Die Reform der Beamtenschaft in den Rheinbundstaaten," in *Reformen im Rheinbündischen Deutschland*, ed. E. Weis, 181–93 (Munich: De Gruyter, 1984), 188.
15. Max Weber, "Wirtschaft und Gesellschaft," in *Gesamtausgabe*, vol. 22.4 (Tübingen: Mohr, 2001), 157. Cf. Stefan Brakensiek, *Fürstendiener, Staatsbeamte, Bürger. Amtsführung und Lebenswelt der Ortsbeamten in niederhessischen Kleinstädten (1750–1830)* (Göttingen: Vandenhoeck & Ruprecht, 1999).
16. Koselleck, *Preußen zwischen Reform und Revolution*, 114.
17. Ute Frevert, "Das jakobinische Modell. Allgemeine Wehrpflicht und Nationsbildung in Preußen-Deutschland," in *Militär und Gesellschaft im 19. und 20. Jahrhundert*, 17–47 (Stuttgart: Klett-Cotta, 1997).
18. Hans-Ulrich Wehler, *Deutsche Gesellschaftsgeschichte*, vol. 1, *Vom Feudalismus des Alten Reiches bis zur defensiven Modernisierung der Reformära 1700–1815* (Munich: Beck, 1987), 249; Ute Frevert, *A Nation in Barracks: Conscription, Military Service and Civil Society in Modern Germany* (Oxford: Berg, 2004), 11.
19. Frevert, *A Nation in Barracks*, 48–49; Thomas Nipperdey, *Deutsche Geschichte 1800–1866: Bürgerwelt und starker Staat* (Munich: Beck, 1983), 54–56.
20. Fahrmeir, *Citizens and Aliens*, 16. Peter Franke, "Stadt und Bürgerrechtsentwicklungen im 19. Jahrhundert. Das Beispiel Preußen," in *Agrarische Verfassung und politische Struktur. Studien zur Gesellschaftsgeschichte Preußens 1700–1918*, ed. Wolfgang Neugebauer and Ralf Pröve, 123–43 (Berlin: Spitz, 1998), 124. In the Prussian configuration, however, this also still entailed "traditional" rights to exercise certain crafts and acquire property in the town.
21. Fahrmeir, *Citizens and Aliens*, 20.
22. *Das Strafgesetzbuch und die Strafproceßordnung für das Königreich Sachsen* (Leipzig, 1855), §36.
23. Diethelm Klippel, "Das Privileg im deutschen Naturrecht des 18. und 19. Jahrhunderts," in *Das Privileg im europäischen Vergleich*, ed. Barbara Dölemeyer and Heinz Mohnhaupt, vol. 2, 329–45 (Frankfurt a.M.: Klostermann, 1997), 336.
24. Karl Salomo Zachariae, *Vierzig Bücher vom Staate*, vol. 6 (Heidelberg: Winter, 1842), 219.
25. Ernst Friedrich Iphofen, "Ueber politische Ehrenrechte II," *Zeitschrift für Rechtspflege und Verwaltung* 25 (1864): 314–48, 330.
26. Karl Binding, *Grundriß des deutschen Strafrechts. Allgemeiner Teil*, 6th edn. (Leipzig: Engelmann, 1902), 205.
27. Friedrich Noellner, *Das Verhältniss der Strafgesetzgebung zur Ehre der Staatsbürger. Ein Beitrag zur Reform der deutschen Strafsysteme, vom philosophischen, legislativen und praktischen Standpunkte* (Frankfurt a.M.: Bayrhoffer, 1846), vi.
28. On the dominance of this penal discourse, see Désirée Schauz, *Strafen als moralische Besserung: Eine Geschichte der Straffälligenfürsorge 1777–1933* (Munich: Oldenbourg, 2008).
29. Friedrich Noellner, *Das Verhältnis der Strafgesetzgebung*, 66.
30. Ideas similar to Noellner's can be found in Dietrich Georg Kieser, *Zwei akademische Reden. Ueber das Verhältniß der Philosophie der Natur zur Religion und über die Emancipation des Verbrechers im Kerker* (Jena: Cröker, 1845), 35; Carl Joseph Anton Mittermaier, *Die Strafgesetzgebung in ihrer Fortbildung. Geprüft nach den Forderungen der Wissenschaft und nach den Erfahrungen über den Werth neuer Gesetzgebungen, und über die Schwierigkeiten der Codifikation*

(Heidelberg: Winter, 1841); Ludwig Hugo Franz von Jagemann, "Die Bürgerliche Ehre im Verhältnisse zum Strafgesetze," *Archiv des Criminalrechts* 4 (1838): 248–72; Ferdinand Carl Theodor Hepp, *Das Strafen-System des neuen Entwurfs eines Strafgesetzbuches für das Königreich Württemberg vom Jahr 1835. In Vergleichung mit dem gemeinen Rechte, dem Strafedicte und neueren Legislationen* (Heidelberg: Mohr, 1836), 48.
31. Timon de Groot, "Politieke misdadigers of eerloze criminelen?," *Tijdschrift voor Geschiedenis* 132, no. 1 (2019): 21–47. Chapter 2 contains more on the context of the revolutions of 1848–49.
32. René Wiese, ed., *Vormärz und Revolution: Die Tagebücher des Grossherzogs Friedrich Franz II. von Mecklenburg-Schwerin 1841–1854* (Cologne: Böhlau Verlag, 2014), 115.
33. Ferdinand Carl Theodor Hepp, "Die Reform des Infamiesystems," *Der Gerichtssaal* 2, no. 1 (1850): 416–38, 416.
34. Adolf von Wick, *Über Ehrenstrafen und Ehrenfolgen der Verbrechen und Strafen. Eine Abhandlung aus dem Gebiete der Strafgesetzgebung* (Rostock: Stiller, 1845), 32.
35. Ibid., 163.
36. Cf. Martin Reulecke, *Gleichheit und Strafrecht im deutschen Naturrecht des 18. und 19. Jahrhunderts* (Tübingen: Mohr Siebeck, 2007), 332.
37. Julius Merkel, "Ueber Verlust der bürgerlichen Ehrenrechte und über Wiederherstellung derselben," *Allgemeine Gerichtszeitung für das Königreich Sachsen* 7 (1863): 1–24, 4.
38. Marc de Wilde, "Just Trust Us: A Short History of Emergency Powers and Constitutional Change," *Comparative Legal History* 3, no. 1 (2015): 110–30.
39. During the nineteenth century, Austrian and Prussian citizenship was only granted to foreigners as an act of sovereign mercy. This also underlines the character of citizenship as a privilege. See Gosewinkel, *Einbürgern und Ausschließen*, 35, 97.
40. Cited in Ute Frevert, *Vertrauensfragen. Eine Obsession der Moderne* (Munich: Beck, 2013), 161.
41. Ibid., 160.
42. In the literature on electoral theory, this is also known as the "broken contract" argument for felony disfranchisement. See Claudio López-Guerra, *Democracy and Disenfranchisement: The Morality of Electoral Exclusions* (Oxford: Oxford University Press, 2014), 110–12.
43. Adolf Wick most frequently used the notions of common trust (*Gemeinvertrauen*), public loyalty and faith (*öffentliche Treue und Glauben*), or the Latin phrase *publica fides*.
44. Cited in Ernst Friedrich Iphofen, "Ueber politische Ehrenrechte," *Zeitschrift für Rechtspflege und Verwaltung* 24 (1863): 299–342, 315.
45. Wick, *Über Ehrenstrafen und Ehrenfolgen*, 233. Wick mentioned "hate" and "revenge" as motives that did not make an act dishonorable.
46. Wick emphatically distinguished disposition from intention or motive; ibid., 230.
47. Cf. *Motive zum Entwurf des Strafgesetzbuchs für die Preussischen Staaten* (Berlin, 1851), 9–10.
48. Nipperdey, *Deutsche Geschichte 1800–1866*, 290, 377–80.
49. Peter Becker, *Verderbnis und Entartung. Eine Geschichte der Kriminologie des 19. Jahrhunderts als Diskurs und Praxis* (Göttingen: Vandenhoeck & Ruprecht, 2002), 12, 38, 47–49.
50. Ibid., 44–53.
51. Becker called these early criminologists "criminalists" (*Kriminalisten*) and distinguished their later counterpart through the use of the term "criminologists" (*Kriminologen*).
52. Wick, *Über Ehrenstrafen und Ehrenfolgen*, 225. Nonetheless, Wick did not completely do away with estate privilege in his theory: for less serious crimes, he believed that *custodia honesta* could be a "surrogate" punishment for people from the higher classes. Wick therefore took a middle position between those who argued that *custodia honesta* should be a surrogate for all offenders from the higher classes and those who argued that *custodia honesta* was an alternative punishment for people who had committed an offense despite having an honorable disposition. Cf. Karl Richard Sontag, *Die Festungshaft* (Leipzig, 1872), 74–118.

53. Wick, *Über Ehrenstrafen und Ehrenfolgen*, 232.
54. Ibid., 173.
55. For an example of the significance of the religious interpretation of the act of perjury and its relation to the exercise of power in an early modern German village, see David Warren Sabean, *Power in the Blood* (Cambridge: Cambridge University Press, 1984), 144–73, in particular, 172: "What is interesting here is the way in which the issue was hung on conscience and the way state officials used conscience in the practice of authority . . . individual responsibility and public confession were the central theological concepts buttressing state power."
56. *Constitutio Criminalis Theresiana* (Vienna, 1769), part 2, art. 59.
57. Ludwig von Bar, *Geschichte des deutschen Strafrechts und der Strafrechtstheorien, Handbuch des deutschen Strafrechts*, vol. 1 (Berlin: Weidmann, 1882), 156.
58. Franz von Liszt, *Meineid und falsches Zeugnis. Eine strafrechts-geschichtliche Studie* (Vienna: Manz, 1876), 128–35; Franz Grünberg, *Zur systematischen Stellung des Meineides* (Berlin: A. Hendebett, 1900), 15.
59. Hans Ernst von Globig and Johann Georg Huster, *Abhandlung von der Criminalgesetzgebung. Eine von der ökonomischen Gesellschaft in Bern gekrönte Preisschrift* (Zurich: Füessly, 1783), 222.
60. *Allgemeines Gesetzbuch über Verbrechen und derselben Bestrafung* (Vienna, 1787), §149. Cf. Liszt, *Meineid und falsches Zeugnis*, 136.
61. Helmut Reinalter, "Aufgeklärter Absolutismus und Josephinismus," in *Der Josephinismus. Bedeutung, Einflüsse und Wirkungen*, ed. Helmut Reinalter, 11–21 (Frankfurt a.M.: Peter Lang, 1993); Charles W. Ingrao, *The Habsburg Monarchy, 1618–1815*, 197–200 (Cambridge: Cambridge University Press, 2000). Wunder, *Geschichte der Bürokratie in Deutschland*, 18–19.
62. Liszt, *Meineid und falsches Zeugnis*, 129.
63. Carl Josef Anton Mittermaier, "Ueber den Meineid nach dem gemeinen Rechte und den Bestimmungen der neuesten Strafgesetzbücher," *Neues Archiv des Criminalrechts* 2 (1818): 85–120, 110.
64. Ferdinand Carl Theodor Hepp, *Die politischen und unpolitischen Staats-Verbrechen und Vergehen nebst angränzenden Amtsverbrechen und Polizei-Uebertretungen* (Tübingen: Zu-Guttenberg, 1846).
65. Cited in Grünberg, *Zur systematischen Stellung des Meineides*, 19.
66. "Verbrechen und Vergehen wider die öffentliche Ordnung"; RStGB, §153.
67. French Enlightenment philosopher Jean-Jacques Rousseau used a similar "broken contract" argument in his defense of criminal punishment, but he explicitly discussed it in the context of the crime of murder and to justify the exercise of the death penalty: Jean-Jacques Rousseau, *Discourse on Political Economy and the Social Contract*, trans. Christopher Betts (Oxford: Oxford University Press, 1999), 71–72. Wick's account clearly differs from this since he regarded breaches of public trust as so much more important than violent crimes like murder.
68. Wick, *Über Ehrenstrafen und Ehrenfolgen*, 234.
69. Pieter Spierenburg, *Violence and Punishment: Civilizing the Body through Time* (Cambridge: Polity, 2013), 7.
70. Classic accounts of this thesis include Douglas Hay et al., *Albion's Fatal Tree: Crime and Society and Eighteenth-Century England* (London: Allen Lane, 1975); E. P. Thompson, *Whigs and Hunters* (London: Allen Lane, 1975).
71. Rebekka Habermas, *Diebe vor Gericht. Die Entstehung der modernen Rechtsordnung im 19. Jahrhundert* (Frankfurt a.M.: Campus, 2008), 69–74.
72. Johann Gottlieb Fichte, *Grundlage des Naturrechts nach Principien der Wissenschaftslehre*, vol. 2 (Jena: Gabler, 1797), §19, H.
73. Wick, *Über Ehrenstrafen und Ehrenfolgen*, 236.
74. Ibid., 238.

75. Cf. Becker, *Verderbnis und Entartung*, 196–201.
76. Ibid., 236.
77. Dirk Blasius, *Geschichte der politischen Kriminalität in Deutschland, 1800–1980* (Frankfurt a.M.: Suhrkamp, 1983).
78. Karl Biedermann, "Der Polenprozeß in Berlin," *Unsre Gegenwart und Zukunft* 9 (1847): 205–53, 211.
79. Cf. Sylvia Kesper-Biermann, "'Nothwendige Gleichheit der Strafen bey aller Verschiedenheit der Stände im Staat'? (Un)Gleichheit im Kriminalrecht der ersten Hälfte des 19. Jahrhunderts," *Geschichte und Gesellschaft* 35, no. 4 (2009): 603–28.
80. Cf. James Q. Whitman, *Harsh Justice: Criminal Punishment and the Widening Divide between America and Europe* (Oxford: Oxford University Press, 2005), 135.
81. Wick, *Über Ehrenstrafen und Ehrenfolgen*, 29–30.
82. Becker, *Verderbnis und Entartung*, 180–82.
83. Cf. Joel Feinberg, "The Expressive Function of Punishment," in *Doing and Deserving: Essays in the Theory of Responsibility*, ed. idem, 95–118 (Princeton, NJ: Princeton University Press, 1970).
84. Gallus Aloys Kleinschrod, *Systematische Entwicklung der Grundbegriffe und Grundwahrheiten des peinlichen Rechts nach der Natur der Sache und der positiven Gesetzgebung* (Erlangen: Johann Jakob Palm, 1799), 143.
85. Cited in Iphofen, "Ueber politische Ehrenrechte," 345.
86. See Introduction.
87. Émile Durkheim, *The Division of Labour in Society*, trans. W. D. Halls (London: Macmillan, 1984), 56.
88. Simonin, *Le déshonneur*, 307–15. The notion of *éthocratie* is a reference to Baron d'Holbach's 1776 book *Éthocratie ou le Gouvernement fondé sur la morale* (Amsterdam, 1776).
89. Cited in Carol J. Greenhouse, "Solidarity and Objectivity. Re-Reading Durkheim," in *Crime's Power: Anthropologists and the Ethnography of Crime*, ed. Philip C. Parnell and Stephanie C. Kane, 269–91 (New York: Palgrave Macmillan, 2003), 276.
90. Friedrich Julius Stahl, *Die Philosophie des Rechts*, vol. 2 (Heidelberg: Mohr, 1846), 543.
91. Mittermaier, *Die Strafgesetzgebung*.
92. Cf. Julius Friedrich Heinrich Abegg, *System der Criminal-Rechts-Wissenschaft mit einer Vorrede über die wissenschaftliche Behandlung des Criminalrecht* (Königsberg: Unzer, 1826), 255–58.
93. Wick, *Über Ehrenstrafen und Ehrenfolgen*, 37.
94. Jürgen Kocka, *Arbeitsverhältnisse und Arbeiterexistenzen. Grundlagen der Klassenbildung im 19. Jahrhundert* (Bonn: Dietz, 1990), 112–13; Dieter Schwab, "Familie," in *Geschichtliche Grundbegriffe. Historisches Lexikon zur Politisch-Sozialen Sprache in Deutschland*, ed. Otto Brunner, Werner Conze, and Reinhart Koselleck, vol. 2, 253–301 (Stuttgart: Klett-Cotta, 1975).
95. Thomas Vormbaum, *Politik und Gesinderecht im neunzehnten Jahrhundert vornehmlich in Preußen 1810–1918* (Berlin: Duncker & Humblot, 1980), 109–11.
96. Friedrich von Wick, *Über Fürsorge für entlassene Sträflinge, insbesondere über Organisirung einer kirchlichen Fürsorge für dieselben* (Rostock: Hirsch, 1856), 15.
97. Falk Bretschneider, *Gefangene Gesellschaft. Eine Geschichte der Einsperrung in Sachsen im 18. und 19. Jahrhundert* (Konstanz: Universitätsverlag Konstanz, 2008), 483.
98. Oscar Stillich, *Die Lage der weiblichen Dienstboten in Berlin* (Berlin: Akademie Verlag, 1902), 32.
99. Kocka, *Arbeitsverhältnisse und Arbeiterexistenzen*, 126.
100. On the fear of increased mobility in relation to crime, see Becker, *Verderbnis und Entartung*, 186–93.
101. Wick, *Über Ehrenstrafen und Ehrenfolgen*, 33–34.
102. Ibid., 3.

103. "Gesetz, die Abänderung einiger Bestimmungen in der allgemeinen Städteordnung betreffend, 09.12.1837," in *Gesetz- und Verordnungsblatt für das Königreich Sachsen* (Dresden, 1837), 140–41.
104. Cf. Iphofen, "Ueber politische Ehrenrechte," 311–13.
105. LAV NRW R, BR 0007, no. 8895, *Amtsblatt der Regierung zu Düsseldorf*, 28.11.1845.
106. Carl Theodor Welcker and Carl von Rotteck, *Das Staats-Lexicon. Encyklopädie der sämmtlichen Staatswissenschaften für alle Stände in Verbindung mit vielen der angesehensten Publicisten Deutschlands*, 3rd edn., vol. 12 (Leipzig: Brockhaus, 1865), 423.
107. LAV NRW R, BR 0005, no. 2278, ministerial order of the Ministry of the Interior, 05.03.1822.
108. Adolf von Wick, "Zur Gesetzgebung über die Ehrenfolgen der Verbrechen," *Archiv des Criminalrechts* 32, no. 1 (1851): 1–39, 14.
109. Wilhelm von Brauer, "Ueber die Rehabilitation Verutheilter," *Der Gerichtssaal* 11 (1857): 321–39, 333.
110. Ibid., 326–27.
111. Reinhart Koselleck, "Einleitung," in *Geschichtliche Grundbegriffe*, ed. Otto Brunner, Werner Conze, and Reinhart Koselleck, vol. 1 (Stuttgart: Klett-Cotta 1979).
112. Ute Frevert, "Vertrauen—eine historische Spurensuche," in *Vertrauen. Historische Annäherungen*, ed. idem, 7–66 (Göttingen: Vandenhoeck & Ruprecht, 2003), 14; Frevert, *Vertrauensfragen*, 154–56.
113. Konrad Franz Roßhirt, *Geschichte und System des deutschen Strafrechts*, vol. 3 (Stuttgart: Schweizerbart, 1839), 13.
114. The German word *Gut* could also be translated as "commodity," although, in this context, "good" is simply more accurate. The notion of *Rechtsgut* is most commonly translated as "legal interest," but this use has been criticized by Markus Dubber and others. The translation "legal good" is therefore to be preferred for its straightforwardness.
115. Markus D. Dubber, "Theories of Crime and Punishment in German Criminal Law," *American Journal of Comparative Law* 53 (2006): 679–707, 684–89.
116. Durkheim, *The Division of Labour in Society*, 56.
117. Ernst Rethwisch, *Ueber den Werth der Ehrenstrafen. Juristischer Essay* (Berlin: Puttkammer & Mühlbrecht, 1876), 20.
118. Otto von Gierke, *Deutsches Privatrecht*, vol. 1 (Leipzig, 1895), 427–29. Cf. Justus von Olshausen, *Kommentar zu den Strafgesetzen des Deutschen Reiches*, 4th edn., vol. 1 (Berlin: Vahlen, 1892), 692.
119. Konrad Maurer, "Ehre," in *Deutsches Staats-Wörterbuch*, ed. Johann Caspar Bluntschli and Karl Brater (1858), 226–87, 227; cf. Ute Frevert, "Ehre— Männlich/Weiblich. Zu einem Identitätsbegriff des 19. Jahrhunderts," *Tel Aviver Jahrbuch für Deutsche Geschichte* 21 (1992): 21–68.
120. "Die Ehrenstrafen nach dem neuen preußischen Strafgesetzbuche beleuchtet von einem practischen Juristen," *Hitzigs Annalen der Deutschen und Ausländischen Criminal-Rechtspflege* 27 (1851): 1–23, 8.
121. "Die staatsbürgerliche Gleichheit von Recht und Ehre," in Friedrich Zunkel, "Ehre, Reputation," in *Geschichtliche Grundbegriffe. Historisches Lexikon zur politisch-sozialen Sprache in Deutschland*, ed. Otto Brunner, Werner Conze, and Reinhart Koselleck, vol. 2, 1–63 (Stuttgart: Klett-Cotta, 1975), 32.
122. For example, in Ernst Delaquis, *Die Rehabilitation im Strafrecht* (Berlin: J. Guttentag, 1907), 123.
123. Paul Felix Aschrott and Franz von Liszt, *Die Reform des Reichsstrafgesetzbuchs* (Berlin: Guttentag, 1910), 311. Cited in Ann Goldberg, *Honor, Politics, and the Law in Imperial Germany, 1871–1914* (Cambridge: Cambridge University Press, 2010), 45.

124. Ute Frevert, *Men of Honour. A Social and Cultural History of the Duel* (Cambridge: Polity Press, 1995), 138.
125. Herrmann von Gauvain, "Das Duell," *Berliner Revue* 43, no. 4 (1865): 138.
126. Georg Wilhelm Friedrich Hegel, *Vorlesungen über die Aesthetik*, vol. 2 (Berlin, 1843), 167.
127. Wilhelm von Humboldt, *Ideen zu einem Versuch, die Gränzen der Wirksamkeit des Staats zu bestimmen* (Breslau: Trewendt, 1851).
128. "Meine Ehre steht in niemandes Hand als meiner eigenen und niemand ist Richter darüber und kann entscheiden, ob ich sie habe," *Stenographische Berichte über die Verhandlungen des Reichstages*, vol. 66 (Berlin 1881), 61. Translation: Frank Henderson Stewart, *Honor* (Chicago: University of Chicago Press, 1994), 52.
129. Cf. Aschmann, *Preußens Ruhm und Deutschlands Ehre*, 28–29; Zunkel, "Ehre, Reputation."
130. The irony and complexity of the fact that they were subordinated to this code while they were distancing themselves from it is discussed in Frevert, *Men of Honour*, 169–71.
131. Zunkel, "Ehre, Reputation," 31.

Chapter 2

INSTITUTIONS OF HONOR
A Leveling Society Seeking to Protect Its Institutions

Felony disenfranchisement was essentially an instrument of exclusion: it aimed to exclude serious offenders from participating in certain aspects of society. Crucially, however, debate about the function of this punishment often occurred in the broader context of discussions about greater inclusion in certain institutions. This chapter deals with the dynamics of exclusion/inclusion in questions of membership in important institutions in Imperial Germany. It shows how felony disenfranchisement frequently came to occupy a pivotal role in the debates about the honor of these institutions. Modern demands for inclusion often conflicted with ideas about honor and honorability. Many politicians, political commentators, and social activists instrumentalized felony disenfranchisement to stress the importance of exclusion and defend the honorability of these institutions against these demands.

This chapter looks specifically at the dynamics of inclusion/exclusion in the context of two important leveling trends in German society: the expansion of the system of military conscription and the implementation of universal male suffrage. The chapter then explores other contexts in German society in which disenfranchisement played an ambivalent role in privileges being granted to an extended group of citizens, for instance, in the emerging welfare state and in the existing legal regime as modern penal policy was adapted to make it compatible with it.

The demand for inclusion was also a prominent aim of the bourgeoning field of criminology and the prison reform movement, in which offenders' reform potential was increasingly emphasized.[1] The exclusion of felony disenfranchisement often conflicted with the aim of reintegrating and resocializing "corrigible" offenders, yet modern scholars hardly rebelled against it. Rather, they tried to appropriate the vocabulary of honor and exclusion that underpinned the policy

---

Notes from this chapter begin on page 75.

of felony disenfranchisement—and they tried to make felony disenfranchisement appropriate within their own agenda.

Barring Criminals from the Army

In 1905, Robert Schmölder, a conservative commentator and judge at the supreme court of Hamm, published an article in the *Deutsche Juristenzeitung* in which he urged army officers to deploy the army in the social battle against crime. He suggested that the army could function as a "school" that could reform criminal youths by teaching them the core principles of military discipline. His proposal was born of an anxiety about the influence of modern city life on German youths as the average age of offenders was rather young: official statistics in the German Empire showed that men between the ages of eighteen and twenty-one were most inclined toward criminal behavior. Consequently, Schmölder believed that the best solution to this problem was to force young offenders to join the army after their release from prison (that is, if they were still in the eligible age range). The army could teach them manly discipline and discourage them from choosing a life of crime. He concluded that, with this solution, "the army and navy would become in a wider sense the educators of the people, and this educational function would be of the greatest imaginable importance to criminal policy."[2]

Forcing offenders to join the army after their release from prison, however, was legally impossible if offenders had been incarcerated in a penitentiary (*Zuchthaus*) or had otherwise lost their civil privileges. Schmölder's plan thus ran completely counter to the aspirations of lawmakers who wanted ex-convicts excluded from the military. Schmölder's most important recommendations for the penal policy of the German Empire was, therefore, that §31 should be abolished from the Reich Penal Code and that the policy of felony disenfranchisement should be reconsidered. This article stated that all persons sentenced to the penitentiary permanently lost their rights to serve in the military and to take up public office. By contrast, he argued that former penitentiary inmates should be required to fulfill active military duty just as other male German citizens were.

Reactions to Schmölder's proposal were vehemently negative. The intensity of these reactions demonstrates how little army officials were interested in questions of criminal policy. Most trenchant in his criticism was Heinrich Dietz, a member of the war council who was highly dismissive of Schmölder's essay. In his view, Schmölder's suggestions did not promote the interests of the state at all—on the contrary, they seriously threatened them. In his response, Dietz presented the conflict between the interests of the army and those of criminal policy as a zero-sum game: he agreed that Schmölder's suggestions might contribute to reducing the crime rate among adolescent men, but this advantage would not outweigh the harm this would cause the army and (by implication) German society in general. The moral authority of the army, Dietz argued, existed in the virtues of "loyalty, subordination, companionship, and self-denial." Every member of the army needed to possess these qualities because, "as history teaches us, it is the moral soundness of an army that is frequently decisive."[3] If a greater number of ex-convicts joined the ranks, these virtues would be in grave danger and the honor of the army would be damaged. The army needed to be safeguarded from these morally incompetent soldiers in order to remain "honorable." [4]

Thus, for Dietz and other army officials, the honor of the military existed by virtue of its exclusivity. This idea is important to the militarization thesis in German history, whose significance for the historiography of the Wilhelmine Empire can hardly be overstated. It might be—as historian Benjamin Ziemann argued—the final bastion of the German *Sonderweg* thesis: that Germany's history in modern times deviated significantly from that of other Western European countries.[5] One component of this thesis is that the army, and specifically army officers, had a privileged position in German society.[6] From 1871 onwards, the army did, indeed, stand outside of the legal sphere of the German constitution, and until 1890 officers came exclusively from the nobility. The army functioned as something of an autonomous power in the German Empire, with its officials frequently being regarded as constituting a genuine "caste" (*Kaste*)—an important stratum in German society with its own code of honor.[7] The army's loyalty to the crown strongly influenced the military establishment. After 1890, when restrictions keeping "normal citizens" from becoming officers were dropped, the army still demanded that officers have a certain character and claimed that only those with "nobility of temperament" (*Adel der Gesinnung*) could successfully become officers.[8] The notion of honor thus served to mark the army's exceptionalism.

Military officials in Imperial Germany also frequently argued that it took a certain sense of honor—one that was somehow different from that of normal citizens—for someone to become a member of the army. Without this, they claimed, the army could not function properly. When universal conscription was introduced, however, officials could be less restrictive in their recruiting, so people could be selected even if they lacked this "special sense of honor."

The militarization thesis also includes the idea that the German military militarized all aspects of society. That is, many German citizens adopted the behavioral norms central to army discipline; the normal male "habitus" derived from army discipline—a process captured in the notion of German *Sozialmilitarismus*.[9] Indeed, the German/Prussian army was increasingly valued for its pedagogy, often being described as a "school" of masculinity.[10] In most European countries, army discipline pervaded specific parts of society, such as the internal governance of the institutions of confinement, as Michel Foucault (among others) convincingly demonstrated, but in Germany, army discipline infiltrated nearly all parts of society.[11]

As the army began to recruit a wider range of people and its ideology increasingly pervaded other aspects of society, one might suspect that the importance of the notion of honor in German society would have diminished. This development theoretically could have prompted the army to also open its doors to ex-convicts. After all, a certain current of sociological literature suggests that the less a society reinforces existing hierarchies with its policies and the more leveled it becomes, the less room there is for a notion of honor; this sets ideas of "honor" in opposition to modern egalitarianism.[12] The case of conscription policy in the German Empire, however, disproves this theory. In fact, the opposite happened: suggestions regarding the broadening of membership in official institutions, such as the suggestion made by Schmölder that former inmates should serve in the army, often triggered reactions that emphasized protecting those institutions' honor even more. This dynamic is discussed in more detail below.

The Economy of Punishment

The debate about whether "dishonored felons" should be barred from the army started in the context of discussions surrounding the introduction of the penal code for the North German Confederation (1869), the code preceding the German Empire's penal code of 1871. The contentious point pertained to whether the code should include "dishonoring" elements. Questions of population management were central to the discussion, as when the young legal scholar Karl Binding spoke of the "economy" of punishment.[13] In his view, a legal punishment was an evil perpetrated on the culprit because it damaged what people hold most dear: life, liberty, property, and honor. Yet, he continued, punishments were also an evil for the society that administered them because they damaged the legal products that made society function, often in ways that were unmeasurable to the general observer. The physical and moral ruin of offenders, for instance, could be an unintended effect of punishment, and society ran the risk of disintegration if this happened to too many of its citizens. Thus, Binding argued that lawmakers should seek to strike a balance between the damage caused by punishment and the need for retribution and concluded that society had to be "economical" in administering punishments. This conclusion echoed the liberal creed of the legal philosopher Rudolf Jhering, who famously stated that the history of punishment was that of its demise.[14]

The influential legal scholar Carl Mittermaier—famous for his opposition to the death penalty, among other things—had criticized felony disenfranchisement for "robbing" too many offenders of their honor in the early 1860s. Because of the automatic connection between penitentiary (*Zuchthaus*) sentences and felony disenfranchisement in the penal codes of many of the German states, all persons who had served time in the penitentiary were permanently deprived of their civil privileges. He argued that this state of things created an enormous class of "frightening enemies" (*furchtbare Feinde*) of the state.[15] Reducing the application of this punishment, he asserted, was essential for maintaining a sense of order in the German-speaking countries.

The political climate of the era made the matter even more pressing as rates of incarceration grew significantly from the 1840s onward. At first, this rise resulted from increasing social unrest punctuated by occasional riots.[16] This social unrest had a lot to do with the "double crisis" of the 1840s: the combination of a low economic cycle in supply and demand and consecutive bad harvests.[17] The increase in incarceration not only filled penitentiaries beyond capacity but also stripped many more people of their civil privileges. Later, in reaction to the revolutions of 1848 and as a consequence of the new penal code of 1851, Prussia incarcerated more people than ever before.[18]

The number of disfranchised citizens also became an urgent political matter during the debates in the Frankfurt Parliament in 1849. A year earlier, a pamphlet by Eduard Forsberg, an active participant in the 1848 March revolts in Berlin, had already pointed out the injustice of "dishonoring" such a large number of people, as well as the political consequences. Among other things, the pamphlet highlighted the suffering of 300,000–400,000 people excluded from voting in the national assembly elections in 1848 due to criminal convictions.[19] Forsberg criticized the automatic connection between incarceration and the loss of civil privileges precisely because it created this large class of "dishonored criminals." As a result, the debate among members of the Frankfurt Parliament on a bill about the franchise for a national German parliament (Reichsgesetz über die Wahlen der abgeordneten zum Volkshause) was contentious. Many participants felt that the number of political offenders that would be disenfranchised, according to regulations in many of the individual states, would be too large.

Before the Frankfurt Parliament, Mittermaier (who, in addition to being a professor of law, was also a member of this parliament) emphasized that if every person sentenced to a "dishonoring" punishment were to be excluded from the national elections, this would effectively encompass an enormous group of citizens: both political offenders and "common criminals." He suggested that only those convicted of "really dishonoring" crimes, such as theft, embezzlement, and fraud, should be excluded.[20] Although Wilhelm Zimmermann (a delegate from Stuttgart) and Carl Esterle (Trentino) also supported Mittermaier's view, the bill kept the formulation that everyone deprived of their civil privileges was excluded from the franchise.[21] Bruno Adolph Sturm, a delegate from Sorau, represented the other side of the argument: he stressed the importance of felony disenfranchisement for retaining the "honor" of the franchise. He claimed that it would help to create the necessary respect for participation in these elections:

> If you wish to get rid of the indifference that has shown itself during all the elections so far, then you should help make it such that every person considers it the highest

honor to participate in elections. You would accomplish this directly by excluding all unworthy subjects. Make the right to vote the pride of good citizens and an incentive to reform for those gone astray and you will achieve a victorious feat for morality.[22]

The conflict between Mittermaier and Sturm illustrates the problem with disenfranchisement. Although the exclusion of serious offenders was supposed to uphold the honor of the franchise, the idea of the popular will was undermined when so many men were barred from voting. Consequently, the policy contradicted the "economical" administration of punishment.

Disenfranchisement was considered particularly problematic in the case of "political offenders." After the revolutions of 1848/49, many people who had participated in the revolts were incarcerated in local penitentiaries and disenfranchised. Afterward, many people could clearly recall the image of incarcerated "honorable" political offenders. For example, at the time of German unification in 1871, a journalist recalled in the *Flensburger Zeitung* how both "professors" and "youthful zealots" had been sent off to penitentiaries after the uprisings of 1848/49—in his mind, there was nothing dishonorable about having "misplaced love of the fatherland" or engaging in "political enthusiasm."[23] Likewise, August Bebel recalled in his personal memoirs that many of the penitentiaries in Saxony (especially Waldheim in Zwickau) were filled beyond capacity with political offenders after the 1848/49 revolutions. This left a great impression on him.[24]

The fact that so many people were deprived of their civil privileges without having committed a crime that people considered dishonorable prompted the debate to revise the penal system and sever the automatic connection between a penitentiary sentence and felony disenfranchisement.[25] Nonetheless, some people retained a vivid interest in excluding people from certain privileges. This conflict was debated during the codification of the Reich Penal Code.

Codifying Penal Law in the Context of German Unification

In the early 1860s, the legal integration of the different German countries became a high priority for legal scholars. These scholars often had a twofold relationship with the state and its laws. On the one hand, they frequently acted as consultants for politicians in the design of penal codes. But, on the other, they were also required to explain and criticize the content of the penal code and its underlying principles. At the same time, legal scholars comprised a peculiar stratum of Germany society. As classical examples of the German *Bildungsbürger*, they were often employed as high officials in the Prussian and other German governments. As university degrees were required for high-ranking civil servant positions after 1817, German universities largely came to be regarded as training grounds for public officials.[26]

Legal scholars from the different German states shared a common interest in legal integration—an interest that manifested itself during a remarkable event in 1860: on the initiative of the prominent legal scholar Franz von Holtzendorff, a conference for legal scholars from all the German states was organized with the aim of debating the possibilities for legal integration. This came to be known as the Juristentag and was a great success from the outset.[27] Its pan-German agenda became immediately clear: in preparation for the discussion during the Juristentag, Rudolf von Kräwel—a Prussian jurist—drafted a design for a pan-German criminal penal code.[28] The Juristentag's pan-German ambition was made most explicit in 1862 when the third conference was hosted in Vienna; this choice of location showed that the Austrian Empire was conceived as an important part of this ambition, too.

This third conference in Vienna was the first to put felony disenfranchisement on the agenda. The conference organizers suggested that participants prepare by reading the articles written by Austrian scholar Emil Wahlberg for the Österreichische *Gerichtszeitung*.[29] One of Wahlberg's most important points was that felony disenfranchisement should be temporary; lifelong consequences for incarceration should be abolished. At that time, the 1857 Penal Code of the Grand Duchy of Oldenbourg was the only code that placed absolute limits on how long felons could be deprived of their civil privileges; the Prussian Penal Code, by contrast (like most others), still allowed for the possibility of permanent sentences (although these were not required).[30] At the Vienna conference, Austrian minister Anton Hye von Glunek introduced the topic and defended the then provocative thesis that all forms of disenfranchisement should be abolished from the penal codes.[31] Although his idea found little resonance, the assembled scholars agreed with Wahlberg's suggestion that offenders should never be stripped of their rights permanently but always only for a limited period of time.

The course of the scholarly debate on penal law and codification was, however, closely interwoven with international developments. After the Austro-Prussian War of 1866 and Bismarck's reconciliation with parliament in the wake of a budget conflict that year, the integration of Austria into a pan-German legal code was further away than ever.[32] The conflict thus ruined the ambitions of the scholars gathered in the Juristentag, and when Austria introduced its reformed penal code in 1867, the two empires took divergent paths once and for all. Even so, the idea of a German penal code gained momentum in the North German Confederation, with its members deciding to continue developing one. In 1866, Bismarck and Adolph Leonhardt (the Prussian Minister of Justice) appointed a committee headed by the high Prussian official Heinrich von Friedberg and the influential judge Ernst Traugott Rubo to develop such a code. They presented their first draft in June 1869.[33]

The draft clearly acknowledged the influence of the Prussian Penal Code but also noted that there were some radical changes—most significantly in the treatment of honor and dishonor connected to criminal convictions. Underlying the commission's propositions was the general idea of distinguishing the crime from the punishment, which they expressed as follows:

> public opinion holds that the place where a person sits out his punishment must serve as the measure for whether the punishment itself should be viewed as dishonorable or not, and [the public] generally associates the penitentiary with dishonor. . . . It behooves the legislator to prohibit such a popular notion from becoming law. It is his task to show that a punishable act is not dishonorable because of the type of punishment meted out, nor because of where the culprit does his time.[34]

The prison system of the German states before unification distinguished between several forms of imprisonment, with the distinctions between prisons being based on how "infamous" they were.[35] A penitentiary (*Zuchthaus*) was considered inherently dishonoring, while a normal prison (*Gefängnis*) had no legal effects on the honor of the convict. Fortress confinement (*Festungshaft*), furthermore, was a sentence for people convicted of offenses motivated by an "honorable disposition" (*ehrenhafte Gesinnung*)—in general, people who were sentenced for dueling.[36] As James Whitman put it in his comparative history of penal culture in the United States and on the European continent, "German prisons were, strikingly enough, differentiated according to their degree of 'dishonorability'."[37]

Since the end of the eighteenth century, multiple attempts had been made to abolish such associations with certain punishments from the law, but a penitentiary sentence retained the stigma of "dishonor."[38] An important element of this was the codification of disenfranchisement as an automatic consequence of such a sentence. For instance, this was the case in the Prussian Penal Code of 1851, which stipulated that a penitentiary sentence entailed the legal suspension of one's "civil honor."[39] The permanent suspension of one's civil privileges after this sentence bolstered the dishonor associated with being sent to the penitentiary.

Cutting loose from this aspect of the Prussian Penal Code, the drafters of the penal code for the North German Confederation left it to a judge's discretion whether an offender was to be deprived of his privileges; it would no longer be an automatic consequence of a certain type of incarceration.[40] To the experts on the commission, this was the only way to do justice to the principle of distinguishing between the crime and the punishment. Still, they maintained the distinctions between different prison sentences, allowing the dishonoring aspect of the penitentiary to eventually slip back in through the backdoor.

The General Staff Intervenes

As simple as the recommendation to disconnect the punishment of felony disenfranchisement from the penitentiary sentence sounded, it turned out to be one of the most controversial issues in devising the penal code for the North German Confederation and the later code for the German Empire. The conflict became clearest in the contrast between the original design for the penal code and its form upon implementation in 1869. Since the legal scholars on the commission constantly had to make compromises with each other and with members of parliament, all of whom wanted to see their own ideas included, the result differed significantly from the initial draft. A closer inspection of how the regulations surrounding disenfranchisement were justified during the drafting process therefore also shows that penal codes were not just the ideas of legal scholars put into practice.[41]

The second and final draft of the penal code for the North German Confederation added an extra article on the suspension of civil privileges. The additional article (§31 both in the penal code for the North German Confederation and in the Reich Penal Code) stated that all persons sentenced to the penitentiary permanently lost their rights to serve in the military and to take up public office. This diverged significantly from the intention expressed in the first draft, namely, the abolition of all automatic connections between a type of incarceration and the offender's "loss of honor." Even though this much-disputed paragraph did not explicitly use the notion of honor, and it was isolated from the "actual" punishment of disenfranchisement, it still (potentially permanently) stripped criminals of two core civil privileges (the rights to join the army and to hold public office) after a penitentiary sentence.

The course of the debate suggests that army officials decisively influenced the introduction of §31, especially since most support for the measure came from delegates who were directly involved with the Prussian army. The Prussian Field Marshal Helmuth von Moltke, for instance, strongly endorsed this addition to the code and defended it as a self-evident principle. He held it to be a traditional Prussian (perhaps even Germanic) principle for dishonored members of society to be ineligible for military service.[42] Moltke feared that the inclusion of former penitentiary inmates would not only exert a negative influence on army discipline but also undermine the army's general self-esteem (*Selbstgefühl*) because it was an institution "that lives by honor and [whose members] do not deserve to have to serve with those who do not have it."[43] Prussian War Minister Albrecht Theodor von Roon had expressed similar sentiments in a letter to Bismarck in 1869, arguing that German soldiers would consider it a huge disgrace to have to serve with former penitentiary inmates.[44]

The opponents of the introduction of §31, who were mostly members of the National Liberal Party, felt that this article granted the army a privileged position and feared that it implicitly constructed a difference between the honor of army membership and the honor of exercising other civil privileges.[45] This framing of the debate put the definition of honor at stake. Another important Prussian army officer, Karl von Steinmetz, disagreed in particular with opponents of the article who argued that the implied divide between types of honor would grow wider. He rejected the idea that the article implied a distinction between types of honor because citizenship and the army stood in close relation to one another as everybody with citizenship rights was expected to join the army. Moreover, he affirmed one principle especially—"dishonorable (*ehrlos*) = defenseless (*wehrlos*)." In stating this principle in this way, he was playing on the catchphrase "defenseless = dishonorable," which was used to defend the necessity of a large standing army. Believing that it took honor for someone to be able to defend himself and his country, Steinmetz held that it was equally in the interest of the army and the German nation to exclude dishonored ex-offenders from military service.[46]

What is important in both Steinmetz's and Moltke's positions is that the two men used the popular association between the penitentiary and "dishonor" to support them, regardless of whether the penitentiary was connected to the deprivation of an offender's civil privileges. As long as people believed the penitentiary to be dishonoring, they advocated that ex-convicts should be excluded from the army. Many other prominent conservative members of the Reichstag, like Botho zu Eulenburg, backed Steinmetz and Moltke.[47] Even Heinrich von Friedberg, the head of the commission that drafted the original text, later acknowledged that §31 was in the nation's best interest despite being inconsistent with the principle of distinguishing the crime from the punishment.[48]

In the end, the intervention of army officials in the Reichstag debate suggests that they were inspired to promote the addition of §31 by their fear that requirements for participating in state institutions like the army would be made less rigorous. Hence, their support for §31 should be viewed in the context of the movement toward universal conscription. At the time, the criteria for eligibility to join the army were already being softened, and a growing number of young men were being recruited.[49] This change was not as sudden as the introduction of universal male suffrage for the Reichstag (introduced in 1871), but the army increasingly took on the character of a national institution consisting of all (male) citizens of the nation. Around 1870, there was already something close to universal conscription.

That the move toward universal conscription largely motivated army officials in their push to exclude former penitentiary inmates from the army became even clearer in a speech by Helmut von Moltke at the Reichstag in 1872, when a new military code was under discussion:

> When everybody takes up arms, it is only natural that the bad people—and every nation has some—also take up arms. We have to take everyone, every man who is of the right age, who is healthy and of such and such physical stature. The recruitment commission cannot vet the morals of the recruits. Thus, we get people who might belong in the penitentiary if strict military discipline did not keep them from this misfortune.[50]

Even though he acknowledged that the times demanded universal conscription, Moltke clearly expressed his discomfort with the idea. He likewise remained fiercely opposed to the army having officers from a middle-class background.[51] However, the new criteria made it difficult to preserve the exclusive character of the army, leaving only one ground for exclusion: having served time in the penitentiary. Moltke believed that excluding dishonored felons would, at the very least, uphold the honor of the army. In this way, the German government could still safeguard the army from the influence of "morally inferior" people.

"The Army Is Not an Institution of Moral Reform"

The debate over §31 shows how discussions regarding the expansion of institutions like the army and the lowering of eligibility hurdles triggered reactions that highlighted the notion of honor. Advocates of policies for maintaining honor, however, no longer focused on the personal status of high-born individuals, focusing instead on the abstract honor of the army as an institution needing protection. Despite this difference in the notion of honor, its advocates defended it with just as much passion. This way of protecting the honor of the army continued to exist in the German Empire. As illustrated by the vehement reactions to Schmölder's suggestion that felons be included in conscription (described in the opening of this chapter), army officials cherished the principle of excluding "dishonored felons"—even thirty years after the Reich Penal Code was drafted.

At that time, combating crime was a top priority for conservative imperial authorities. They believed that they could unify the populations of this newly founded state with harsh punishments, surveillance methods, and the expulsion of minorities, but few thought of the army as bearing any responsibility in the prevention of crime.[52] The idea that the army could reform ex-convicts was completely unheard of. In a way, this is striking because the military had already permeated many aspects of society in the German Empire. The militarization of society manifested itself, for example, in the penal landscape as prison wardens were often recruited from the pool of former army officers.[53] Therefore, the application of severe army discipline to prisoners was not the point of contention. Furthermore, in this period of German history, under the influence of the "modern school" of criminal law, the idea that punishment should have a social purpose increasingly took hold; the focus gradually shifted from retribution to the reform potential of criminals. Thus, questions arose more often about how the army could contribute to this aim.

In fact, criminal policy at that time was engaged in an intellectual dispute about the nature and purpose of criminal law that came to be known as the *Schulenstreit* (the school dispute) between the adherents of the "classic" school and those of the "modern" one. The precise difference between the two schools is a matter of debate. Historian of crime and criminology in modern Germany Richard F. Wetzell argues that the "classic" movement largely focused on protecting the individual from the state "by limiting the state's penal power."[54] This group was associated with the works of the devout legal positivist Karl Binding and scholars like Karl Birkmeyer and Friedrich Oetker. The purpose of criminal law, they argued, was to administer retribution to deter people from criminal behavior. The notion that there was a "classic school," however, emerged in reaction to a group of scholars who started to actively fashion themselves as "moderns."[55] The "modern" movement had a more holistic, scientific approach to criminal justice and sought to integrate the disciplines of criminology and moral statistics. The journal *Zeitschrift für die gesamte Strafrechtswissenschaft* functioned as the main platform for this movement.[56]

The idea that offenders could be reformed by recruiting them for the army arguably fit well with the ideas of the modern school about offenders' reform potential. Some scholars who identified with this movement had, in fact, pointed out the counterproductive and criminogenic effects of excluding former penitentiary inmates from the army. Legal scholar Julius Medem, for instance, observed in an 1887 essay that people were motivated to "visit" the penitentiary in order to avoid conscription.[57] Franz von Liszt, the main advocate of the modern movement, had remarked in one of his many programmatic essays that he wanted §31 abolished for that very reason.[58] Yet, in both Medem's and Liszt's case, their dismissal of felony disenfranchisement was not connected with thoughts about the pedagogical function of the army, and they put little effort into actively encouraging the abolition of these punishments.

Like Medem and Liszt, Schmölder pointed out the paradox of young people, in particular, being motivated to engage in criminal activity by "dishonored" felons' exclusion from the army, arguing that they often preferred a stay in the penitentiary over military conscription.[59] However, Schmölder was the first scholar up until then to seriously argue that the army should take responsibility for combating crime in society and one of the few commentators to point out the overlapping interests of the army and the prisons.

Curiously, Schmölder identified with the "classic school" in the *Schulenstreit*. In 1904, he published an article in the *Preußische Jahrbücher* on "modern" ideas of imprisonment, expressing many concerns about these. Prisons, he argued, were neither "sanatoria" nor "boarding schools" but primarily institutions of punishment. Inmates were thus supposed to experience incarceration as malicious, not as a comfort. The growing influence of "modern" scholars on the actual management of local prisons, he believed, was to blame for this development.[60] Yet serious offenders should have to face something they really fear: the military. As he stated, "The young rowdies and pimps of our big cities fear nothing more than the iron discipline that awaits them in the military."[61] Schmölder's stance shows that it was not only adherents of the modern school who entertained ideas about moral reform.

Meanwhile, the rhetoric that army officials used to justify the exclusion of dishonored felons became more medicalized, focusing on the "hygiene" of the army and similar institutions. Conservative army officials, who were arguably more inclined toward "classical" ideas of punishment, were influenced by modern ideas about the connection between medical issues and the causes of crime. In this framework, moral incompetence was regarded as a form of physical degeneration.[62] In the second half of the nineteenth century, hygiene discourse—with a focus on preventing sickness and creating the conditions for healthy living—increasingly dominated debates over social questions, including policing and criminal law.[63]

In this context, Hermann Simon, a medical scholar and army physician, classified former penitentiary inmates together with psychiatric patients, advising against allowing either into the army. In his argument, the connection between physical and mental degeneration and the moral unworthiness of ex-convicts was very clear:

> The ideal purpose of our standing army is to bring the best of our people together to forge a strong and reliable defense of the fatherland. It is not supposed to be an institution of moral reform and education for feeble-minded, morally degenerate youths.[64]

In his response castigating Schmölder's reform suggestions, discussed above, war council member Heinrich Dietz also presented many arguments based on statistical research into the ever-growing rates of offenses recorded within the Prussian army of the German Empire. In particular, he tied growing number of offenses to the growing amount of sick leave.[65] Judging by sick-leave statistics, the labor divisions were the most underachieving ones in the army because sick leave was six times as high as in other divisions, he argued. In fact, the labor divisions consisted mainly of people who were considered unworthy of joining the armed forces, mostly ex-convicts, who were nevertheless eligible to join the labor divisions. He concluded from this that if more former convicts joined the ranks, morale among the soldiers would decline dramatically.[66] Thus, his final argument was that ex-convicts would only contribute to the further degeneration of the army.[67]

Schmölder's only real supporter was Alexis Küppers, a professor from Bonn who shared his concerns about the criminogenic effects of ex-convicts being exempt from military service. In a 1912 article for the progressive *Monatsschrift für Kriminalpsychologie und Strafrechtsreform*, Küppers wrote that offenders favored the penitentiary sentence over a normal prison sentence in certain respects since the former precluded them from having to fulfill the compulsory military service after their release.[68] Küppers's article reiterated much of what

Schmölder had argued six years earlier, but unlike Schmölder's classic school orientation, he was a scholar of Liszt and based his ideas on "modern" principles. These scholars with opposite backgrounds and conflicting ideas about criminal policy eventually found common ground in the idea of using the army to morally reform ex-convicts. Nonetheless, Küppers, even as an advocate of the modern school, was very careful about protecting the honor of the army, which showed that supporting ex-cons' participation in the institution required a delicate balance.[69] Army officials dismissed Küppers's suggestions just as vehemently as they had Schmölder's.[70]

The opposition of the General Staff and others to recruiting ex-convicts was echoed in journals and newspapers criticizing the French policy of enlisting such individuals. The Foreign Legion was often raised as a negative example for German army policy because of the immoral character its soldiers displayed.[71] German commentators also highlighted the French policy of recruiting ex-convicts for regular army units.[72] The German policy, by contrast, decidedly isolated the prison from the army. The army authorities stubbornly adhered to their core principle that only law-abiding citizens in full possession of their civil privileges were eligible for the specific honor of serving in the army and defended it with vigor.

Disenfranchisement for the Benefit of Electoral Policy

The previous sections show that the stipulations on disenfranchisement in the Reich Penal Code constituted a complicated trade-off between the opposing demands of inclusion and exclusion. In other words, it codified the expansion of civil privileges to include a larger group of citizens only insofar as a certain class of "degenerates" remained excluded. Therefore, disenfranchisement played a crucial and ambivalent role in the leveling trends within the German Empire, both in the expansion of military conscription and in the development of suffrage rights.

The expansion of the privilege of voting to achieve universal male suffrage generated similar anxieties as the introduction of universal conscription, particularly among the higher classes, who feared that this gave the "rougher" crowd coveted state powers. Anthropologist Otto Ammonn, a vehement critic of expanding voting rights, summed up this sentiment in 1895: "the most common screamers and gossipers are the privileged people of universal suffrage; troublemakers will return from the ballot box adorned with the laurel of victory, something that was in the past considered a moral impossibility."[73] To safeguard the "honor" of this institution, he maintained, dishonored offenders had to remain excluded.

Interestingly, the exclusion of dishonored felons from the ballot box was hardly ever contested in the public arena of Imperial Germany.[74] Schmölder, for instance, in arguing that ex-convicts should be conscripted, emphasized that this certainly did not mean that their voting rights should be restored as well. For him, this issue was beyond debate.[75] Even Social Democrats, who were generally highly critical of the German suffrage system, hardly ever criticized this aspect of German penal policy. In the state of Prussia, this lack of fundamental criticism was likely due to critics of the electoral system having other, more fundamental concerns, including the *Dreiklassenwahlrecht* (the three-class franchise system) that had existed in Prussia since 1849. Many liberals and Social Democrats criticized it as gravely unjust because it marginalized ethnic minorities and the poor. In this system, the votes of low-income people carried very little weight, so people presumably felt that making a case to restore voting rights to disenfranchised felons would not be worthwhile. In fact, opponents of Prussia's three-class franchise system generally favored the implementation of the electoral system for the Reichstag in Prussia, which included provisions for felony disenfranchisement.[76]

Prussia's three-class franchise system even inspired mockery in satirical magazines, whose cartoons suggested that the system equated Prussia's lower-class people with "dishonored" felons. For example, a 1908 cartoon in the Bavarian satirical magazine *Simplicissimus* depicted a man sentenced with disenfranchisement. As he does not know what this means, the judge explains that he has lost his right to vote, to which he responds, "Alas, I shall become a Prussian."[77]

The publication date of 1908 was significant: that year, the outcry about the electoral system reached a high point in Prussia.[78] Efforts to change electoral policy prompted renewed support for felony disenfranchisement, which was used to make a case for including the "law-abiding" poor in the franchise.

Sociologist Ferdinand Tönnies, for instance, argued in an article for the progressive magazine *Das freie Wort* that stricter enforcement of felony disenfranchisement could compensate for an expansion of the right to vote: "As is well known, people can be deprived of their civil privileges as a secondary punishment. But society could and should make more drastic use of this, not for the benefit of criminal policy, but for the benefit of electoral policy."[79] Tönnies argued that felony disenfranchisement was a political necessity in response to opponents who feared that the franchise would lose its "honorable character" if the electoral system were reformed. A stricter policy of felony disenfranchisement, he maintained, would safeguard the honor of the franchise while reversing the "disgrace" of the poor being excluded from it.

The punishment of disenfranchisement was included in arguments concerning the expansion of civil privileges on other occasions as well, such as in the struggle for women's suffrage. Ottilie Baader, a pioneer of the socialist feminist movement, for example, argued that women's exclusion from the franchise was disgraceful in that, among other reasons, it treated them as equivalent to "dishonored felons."[80] These dynamics of inclusion and exclusion demonstrate what French philosopher Étienne Balibar calls the "antinomy of citizenship": citizenship, he argues, can essentially be understood in two senses, one exclusive and

Figure 2.1. Cartoon by Eduard Thöny. Image reads: "So you've lost your honor for three years, do you know what that means? – No – For example, you are not allowed to exercise the right to vote – (in slang) Alas, I shall become a Prussian." Eduard Thöny, "Harte Strafe" (Harsh Punishment), *Simplicissimus* 13, no. 2 (1908): 23. Courtesy Klassik Stiftung Weimar.

the other inclusive. "Statutory" citizenship is exclusive in that the state limits access to it; it primarily revolves around one's membership in and obligations to the state, and citizens are primarily understood as its subjects. In an inclusive understanding of citizenship, on the other hand, people who claim citizenship contribute to the process of constituting the state. In this way, they themselves determine the boundaries of citizenship.[81]

Membership, Eligibility, and State Honor

Importantly, the dynamics of inclusion and exclusion applied not only to the right to join the army and the right to vote for state parliaments. Disenfranchisement, in particular, had many exclusionary effects that transcended the provisions in the penal code. In a sense, one could argue that the policy of disenfranchisement pervaded all of German society. For instance, it was interwoven into the emerging German social state in many ways. In the 1870s, a state-regulated social security system was first set up in Germany, which, for the most part, mandated privately organized insurance funds. This was an important first step in the creation of a welfare state.[82] Social insurance policy was founded on a regime of trust based on objective data and the expertise of medical authorities.[83] In this context, "moral hazards" were considered a great threat to the insurance funds because as these grew larger, they became potentially easier to abuse.[84] Disenfranchisement then served as an important objective criterion for (partially) excluding "dishonored" felons to prevent this moral hazard.

Most of the miners' insurance funds (*Knappschaften*), for instance, required "the full possession of civil privileges" for "first-class" membership,[85] which provided full entitlement to benefits. The mine workers' insurance fund of Bochum, for instance, stipulated this condition in its statutes.[86] The Prussian government's general directives on miners' insurance funds also included the possibility of refusing membership to dishonored felons.[87] Furthermore, the punishment of disenfranchisement was included in the second version of the national health insurance law of 1892 as a criterion municipalities could use to deny benefits to possibly fraudulent applicants.[88] In many ways, therefore, disenfranchisement nullified one's entitlement to benefits in the emerging social security state.

The condition of being "in full possession" of one's civil privileges was found in the statutes of many more organizations that operated in the domain between private initiative and state regulation, such as social clubs, workers' unions, and political organizations. The Christian Workers' Union of Essen, for instance, included such a provision, and even unions that included mostly women, such as the Gewerkverein der Heimarbeiterinnen für Kleider- und Wäschefabrikation, had similar rules.[89] In such organizations, disenfranchised citizens might be excluded from membership entirely, stripped of the right to vote during assemblies, or prevented from joining a board.[90] Disenfranchised citizens were also excluded from the works councils that arose in this period.[91]

Similarly, the Reich Commercial and Industrial Code (Reichsgewerbeordnung), introduced by the North German Confederation in 1869, stipulated civil privileges as a condition for many types of employment.[92] For many professions, it was mandatory for applicants to have an official certificate licensing them to practice a certain craft (predominantly in the trades) that they could only obtain if they were in full possession of their civil privileges. In this sense, the distinction between state and market affairs was more an idea than a reality. As I argued in the Introduction, the punishment of disenfranchisement rested on the strict separation of state affairs and the free market. Many penal reform proposals emphasized that disenfranchisement was not supposed impact people's position in the market.[93] In legal terms, this meant that it was only supposed to have consequences in public law and not in private law. Thus, one could easily conclude that these regulations frustrated the intended function of the punishment as they failed to fully implement the ideological emancipation of the market from the state.

Yet, one could also argue that these examples show that the state-centered notion of honor truly became hegemonic at this time as it penetrated many realms of German society. After all, unions and semi-private organizations relied on these penal provisions for determining social insurance and employment eligibility, which suggests that these organizations had largely transferred their sanctioning powers to the state. In this sense, the state became the sole arbiter of who was "honorable enough."

Disenfranchisement in a Cluttered Penal Landscape

Even within the prison system, the presence of disenfranchised felons had complicated and ambivalent effects. In writings on prison administration in the German Empire, there was a broad consensus that the distinctions in the Penal Code between "dishonored" offenders and regular convicts had no bearing on the way these people were treated inside prison facilities. In fact, whether criminals were sentenced to a deprivation of their civil privileges or not, they were often sent to the same facility, be it a prison or a penitentiary. This went against the clear-cut distinction behind dishonoring sentences that stipulated incarceration in a penitentiary, separate from those who were not so dishonored, as was succinctly formulated by Carl Mittermaier as early as 1843: "the distinction between dishonorable and non-dishonorable punishments must be made clear by the building itself."[94] In Wilhemine Germany, however, it was usually only long-term penitentiary convicts (above one year) who were sent to larger penitentiaries, like the bigger facilities in Moabit, Bruchsal, or Rawicz. Other convicts were usually placed together in smaller institutions across Germany.[95]

In this context, it is important to note that the German penal landscape was diffuse; there was no uniform code of prison administration, so few regulations were upheld on a national level.[96] As penal expert Karl Krohne argued in 1881, the institution in which one was incarcerated made all the difference.[97] Liszt, adding to Krohne's observation, noted that one could witness every imaginable method of incarceration being applied at the same time across the German Empire.[98] Nobody could guarantee that the distinctions between prison and penitentiary inmates would be upheld in all the facilities, and gradually prison experts started to argue that the distinction between a penitentiary and a prison was merely a difference in words.[99]

Interestingly, however, the mixing of inmates made the question of differences in treatment more significant. From several discussions that took place in the *Blätter für Gefängniskunde* (the official journal for prison wardens) in the 1890s and 1900s, one can conclude that many prison wardens at least tried to treat "dishonored" offenders differently from "regular" inmates. A frequent topic was how "dishonored" felons should be addressed. Although the practice varied from prison to prison, many prison wardens used disenfranchisement as their criterion for using the informal *du* instead of the formal *Sie*. Disenfranchised prisoners were addressed more frequently with *du*, while other inmates were addressed with *Sie* out of respect for their untainted status.[100]

What often happened in mixed facilities, moreover, was that penitentiary convicts and regular prisoners were assigned different uniforms (traditionally regular prisoners wore blue ones and penitentiary inmates wore brown ones). Adolf Streng, a prison warden from Hamburg, described the clothing policy as an integral part of the system of dishonor because he considered the prison garment a form of *capitis deminutio*, a measure to deliberately demean the convict. At the same time, he noted that some prison wardens had become more liberal in assigning the outfits to inmates and also in placing inmates in different wings of their facilities.[101]

In the context of labor supply, the question of distinguishing different kinds of inmates was particularly pertinent. A governmental tract from 1897 titled "Die Grundsätze welche bei dem Vollzuge gerichtlich erkannter Freiheitsstrafen bis zu weiterer gemeinsamer Regelung zur Anwendung kommen" (The Principles which Are Applied in the Execution of Judicially Enforced Custodial Sentences until Further Arrangements Are Made; hereafter "Grundsätze") was an attempt to introduce a uniform prison policy in Prussia. The tract stated that inmates still in possession of their privileges were entitled to milder treatment, particularly where labor was concerned.[102] This tract elaborated on the rather unclear regulations in the Reich Penal Code: §15 and §16 of the Reich Penal Code stipulated that penitentiary inmates were to be subjected to forced labor, whereas regular prisoners could be assigned to work "that fit his or her qualities."[103] The 1897 tract, however, stated more explicitly that people in possession of their civil privileges deserved "individualized" treatment. Their work should fit their health status, their competencies, their future ambitions, and their level of education. They should be able to choose how they wanted to be occupied.[104] Finding "fitting work" was thus seen as a sign of respect for their status as "regular" prisoners.

A circular from the Prussian Minister of Justice that same year made it clear that the stipulations in the "Grundsätze" were partly motivated by worries about some "regular" inmates having a damaged "sense of honor":

> It has been noticed that more highly educated and upstanding inmates, who have not been convicted of dishonorable crimes and have not been stripped of their civil privileges, are instructed to do work of the most inferior kind. I do not underestimate the difficulties of finding appropriate occupation, but I do find it necessary and feasible that the individual characteristics of prisoners be taken into proper consideration in the distribution of labor.[105]

Apparently, the structurally demeaning treatment of prisoners from a higher educational background worried the Prussian Minister of Justice. This document gave prison officials a tool both for justifying privileges for some prisoners and for treating others more harshly.

The organization of labor was, in fact, one of the greatest difficulties prison wardens faced, as prison expert Hermann Kriegsmann acknowledged in his handbook of 1912.[106] In the smaller mixed institutions, in particular, it was difficult to find tasks for the inmates, which made the requirements stipulated in the "Grundsätze" even more problematic. Sometimes the inmates had no work at all.[107] According to a statistic from 1905, almost 14 percent of the inmates of smaller institutions were not engaged in any form of labor.[108] This is partly explained by the critical attitude toward prison labor, which was seen as spoiling the national economy. Many German political parties, for instance, made curtailing prison labor a core issue in their programs.[109]

Most often, prisoners were given work that was easy to organize, like the upkeep and maintenance of the facility. But more highly educated prisoners who had not been dishonored considered this sort of work demeaning. This also applied to tasks like basket weaving and garment manufacturing. Some critics of the penal system at that time decried the "feminine" nature of the prison labor as damaging to male convicts' masculine honor.[110]

One possible solution to the labor problem was "prisoner leasing," that is, sending prisoners out to work for a wage for an outside company or the government. In the German Empire, this gradually became more accepted but happened mostly for state enterprises.[111] In this context, too, however, the division between "honorable" and "dishonoring" work was carefully maintained. In 1902, for instance, although the local welfare society for prisoners in Aachen had advocated that prisoners be employed for road and railway maintenance, the authorities of the governmental district were reluctant to employ prisoners thus because they feared doing so would diminish the reputation of this kind of work. As the

District Commissioner of Düren stated, since prisoners had committed crimes, they must have a "dishonorable" or "rough" disposition and be excluded from this kind of work. The police commissioner of Aachen, too, worried about the adverse effect on the reputation of public enterprises.

Figure 2.2. Cartoonist Thomas Theodor Heine mocking the reverence for people working in public service: "Can you please tell the way to the Grimmaische Strasse?" – (in slang) "You, listen, a decent man keeps his hat in his hand when he's talking to a royal official." Thomas Theodor Heine, "Durchs dunkelste Deutschland 9: der Beambte," *Simplicissimus* 6, no. 42 (1901): 329. Courtesy Klassik Stiftung Weimar.

The District Commissioner of Aachen, for his part, suggested that prisoners could be employed in this sector after they had served their sentences. If these prisoners knew that the state enterprises wanted to employ them after they served their time, it might inspire a sense of honor of the prisoners who were willing to work, he argued.[112] Despite their diverging opinions, these authorities were all clearly concerned about the "honor" of such prisoner leasing. They believed that state service clearly had a more "honorable" character than other kinds of work and that the exclusion of dishonored felons from such "honorable work" was essential for the protection of its honor.

Two Penal Reform Proposals

As these individual cases show, German penal authorities thought less about properly "dishonoring" serious felons than they did about protecting "regular" inmates. This was largely motivated by their ambition to reintegrate "corrigible" offenders as they felt that it would be more difficult to resocialize offenders whose sense of honor had been damaged. This also explains why many legal scholars, instead of lobbying to abolish the "empty" distinctions in the penal code, believed that the factual erosion of the distinction between different prisoners and between different institutions was a problem that needed to be solved. In fact, better observance of the distinction in prisoners could boost the spirits of prisoners whose honor was not legally damaged. Consequently, the spatial separation and differentiated treatment of "dishonored" convicts and "regular" prisoners needed to be restored.

During their annual meetings from 1887 to 1889, members of the Northwest German Prison Association (Nordwestdeutscher Gefängnisverein) also concluded that the legal distinction between "dishonored" and regular offenders needed to be maintained. In their view, it corresponded to the legal consciousness, or *Rechtsbewusststein*, of the common people, who held that a distinction between certain crimes—and thus between certain kinds of imprisonment—was of great moral value.[113] The association's refusal to support the abolition of the hierarchical differentiation in prisons and prisoners demonstrates the enduring appeal the idea still had to many prison experts and other citizens of the German Empire. Even the progressive legal scholar Liszt, in his earlier work, had advocated a clearer distinction between the two kinds of prisoners and proposed that the contemporary practice of putting penitentiary inmates and other convicts in the same institution be prohibited.[114]

In the first decade of the twentieth century, the German government had decided that, after more than thirty years, it was time for the Reich Penal Code to undergo a thorough revision. This gave many experts an opportunity to propose solutions to the problem of blurring boundaries in the penal landscape. The commission responsible for the reform presented its first draft in 1909, preceded by a massive scholarly work that systematically compared the penal systems across the world, the nine-volume *Vergleichende Darstellung des deutschen und ausländischen Strafrechts*.[115] The draft for the new penal code largely maintained the ideas of the "classic" school, only marginally adopting some of the ideas of the "modern" school.[116]

The "classic" school orientation manifested itself in, among other things, the draft's strong emphasis on the legal distinction between the types of incarceration. Some journalists observed that tightening up regulations was a main aim of this legal reform,[117] which may have motivated the clarifications. It is very likely that public debate about the general "intensification" (*Verschärfung*) of penal measures also played a role. For instance, many German newspapers, and particularly conservative ones like the *Deutsche Tageszeitung* and the *Hamburger Nachrichten*, called for corporal punishment to be reintroduced.[118] Numerous conservative commentators and politicians saw this as essential as a potential harsher punishment for "dishonored" offenders.

Yet, prison wardens objected that such "disciplinary measures" were not really fit for people deprived of their privileges because they believed there was no hope of inciting a sense of honor in such individuals. Corporal punishment, they believed, only had a pedagogical effect on youthful offenders as it could strengthen their weak sense of honor. However, youths were not commonly deprived of their privileges.[119] In the end, corporal punishment was not included in the draft of the reformed penal code.

Even though the commission did not include corporal punishment, its members took the idea seriously. They acknowledged that there were good justifications for it but argued that greater emphasis on the separation between "regular" prisoners and penitentiary inmates could help to achieve the same goals as it would protect the honor of "regular" inmates while making the harsher punishment of "serious criminals" more feasible.[120] Thus, it was important for penitentiary sentences to be carried out in institutions specifically designed for that purpose.[121]

Even "modern" legal scholars' counterproposal, which was published a year after the 1909 draft, left the regulations between "dishonored" felons and regular inmates unchanged.[122] They did suggest that the legal distinction should be based on an offender's character rather than the nature of the offense. This would grant prison wardens more power to judge how sentences would be carried out by personally assessing the character of the offender. This was a way for "modern" school adherents to introduce the categories of the "incorrigible" and "corrigible" offenders and make them compatible with the traditional legal distinction between "dishonored" felons and regular prisoners in the penal code.[123]

In the end, however, the penal code was not reformed, and the laws remained as they were. Unlike Foucault, who observed that imprisonment was a "gray" and "uniform" sentence,[124] nineteenth-century commentators and penal experts believed in the possibility and use of differentiating offenders inside penal facilities, even if Foucault was evidently right that these differences were hardly considered in practice. Consequently, the idea of differentiation greatly influenced their debates about penal reform.

The Right to Be Trusted and Not to Be Stripped

In many ways, the presence of "dishonored" felons could function as an argument for granting more privileges to other convicts. Thus, debates about the possibility of expanding privileges for prisoners were always accompanied by a plea for stricter rules for disenfranchised felons. The previous section showed how this worked in the context of the internal administration of prisons, but it also happened outside prison facilities. Chapter 1 already laid out how the penal code was the primary place where civil privileges were defined and argued that the question of civil privileges became intimately connected with the topic of crime and punishment. A consequence of this was that penal law also became an important instrument for protecting German citizens' civil privileges. In other words, criminals who were not disenfranchised could insist on certain rights and privileges.

For instance, the "right to be trusted" played a role in the introduction of an indemnity law that passed the Reichstag in 1905. This law regulated the financial compensation that citizens who were later deemed innocent could claim from the government after being held in pretrial detention (*Untersuchungshaft*).[125] One effect of this law was that state prosecutors had to be more cautious about detaining citizens suspected of criminal activity.[126] However, the law also stipulated that these regulations did not apply to all citizens equally. People who were not in possession of their civil privileges or who had been discharged from the penitentiary within one year prior to their detention were not eligible. This important clause clarified that authorities believed that their previous conviction alone constituted a reasonable suspicion to justify detaining them. As the official text of the law declared, "[in these cases], the suspicion that led to their arrest is the unavoidable consequence of their previous criminal activity, which has not yet been erased from the minds of their fellow citizens."[127]

Initially, the law stipulated that people were not eligible to make an indemnity claim if they had been sentenced for a felony any time in the five years prior to being taken into custody or if they had been sentenced for begging, vagrancy, "refusal to work," or similar offenses. However, many Reichstag representatives criticized the unjust nature of this exception, and Social Democrat Adolf Thiele, who otherwise supported the law, harshly criticized its many limitations.[128] In the end, the Social Democrats voted against the law, even though they had long been advocating for it.[129] But after the debate in the Reichstag, the eligibility limitations were narrowed so that only disenfranchised citizens remained excluded. This satisfied everyone. The lawmakers granted falsely convicted citizens in possession of their civil privileges the right to restitution while maintaining part of their policy of "reasonable suspicion" against the dishonored segment of the population.[130] It is clear from the Reichstag's broad consensus that disenfranchisement was universally accepted as a measure justifying a person's detention.

The Problem of Overlapping Jurisdictions

In the rather confusing landscape of overlapping jurisdictions in the German Empire, the punishment of disenfranchisement also created legal protection against the arbitrary loss of one's privileges. As argued in chapter 1, civil privileges were only listed in the article of the penal code that concerned their possible suspension. As a result, the Reich Penal Code constituted the primary source upon which to base decisions to deprive German citizens of their civil privileges. For instance, one important stipulation was that disenfranchisement could only be imposed in combination with a "primary" punishment (that is, imprisonment); disenfranchisement was thus only a "secondary punishment" (*Nebenstrafe*).

An example helps to clarify how this protected one's privileges. Adolf Jacobsen, a leather manufacturer and member of the Reichstag for the Freisinnige Volkspartei, was placed in legal detention for approaching insolvency in 1899. A great deal of debate ensued in academic journals about whether this affected his mandate. However, a novelty of the Reich Penal Code was its distinction between "simple" and "fraudulent" bankruptcy: only in the latter case was the culprit disenfranchised.[131] Moreover, Jacobsen had not officially been declared bankrupt but had only been detained. Nonetheless, another Reichstag member, Julius Kopsch, petitioned for Jacobsen to be dismissed from the Reichstag. The members of a commission tasked with deciding on this, however, saw it differently. They voted against dismissal since they pointed out that Jacobsen was still in full possession of his civil privileges.[132] Legal scholars used this opportunity to reflect on the legal principles underlying this question. And, indeed, many argued that—even though it was questionable whether a bankrupt person could remain a member of the Reichstag—there was no legal reason to rescind Jacobsen's mandate.[133]

Disenfranchisement was also prominently relevant for honorary titles. In the Reich Penal Code, §33 entailed the permanent suspension of all titles, orders, and decorations for offenders convicted of dishonorable crimes. Some scholars believed that, since honorary titles were awarded as a special act of sovereign grace (*landesherrlicher Gnade*), dishonored criminals should be stripped of them as well,[134] but this position was highly disputed. This was particularly problematic in the case of army officers on reserve; they comprised a large segment of society, and their legal status was not always clear.

At the turn of the century, numerous inactive officers were summoned before military courts of honor for allegedly insulting other (former) army officers in public. One officer so charged was the Bavarian military officer Rudolf Krafft, who had published a book entitled *Shining Misery*, a vehement critique of soldiers' maltreatment by officers in the Bavarian army.[135] After his hearing in the military court of honor, he was stripped of his titles and pension and deprived of his right to wear his uniform.[136] Another example was the inactive officer Fritz Hoenig, who wrote historical accounts of the Franco-Prussian War after completing his military service. His tracts, however, prompted the General Staff to accuse him of insulting former officers by implying that their cowardice had caused the loss of the Battle of Villepion in 1870. Like Krafft, Hoenig was stripped of his titles and his pension because he refused to apologize or to grant the officer's son satisfaction for the insult to his father.[137] These dishonoring sentences were controversial in that they were meted out alone, even though the penal code stated that they could only supplement prison sentences.

A journalist for the left liberal journal *Berliner Tageblatt*, Richard Gädke, an inactive army officer who had himself been expelled from army service without being sentenced for a crime punishable by imprisonment,[138] took up with the fate of these former officers in several articles. Highly critical of these sentences and the policy of stripping the titles of officers on reserve, Gädke argued that these proceedings enabled the General Staff to dishonor former officers simply for their opinions.[139] The words of this journalist did not impress the military authorities.

However, the military authorities were impressed when Paul Laband, one of the greatest authorities on constitutional law during the Wilhelmine period, devoted an article to the matter in the *Deutsche Juristenzeitung* in 1907.[140] In it, he argued that honorary titles ought not be arbitrarily stripped since they had been awarded as an "honor." Laband contended that even though titles were granted by a special act of grace, they still became a subjective right immediately upon bestowal and were therefore protected by law.[141] The Reich Penal Code, he concluded, protected these people from the suspension of their titles as long as they had not been sentenced for a crime that prescribed their rescission. Thus, he backed up Gädke's criticism of this practice and pointed out the injustice of these sentences. Laband's doctrine thereafter became generally accepted among legal scholars. As another journalist of the *Berliner Tageblatt* remarked, the laws on disenfranchisement were primarily intended to guarantee the protection of people's honor, and that of soldiers, in particular.[142] Combined with the generally accepted rule of *nulla poena sine lege* (no punishment without a law), these legal debates about the loss of privileges and honors could be interpreted as another sign that the legal system in the German Empire increasingly allowed citizens to more effectively defend their rights before a court of justice.[143]

In a short treatise on the legal status of honor from 1892, Karl Binding shared his thoughts about the motivation behind the codification of felony disenfranchisement in the Reich Penal Code: "Disenfranchisement does not take one's honor but takes the rights of him who has already lost his honor."[144] In other words, the punishment was nothing more than the symbolic expression of a loss of honor that had already occurred, in his view. This statement highlights that German authorities considered disenfranchisement important as one means of making citizenship exclusionary: people who had disgraced themselves had no entitlement to the privileges of citizenship. Yet other citizens and social activists considered felony disenfranchisement important on account of its inclusionary function. It elevated the character of "ordinary citizenship" by clarifying who did not belong to that group. The philosopher and pedagogue Friedrich Paulsen argued along these lines when he stated that the mere existence of honor punishments proved that "ordinary" citizens (*Staatsbürger*) were a privileged political class with a specific kind of honor; all who had not disgraced themselves were worthy of this honor.[145]

All in all, disenfranchisement in the German Empire was remarkable as a result of both its inclusionary and exclusionary functions. It not only excluded dishonored criminals from various memberships but also provided a stronger argument for granting privileges to those who had not received such a sentence. In the German Empire, society was growing more inclusive; larger groups of citizens were gaining access to certain institutions, such as the army, the franchise, certain labor regulations, and insurance funds. In debates about inclusion, the interests of population management and state institutions were often weighed against one other. People who emphasized the "honor" of official institutions and the privileges they entailed nearly always resisted suggestions to broaden membership. Meanwhile, several scholars critical of exclusionary practices feared that excluding too many citizens from certain occupations, state enterprises, and other institutions would disturb the "economy" of honor. They sought to find a balance between shielding the honor of state institutions while insisting on the "dishonored" status of ex-convicts without labeling too many people dishonorable and thus contributing to social disintegration. This dialectic was an essential part of many reforms that affected the core components of German citizenship.

Control over membership in these institutions fully relied on "civil honor" as stipulated in the penal code. Although this notion belonged more to the vocabulary of conservative authorities and traditional scholars, even scholars who sought to distinguish between corrigible and incorrigible offenders and to resocialize the former did not dismiss it outright. In fact, the many penal reform proposals that "modern school" adherents shared with those of the "classic school" in the early twentieth century showed that even modern-leaning legal experts believed in the compatibility of the categories of honor and dishonor with modern ideas about criminal policy and rehabilitation. This underscores the truly hegemonic status of the German Empire's notion of honor.

Notes

1. Richard F. Wetzell, "Introduction," in *Crime and Criminal Justice in Modern Germany*, ed. Richard F. Wetzell, 1–28 (New York: Berghahn Books, 2014); Christian Müller, *Verbrechensbekämpfung im Anstaltsstaat: Psychiatrie, Kriminologie und Strafrechtsreform in Deutschland 1871–1933* (Göttingen: Vandenhoeck & Ruprecht, 2004), 125–70.
2. Robert Schmölder, "Die Wehrpflicht der Verbrecher," *DJZ* 10, no. 21 (1905): 982–85, 985. On urban youth in the German Empire, see Klaus Tenfelde, "Großstadtjugend in Deutschland vor 1914. Eine historisch-demographische Annäherung," *Vierteljahrschrift für Sozial- und Wirtschaftsgeschichte* 69, no. 2 (1982): 182–218.
3. Ibid., 227.
4. Heinrich Dietz, "Keine Wehrpflicht der Verbrecher!," *GAS* 53, no. 4 (1906): 225–35.
5. Benjamin Ziemann, "Sozialmilitarismus und militärische Sozialisation im deutschen Kaiserreich 1870–1914," *Geschichte in Wissenschaft und Unterricht* 53, no. 3 (2002): 148–64.
6. Ibid.
7. Thomas Nipperdey, *Deutsche Geschichte 1866–1918. Machtstaat vor der Demokratie* (Munich: Beck, 1992), 224.
8. Gordon A. Craig, *The Politics of the Prussian Army, 1640–1945* (Oxford: Clarendon Press, 1955), 235.
9. Ziemann, "Sozialmilitarismus und militärische Sozialisation," 153.
10. Ute Frevert, "Das Militär als Schule der Männlichkeit. Erwartungen, Angebote, Erfahrungen im 19. Jahrhundert," in *Militär und Gesellschaft im 19. und 20. Jahrhundert*, ed. Ute Frevert, 145–73 (Stuttgart: Klett-Cotta, 1997).
11. Michel Foucault, *Surveiller et punir. Naissance de la prison* (Paris: Gallimard, 1975); see the section on *"le carcéral,"* 343–60, in particular; Thomas Nutz, *Strafanstalt als Besserungsmaschine. Reformdiskurs und Gefängniswissenschaft 1775–1848* (Munich: Oldenbourg, 2001), 95.
12. Peter Berger, "On the Obsolescence of the Concept of Honor," *Archives Européennes de Sociologie* 11 (1970): 339–47.
13. Karl Binding, *Der Entwurf eines Strafgesetzbuchs für den norddeutschen Bund in seinen Grundsätzen* (Leipzig: Engelmann, 1869), 9–10.
14. "Die Geschichte der Strafen ist ein fortwährendes Absterben derselben," cited in ibid.
15. Carl Josef Anton Mittermaier, "Die entehrenden Strafen," *Allgemeine deutsche Strafrechtszeitung* 1, no. 12 (1861): 177–82, 180.
16. Richard H. Tilly, *Kapital, Staat und sozialer Protest in der deutschen Industrialisierung. Gesammelte Aufsätze* (Göttingen: Vandenhoeck & Ruprecht, 1980), 154–55.
17. Wolfram Siemann, *Die Deutsche Revolution von 1848/49* (Frankfurt a.M.: Suhrkamp, 1985), 46.
18. Carl Krohne, *Die Strafanstalten und Gefängnisse in Preußen* (Berlin: Heymann, 1901), xxi; Dirk Blasius, *Geschichte der politischen Kriminalität in Deutschland, 1800–1980* (Frankfurt a.M.: Suhrkamp, 1983), 49–50.
19. Eduard Forsberg, "Gerechtigkeit für den Bestraften," 1848; *Sammlung Deutsches Historisches Museum*, Do 69/258 I.
20. Franz Wigard, *Stenographischer Bericht über die Verhandlungen der deutschen Constituirenden Nationalversammlung zu Frankfurt am Main*, vol. 7 (Frankfurt a.M.: Sauerländer, 1849), 5367.
21. *Reichsgesetz über die Wahlen der Abgeordneten zum Volkshause* (Frankfurt a.M., 1849), §3.
22. Wigard, *Verhandlungen der Deutschen Constituirenden Nationalversammlung*, vol. 7, 5370.
23. GStA PK, Rep. 84a, Nr. 8028, *Flensburger Norddeutsche Zeitung*, 1871, 128.
24. August Bebel, *Aus meinem Leben*, vol. 1 (Stuttgart: Dietz, 1910), 56.
25. For a comparison between Dutch and German codifications of dishonoring sentences, see: Timon de Groot, "Politieke Misdadigers of Eerloze Criminelen?," *Tijdschrift voor Geschiedenis* 132, no. 1 (2019): 21–47.

26. Wunder, *Geschichte der Bürokratie in Deutschland*, 38–39; Koselleck, *Preußen zwischen Reform und Revolution*, 398–404.
27. Esther Hartwich, *Der deutsche Juristentag von seiner Gründung 1860 bis zu den Reichsjustizgesetzen 1877 im Kontext von Nationsbildung und Rechtsvereinheitlichung* (Berlin: Berliner Wissenschafts-Verlag, 2008), 20–22.
28. Rudolf von Kräwel, *Entwurf nebst Gründen zu dem allgemeinen Theile eines für ganz Deutschland geltenden Straf-Gesetzbuchs unter besonderer Berücksichtigung der geltenden deutschen Straf-Gesetzbücher, sowie des baierischen und Lübeck'schen Entwurfs* (Halle: Buchh. des Waisenhauses, 1862).
29. See *Wiener Zeitung*, 28 June 1862.
30. Franz von Holtzendorff, "Strafarten," in *Deutsches Staats-Wörterbuch*, ed. Johann Caspar Bluntschli and Carl Ludwig Theodor Brater, vol. 10, 279–314 (Stuttgart, 1867), 310.
31. *Verhandlungen des dritten deutschen Juristentages* (Berlin, 1862), 406–43.
32. Thomas Nipperdey, *Deutsche Geschichte 1800–1866. Bürgerwelt und starker Staat.* (Munich: Beck, 1983), 749–70.
33. Werner Schubert, *Entstehung des Strafgesetzbuchs*, vol. 1 (Baden-Baden: Nomos Verlag, 2002), xv.
34. *Entwurf eines Strafgesetzbuches für den Norddeutschen Bund* (Berlin: Decker, 1869), 51.
35. See Kesper-Biermann, *Einheit und Recht*, 20–21.
36. Local terminology sometimes varies, but I use these translations as an analytical distinction. The meaning of the words "penitentiary" and "prison" are as historically variable as *Haft, Gefängnis,* and *Zuchthaus* were in German. See Pieter Spierenburg, *The Prison Experience. Disciplinary Institutions and Their Inmates in Early Modern Europe* (Amsterdam: Amsterdam University Press: 2007), 8–10. The Prussian Penal Code also drew a distinction in criminal acts between contraventions (Übertretungen), misdemeanors (*Vergehen*), and felonies (*Verbrechen*). In general, only felons were deprived of their civil privileges.
37. Whitman, *Harsh Justice*, 132.
38. Nutz, *Strafanstalt als Besserungsmaschine*, 60–61.
39. *Strafgesetzbuch für die Preußischen Staaten* (Berlin, 1851), §11: "Die Verurtheilung zur Zuchthausstrafe zieht den Verlust der bürgerlichen Ehre von Rechtswegen nach sich."
40. This constituted a remarkable contrast not only with the Prussian Penal Code but also with the Austrian Penal Code of 1867 as the Austrian Penal Code was widely regarded as restricting a great deal of a judge's discretionary powers in comparison with other codes. Fifty years later, during World War I, when legal scholars started arguing for a common "Central European" criminal code, these differences remained one of the biggest obstacles to legal integration between Germany and Austria-Hungary. "Die Freiheit des richterlichen Ermessens [ist] der 'Zentralnerv'," James Goldschmidt argued during World War I: James Goldschmidt, "zur mitteleuropäischen Strafrechtsvereinheitlichung," *ZStW* 38, no. 1 (1917): 417–36, 429. See Michael Kubiciel, "Einheitliches europäisches Strafrecht und vergleichende Darstellung seiner Grundlagen," *Juristenzeitung* 70, no. 2 (2015): 64–70.
41. Diethelm Klippel, Martina Henze, and Sylvia Kesper-Biermann, "Ideen und Recht. Die Umsetzung strafrechtlicher Ordnungsvorstellungen im Deutschland des 19. Jahrhunderts," in *Ideen als gesellschaftliche Gestaltungskraft im Europa der Neuzeit. Beiträge für eine erneuerte Geistesgeschichte*, ed. Lutz Raphael and Heinz-Elmar Tenorth, 372–94 (Munich: Oldenbourg, 2006).
42. *Verhandlungen des Reichstages des Norddeutschen Bundes*, vol. 10, 207.
43. Ibid., vol. 10, 208.
44. Cited in Klippel, Henze, and Kesper-Biermann, "Ideen und Recht," 385.
45. This criticism was voiced most prominently by Eduard Lasker, Friedrich Meyer, and Hugo Friedrich Fries: *Verhandlungen des Reichstages des Norddeutschen Bundes*, vol. 10, 208–10.
46. Ibid., vol. 10, 211.

47. Ibid.
48. Ibid., vol. 10, 209.
49. Frevert, *A Nation in Barracks*, 149.
50. *Stenographische Berichte über die Verhandlungen des Reichstages*, vol. 2 (Berlin 1872), 815.
51. Frevert, *A Nation in Barracks*, 158.
52. Eric A. Johnson, *Urbanization and Crime: Germany, 1871–1914* (Cambridge: Cambridge University Press, 1995); Silviana Galassi, *Kriminologie im deutschen Kaiserreich. Geschichte einer gebrochenen Verwissenschaftlichung* (Stuttgart: Steiner, 2004), 89–104; Matthew P. Fitzpatrick, *Purging the Empire: Mass Expulsions in Germany, 1871–1914* (Oxford: Oxford University Press, 2015).
53. Schauz, *Strafen als moralische Besserung*, 170–71.
54. Richard F. Wetzell, *Inventing the Criminal: A History of German Criminology, 1880–1945* (Chapel Hill: University of North Carolina Press, 2000), 34; Müller, *Verbrechensbekämpfung im Anstaltsstaat*, 126–40.
55. Monika Frommel, *Präventionsmodelle in der deutschen Strafzweck-Diskussion* (Berlin, 1987).
56. Sylvia Kesper-Biermann, "Wissenschaftlicher Ideenaustausch und 'kriminalpolitische Propaganda'. Die Internationale Kriminalistische Vereinigung (1889–1937) und der Strafvollzug," in *Verbrecher im Visier der Experten. Kriminalpolitik zwischen Wissenschaft und Praxis im 19. und frühen 20. Jahrhundert*, ed. Désirée Schauz and Sabine Freitag, 79–97 (Stuttgart, 2007), 81–82; Wetzell, *Inventing the Criminal*, 16.
57. Rudolf Medem, "Strafzumessung und Strafvollzug," *ZStW* 7 (1887): 135–74, 143.
58. Franz von Liszt, "Kriminalpolitische Aufgaben," *ZStW* 10 (1890): 51–83, 63.
59. Schmölder, "Die Wehrpflicht der Verbrecher," 984.
60. Robert Schmölder, "Die alte und die neue Kriminalistenschule und der Strafvollzug," *PJ* 115, no. 9 (1904): 489–96.
61. "In unseren großen Städten fürchten die jugendlichen Rowdies und Zuhälter nichts auf der Welt so sehr wie die eiserne Disziplin, die ihrer demnächst beim Militär harrt," Schmölder, "Die Wehrpflicht der Verbrecher," 983.
62. Richard F. Wetzell, "The Medicalization of Criminal Law Reform in Imperial Germany," in *Institutions of Confinement. Hospitals, Asylums, and Prisons in Western Europe and North America, 1500–1950*, ed. Finzsch and Jütte, 275–84 (Cambridge: Cambridge University Press, 2003); Müller, *Verbrechensbekämpfung im Anstaltsstaat*, 64–71.
63. Greg Eghigian, *Making Security Social: Disability, Insurance, and the Birth of the Social Entitlement State in Germany* (Ann Arbor: University of Michigan Press, 2000), 60.
64. Hermann Simon, *Ein Beitrag zur Kenntniss der Militärpsychosen* (Saargemünd: Völcker, 1898), 88.
65. The statistical data came from Ewald Stier, *Fahnenflucht und unerlaubte Entfernung. Eine psychologische, psychiatrische und militärrechtliche Studie*. Halle: Marhold, 1905.
66. Dietz, "Keine Wehrpflicht der Verbrecher!," 231.
67. Ibid., 228.
68. See Alexis Küppers, "Die Unfähigkeit der zu Zuchthaus Verurteilten, in das deutsche Heer und die Kaiserliche Marine einzutreten," *MKS* 8 (1912): 630–36, 633.
69. Ibid., 634.
70. Ewald Stier, "Die Wehrpflicht der Verbrecher," *MKS* 9 (1913): 272–77.
71. See BA–BL, R 3001/6037, "Gegen die Fremdenlegion," *Kölnische Zeitung*, 17 August 1913. See also a review of Erwin Rosen's book, *In der Fremdenlegion. Erinnerungen und Eindrücke* (Stuttgart, 1909) in *PJ* 142 (1910): 127, in which the reviewer emphasized the immoral character of most recruits in the French Foreign Legion.
72. "Der ungenügende Bevölkerungszuwachs in Frankreich und sein Einfluß auf die Armee," *PJ* 142 (1910): 143–49.

73. Otto Ammon, *Die Gesellschaftsordnung und ihre natürlichen Grundlagen. Entwurf einer Sozial-Anthropologie zum Gebrauch für alle Gebildeten, die sich mit sozialen Fragen befassen* (Jena: G. Fischer, 1895), 198–99.
74. Noted also in Emil Spira, "Die Wahlfälschung in Theorie und Legislation," *Zeitschrift für das Privat- und Öffentliche Recht der Gegenwart* 35 (1908): 479–588, 505–8.
75. Schmölder, "Die Wehrpflicht der Verbrecher."
76. Hellmut von Gerlach, *Die Geschichte des preussischen Wahlrechts* (Berlin: Buchverlag der "Hilfe," 1908).
77. "Harte Strafe," *Simplicissimus* 13, no. 2 (1908): 23.
78. Hedwig Richter, *Moderne Wahlen: Eine Geschichte der Demokratie in Preußen und den USA im 19. Jahrhundert* (Hamburg: Verlag des Hamburger Instituts für Sozialforschung, 2017), 463–67.
79. Ferdinand Tönnies, "Das Reichstagswahlrecht für Preussen," *Das freie Wort* 7 (1907): 492–97.
80. "Aus der Frauenbewegung," *Vorwärts*, 17 January 1907, 6.
81. Étienne Balibar, *Equaliberty*, trans. James Ingram (Durham, NC: Duke University Press, 2014), 1–32.
82. Gerhard A. Ritter, *Sozialversicherung in Deutschland und England: Entstehung und Grundzüge im Vergleich* (Munich: Beck, 1983), 28–51.
83. Eghigian, *Making Security Social*, 65–66.
84. Timothy W. Guinnane and Jochen Streb, "Moral Hazard in a Mutual Health Insurance System: German Knappschaften, 1867–1914," *Journal of Economic History* 71, no. 1 (2011): 70–104.
85. Adolf Arndt, *Bergbau und Bergbaupolitik* (Leipzig: Hirschfeld, 1894), 126–27. See Gierke, *Deutsches Privatrecht*, 430.
86. *Statut des Allgemeinen Knappschafts-Vereins zu Bochum* (1890), §15.
87. "Zur Frage wegen der Arbeiterversicherungskassen," *Die Post*, 28 October 1880, cited in *Quellensammlung zur Geschichte der deutschen Sozialpolitik: 1867 bis 1914*, vol. 1.6, ed. Karl Erich Born, Peter Rassow, and Florian Tennstedt (Stuttgart: Fischer, 2002), 430–39.
88. "Gesetz über die Abänderung des Gesetzes, betreffend die Krankenversicherung der Arbeiter, vom 15. Juni 1883," *Deutsches Reichsgesetzblatt* 20 (1892), §6a; Moritz Stelzer, "Die Beschränkung, Versagung und Aufrechnung von Leistungen der Krankenversicherung," *Volkstümliche Zeitschrift für die Gesamte Sozialversicherung*, 34.14 (July 1928).
89. *Statuten des christlichen Arbeitervereins in Essen* (1870), §29; Dieter Schuster, *Chronologie der deutschen Gewerkschaftsbewegung von den Anfängen bis 1918*, electronic edition (Bonn, 2000), 1899, available at http://library.fes.de/fulltext/bibliothek/tit00148/00148031.htm (last accessed 31 January 2022).
90. Some examples: Allgemeiner Deutscher Gärtnerverein, *Haupt-Statut des Allgemeinen Deutschen Gärtnervereins* (Berlin, 1903) §3: "Any gardener who . . . is in possession of civil rights can be accepted as a member"; Verband der in Gemeinde- und Staatsbetrieben Beschäftigten Arbeiter und Unterangestellten, *Statut des Verbandes der in Gemeinde- u. Staatsbetrieben Beschäftigten Arbeiter und Unterangestellten* (Berlin, 1903), §3: "Expulsion from the association takes place . . . if a member is guilty of dishonorable actions"; Deutscher Techniker-Verband, *Erneuerte Satzungen des Deutschen Techniker-Verbandes* (Berlin, 1894), §4: "Every German technician who is in good standing can . . . be accepted as an individual member"; *Statut des Verbandes der Lithographen, Steindrucker und Verwandten Berufe* (Berlin, 1907), §4.
91. "Anlage zum Schreiben des Staatssekretärs des Reichsamtes des Innern an den preußischen Handelsminister," 10 November 1907, *Quellensammlung zur Geschichte der deutschen Sozialpolitik*, vol. 3.1 (Stuttgart: Fischer, 1994), 162–63.
92. *Die Reichsgewerbeordnung in ihrer neuesten Gestalt nebst Ausführungsvorschriften* (Berlin, 1892).
93. See the Introduction.

94. Carl Josef Anton Mittermaier, "Strafarten," in *Staats-Lexikon*, ed. Carl von Rotteck and Carl Welcker, vol. 15, 184–215 (1843), 209.
95. Karl Krohne, *Lehrbuch der Gefängniskunde unter Berücksichtigung der Kriminalstatistik und Kriminalpolitik* (Stuttgart: Enke, 1889), 223–29.
96. Christina Schenk, *Bestrebungen zur einheitlichen Regelung des Strafvollzugs in Deutschland von 1870 bis 1923. Mit einem Ausblick auf die Strafvollzugsgesetzentwürfe von 1927* (Frankfurt a.M.: Lang, 2001). See also Martina Henze, *Strafvollzugsreformen im 19. Jahrhundert. Gefängniskundlicher Diskurs und staatliche Praxis in Bayern und Hessen-Darmstadt* (Darmstadt: Selbstverlag der Hessischen Historischen Kommission, 2003).
97. Karl Krohne, "Der gegenwärtige Stand der Gefängniswissenschaft," *ZStW* 1 (1881): 53–92, 71. See Berthold Freudenthal, *Die staatsrechtliche Stellung des Gefangenen* (Jena: G. Fischer, 1910), 20.
98. Franz von Liszt, "Preussen, Königreich Sachsen und die übrigen Norddeutschen Staaten," in *Handbuch des Gefängnißwesens*, ed. Franz von Holtzendorff, 161–84 (Hamburg: Richter, 1888), 165.
99. See, for instance, Adolf Schrenk, *Die bedingte Verurteilung* (Erlangen: Jacob, 1892), 4; Otto Mittelstädt, "Die Reform des deutschen Gefängniswesens," *PJ* 40 (1877): 425–35 and 487–99, at 490.
100. F. Szuhany, "In welcher Weise sollen die Strafgefangenen angeredet werde," *BfG* 2 (1867): 264–69. See Richard Braune, "Die Freiheitsstrafen einst und jetzt," *ZStW* 42, no. 1 (1922): 14–32, 17–18; Krohne, *Lehrbuch*, 226–27.
101. Adolf Streng, *Studien über Entwicklung, Ergebnisse und Gestaltung des Vollzugs der Freiheitsstraf in Deutschland* (Stuttgart: Enke, 1886), 141.
102. "Die Grundsätze welche bei dem Vollzuge gerichtlich erkannter Freiheitsstrafen bis zu weiterer gemeinsamer Regelung zur Anwendung kommen," *Central-Blatt für das Deutsche Reich* 25 (1897): 308–13, §17.
103. "Die zur Gefängnißstrafe Verurtheilten können in einer Gefangenanstalt auf eine ihren Fähigkeiten und Verhältnissen angemessene Weise beschäftigt werden; auf ihr Verlangen sind sie in dieser Weise zu beschäftigen," RStGB §16.
104. Report from prison warden Michaelis (Aachen) at the general assembly of prison governors in Darmstadt 1898, in *BfG* 32 (1898): 116–23, 119.
105. See Verfügung 13.02.1897, *Zeitschrift des Rheinpreussischen Amtsrichter-Vereins* (1898).
106. Hermann Kriegsmann, *Einführung in die Gefängniskunde* (Heidelberg: Winter, 1912), 206.
107. Franz von Liszt, *Die Gefängnisarbeit* (Berlin: Guttentag, 1900), 6.
108. Cited in Leonore Seutter, *Die Gefängnisarbeit in Deutschland mit besonderer Berücksichtigung der Frauen-Gefängnisse* (Tübingen: Laupp, 1912), 26.
109. For example, the Christlich-Soziale Partei (conservative), the Deutsche Volkspartei (progressive liberal), and the Nationalliberale Partei (conservative liberal) all explicitly mentioned the strong reduction of competition by prison labor as part of their political programs in 1909. See Karl Mahler, *Die Programme der politischen Parteien in Deutschland* (Leipzig: Gracklauer, 1909).
110. For instance, in Max Treu, *Der Bankrott des modernen Strafvollzuges und seine Reform* (Stuttgart: R. Lutz, 1904), 11. Prisoners who were engaged for multiple years in a row in these "feminine" forms of occupation could only display feminine and childish behavior, Treu argued: "Just observe these prisoners, how vain they have become, how they comb their hair and use every windowpane as a mirror, tie their scarf and shirt-collar—indeed, how they even often play the part of the woman when engaging in sexual excesses!"
111. Liszt, *Gefängnisarbeit*.
112. LAV NRW R, BR 0005, no. 24172.
113. GStA PK, I. HA. Rep. 84a, *Nordeutsche Algemeine Zeitung*, 6 November 1889.

114. Liszt, "Kriminalpolitische Aufgaben III," 60–61.
115. Karl von Birkmeyer and Oscar Netter, eds., *Vergleichende Darstellung des deutschen und ausländischen Strafrechts. Vorarbeiten zur deutschen Strafrechtsreform*, 9 vols. (Berlin: Liebmann, 1905–9).
116. BA–BL, R 3001/6035, Karl Birkmeyer "Strafrechtsreform," *Münchner Neuesten Nachrichten*, 9 November 1909.
117. See the collection of newspaper articles in BA–BL, R 3001/6027 and BA–BL, R 3001/6035.
118. This is most prominently defended in BA–BL, R. 3001/6035, "Die Prügelstrafe," *Hamburger Nachrichten*, 7 December 1909. Some legal scholars also defended the idea in academic journals. For instance, see Langer, "Gedanken über neue Strafarten," *DJZ* 11 (1906): 456–60.
119. Report from prison governor Böhmer (Zwickau) in *BfG* 27 (1893): 175–91, 187.
120. See "Der Strafvollzug im neuen Gesetzentwurf," *Neue Preußische Zeitung*, 12 November 1909.
121. *Vorentwurf zu einem Deutschen Strafgesetzbuch*, vol. 2 (Berlin: Guttentag, 1909), 82ff.
122. Wilhelm Kahl et al., *Gegenentwurf zum Vorentwurf eines deutschen Strafgesetzbuchs* (Berlin: Guttentag, 1911).
123. Liszt, *Der Zweckgedanke im Strafrecht*, 24.
124. Foucault, *Surveiller et punir*, 119.
125. See Eduard Burlage, *Die Entschädigung der unschuldig Verhafteten und der unschuldig Bestraften* (Berlin: O. Liebmann, 1905).
126. This effect of the law was discussed but rejected by the state prosecutor Oskar Hamm in his "Der Entwurf eines Gesetzes betreffend die Entschädigung für unschuldig erlittene Untersuchungshaft," *DJZ* 9, no. 4 (1904): 177–85.
127. *Stenographische Berichte über die Verhandlungen des Reichstages*, vol. 206 (Berlin: J. Guttentag, 1904), 858–59.
128. *Stenographische Berichte über die Verhandlungen des Reichstages*, vol. 200 (Berlin: J. Guttentag, 1904), 2889–91. See *Protokoll der Verhandlungen des Parteitages der Sozialdemokratischen Partei Deutschlands abgehalten zu Bremen vom 18. bis 24. September* (Berlin: J. Guttentag, 1904), 95–96.
129. Karl Frohme had already placed a petition for this in the Reichstag in 1882: Burlage, *Die Entschädigung*, 1. For more on the excessive use of pre-trial detention by the German police in that period, see Wilhelm, *Das deutsche Kaiserreich*, 454ff.
130. See Max Treu, "Vorbestraft," *Der Türmer* 6, no. 9 (1904): 290–97; J. A. Amrhein, *Strafprozess-Reform* (Zürich, 1908).
131. Klaus Tiedemann, *Konkurs-Strafrecht* (Berlin: De Gruyter, 1985), 16.
132. *Stenographische Berichte über die Verhandlungen des Reichstages*, vol. 176 (Berlin: J. Guttentag, 1900), 3354.
133. Julius Guttmann, "Geht ein Abgeordneter durch Eröffnung des Konkursverfahrens über sein Vermögen seines Mandats verlustig?" *DJZ* 5 (1900): 40–42; Guido Leser, *Untersuchungen über das Wahlprüfungsrecht des Deutschen Reichstags* (Leipzig: Duncker & Humblot, 1908), 15.
134. E. Braun, "Die Zurückziehung von Titeln, Orden und Ehrenzeichen nach dem Verwaltungsrecht Preussens," *Archiv für öffentliches Recht* 16 (1901): 528–74, 564.
135. Rudolf Krafft, *Glänzendes Elend* (Stuttgart: Lutz, 1895). See Nicholas Stargardt, *The German Idea of Militarism: Radical and Socialist Critics, 1866–1914* (Cambridge: Cambridge University Press, 1994), 40.
136. Richard Gädke, "Offiziersehre und Militärehrengerichte," *Berliner Tageblatt*, 31 January 1905.
137. Fritz Hoenig, *Mein Ehrenhandel mit dem Oberst und Flügeladjutant v. Schwartzkoppen und dem Oberst und Abteilungschef im Generalstabe von Bernhardi* (Berlin: H. Walther, 1902), 13–15.
138. "Offiziersehre und Militärehrengerichte," *Berliner Tageblatt*, 31 January 1905.
139. "Ein Ritter der Standesehre," *Berliner Tageblatt*, 5 November 1905.

140. Michael Stolleis, *Geschichte des öffentlichen Rechts in Deutschland*, vol. 2, *Staatsrechtslehre und Verwaltungswissenschaft: 1800–1914* (Munich: Beck, 1992), 343.
141. Paul Laband, "Das Recht am Titel," *Deutsche Juristenzeitung* 12, no. 4 (1907): 200–7, 203.
142. "Professor Laband über Entziehung von Titeln," *Berliner Tageblatt*, 17 February 1907.
143. The Prussian constitution of 1851 had already stipulated that "Strafen können nur in Gemäßheit des Gesetzes angedroht oder verhängt werden." On the development of the rule of law in the German Empire, see Kenneth F. Ledford, "Formalizing the Rule of Law in Prussia: The Supreme Administrative Law Court, 1876–1914," *Central European History* 37, no. 2 (2004): 203–24.
144. Karl Binding, *Die Ehre und ihre Verletzbarkeit* (Leipzig: Duncker & Humblot, 1892), 9.
145. Friedrich Paulsen, *System der Ethik mit einem Umriss der Staats- und Gesellschaftslehre*, vol. 2 (Berlin: Hertz, 1900), 88–89.

Chapter 3

POLITICAL OFFENDERS VS. COMMON CRIMINALS
Challenging the Distinction

In their daily practice of trying and sentencing offenders, state prosecutors and judges in the German Empire could draw on precedents compiled in manuals made for precisely that purpose. And, of course, the books contained sample verdicts that entailed the punishment of disenfranchisement. A case tried in Kassel in 1899 is representative of the kind of cases described in the books. A trial by jury, the case involved Johann Groß, a plumber from Wabern, and Wilhelm Schmidt, an engraver from Bebra. The jury found both men guilty of counterfeiting, and the judge sentenced Groß and Schmidt to five and three years in the penitentiary, respectively. He also sentenced both men to deprivation of their civil privileges for five years and ordered them to pay all the legal costs. The manual instructed that it was important to give reasons for such a verdict and to explain, for example, why one received a harsher sentence than the other. The reason in this case was that Groß had orchestrated the criminal scheme. Judges also had to justify the convicts' disenfranchisement. In accordance with §32 of the Reich Penal Code, they did so by explicitly mentioning that the culprit showed a "dishonorable disposition" in his actions.[1] As argued in previous chapters, "the dishonorable disposition" was the crucial concept justifying the existence of the punishment of disenfranchisement. By pronouncing the judgment, the judge transformed the accused into a dishonorable felon.

Disenfranchisement was thus not only a tool for excluding criminals from participation in society; disenfranchising someone was a performative act of transforming a citizen into a dishonored felon. Arguably, however, counterfeiting was one of the least controversial crimes associated with a "dishonorable disposition," which is presumably why this case was chosen for the instruction manual. Furthermore, it was not necessary for the judge to elaborate further on

---

Notes from this chapter begin on page 117.

the verdict, which demonstrated the dishonorable disposition of the accused by definition. In the German Empire, however, there were many criminal cases that were much more controversial than this one and the application of the notion of the "dishonorable disposition" was contested in such cases. Frequently, these were cases in which political ideology played a major role. Controversy often erupted when a court ruling turned a politician into a disgraced criminal.

The punishment of disenfranchisement had an "apolitical" claim, meaning that it was only supposed to be imposed only if the act reflected the offender's "dishonorable disposition." It was not supposed to be used to silence political opponents out of partisan interest—something the German political scientist Otto Kirchheimer later defined as "political justice."[2] Precisely because this punishment was allegedly apolitical, however, it sparked a great deal of controversy whenever seemingly "political offenders" were sentenced with disenfranchisement for having a "dishonorable disposition." In criminal procedures of the German Empire, the concept of a "dishonorable disposition" thus crucially helped to draw the line between "political offenses" and morally condemnable, criminal behavior.

The function of disenfranchisement—to demarcate the line between political offenses and condemnable criminal conduct—is central to this chapter. As anthropologists Jean and John Comaroff expounded, "sovereign power" resides "in the capacity to authorize and enforce" the distinction between political and non-political crime.[3] This chapter therefore outlines the extent of sovereign power in the German Empire by looking at instances in which the authorities tried to redefine certain "political" offenses as "common criminal activity." The chapter also scrutinizes the instances in which a mutually accepted consensus on the distinction between "common criminals" and "political offenders" limited the state's options for punishing political opponents. Whereas a consensus about "mutually accepted rules of the game" regarding how to treat political prisoners "enabled other societies to contain their political quarrels," historian Alex Hall argues, the German Empire lacked such a consensus, resulting in frequently harsh sentences against them, particularly if they advocated socialist ideas.[4] Nevertheless, this chapter seeks to show that there was, in fact, a consensus in the German Empire about criminal law and its relation to political offenders, with disenfranchisement being a central component to this consensus.

But it is crucial to distinguish between two levels here. The first level is the debate about the very idea that political offenders should be entitled to privileged treatment. The second level concerns the question of which offenses should be considered political. I argue that there was a delicate consensus on the first level, whereas the second level was more problematic. It is, therefore, important not to take the concept of political crime at face value. Thus, the chapter seeks to analyze how judges and public prosecutors defined "political crimes" in their actual sentencing practices, as well as seeking to determine the grounds they used to grant some defendants consideration as political offenders while denying it to others.

The 1890s was a crucial period: the Anti-Socialist Laws had recently been repealed and the authorities repeatedly attempted to include political activists in the category of "serious criminals." These attempts sparked tremendous outcry as they ran counter to the consensus that political offenders should be entitled to privileged treatment. This consensus that political offenders should be punished "mildly," therefore, was an indispensable condition of many commentators' criticisms of the policy of the 1890s, which, in turn, helped to lend these disputes their controversial air.[5] This chapter does not aim to dismiss the sometimes severe criticisms of Imperial Germany's legal system, including allegations of "class justice" and an often-proclaimed "crisis of trust" in the judiciary. But it does aim to show that criticism did not mean there was no consensus.

A "Perjury Plague"?

It is clear from the crime statistics of the German Empire that disenfranchisement was not usually imposed for offenses normally classified as political ones. In fact, disenfranchised felons were sentenced for a variety of offenses: from perjury to statutory rape, and from embezzlement to manslaughter.[6] Convictions for nearly all offenses could prompt disenfranchisement if the judge decided that the criminals had committed their crimes due to their "dishonorable dispositions." This was a major consequence of the judicial discretion introduced with the Reich Penal Code. However, the legal and historical literature on criminal law in the German Empire presents a broad consensus that disenfranchisement was only to be imposed in cases of perjury.[7] Yet, in reality, only 2 to 5 percent of all people sentenced with disenfranchisement were convicted of perjury. Of course, this did not change the broad perception of perjury as a dishonorable crime; 60 to 80 percent of people found guilty of perjury annually were deprived of their civil privileges, which meant that they were generally perceived to have acted out of a dishonorable disposition.

According to the crime statistics, the largest percentage of disenfranchised felons were those sentenced for theft (most of them either recidivist thieves or those convicted of "grand theft").[8] As seen in figure 3.1, theft constantly dominated statistics of felony disenfranchisement from 1882 to 1914. The numbers also show interesting changes, including, for instance, that disenfranchisement was increasingly imposed on people sentenced for sexual assault (especially against minors). This was a direct result of the implementation of the so-called *Lex Heinze* in 1892/1900, which defined sex offenses and other crimes against public morality more rigorously and instituted harsher penalties for these crimes, particularly soliciting sex from a prostitute. More generally, this can be interpreted as arising from criminal experts' shifting their focus away from "malicious" individuals and toward "perverted" people, as well as a growing awareness that society

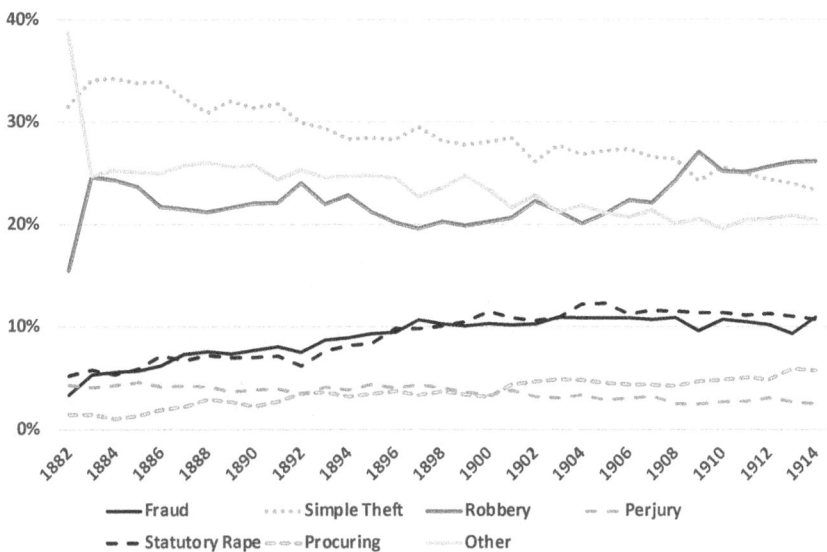

Figure 3.1. Sentences of disenfranchisement divided by criminal offense, 1882–1914. Source: *Statistik des deutschen Reichs, 1882–1914.* © Timon de Groot.

had a duty to protect children from sexual abuse.[9] In other words, the public increasingly condemned these immoral crimes, and the legislature supported this shifting perspective.

For perjury, however, the number of convictions does not necessarily reflect citizens' judgment of its seriousness. In fact, perjury was an emotionally laden subject in the German Empire.[10] Traditionally, the oath one took (and still takes) before testifying was meant to protect the judicial system against double-crossing and dishonorable behavior, and while jurists were supposed to trust that it deterred people from lying, in practice it often did not work. People still committed perjury, a fact that contemporaries generally ascribed to diminishing respect for the sanctity of the oath and the honor of the court. This implied a decline in people's moral credibility, which was frequently attributed to the diminished piety of German society.[11] Perjury remained the paradigmatic offense against public trust, so criminal experts saw it as clearly reflecting a dishonorable disposition, and, almost by definition, regarded the perjurer as a malicious individual intentionally trying to con the system. Consequently, they strongly correlated the number of perjury convictions with the "honor" and moral character of the German citizenry.

Nevertheless, the total number of people convicted of perjury during the German Empire actually declined, with only a little more than a thousand such convictions occurring in 1882. The rate steadily dropped to between five hundred and six hundred between 1905 and 1913. These statistics potentially support the

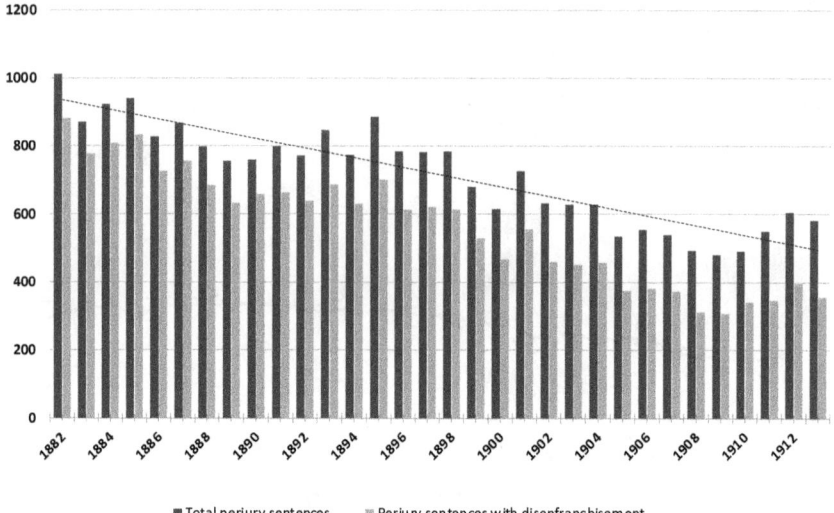

Figure 3.2. Annual number of perjury sentences, 1882–1914. Source: *Statistik des deutschen Reichs, 1882–1914*. © Timon de Groot.

view that the German authorities lost interest in perjury. Paradoxically, though, many people, including Ulm judge Gustav Pfizer writing in the *Grenzboten* in 1886, felt that a "perjury plague" was threatening the empire's judicial system, even though there were fewer convictions.[12]

However, the statistical evidence was somewhat controversial. Although "dark numbers" were not part of German criminal experts' crime statistics (until 1908, when Japanese/German mathematician Shigema Oba used the German equivalent *Dunkelziffer* in his book, which influential statisticians like Georg von Mayr then picked up), they had long been aware that statistical knowledge of crime had its limitations.[13] Indeed, this awareness underlay a great deal of anxiety about criminals passing as normal citizens and perjurers double-crossing the judicial system.

The intellectual father of so-called *Moralstatistik* in Germany, Alexander von Öttingen, had already pointed out these limitations in crime statistics in an article he published in the first volume of the *Zeitschrift für die gesamte Strafrechtswissenschaft* in 1881. Öttingen argued that one should not focus too much on the number of actual criminal convictions if one wanted to make claims about the nation's "public morality" (*öffentliche Moral*). Instead, he believed that assessment of a nation's moral development had to include the "great number of illegal acts that are not prosecuted, that take up the energies of the entire people but are never dealt with in court."[14] Similarly, Otto Mittelstädt (commenting on Wilhelm Starke's book *Verbrechen und Verbrecher in Preußen 1854–1878*) pointed out that only a small portion of the "mass of criminal substance" was prosecuted and urged criminal experts to be cautious when interpreting crime statistics: "The statisticians, who despite this fact continue to work with these inconclusive, arbitrary numbers, cannot be warned enough to use caution."[15]

Experts also exhorted caution in relation to the official numbers. Alfred Kloss, an influential state prosecutor from Halle who authored an official textbook for his profession, found the official crime statistics for perjury unconvincing; he presented his own alternative findings based on his experiences at the criminal court in Halle in a 1904 lecture for the Saxon Prison Society. He believed that, in a year, he had witnessed six cases of false testimony in which the perjurer had been acquitted or not prosecuted. Based on the number of oaths annually sworn in German criminal courts, he concluded that the real number of perjurious acts that year was about 11,321—almost twenty times the number of convictions for such acts.[16] In other words, even though conviction rates were dropping rapidly, the panic about perjury hardly subsided. Paradoxically, the publication of the numbers actually heightened anxiety about perjury as people became more aware of the large number of cases that went unpunished. Some even argued that the more oaths people swore, the more people committed perjury.[17]

The Public's "Excitability about Crime"

Crime statistics were both a sign and a signifier in the public debate on the magnitude and seriousness of crime in German society. Perjury statistics played an important role in this debate because they could easily be manipulated to discredit an entire group for its lack of moral credibility. Given the perceived religious nature of the judicial oath, it could, for instance, be used to discredit Christians of other denominations. Indeed, some people claimed that crime statistics proved Catholics' greater tendency to commit perjury, an allegation often made in the context of the *Kulturkampf*.[18] Antisemitic sentiments also crept into this discussion.[19] Jewish citizens were overrepresented in perjury statistics, which antisemites exploited to argue that Jews were less trustworthy than others on racial grounds. The influential author and active member in the *Wandervogel* movement, Heinrich Sohnrey, for instance, used these statistics to turn the perjury discussion into an entirely Jewish problem.[20] Most commentators, however, provided different explanations for these statistics, pointing out that Jewish people usually practiced professions in which perjury and fraud were more commonly encountered.[21] The Jewish organization Verein zur Abwehr des Antisemitismus shared this view.[22]

In general, there was no indication in the crime statistics that one ethnic or religious group was disenfranchised significantly more than others. An overview by the statistical bureau of Prussia of criminality among different confessions in

1911, for instance, indicated an overrepresentation of Jews within certain typical "dishonorable" crimes, such as fraud and forgery, but a significant underrepresentation in crimes such as theft and robbery.[23] In fact, statistician Rudolf Wassermann argued that one would expect an even higher rate of crimes (what he called *soll-Kriminalität*) with a profit-seeking motive among Jewish Germans than the current numbers (*ist-Kriminalität*) showed, given the fact that Jews were more represented in professions where these crimes were more common.[24]

These discussions surrounding perjury and perjury convictions show that the official publication of crime statistics reinforced anxiety about "unknown" aspects of crime and punishment, and vice versa. The more statistics generated knowledge about crime and prosecution, and the more this knowledge was published and distributed via the national media, the more anxiety people had about offenses going unpunished.[25] This cycle created a demand for more knowledge about "actual" crime and was, in the words of the influential law professor Herman Seuffert, a result of the German public's "excitability about crime." In his view, one testament to this growing nervousness was the rise in denunciations.[26] In short, crime statistics did little to calm the panic around crime and criminals passing as "normal" citizens. Instead, they often fueled these anxieties in unforeseen ways.

Consequently, when, according to the Reich crime statistics, the total number of people sentenced with disenfranchisement dropped after the founding of the German Empire, this prompted an anonymous public prosecutor from southern Germany to express his dismay about the empire's "mild" penal policy. Calling for "more honor punishments!," he complained in a letter to the *Deutsche Tageszeitung* in July 1914 (shortly before the outbreak of World War I) that this punishment had grown less significant after the Reich Penal Code was introduced.[27] Indeed, there had been a steady decline in the imposition of disenfranchisement in Germany since 1882.[28] In 1882, the civil privileges of 20,507 individuals were suspended, mostly for robbery convictions.[29] In 1900, the number was 14,029, and it reached a low point in 1907, when 11,506 individuals lost their civil privileges. The number increased slightly after 1907 (12,552 in 1911), but it never reached the same level as in 1882.[30]

However, in this case, too, one must be suspicious of the conclusion, based on a decline in convictions, that "honor punishment" had lost its significance. Despite the drop, the rate of people sentenced with disenfranchisement stood at 8.5 percent in 1882 and remained around or above 5 percent in the decades thereafter (except during World War I).[31] In fact, throughout the empire's existence, disenfranchisement was imposed more frequently than the penitentiary. Therefore, when compared to the total number of penitentiary sentences, it is evident that disenfranchisement certainly had a prominent place in the penal system of the German Empire.

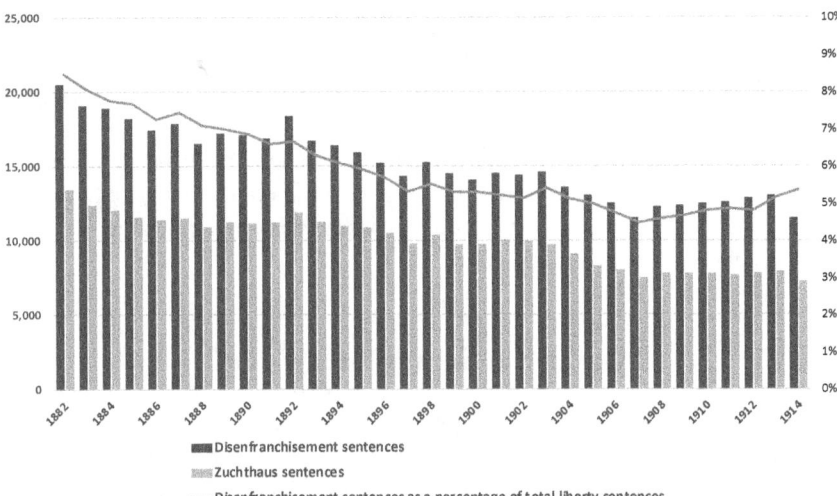

Figure 3.3. Annual number of disenfranchisement sentences compared to penitentiary (*Zuchthaus*) sentences, 1882–1914. Source: *Statistik des deutschen Reichs, 1882–1914*. © Timon de Groot.

This is peculiar since disenfranchisement and the penitentiary had long gone hand in hand. In the Prussian Penal Code, disenfranchisement was still codified as an automatic consequence of a penitentiary sentence (see chapter 2). The permanent suspension of civil privileges after a penitentiary sentence bolstered the dishonorable nature of the latter. The Reich Penal Code, by contrast, stipulated that the decision to deprive an offender of his civil privileges should be left to the judge's discretion. Thus, this penal code officially disconnected the two punishments. The statistics suggest that judges frequently exercised their discretionary powers because they often supplemented regular prison sentences with dishonoring punishments. From this perspective, the anonymous public prosecutor seems to have been misguided in concluding that fewer disenfranchisement sentences in the crime statistics meant that the punishment was falling into disuse.

The anonymous public prosecutor, however, had a much larger concern. Beyond the drop in disenfranchisement, he was worried that certain types of offenders—especially procurers, sex offenders, and, most notably, political offenders—were all too frequently coming off unscathed. He felt that this was a clear sign of the German penal system's "mild" treatment of such offenders compared to how they had been treated in the past. Yet the data did not really support this claim since the rate of procurers and sex offenders being sentenced increased. Even though the prosecutor was mistaken about certain facts, though, the article confirms that people generally ascribed a moral function to the punishment of disenfranchisement: it should be used to punish those convicted of the most morally condemnable of crimes. This article was also remarkable in that the anonymous prosecutor broke with a long-standing consensus about the use of disenfranchisement by singling out political offenders for harsher punishment—a position that was only very gradually beginning to take hold. In fact, most legal scholars at that time conceived of disenfranchisement as "apolitical" by its very nature: it was not to be used against political offenders but only against those considered dangerous to the public whose actions had indicated that they were somehow lacking in morality.

"Opinion as Such Is Not a Crime"

As mentioned, the crucial notion in disenfranchisement was that offenders so sentenced presumably had a "dishonorable disposition." But the legal literature hardly ever explained exactly what this was. As a result, the only point of universal consensus was that political offenses should not suggest that the offenders had such a "dishonorable disposition." That is, a "dishonorable disposition" was considered a politically neutral category; political crimes—despite being illegal actions—were, thus, typical "non-dishonoring" offenses.

A famous trial often mentioned in this context was that of lèse-majesté against Johann Jacoby in 1842. After he had published his critical treatise *Four Questions Answered by an East Prussian*, he was found guilty and sentenced to two years of fortress confinement—not penitentiary confinement—and his privileges remained intact. The presiding judge defended his decision to sentence him to fortress confinement with the following remarks:

> Questions of politics, principles of the general welfare, debates on the utility or reprehensibility of state institutions and constitutions . . . cannot be made into an object of juridical decision. Such discussions belong to a domain from which the judiciary is excluded and thus from which it must maintain its distance. . . . Opinion as such is not a crime.[32]

At the time, the sentence was controversial; in fact, it led Friedrich Wilhelm IV to be stricter with criminal judges.[33] But in the subsequent decades, legal experts commenting on political trials frequently cited it to argue that political offenders, particularly people convicted of high treason, were supposed to be treated in a more privileged manner than other offenders were.[34]

Legal scholars' general attitude toward political offenders was not just based on the case against Jacoby but was, in fact, derived from Immanuel Kant's philosophy of the nature of positive law and a distinction drawn between it and morality. Prussian legal philosopher and politician Julius Kirchmann prominently drew upon this distinction:

The distinction between the two is clear to all. Legal duties have a compulsory character, while such a compulsion cannot be brought to bear on moral duties, not even when it concerns the most important and holy of things. Another distinction is that the law does not consider one's conscience or one's inner motive to act. It only sees the external action, whereas morality also encompasses the motive.[35]

Such arguments implied that political offenders had to be punished for transgressing the norms dictated by positive law, but that the state had to refrain from making moral judgments about such offenders' general disposition. In this sense, the state basically claimed it would not pass judgment on the political ideas that motivated a transgression of the law. The opposite of this idea was called *Gesinnungsstrafrecht*—sentencing people for having a certain conviction—a type of law that was heavily contested, mostly by liberal legal scholars.[36]

An important consequence of this distinction between positive law and morality was that it allowed scholars to view disenfranchisement as a punishment that clearly expressed a strong moral judgment about the motivation of the offender beyond the sphere of legality.[37] The legal scholar Richard John expressed this view pointedly in 1869. Punishing an offender with disenfranchisement, he argued, entailed "a judgment against his honorability, his morality."[38] In other words, depriving offenders of their civil privileges suggested that they had served their time but had not yet "morally" atoned for their crimes. The punishment thus formed a vital part of the moral economy of the German Empire, making those regarded as morally reprehensible pay more to atone for their crimes than political offenders did.[39]

Fritz von Calker, a law professor at the University of Strasbourg, championed this idea of treating "malicious," morally reprehensible criminals more harshly.[40] A consequence of this view was that it gave more weight to the character of the offender than it did to the nature of the criminal act. For this reason, Calker fiercely opposed the Reich Penal Code's statutes, claiming that certain offenses testified to a dishonorable disposition by definition (perjury being the prime example).[41] He argued that disposition should be judged on a case-by-case basis as judges should individually assess the moral convictions behind each offender's actions.

The difficulty for many scholars was that several other conclusions could be drawn from such a distinction between positive law and morality. Some scholars, for instance, started arguing that the philosophical distinction between law and morality actually meant that the state only had the legitimate power to punish transgressions of the law and was not entitled to make judgments about the moral character of serious felons, as this would constitute another form of *Gesinnungsstrafrecht*. Calker, on the other hand, did not think that focusing on offenders' character contradicted the principle of punishing only actions. Instead, he viewed it as a more thorough way of determining culpability.[42]

This idea of a deeper understanding of culpability came up in the context of the *Schulenstreit* between the "classic" and "modern" schools of law.[43] With his emphasis on the question of culpability, Calker presented himself as an adherent of the "classic" school. In Liszt's modern school, however, safeguarding society from potentially dangerous individuals was a key point on the agenda. This prompted modern school adherents to place more emphasis on assessing individuals' character, but they also advocated that the moral distinction between "honorable" and "dishonorable" dispositions should be abolished.

This idea only gradually took hold in Liszt's own writings. In his 1889 and 1890 essays on the tasks of criminal policy, he wrote that the distinction between dishonoring and regular punishments was crucial to the German system of criminal justice.[44] Six years later, however, he argued to the contrary that judges should be careful about passing judgments on an offender's morality or the degree to which a crime should be viewed as morally reprehensible.

By this time, he considered it wrong to replace a purely legal judgment with both moral and "aesthetic" ones, arguing that it was a mistake to use the supposedly honorable or dishonorable disposition of the offender in determining the severity of a punishment: "The times in which honor and right were closely related concepts are long gone."[45] One of Liszt's suggestions was to replace the notion of the "dishonorable" disposition with an "anti-social" disposition, because he believed that "anti-social" did not imply a judgment about a person's intrinsic moral character but only conveyed a judgment about the risks that person posed to society.

Proponents of the "classic" view frequently accused the modern school of propagating a form of *Gesinnungsstrafrecht* by focusing on an offender's character and the protection of society.[46] They worried, for instance, that the "modern" position led to people being punished without having actually committed a crime. In the end, however, both arguments placed weight on the character of the offender. Yet, it was mostly "classic" school adherents who combined this with the idea that certain crimes testified to a morally reprehensible disposition, which they used, in turn, to justify harsher punishments.[47] For the same reason, those of the classic school were more supportive of existing regulations in the Reich Penal Code, while the moderns pushed more for its reform. Erik Wolf, a twentieth-century philosopher of law, depicted the difference between the two schools as the difference between Berlin—the seat of legislative power—and Leipzig—where the imperial court of justice resided. Liszt was a professor at the University of Berlin and Binding was a professor in Leipzig. According to Wolf, the conflict was between the joy of persistence (*beharrungsfreude*) that characterized the power of jurisdiction (Leipzig) and the pleasure in progress (*fortschrittslust*) that characterized the power of legislation (Berlin).[48]

Academic Literature on High Treason

The distinction between positive law and morality was arguably the dominant mode of justifying harsher punishments for "serious" criminals and lighter punishments for political offenders, but this proved to be much more difficult in practice than in theory. It was not always easy for jurists to determine where the line between a political and a dishonorable crime should be drawn. The regulations in the Reich Penal Code did not help much in answering this question since the code stated that the special category of offenses listed as high treason (*Hochverrath*) could be punished in various ways. Only one act of high treason—assassination of the head of state—prescribed a single possible sentence: the death penalty.[49] For all other forms of high treason, the law stipulated that offenders were either to be punished with a stay in the penitentiary, or, if there were special circumstances, in fortress confinement. The penal code did not provide for the possibility of depriving these offenders of their civil privileges. Given this fact, one might argue that high treason was not dishonoring by definition.[50]

However, this was problematized by the definition the code provided for extenuating circumstances, with §20 being most crucial in this matter: "where the law offers the choice between the penitentiary and open custody, the penitentiary may only be chosen when it is clear that the punishable act arose out of a dishonorable disposition."[51] This article exacerbated the dishonoring nature of the penitentiary sentence. In chapter 2, I discussed the problematic definition of the penitentiary sentence and its relation to the notion of honor; it was problematic because the penitentiary sentence made ex-offenders ineligible to hold public office or to join the army or marines. In reality, the penitentiary sentence still had an element of disenfranchisement to it. But this article made it even more problematic. During debate on the law in the Reichstag, many members argued that fortress confinement should be the standard punishment for political offenders, implying that political offenders generally acted out of an honorable disposition and that they should thus only be sentenced to the penitentiary in exceptional cases.[52] Yet, despite the reflections on this notion in academic literature, lawyers had few formal legal prescriptions for deciding what was "dishonorable."[53]

In a 1921 book devoted to the topic of the "dishonorable disposition," law student Eduard Guckenheimer, who was trained in Liszt's "modern" school and supervised by Liszt's protégé Moritz Liepmann, addressed the lack of a satisfactory definition of a dishonorable disposition. Neither the law nor jurisprudence had provided one. He also pointed out that members of the Reichstag, while discussing the Reich Penal Code, had in fact actively supported leaving the notion undefined. Influential Reichstag member Eduard Lasker, for instance, justified this by arguing that judges were not supposed to base their decisions on some kind of template but should proceed on a case-by-case basis, trusting their intuition about what motivated the act.[54]

The only consensus about the definition of dishonorable disposition found in the legal literature was that the notion of honor was explicitly to be understood not as a form of estate honor but as a truly ethical notion.[55] Given the charged nature of these decisions, trial by jury was often prescribed for offenses that could lead to these harsh punishments. In such cases, a group of the defendant's peers could assess his motives and character and secure a fair sentence.[56] But these jurors, too, essentially had to trust their moral instincts in making such decisions. This meant that it was truly up to judges and juries to determine which crimes suggested a dishonorable disposition. In some cases, this meant that they had the power to really determine the distinction between "politics" and "crime."

"Insidious Attacks" and "Catchphrases about Class Struggle"

The question of how the system should handle political crimes became especially relevant in the political struggle during the first two decades of the German Empire. Amid a protracted economic recession that began in 1873, when authorities grew more concerned about the expansion of Social Democracy, Chancellor Bismarck launched a campaign to severely suppress the actions of its adherents. This suppression manifested itself in several important measures: the creation of the "political police" in 1873 and, after two failed assassination attempts on Chancellor Bismarck, the introduction of the Anti-Socialist Laws of 1878. The Anti-Socialist Laws remained in force for twelve years, an era of intense political persecution and the state's struggle against Social Democrats. During this time, the concept of what constituted a "political crime" was also seriously questioned. Importantly, though, despite the strict policies of oppression targeted at Social Democracy, the Anti-Socialist Laws by and large continued the policy of "mildly" punishing political offenders: the possibility of disenfranchisement was not included in these measures. Only after the Anti-Socialist Laws were repealed in 1890 did the German authorities try more actively to get Social Democrats convicted as "common criminals."

The first high treason trial against Wilhelm Liebknecht and August Bebel in 1872 was clearly conducted on the assumption that they were to be treated "mildly" as political offenders. In 1872, they were put on trial for founding the Socialist Party, and the principle of privileged punishments for political offenders was applied without reservation. The judges never truly considered the idea that Liebknecht and Bebel should be disenfranchised, nor did the public prosecutor seek this punishment.[57] Even though they were the most prominent victims of Bismarck's politics targeting Social Democrats in the early years of the German Empire, the judiciary treated them according to the consensus among legal scholars. Liebknecht and Bebel were thus sentenced to open custody for high treason and were detained in the Hubertusburg fortress for two years. It turned out to be quite significant for the two that they were not sent to the penitentiary, nor deprived of their civil privileges. They did not lose their eligibility to be representatives in any of the German houses of parliament, and they were thus able to remain members of the Saxon Landtag and the Reichstag, respectively, after they had served their time.

Even as the persecution of Social Democrats grew more intense when the "political police" force was founded and the Anti-Socialist Laws of 1878 were introduced, general ideas about the punishment of political crimes did not seem to change that significantly.[58] For example, no offense in the Anti-Socialist Laws was punishable with a penitentiary sentence or with the deprivation of civil privileges: membership in an outlawed socialist organization could be punished with a stay in a "regular" prison of up to three months (§17), while the distribution of illegal pamphlets could lead to a sentence of up to six months of imprisonment (§19).[59] In fact, legal commentators commonly evaluated the nature of punishments in the Anti-Socialist Laws in different terms than the punishments in the actual Reich Penal Code. The Anti-Socialist Laws were often described as "police measures," whereas punishments from the actual penal code were termed "criminal punishments."[60] The state could thus argue that the policy against Social Democrats was justified because the "mild" sentences were proportional to the political nature of their offenses.

Because political offenders enjoyed privileged treatment in accordance with contemporary discourse on penal law, they initially seemed willing to accept their punishment without much consternation. This explains why Wilhelm Liebknecht and other leaders of the Social Democratic movement chose law-abiding tactics in the early years of the Anti-Socialist Laws; hoping this would lead to a more lenient execution of the law, they thought it reasonable that people who violated the laws should be punished in accordance with them.[61] However, Liebknecht did not foresee the severity with which the Anti-Socialist Laws would be implemented, including the suppression of the main socialist media outlets, the dissolution of socialist unions, and the imposition of the Lesser State of Siege. After the emperor proclaimed a period of "mild practice" for the Anti-Socialist Laws in 1881, compliance again seemed a reasonable tactic for the Social Democrats. This ended in 1886, though, when the laws were more rigorously enforced once again.[62]

Despite the "mild" punishments in the Anti-Socialist Laws, however, the judges and public prosecutors still had the important power to determine who was considered a "political" offender and who had committed a "dishonorable" crime. They had this authority especially in their judgments about high treason. After the introduction of the Code of Criminal Procedure in 1877, cases of high treason came under the jurisdiction of the highest court of the German Empire (the Reichsgericht), so the judges of this court were responsible for distinguishing whether high treason was committed out of "political" motives, or, rather, "criminal" ones.[63] The importance of this power became clear in high treason trials following the introduction of the Anti-Socialist Laws. These trials showed that defendants could be categorically denied the privilege of being treated as "political" offenders, and this was pertinent to the publicly accepted definition of "dishonorable disposition."

In 1881, the Reichsgericht tried a group of people from Frankfurt and Berlin who had allegedly formed a secret society to plan attacks on police officers who were actively persecuting anarchists. The group from Frankfurt, which received the most media attention, was led by a shoemaker named Joseph Breuder; another prominent member was the Belgian intellectual Victor Dave. The public prosecutor officially charged the organization with conspiring to violently attack the state in several different ways, including plotting to attack the notorious Frankfurt police officer Ludwig Rumpf (the man popularly described as the "anarchist eater") with acid.[64] It was Rumpf, in fact, who had been responsible for their arrest. He had people infiltrate the group and had key witnesses who could testify that the group had been plotting against the authorities. The accused had also been in possession of material that supported anarchistic ideals, which was used as evidence in the case. The most important documents were copies of the magazine *Freiheit* and other works by the prominent anarchist Johann Most, which wholeheartedly promoted the propaganda of the deed. Furthermore, the state prosecutor also argued that the group was organized along the lines that David Most had outlined in his pamphlets.[65] All of the defendants pleaded not guilty, contending that their organization had different aims than those they were accused of pursuing. However, the judge considered it proven beyond doubt that the organization wanted to "destroy the social order."

Figure 3.4. The trial of high treason against Joseph Breuder and accomplices before the supreme court in Leipzig in 1881. Fritz Waibler, "Der Socialisten-Hochverrathsproceß vor dem Reichsgericht in Leipzig," *Illustrirte Zeitung*, 29 October 1881.

Besides the question of guilt, the question of whether the offenders should be disenfranchised played a crucial role in the trial. In the end, although some of them were acquitted due to lack of evidence, most of them were sentenced to time in the penitentiary and deprived of their civil privileges. The public prosecutor had argued that the criminals had been motivated by ideas so morally reprehensible that the judiciary needed to highlight the offense's dishonorable nature—that it was not an "honorable" political offense. When exercising violence against the state constituted an integral part of offenders' political philosophy, the disposition of those acting upon it could no longer be deemed honorable, he had said. The distinction between violent action and mere attempts to practice political ideas was crucial for determining whether offenders had acted honorably.[66] Karl Braun, a state attorney from Leipzig who provided a detailed commentary on the case in the newly established journal *Das Tribunal*, maintained that the convicts' sentences, including the penitentiary and disenfranchisement, were not controversial but regarded as the just deserts for their crime.[67]

Did this constitute a break with the philosophical consensus about political offenders? It is possible to argue that it did. However, the judges and the prosecutor wanted to ensure that this verdict would not be understood in this way. Thus, they did everything in their power to argue that the accused had not been trying to translate political convictions into practice, but were simply low-life criminals motivated by their "dishonorable dispositions." The prosecutor's own account of the case shows how he actively sought to depict this group as a criminal organization, drawing on popular descriptions of the criminal underworld and the discursive resources provided by the criminal sciences. He used notions like rogue deeds (*Schurkenstreichen*) and insidiousness (*Heimtücke*) and contrasted them with the "German virtues" of manliness and courageousness:

> in a sense, this insidious assault, this lying in wait in the dark to attack an unsuspecting person taking a walk, is much more dishonorable and reprehensible than the use of means of violence in an uprising, in struggles at the barricades, in the honest face-to-face fight.[68]

In other words, the prosecutor made sure to say that overt, public political opposition was not dishonoring, but that the actions planned by the anarchists should not be confused with political action. The definitive attribute for the prosecutor was the distinction between public and secretive action: secrecy was the key feature that allowed him to associate the anarchists with "common" criminal organizations. Secrecy combined with the aim to subvert the state order was indeed a common trope in criminological treatises of the time that depicted criminal organizations as a "counterworld" (*Gegenwelt*) within society.[69]

The authorities' suspicion that the group was a criminal organization and not a legitimate political organization was bolstered by the notion that political ideologies could be used as a cover-up for "normal" crime. Public prosecutor Gustav

Otto articulated this belief in his popular book *Berlin's Criminal World* of 1886. Criminal organizations that were determined to subvert the order of society, he argued, occasionally embellished their "insidious" attacks on society with catchphrases about class struggle:

> what used to be a simple struggle for one's own existence only need be deemed a good thing, a justified war against capital, and use other nice catchphrases to be brought into good form and the monsters like Stellmacher and Kammerer are ready-made.[70]

Hermann Stellmacher and Anton Kammerer were Viennese men who shot a police officer in 1884. The media typically interpreted attacks on police officers as anarchistic because police officers were responsible for keeping an eye on anarchist and socialist organizations. What Otto observed in this passage was what he believed to be the thin line between ideological action and common criminality; his greatest worry was that "common" criminals would cunningly make use of this slippery slope. In other words, Otto believed that many "common" criminals pretended to be ideologically inspired champions of good causes when they were in fact acting out of selfish motivations. This thought had clearly inspired the judges and prosecutors in the trial against Breuder and his Frankfurt group.

For precisely the same reason, prominent Socialist Party members were mostly supportive of these verdicts against anarchist offenders. Many of them actively tried to distance themselves from anarchists and the so-called propaganda of the deed by deploying similar tropes of the "criminal" and dishonorable nature of anarchism.[71] Wilhelm Liebknecht, for instance, used such arguments in his speech at the 1887 convention of Social Democrats in St. Gallen, incorporating words that recall Otto's descriptions in *Berlin's Criminal World*:

> People who commit robbery, homicides and arson are common criminals, even when they justify their crime under the guise of anarchism. The fact that common criminals tout themselves as bearers of higher ideas is nothing new.[72]

Although Liebknecht did not group people who supported the propaganda of the deed together with "common criminals" who masked their deeds behind a political ideal, he did point out the slippery slope of the propaganda of the deed. He also used other notions, like "phrase revolutionaries" (*Phrasenrevolutionären*)—that is, revolutionaries in word only—on some occasions to attack the hypocritical nature of such groups.[73] It is thus significant that many prominent members of the Socialist Party approved of the verdict against Breuder and Dave, reinforcing the image of anarchists as "common criminals."

Otto's description of common criminals using political phrases as a cover-up underscores another key attribute of the so-called dishonorable disposition: selfishness. This category, in fact, played a dominant role in the verdict against Victor

Dave. Because of Dave's rather exceptional status in this trial, the public prosecutor had a more difficult time justifying sentencing him to the penitentiary. Dave's lawyers explicitly argued that it was unjust for him to be sent to the penitentiary because they believed that this would have a much more detrimental effect on him than on the other members of this organization due to his being a more educated person. The state prosecutor, however, used Dave's Belgian citizenship to accuse him of a specific kind of egoistic opportunism. Dave, he argued, belonged to a group of people who traveled to other countries to mobilize working-class people but returned to the safety of their home countries once they were prosecuted, while the actual protesters were punished for their actions.[74] The kind of egoism and opportunism that this behavior reflected, the prosecutor claimed, was all the more reason to view Dave as having been motivated by his dishonorable disposition.[75] Thus, while his lawyers tried to emphasize Dave's intellectual character—implying that he was not a man of action but of "spirit"—the judge had a different opinion and declared that Dave was not just an "idealistic fanatic" but truly a man capable of "dishonorable" action.[76]

Indeed, the contrast between acting selfishly or idealistically became a prominent part of the distinction between political offenses and "dishonoring" crimes. As the prominent Swiss legal scholar Carl Stooß argued in his 1892 textbook on criminal justice: "The person convicted of high treason who acts selflessly in the name of ideals may not be punished as a common criminal."[77] Guckenheimer also drew on this distinction when he later argued that the one juridical notion that defined the dishonorable disposition was egoism.[78] In fact, Guckenheimer argued that the judges in the trial against Breuder and his group believed that many of the defendants had indeed been motivated by personal profit, which made them even more "dishonorable."[79]

The trial against Breuder and his group became notorious in many ways. The controversial methods Rumpf had used to get the members of the organization arrested were widely criticized and denounced, even by more conservative commentators. The use of *agents provocateurs*, in particular, was regarded as being unworthy of the dignity of the state.[80] Many saw Rumpf's assassination four years later as an act of revenge for the whole debacle.[81] But the trial was extremely significant in determining how "dishonorable disposition" was defined in the jurisprudence of the German Empire because it marked the first time that the Reichsgericht had used its discretionary powers to define the extent of political crime. Consequently, the verdict created a precedent for treating anarchism and the propaganda of the deed as a form of common, dishonorable criminality rather than political action. This judicial precedent, together with the assassination of Rumpf, contributed to the state's growing persecution of anarchists and to them being portrayed more starkly as true "criminal" enemies of the state. The Reichsgericht itself drew on the precedent again in another high-profile high treason trial it heard in 1886.[82]

The Lawyer and the Anarchist

In the end, the mere suspicion of anarchism was enough to prompt many prosecutors to treat the accused as people with "dishonorable dispositions." All in all, however, surprisingly few cases of high treason were brought before the Reichsgericht in the German Empire.[83] Yet, the judicial consensus about the "dishonorable" nature of anarchism also influenced the process of legislation, for instance, the law on explosives that was introduced in 1884, which was clearly inspired by the fear of anarchist attacks. In contrast to the Anti-Socialist Laws, this law included dishonoring sentences like the penitentiary, disenfranchisement, and the death penalty.[84] Prominent champions of the anarchist cause, like Sepp Oerter in 1893, were sent to the penitentiary after being accused of violating the new law.[85]

This prompted controversy about whether the attribution of the term "anarchist" was justified. Sometimes, two people were put on trial for a similar offense, but one was considered an anarchist and the other was not. This happened, for instance, in 1907 and 1908, when the Reichsgericht in Leipzig heard two other prominent trials for high treason. The context of these trials was that left-wing commentators increasingly criticized what they saw as the "militarization" of German society. Leftists and Social Democratic politicians often wrote about the maltreatment and physical abuse suffered by low-ranking soldiers at the hands of their commanding officers, and they frequently combined their criticisms with a call for general disarmament, arguing that the army was one of the most pernicious elements of modern society.[86]

A prominent figure in this opposition was the young defense attorney Karl Liebknecht, the son of Wilhelm Liebknecht, who published many articles on the topic for the magazine *Die junge Garde*. In an article from 22 September 1906, titled "Goodbye Recruits," Liebknecht had argued, for instance, that conscription should be seen as a form of modern slavery. In light of the assault on soldiers and the roughness of the barracks, enlisted proletarians would soon come to view their former lives in poverty as a "symbol of freedom," he held.[87]

Government officials and conservative politicians had become concerned about the "hostile agitation against the army," which they felt gravely threatened the stability of the army and society. They were particularly worried about the influence this kind of agitation might have on adolescents ready for conscription. In 1897, for instance, Prussian War Minister Heinrich von Goßler argued in the *Kreuzzeitung* that Social Democrats had contributed to the coarsening of manners among the German youth, with statistics revealing a remarkable percentage of conscripted soldiers with criminal records.[88] He claimed that these youngsters were inspired by anti-military rhetoric and undermined army discipline. Moreover, the number was increasing, and he unambiguously blamed Social Democratic political ideas for this—an accusation that August Bebel fiercely rebuked in the Reichstag.[89] Nonetheless, *heeresfeindliche agitation* (hostile agitation against the army) concerned many people, and even prominent criminal experts wrote about its dangers.[90]

The defendant in one case was a resident of Kiel named Rudolf Oestreich, the editor of the anarchist journal *Freier Arbeiter*, who was charged with high treason for publishing an article titled "Anarchism and Antimilitarism." The article dealt with the International Anarchist Congress organized in Amsterdam in 1907, where the international politics of anti-militarism had been discussed. The charge against Oestreich was allegedly based on one specific sentence from the article stating that his group believed that there were men among their ranks who were prepared to put these decisions into action and thus "to get rid of one of the worst institutions of today's social order."[91]

The defendant in the other case was Karl Liebknecht himself, who published his treatise *Militarism and Anti-Militarism*, which brought together all his views on the detrimental effects of German militarism. He was charged with high treason and brought before the Reichsgericht in 1907. Justus Olshausen, a high-profile lawyer whose interpretation of the Reich Penal Code was seen as authoritative, was assigned as the prosecutor.[92] Olshausen saw Liebknecht's treatise as a piece of "anarchistic writing," so he was eager to argue that Liebknecht's publication of this essay clearly expressed his dishonorable disposition. In his introductory remarks, Olshausen stated:

> I have no problem saying that the acts of the accused are without honor, because he, a grown man, a jurist who himself wore a uniform and is still a member of the military, should not have agitated against the military in this way. . . . The spitefulness of the accused's agitation and the dangerousness of his action make the matter all the graver.[93]

The judge, Ludwig Treplin, however, explicitly stated the opposite opinion in his verdict, arguing that Liebknecht had no doubt acted out of nothing more than his political conviction. He therefore sentenced Liebknecht to two years in open custody.[94]

For Liebknecht personally, this verdict was of great significance. When some of his fellow lawyers tried to get him banned from practicing law by bringing him before the honor court for lawyers, Liebknecht defended himself by arguing that he was sentenced to open custody, which meant that the judge had officially decided that he had acted out of an honorable disposition. "The only important thing here is the moral appraisal," he noted in his defense, which demonstrated his acceptance of the distinction between law and morality.[95] In fact, he used it to justify his categorization as a political offender, not a dishonorable criminal.

The trial against Oestreich, however, ended differently. The judge and jury considered Oestreich's article evidence of his anarchistic ideology and believed that his writing represented a serious threat to the army. He was thus found guilty of conspiracy to commit high treason. The prosecutor was clear in his assessment of Oestreich's dishonorable disposition: "When somebody negates the existence of the legal order as such, then he cannot be considered honorable within this legal order."[96] He had demanded that Oestreich be sent to the penitentiary for two years, but the court president, Karl von Bülow, went above and beyond and sentenced Oestreich to four years in the penitentiary and deprived him of his civil privileges for another four years.[97]

After he was released from the penitentiary, Oestreich said that the judges and prosecutor clearly acted out of bias:

> As far as my disposition goes, there was no doubt as to its baseness, [because the common wisdom is that] whoever brings the dear German fatherland in danger acts without honor and he must be sent to the penitentiary.[98]

Although there were hostilities between Social Democrats and anarchists, many Social Democratic politicians were critical of the verdict against Oestreich in light of the patently obvious similarities between the Liebknecht and Oestreich trials. Arnold Stadthagen, a Social Democratic Reichstag member, vehemently opposed the verdict in a Reichstag session in 1908. He even noted how an expert witness had stated under oath that the *Freier Arbeiter* was not a magazine that actively professed the propaganda of the deed. But what outraged Stadthagen most was the sentence. Stadthagen believed that Oestreich had clearly acted unselfishly, so the penitentiary sentence and deprivation of civil privileges was nothing more than *Gesinnungsstrafrecht*: "He is only deemed dishonorable because he has a different political conviction," he cynically remarked.[99]

Stadthagen's argument and his use of the penal code to support it underscore his adherence to the general consensus that political offenders should be treated with privilege. But commentators gradually became convinced that members of the German Empire's judiciary were systematically refusing to accept this consensus in their judgments. Liebknecht himself was one of these commentators. He argued that this verdict against Oestreich would have long-term negative effects on the judiciary. In fact, he predicted in response to the verdict that "the value of judicially recognized honor will sink for all independent-minded citizens because of such verdicts."[100] To be sure, the judiciary had the power to define the line between political and common crime, and this happened at first with little criticism, but gradually, when these cases were compared with others, it became more problematic. However, the pertinent question for commentators was whether judges misused this power for political ends. When it appeared that they did, a heightened sense of them being biased against people from lower classes and with other political ideas reinforced this criticism.

After the Anti-Socialist Laws: Criminalizing Political Opposition

Disenfranchisement sentences were not supposed to provoke major controversies. After all, the punishment was understood by its very nature as "apolitical," so sentences had to be based on a common understanding of who was a "common criminal" (*gemeiner Verbrecher*). An assumption that often underlay this philosophy was that upstanding members of society had by definition such an understanding. Even so, controversies about these sentences arose, not least because it was sometimes very difficult to determine what constituted a political crime, aside from the fairly clear-cut matter of high treason. In general, there were three ways the "dishonorable disposition" notion generated political controversy: 1) when it was used to depoliticize certain affairs, 2) when using it created certain new privileges, and 3) when the government tried to impose penitentiary confinement and disenfranchisement for acts that had never prompted such sentences before.

Political crime and the treatment of political offenders—particularly socialists—grew more significant in the 1890s after the Anti-Socialist Laws had been repealed. In this period, the German authorities were becoming increasingly anxious about all kinds of people that they believed wished to subvert the state order, and they no longer had the punitive instrument of the Anti-Socialist Laws at their disposal. Furthermore, there was a series of terrorist attacks across Europe, the labor movement was growing more popular, the SPD won many Reichstag seats in the 1890 elections, and a national strike seemed ever more likely. In this context, all three grounds for controversy emerged.

Punishing Political Agents as Common Criminals

As I argued in chapter 1, disenfranchisement was intended to be both inclusive and universal, meaning that all citizens could be so punished if (and only if) they were found guilty of crimes that exhibited a "dishonorable disposition." Unfortunately, the official statistics did not register the professions of those sentenced with disenfranchisement until 1911, so it is impossible to know how many upper-class people were deprived of their privileges. Nevertheless, the numbers from 1911 show that all kinds of people were so sentenced: working-class men and women as well as bourgeois businessmen and civil servants.[101] Although few were diplomats and higher civil servants, such people could, in principle, be subjected to this punishment too.

For instance, in one of the major political conflicts in the early years of the German Empire—between Chancellor Bismarck and the German consul in Paris, Harry von Arnim—a high-ranking politician was threatened with disenfranchisement, which would have made him a "dishonored" felon. After the Franco-

Prussian War and the fall of the Paris Commune, Arnim became a prominent adversary of Chancellor Bismarck. When Arnim supported France becoming a republic, in contrast to Bismarck, who favored a monarchy, their rivalry intensified.[102] Meanwhile, Arnim had started a public campaign against Bismarck's policies, attempting to publicize information from diplomatic documents. Bismarck ordered Arnim to stand trial for stealing official state documents. Although Arnim was convicted, his crime was not deemed to have resulted from a dishonorable disposition.[103] His lawyers, the prominent scholars Emil Wahlberg and Franz von Holtzendorff, convinced the jury that Arnim had not suppressed and stolen any material from the embassy, which would have been a "dishonorable" crime.[104] Arnim was, nonetheless, sentenced to time in regular prison for a breach of trust in his position at a foreign embassy. Three years later, however, after he had fled to Switzerland and published the anonymous treatise *Pro Nihilo!* containing state secrets, he was sentenced to the penitentiary and deprived of his civil privileges for the act of high treason.[105]

In a commentary on the case, an anonymous professor of law argued that Arnim's actions reflected his base character—he had acted deceitfully. Consequently, the professor believed that Arnim deserved disenfranchisement as he had to be seen as a "common criminal" (*gemeiner Verbrecher*); his status as a nobleman and higher civil servant was irrelevant.[106] Certainly, stifling political opposition was one of Bismarck's main motives for instigating these trials. But Bismarck and his supporters cunningly made use of legal categories to "depoliticize" the conflict. By charging Arnim with crimes that testified to a dishonorable disposition, they could persuasively argue that he had violated the norms of acceptable political behavior. Arnim's case demonstrates that one could instrumentalize the "dishonorable" quality of certain offenses to depoliticize a particular affair. This was only possible because of the penal code's distinction between "dishonoring" and "non-dishonoring" crimes.

Such depoliticization was most successful in cases of perjury. When political defendants were charged with perjury, they came to be cast as "common criminals." This could completely change the outcome of a trial, prompting critics to very frequently argue that perjury trials were used for political ends.[107] Trying people for perjury was thus one of the most prominent ways of stigmatizing political offenders as criminals; even perjury charges could discredit a political opponent.[108] Something like this happened to socialist Reichstag member Karl Ibsen in 1880 when he tried to protect a party-affiliated book printer accused of distributing Bebel's book *Woman and Socialism*. Ibsen was sentenced to three years in the penitentiary and deprived of his civil privileges for five years.[109] The judges, enraging members of the Socialist Party, did not accept Ibsen's attempt to protect another man from being convicted as an excuse.

The government increasingly used this tactic after the socialist laws were repealed in 1890. Critics of socialism more generally started depicting socialist parties as criminal organizations by arguing that they tended to disrespect the oath and encouraged their members to commit perjury. This strategy aimed to delegitimize them as "political" parties. In fact, many criminologists sought a connection between political ideology and crime. They analyzed cases of perjury to support the idea that socialist ideology justified "regular" crimes like perjury, as evident in socialists' attacks on religiosity. An example of this theory can be found in Wilhelm Starke's influential statistical study of the development of crime patterns in Prussia from 1854 to 1878. In the book, Starke identified the spread of socialist ideas as a cause of rising crime because socialist ideas "have disturbed the moral and religious convictions that hold society together, mock veneration and piety, confuse the legal sense of the masses and destroy the respect of the law."[110] In his mind, the growing number of perjury convictions was a strong indicator of the spread of socialism as its godlessness led people to disrespect the sacred oath.[111] While jurists insisted on a strong distinction between political opposition and criminal activity, perjury crimes led to political ideas and morally reprehensible behavior becoming closely associated.

Several scholars and commentators pointed out this association between Social Democrats and perjury. For example, prominent member of the Social Democratic Party of Germany (SPD) Karl Frohme, in his study of the political police of the German Empire, dedicated an entire part of the study to elucidating how the police campaign against Social Democrats deployed perjury.[112] Frohme noted that conservatives and liberals had even started referring to the SPD as the "perjury party," quoting people like the former editor of the influential magazine *Die Grenzboten* Hans Blum as evidence. Blum had argued that Social Democrats actively supported the use of perjury if it was in the party's best interest:

> This mark of shame of the party is the result of their conscienceless rejection of all divine and human discipline and order. Godlessness and lawlessness meet in the soul of the perjurer and lead him to both earthly and eternal punishment and damnation.[113]

The Hamburg prosecutor Anton Romen became another prominent figure in the campaign to portray the SPD as a "perjury party" with the publication of his *Perjury and Social Democracy* in 1892.[114]

Social Democrats grew increasingly worried about this political use of perjury (occasionally called a *Meineidshetze*), which had effects both inside and outside the courtroom. Frohme had no doubt that the political police strategically prosecuted Social Democrats for perjury. He argued that police witnesses systematically distorted the truth in trials against Social Democrats, in which jury members were always hostile to the Social Democratic political ideology, and that the "perjury party" propaganda had two important effects. First, it caused judges and public prosecutors to prejudge the testimonies of Social Democrats as unreliable and dishonest. When there were conflicting accounts in a trial, judges thus usually decided that civil servants spoke the truth and that the other party must necessarily have committed perjury. This made it easy to convict Social Democrats of perjury. Second, the judiciary used the oath as a means of extortion to deter Social Democrats from giving testimony.[115] The abovementioned public prosecutor Romen in Hamburg frequently used both of these strategies, Frohme maintained.[116]

The perjury cases against Social Democrats generated a great deal of public concern and debate.[117] One of the causes célèbres that upset Social Democratic politicians was a trial against the president of the socialist workers' union in Dortmund, Ludwig Schröder.[118] The case was complicated, having begun when libel charges were brought against a journalist who had accused a police officer of beating Schröder to the ground after Schröder had allegedly refused to obey his request to remove himself from a meeting of the Christian miners' union in Bochum. In the ensuing trial, the police officer testified under oath that he had never hit Schröder and was ultimately acquitted. The journalist was found guilty of libel, which led the state prosecutor to charge Schröder and seven other witnesses who had claimed that the police officer had hit Schröder with perjury.[119] This trial, known as the Essen perjury trial, became notorious.

When Schröder and the other witnesses were accused, national media outlets immediately portrayed the trial as a political one in the authorities' struggle against Social Democrats.[120] Victor Niemeyer, the state prosecutor on this case, however, actively tried to reframe the nature of the trial: in his statement before the court, he reminded the jury of the "criminal" nature of perjury, emphasizing that the case against Schröder should be seen as a "simple" perjury trial and nothing more.[121] In other words, Niemeyer strategically used the distinction between "common criminality" and political opposition to deny the defendants the possibility of being treated as "political" offenders.

Furthermore, to support the idea that Schröder had committed perjury, the prosecution actively contrasted the immorality of the socialist workers' union with the piety of the Christian miners' union. Niemeyer emphasized the Christian mine workers' great respect for religion and the sacredness of the oath, in contrast to which socialist workers despised religion and did blasphemous things like comparing the conviction of a fellow worker with the suffering of Christ. Moreover, Niemeyer added that the local magazine of the Socialist Union had actually defended committing perjury to save fellow mine workers from being sentenced.[122] He therefore ultimately tried to make the charge of perjury plausible simply by associating the accused with socialist ideology. Schröder was found guilty of perjury, sentenced to three-and-a-half years in the penitentiary, and deprived of his civil privileges for five years. In response to this verdict, the SPD put Schröder up for election to the Reichstag, but the petition was rejected as he had been deprived of his civil privileges.[123] The verdict against Schröder was only revised in 1911 after investigations proved that the police officer had been lying.[124] In the legal constellation of the German Empire, it was unclear if trade unions were considered "political" organizations, but what is clear is that verdicts like that against Schröder played an important role in state prosecutors' attempts to deny political consideration to union members.[125]

Along with union members, many politicians were charged with perjury, too, and not only members of the SPD. Against the background of the legal authorities' struggle to have Social Democrats convicted of criminal behavior, accusing political opponents of perjury became a common strategy for discrediting them as it seemed a proven method of turning political disagreements into questions of moral character. The leader of the Christian Social Party, Adolf Stöcker, was

Figure 3.5. Mockery of judges considering membership of the Social Democratic Party as an aggravating circumstance. A lawyer pleads: "Even if the crime of robbery and murder, which my client carried out, may be so despicable, I still plead for mitigating circumstances – the accused is namely not a Social Democrat." Hans Gabriel Jentzsch, *Wahre Jacob*, Aug. 1, 1899. Courtesy Klassik Stiftung Weimar.

repeatedly accused of perjury by his political opponents, and Hans Leuss, a member of the notoriously antisemitic German Social Reform Party, was convicted of perjury and sentenced to the penitentiary.[126] In both cases, political opponents played an important role in the persecution of these politicians as "perjured criminals."

A similar mix of political opposition and criminal prosecution seems to have taken place in the infamous Eulenburg affair in 1908, when prosecutors charged the confidant of the German emperor Prince Philipp of Eulenburg with perjury for denying having had sexual relations with multiple men. In newspapers and magazines, however, people actively associated this persecution with Eulenburg's attempted treason. The charge of perjury against Eulenburg cannot be dissociated from a widespread aversion to the politics he and the German emperor stood for at the time. The failure to convict him prompted outcries about class justice and the mild treatment of upper-class citizens.[127] As this case attests, attempts to discredit political opponents as "ordinary criminals" by accusing them of perjury were not always successful. Yet, when used effectively, the strategy took perfect advantage of the philosophical line between political and immoral crimes.

Lèse-majesté Controversies

In addition to perjury charges, the number of charges of lèse majesté—that is, insulting the monarch—exploded in the 1890s, and many of those accused were members of the socialist press.[128] An average of two to three German citizens was charged with lèse-majesté every day.[129] Just as with the perjury trials, the trials for these charges can be viewed, Alex Hall argues, as the continuation of the struggle against Social Democrats "by other means" after the repeal of the Anti-Socialist Laws.[130] However, an important difference between the lèse-majesté and perjury trials was the possible sentences: convictions for lèse-majesté could not lead to disenfranchisement or penitentiary sentences. This meant that critics mostly used other criteria to question these trials. The length of a prison sentence was the most important measure of severity in these cases. One heavily criticized trial, for instance, was that against August Müller, the editor of the *Magdeburger Volksstimme*, who was sentenced to four years in prison for committing lèse-majesté; most in the socialist press considered this excessively long.[131] Together with the arbitrary treatment of prisoners, as well as abusively long periods of pretrial custody for many people accused of lèse-majesté, cases like these contributed to growing anger about such charges and trials.[132] Such abuses contributed to the emergence of the concept of *Klassenjustiz*, or class justice, and the rising number of lèse-majesté charges also gave rise to tremendous distrust in the German judiciary.[133]

Ultimately, however, observers remained interested in the disposition of the accused and whether convicts could be deemed "dishonorable" in cases of lèse-majesté as well. For example, when Maximilian Harden, the famous editor of *Die Zukunft* (who would later break the story of the Eulenburg affair), published a mockery of the German emperor Wilhelm II in the form of a fable about a "poodle monarch" in 1898, his subsequent trial for lèse majesté precipitated a controversy. Although Harden had not explicitly referred to Wilhelm II in the fable, the judge still regarded it as insulting the German emperor.[134] After Harden had been convicted, the judge declared that Harden's actions did not testify to a "dishonorable disposition," so he sentenced him with open custody instead of regular prison.[135] The Reich Penal Code's laws on lèse-majesté left the matter to the judge's discretion, stipulating that this choice was possible given mitigating circumstances. Even so, it did not define these circumstances, nor did it expressly indicate that convicts who had acted out of an "honorable disposition" should receive reduced sentences. Thus, when the judges justified the mild punishment in light of Harden's still "honorable disposition," they implied that all other people convicted of lèse-majesté who were sentenced to regular prison were "dishonorable"—or at least this was the conclusion many commentators drew.

An editor of the *Hamburger Anzeiger* made precisely this point: he believed that one's disposition should never be a determining factor in cases of lèse-majesté.[136] In his view, the laws against lèse-majesté were not aimed at punishing opinions but at sanctioning the form in which they were expressed. Thus, he argued, judges were supposed to refrain from making any judgments about the offender's disposition or moral views and stick to judging the act itself. Harden's disposition, whether "honorable" or "dishonorable," was beside the point. The case illustrates how privileged sentences prompted people to believe that others who were not so treated were implicitly "dishonorable." In addition, when lawbreakers seemed to create a new group of "honorable" political criminals, they themselves were more likely to be suspected of serious crimes. After Harden's trial, convictions for lèse-majesté were immediately seen in a different light. By imposing such a sentence, the critics argued, the judge had changed the penal code's stipulations about the honor of persons convicted of this crime.

The Sedition and Penitentiary Bills:
Imposing Disenfranchisement for New Forms of Sedition

As Harden stood trial, the German government was trying to redefine certain offenses more actively as crimes that testified to a "dishonorable disposition." This would enable it to strip certain acts of their political dimension. Notably, it employed this strategy against people who organized and participated in strikes or any other forms of collective action. According to §152 of the Reich Commercial and Industrial Code, strikes were not punishable by law.[137] However, the penal code still had plenty of articles that the judiciary could utilize to prosecute strikers. For instance, if a judge deemed that a strike had gotten out of hand, the participants could be charged with disturbing the peace or public order, that is, with *Landfriedensbruch*. Moreover, they could also be charged, according to §130 of the penal code, with "incitement to engage in class struggle."[138] Nonetheless, the Reich Penal Code stipulated that convictions for these offenses should lead to regular prison sentences.

The authorities' worries about strikes grew in the years around 1890, when a series of strikes was organized across the German Empire.[139] Initially, the government seemed willing to meet many of the labor movement's demands by passing new, socially minded legislation.[140] But this policy changed around 1894, when the more conservative Hohenlohe administration replaced the Caprivi administration. At the same time, the emperor held two speeches warning of the danger of people who wanted to "subvert the order of society." All of this led the government to take a new approach to strikes; it proposed the notorious so-called Sedition Bill (*Umsturzvorlage*), a set of laws designed to protect society from attempts to subvert the state order, particularly on the part of Social Democrats.[141] The Sedition Bill would have entailed revisions to the penal code that would have stipulated penitentiary sentences instead of prison for certain offenses if they involved a conspiracy to "subvert the state order."

As some commentators in the socialist press remarked, "people with the aspiration to subvert the state order" could basically be translated as "Social Democrats."[142] The bill failed to pass the Reichstag in 1895, but it set the tone for the persecution of people who participated in strikes. After the Hamburg dockers' strikes of 1896 and early 1897, bricklayers' strikes in Leipzig, and many other strikes across the German Empire, the Hohenlohe administration grew more fearful of the violent repercussions of strikes.[143] In particular, they were anxious that some workers might force others to join a coalition. This led to another hotly debated proposal in the Reichstag, the so-called Penitentiary Bill (*Zuchthausvorlage*).[144] Vice-Chancellor Arthur von Posadowsky-Wehner brought this bill before the Reichstag in 1898, but the emperor had already established the mood earlier that year in his "penitentiary speech" in Oeynhausen.[145] The use of "penitentiary" in the title of this bill was clearly vital since it marked these workers' actions as "dishonorable" rather than political.

The Penitentiary Bill explicitly sought to give harsher sentences to people who "obstructed" other workers from exercising their occupation. Some historians describe the Penitentiary Bill as a reckless solo effort by the emperor to further suppress Social Democracy, mobilizing the "weak" government of Hohenlohe for his personal vendetta against the Social Democrats.[146] It should be pointed out, however, that Vice-Chancellor von Posadowsky-Wehner took great pains to justify this policy to the Reichstag. He carefully set out his justifications in a memorandum handed to the Reichstag on "disturbances during labor conflicts" (*Ausschreitungen bei den Arbeitskämpfen*).[147] The language in this memorandum clearly aimed to convince other politicians that such disturbances should be treated as "dishonorable crimes" instead of as actions motivated by moral or political convictions. Importantly, the draft contained about twenty references to "terrorism" committed by strikers against the "people who are willing to work" (*Arbeitswillige*).[148] By using the notion of "terrorism" so frequently, Posadowsky-Wehner sought to associate such strikers with anarchist criminals.

The threat of penitentiary sentences and the repeated use of the notion of terrorism clarifies why the proposed legislation provoked public outrage. The bill's opponents sought to convince others that participation in workers' coalitions was based on moral principle and not on criminal intent. In fact, the entire debate about the "compulsion to join a coalition" (*Koalitionszwang*) was dominated by questions of moral obligations. The authorities argued that strikers obstructed people who only wanted to fulfill their moral duty to work (in their opinion, the notions of *will* and *duty* were closely associated), and that such obstruction constituted an offense against their moral duties, making it "dishonoring." Carl Legien, a union leader and influential SPD member who had drafted another memorandum on this issue, argued that milder punishments were, in fact, more appropriate for these agitators since they were acting out of moral conviction; they had the moral right to form a coalition as workers, and these actions were motivated by their feelings of mutual solidarity.[149] Legien and others stressed the moral righteousness of protesting against labor contracts and stressed the need for a sense of solidarity in such endeavors.[150] Neglecting this moral duty was more "dishonorable" than acting in accordance with it. They often drew comparisons between feelings of solidarity among workers and the feeling of solidarity in the army. After all, the "honor" of military comradeship was beyond dispute. They hoped this comparison would help persuade government officials that strikers had an "honorable" character.[151]

When penitentiary and disenfranchisement sentences were then, in fact, imposed on workers charged with coercing other workers to strike, there was great outrage. An 1899 trial in a Dresden court provides an example. Even though the penitentiary bill had not been ratified, the court seemed to anticipate it passing as it imposed harsh sentences on seven employees of a construction firm from the Saxon town of Löbtau for allegedly obstructing other workers: in total, the group members were sentenced to fifty-three years in the penitentiary and seventy years of disenfranchisement. The very harshness of the sentences made the case into something of a cause célèbre.[152] Immediately after sentencing, a *Vorwärts* editor wrote: "the era of the Penitentiary Bill casts its shadow upon us."[153] The socialist press covered the trial extensively, repeatedly emphasizing that it underscored the "penitentiary course" of the empire's rulers.[154] The media interest illustrates the sense of injustice many commentators felt about sentencing "honest" workers with penitentiary confinement and disenfranchisement.

Figure 3.6. The Penitentiary Bill was meant to protect the people who are "willing to work" by severely punishing people who blocked their access to work. An anonymous Cartoonist depicts the Penitentiary Bill here as a malfunctioning scarecrow, scaring away the wrong things. Anonymous, *Wahre Jacob*, 17 January, 1899. Courtesy Klassik Stiftung Weimar.

In the end, the Penitentiary Bill never passed. Opposition to it was too great, not least because the criticism was not limited to Social Democrats. Among the critics were people like Max Weber, who argued that hampering workers' ability to strike would only worsen the legal position of working-class people.[155] The rejection of the Penitentiary Bill was vital to maintaining the consensus about the function of penitentiary and disenfranchisement sentences. After all, once this bill was rejected, these punishments could not legally be applied to offenders largely regarded as having acted "honorably." In consequence, penitentiary sentences remained the most important way of distinguishing between "political" and non-political offenders.

That the authorities sought to impose more and more "dishonoring" punishments on Social Democrats from 1890 means that the same struggle against Social Democracy was not just being waged "by other means," as Hall argues. Rather, the authorities tried to break with the preexisting consensus on the treatment of political offenders by promoting the idea in public discourse that Social Democrats were not political opponents but serious criminals. This means that the authorities' goals were different, too: they wished not only to repress the activities of Social Democrats but also actually to convict them like common criminals. One should therefore not underestimate the significance of lawmakers' failure to pass both the Sedition and Penitentiary Bills. It shows the limits of the government's powers to punish its political opponents like common criminals.

Social Democrats' Appropriation of Disenfranchisement

The important conclusion to be drawn from the evidence presented in this chapter is that these dishonoring sentences—regardless of whom they were imposed upon, be they high public officials or members of workers' unions—never resulted in a full-blown rejection of disenfranchisement or penitentiary punishments as such, despite the often very fierce public criticism of them. In the end, the criticism remained directed toward the people making the verdicts and sentences, the judges and jurors, whose biases, critics claimed, often ran contrary to the basic principles of the penal code. Accordingly, the most common criticism was that judges displayed a certain "otherworldliness."[156]

Members of the SPD and the media touted the party-made allegations of *Klassenjustiz* and "otherworldliness" more than anyone else. Before the outbreak of the First World War, however, they never explicitly protested the existence of the dishonoring punishments. In fact, one could argue that they not only passively accepted the punishments of disenfranchisement and penitentiary but also even actively supported them. Unfortunately, however, apart from August Bebel's famous remarks in *Woman and Socialism* that there was no crime in the utopian socialist state, it is difficult to reconstruct the SPD's stance on issues of criminal law, and, by extension, to identify its position on disenfranchisement. Still, there is reason to believe that members of the SPD in principle supported the idea of certain felons being considered "dishonorable." As *Vorwärts* editors argued in 1909 in a twelve-part editorial on criminal reform, criminal law was an instrument not just for exercising power over political opponents but also for battling crime.[157] This was also why the SPD was generally positive about police action; the party supported much of the active police policy against deviant members of the working classes.[158]

In addition, one should not forget that the concept of "dishonorable disposition" was used and contested within the SPD. There were frequent battles within the SPD about whether strikebreakers and pieceworkers could be accused of having a "dishonorable" disposition. For example, in 1901 in Hamburg, the local trade unions and Social Democratic Party actively fought over the application of the term "dishonorable," eventually drawing the national party leadership into the fray. A group of around two hundred bricklayers had agreed to work at a piece rate. This initiative violated the collective agreement to abolish piece wages that the local bricklayers' union had made earlier that year. The union leaders of Hamburg viewed the pieceworkers' initiative as a form of backstabbing and "scabbing," fearing, among other things, that the authorities would portray these workers as "willing to work" and the union members opposed to them as obstructers. As the unions were aligned with the German Social Democratic Party, many party members demanded that these pieceworkers be dismissed for their "dishonorable" actions. The interesting thing is that the 1890 bylaws of the SPD said the following: "He who has acted against the principles of the party program or has made himself guilty of dishonorable deeds shall not be admitted."[159]

With this, the SPD membership statutes highlighted the notion of "honor," although it was problematic that "dishonorable actions" were not defined further. Unlike some unions' statutes, it did not explicitly refer to disenfranchisement or any other "dishonoring" sentence. As a result, a special arbitration board had to be appointed to determine whether the incentive workers could be excluded from the party. This special board, chaired by Ignaz Auer, declared that "strikebreaking" was clearly "dishonorable" as it undermined workers' solidarity but that the particular action of the incentive workers did not constitute strikebreaking since members of the local union were not on strike. In the board's verdict, then, these workers' actions were deemed objectionable but not "dishonorable."[160]

Nonetheless, the pieceworkers controversy gave rise to a debate within the party about the meaning of "dishonorable" and prompted some members of the SPD to raise their objections to this verdict at the party congress that year. The president of the Hamburg union, Theodor Bömelburg, declared: "I can't imagine anybody so bad as these people. If their actions are not dishonorable, then I don't know what dishonorable is."[161] Carl Legien, a union leader and prominent party member, also supported this position when he defended a motion to reject the board of arbitration's findings.[162] In the end, the case instigated a debate among several left-wing media outlets about the definition of the "honor of the worker" and whether it differed from the honor of other citizens.[163]

Despite the debate, the arbitration board's verdict was not overturned but was, rather, supported by the party congress. The case of the Hamburg bricklayers demonstrates how the definition of "dishonorable action" was disputed, and not only on the level of penal law: even a political organization that had frequently and vehemently criticized the German Empire's execution of justice used the category. The most interesting aspect, however, was that the arbitration board's definition aligned with the basic principles of the penal code by refusing to regard political opposition and "differences of opinion" as signs of a "dishonorable disposition."

In a similar vein, Alexander Parvus, another prominent SPD party member, considered it unnecessary to label these bricklayers "dishonorable" since, he argued, this notion was reserved for "real criminals": "There is a difference between the bricklayers' lack of discipline and a dishonorable disposition."[164] To his mind, opposition and disagreement were not reasons to declare a person "dishonorable." He added that it would be highly excessive to exclude these workers from the party if the Hamburg conflict resolved itself within a few days. "Dishonorable action," he argued, was a notion that was used to distance themselves (Social Democrats) from the so-called *Lumpenproletariat* and not one for questions of political opposition.[165]

In some cases, national SPD politicians even explicitly supported the use of dishonoring punishments to make sentences more severe. For instance, when the Reich Industrial and Commercial Code was being revised in 1891, Bebel stated that employers making false statements in employees' letters of reference should be punished by being stripped of their civil privileges. In his eyes, these were the most low-life, insidious crimes imaginable.[166] On another occasion, in 1897, Bebel advanced a bill to punish people who trafficked women and participated in prostitution—particularly border agents—with disenfranchisement; the bill ultimately passed.[167] Unsurprisingly, both proposals targeted people who abused the power that came with their privileged position.

"Without Character or Spine": Political Conviction as a Sign of Honor

In the end, what was most pressing was the question of which defendants were entitled to be treated as "political" offenders and thus were able to maintain their right to participation in politics. In many cases, the judiciary drew the distinction. Certainly, the state had a powerful deterrent tool in "dishonoring sentences." But it would be going too far to argue that judges could make unlimited use of them. They were restricted by a consensus about their intended purpose. These sentences were meant to separate "common" criminals from "political" ones. As a result, the notion of honor became increasingly associated with certain moral and political convictions. As Ute Frevert observed, the concept of honor became more and more individualized in the German Empire; people appealed less to lineage and social position and more to personal characteristics in their claim to honor.[168] Adherence to a political belief therefore became a clear indicator of one's worthiness of honor in public discourse.

This view was endorsed from several sides of the political spectrum, both socialist and liberal. In an editorial written for the *Hamburger Echo* in 1908 titled "The Notion of Honor from a Capitalist and a Socialist View," socialist publicist and member of the SPD Franz Laufkötter, whose pseudonym was Brutus, explicitly endorsed the idea that honor mainly consists in one's faithfulness to one's convictions. He argued that people in capitalist society seemed to believe that honor was something exterior, something the authorities could give and take. Yet, honor "in the true sense of the word," he wrote, was really a matter of a person's subjective sense of self-worth and the degree to which he was loyal to his own convictions: "Socialism bases honor on the inner worth of people," and people who only cared about external honor, he argued, were "the most characterless people, without conviction or spine."[169] By pointing out how even Christ had been viewed as dishonorable in the eyes of his peers, he argued that these "external" honor codes were merely relative; he equated these so-called honor codes with time-dependent conventions.

From a different political angle, a liberal judge from Breslau, Paul Albers, made a similar argument in the *Berliner Tageblatt* in 1907. He drew on another example to emphasize how relative the "exterior" definition of honor could be— that of Gottfried Kinkel, a professor and revolutionary activist in the 1848 revolutions whom judges deemed dishonorable after the 1848 revolution but who was later heralded as a national hero. Kinkel was exemplary of someone who was faithful to his beliefs and honorable.[170] These discussions about the concept of honor contributed to it remaining so powerful when invoked.

People could appropriate the often-proclaimed "dual nature" of honor (referring to its exterior and interior aspects) to recover their honor against the claims of the judiciary. But the more this happened, the more it seemed impossible to find common ground for using the notion. At the same time, the suspicion that political ideology could be used to cover up the real motives of a base criminal action influenced the judiciary. Thus, most legal scholars seemed to agree that the difference between a dishonorable and an honorable disposition could be equated with the difference between "real" idealism and egoism. In the German Empire, there seemed to be some common ground in the denouncement of certain "dishonorable" people, but it was gradually crumbling away. For the public prosecutor quoted in the beginning of this chapter, it was self-evident that political offenders should receive harsher sentences. This demonstrates that political offenses were also viewed with more suspicion. Increasingly, because of individual claims to honor, it became harder to find a definition of honor on which the consensus could be based.

Notes

1. Hermann Lucas, *Anleitung zur strafrechtlichen Praxis. Ein Beitrag zur Ausbildung unserer jungen Juristen und ein Ratgeber für jüngere Praktiker* (Berlin: Liebmann, 1902), 286–88.
2. Otto Kirchheimer, *Political Justice: The Use of Legal Procedure for Political Ends* (Princeton, NJ: Princeton University Press, 1961).
3. Jean Comaroff and John L. Comaroff, *The Truth about Crime: Sovereignty, Knowledge, Social Order* (Chicago: University of Chicago Press, 2016), 26.
4. Alex Hall, "By Other Means: The Legal Struggle against the SPD in Wilhelmine Germany 1890–1900," *Historical Journal* 17, no. 2 (2009): 365–86, 386.
5. In *Surveiller et punir*, Foucault thematized the "politicized body" of the criminal. My use of the notion of the "apolitical" might be confusing in light of Foucault's use of politicization. For Foucault, the politicized body is the body that is branded as a "social enemy"—in other words, as an enemy of the political community as such. Cf. Michel Foucault, *On the Punitive Society: Lectures at the Collège de France 1972–1973*, ed. Bernard E. Harcourt (London: Palgrave Macmillan, 2015), 21–42. To make Foucault's use of "politicization" compatible with my argument, it is best to distinguish between "political enemies," that is, members of the "criminal counterworld," and "political opponents." I would, however, also argue that "politicization" is better defined as a process that transforms something into an item of political debate in the public sphere. This aligns more closely with German philosopher Jürgen Habermas's theory of the public sphere and how, for instance, Claus Offe used the notion in his *Contradictions of the Welfare State*, trans. John Keane (London: Hutchinson, 1984). With this definition of politicization, the strategy of depoliticization I describe later in this chapter makes more sense. Within this process, depoliticization presupposes that criminal policy was often viewed as a subsystem of society that was not open for political debate.
6. This picture is clearly confirmed by looking at the crimes people from the Northern Rhine region who were deprived of their civil privileges and wanted their rights restored had been sentenced for. See chapter 4.
7. Henze, Klippel, and Kesper-Biermann, "Ideen und Recht," 384; Ortmann, *Machtvolle Verhandlungen*, 202.
8. The penal code distinguished between 1. *Einfacher Diebstahl* (simple theft), 2. *Einfacher Diebstahl im wiederholten Rückfalle* (repeated instances of simple theft), and 3. *Schwerer Diebstahl* (grand theft).
9. For the *Lex Heinze*, see Otto Müller, *Die lex Heinze* (Freiburg: Lehmann, 1900); Edward Ross Dickinson, *Sex, Freedom, and Power in Imperial Germany, 1880–1914* (New York: Cambridge University Press, 2014), 121–24. On the protection of children from sexual seduction, see Tanja Hommen, *Sittlichkeitsverbrechen. Sexuelle Gewalt im Kaiserreich* (Frankfurt a.M.: Campus, 1999), 53–60. For the shift in focus from criminal experts from the *Gauner* to the sex offender, see Becker, *Verderbnis und Entartung*, 21.

10. Cf. Ortmann, *Machtvolle Verhandlungen*, 200–3.
11. Alexander von Öttingen, *Die Moralstatistik. Inductiver Nachweis der Gesetzmässigkeit sittlicher Lebensbewegung im Organismus der Menschheit* (Erlangen: Deichert, 1868), also argued that diminishing levels of piety explained rising levels of crime.
12. Gustav Pfizer, "Die Meineidspest," *Die Grenzboten* 45 (1886): 344–59 and 392–406.
13. Shigema Oba, *Unverbesserliche Verbrecher und ihre Behandlung* (Berlin: Bahr, 1908). Cf. Georg von Mayr, *Statistik und Gesellschaftslehre*, vol. 3 (Tübingen: Mohr, 1917), 517.
14. Alexander von Öttingen, "Über Die Methodische Erhebung und Beurteilung Kriminalstatistischer Daten," *ZStW* 1 (1881): 414–38, 419.
15. Otto Mittelstädt, "Kulturgeschichte und Kriminalstatistik," *ZStW* 4 (1884): 391–414, 404. For the wider criticism that was expressed on the methods of Starke, see Galassi, *Kriminologie*, 103–5.
16. Alfred Kloss, "Der Meineid in Strafsachen, seine Häufigkeit und verhältnismässig seltene Bestrafung. Die Vorschläge zur Abhilfe," *Jahrbuch der Gefängnis-Gesellschaft für die Provinz Sachsen und das Herzogtum Anhalt* 21 (1905): 1–18.
17. Cf. Bernhard Bauer, *Der Eid. Eine Studie* (Heidelberg: Winter, 1884); "Die Eidesnot," *Die Grenzboten* 53 (1894): 256–61; Wilhelm Kulemann, *Die Eidesfrage* (Eisenach: Thüringische Verlagsanstalt, 1904), 35–37. Cf. Ortmann, *Machtvolle Verhandlungen*, 200–3.
18. See, for instance, Erich Wulffen, *Psychologie des Verbrechers*, vol. 2 (Berlin: Langenscheidt, 1908), 324.
19. Cf. Ortmann, *Machtvolle Verhandlungen*, 30–31.
20. Heinrich Sohnrey, *Der Meineid im deutschen Volksbewußtsein* (Leipzig: Werther, 1894), 53.
21. Bruno Blau, *Die Kriminalität der deutschen Juden* (Berlin: Lamm, 1906), 9–10; Franz von Liszt, *Das Problem der Kriminalität der Juden* (Giessen: Töpelmann, 1907); Georg von Mayr, *Statistik und Gesellschaftslehre*, vol. 3 (Tübingen, 1917), 831–32.
22. Verein zur Abwehr des Antisemitismus (Berlin), *Die Wirtschaftliche Lage, soziale Gliederung und die Kriminalstatistik der Juden* (Berlin: Das Verein, 1912).
23. *Statistisches Jahrbuch für den Preussischen Staat*, vol. 12 (Berlin, 1915), 508–9.
24. See, for instance, Rudolf Wassermann, *Beruf, Konfession und Verbrechen. Eine Studie über die Kriminalität der Juden in Vergangenheit und Gegenwart* (Munich: Reinhardt, 1906), 40–41.
25. This was also noted in the editorial piece in *Vorwärts* on the penal law reform: "Der Vorentwurf zum neuen Strafgesetzbuch," *Vorwärts*, 12 November 1909.
26. Hermann Seuffert, *Die Bewegung im Strafrechte während der letzten dreißig Jahre* (Dresden: Zahn & Jaensch, 1901). Cf. Joachim Radkau, *Das Zeitalter der Nervosität. Deutschland zwischen Bismarck und Hitler* (Munich: Econ, 2000).
27. GStA PK Rep. 84a, Nr. 8028, "Mehr Ehrenstrafen!," *Deutsche Tageszeitung*, 4 July 1914.
28. The official statistics were published from 1882.
29. *Monatshefte zur Statistik des Deutschen Reichs* 59, no. 2 (1883): 71, 81.
30. Cf. Carl Heinrici, "Aberkennung der bürgerlichen Ehrenrechte," *Deutsches statistisches Zentralblatt* 5 (1914): 163–66.
31. I calculated the rate based on the total number of regular prison and penitentiary sentences as disenfranchisement could normally only be added on top of a prison/penitentiary sentence.
32. Verdict of the appeal court in Berlin of 19 January 1843. Reprinted in Johann Jacoby, *Vier Fragen beantwortet von einem Ostpreußen* (Leipzig: Hoff, 1863), 43–44.
33. Koselleck, *Preußen zwischen Reform und Revolution*, 411–14.
34. For instance, this quote was cited by SPD politician Arnold Stadthagen in a speech before the Reichstag in 1911: *Stenographische Berichte über die Verhandlungen des Reichstages*, vol. 263 (Berlin, 1911), 4385.
35. Julius Hermann von Kirchmann, *Die Grundbegriffe des Rechts und der Moral als Einleitung in das Studium rechtsphilosophischer Werke* (Berlin: Heimann, 1869), 105.

36. In principle, positive law aimed first to support the idea that only actions could be punished, not intentions. As a classic 1847 handbook by Heinrich Luden stated: "But the mere will, which has not yet become action, does not belong to the realm of law." Heinrich Luden, *Handbuch des teutschen gemeinen und particularen Strafrechtes* (Jena, 1847), 18. Cf. Gustav Radbruch, *Einführung in die Rechtswissenschaft* (Leipzig: Quelle & Meyer, 1910), 9–10.
37. Of course, this thought was already expressed in Wick's philosophy of the punishment of disenfranchisement, but, as I also indicated in chapter 1, many penal codes still looked at class background in determining the nature of one's disposition by using such categories as the *gebildete Stände* (educated classes), who were presumed to have acted out of honorable dispositions. Increasingly, however, scholars argued that the assessment of a person's disposition was an individual moral judgment. Cf. Whitman, *Harsh Justice*, 132–35.
38. Richard Eduard John, *Entwurf mit Motiven zu einem Strafgesetzbuche für den Norddeutschen Bund* (Berlin: Guttentag, 1868), 126. Cf. Marcuse, *Die Ehrenstrafe*, 29–30.
39. Whitman, too, noted that German lawyers became more preoccupied with morality in the second half of the nineteenth century: Whitman, *Harsh Justice*, 132.
40. Fritz van Calker, *Strafrecht und Ethik* (Leipzig: Duncker & Humblot, 1897); Fritz van Calker, *Ethische Werte im Strafrecht* (Berlin: Liebmann, 1904).
41. Calker, *Strafrecht und Ethik*, 28–29.
42. Calker, *Ethische Werte im Strafrecht*, 36–42.
43. See chapter 2.
44. Franz von Liszt, *Der Zweckgedanke im Strafrecht* (Marburg: Pfeil, 1882), 40; Franz von Liszt, "Kriminalpolitische Aufgaben," *ZStW* 10 (1890): 51–83, 62.
45. Franz von Liszt, "Die psychologischen Grundlagen der Kriminalpolitik," *ZStW* 16 (1896): 477–517, 496n. Similarly, Ernst Sichart, a prison director from Ludwigsburg, argued in a 1901 essay for the *ZStW* that disenfranchisement was a necessary element of German criminal policy, but in a 1905 article for the same journal, he argued that the moral disqualification of offenders only compromised their attempts to reintegrate into society: Ernst von Sichart, "Ein Beitrag zur Revision des Strafgesetzbuches für das Deutsche Reich," *ZStW* 21 (1901): 151–96, 178; Ernst von Sichart, "Fehler und Mängel des deutschen Strafgesetzbuches, welche einem wirksamen Strafvollzuge im Wege stehen, samt Besserungsvorschlägen," *ZStW* 25 (1905): 191–218, 205.
46. Adolf Wach, *Die Kriminalistischenschulen und die Strafrechtsreform* (Leipzig: Duncker & Humblot, 1902), 16; Karl von Birkmyer, *Schuld und Gefährlichkeit in ihrer Bedeutung für die Strafbemessung* (Leipzig: Meiner, 1914), 116–32.
47. It was important to "classic" adherents that judges made these distinctions, whereas it was important to the "moderns" that several experts determined the individual treatment of prisoners—for example, prison wardens.
48. Erik Wolf, "Gustav von Radbruch," in idem, ed., *Grosse Rechtsdenker der deutschen Geistesgeschichte*, 713–67 (Tübingen: Mohr, 1963), 716.
49. In the years before the introduction of the Reich Penal Code, Wilhelm I had *de facto* abolished the death penalty in Prussia by commuting all death sentences with an act of sovereign grace. When Max Hödel and Karl Nobiling both attempted to assassinate the emperor in 1878 (attempts that Bismarck later instrumentalized to introduce the Anti-Socialist Laws), Bismarck had pressured Wilhelm I into executing Max Hödel (Karl Nobiling committed suicide) just as the penal code dictated. The death penalty was thus reinstated for the offense of assassination of the head of state. Richard J. Evans, *Rituals of Retribution: Capital Punishment in Germany 1600–1987* (Oxford: Oxford University Press, 1996), 351–61.
50. For the case of the death penalty, this is more complicated. There had always been a distinction between the dishonoring and non-dishonoring execution of the death penalty, but it had generally been abandoned in the nineteenth century. In general, the death penalty came to

be increasingly seen as dishonoring. However, it could be executed in combination with civil degradation or without, which implied that the distinction could still be made.

51. RSTGB §20.
52. Cf. Kesper-Biermann, *Einheit und Recht*, 337–39.
53. It is important to remember that an "honorable disposition" was also often attributed to people sentenced for dueling. In fact, 92 percent of the people sentenced to open custody in 1904 were convicted of dueling. The dueler, after all, was considered to be acting out of a strong emotional attachment to the code of honor. See James Goldschmidt, "Strafen (Haupt- und Nebenstrafen) und verwandte Maßregeln unter Berücksichtigung der den Inhalt der Strafe bestimmenden Grundsätze des Strafvollzugs," in Karl Birkmeyer et al., eds., *Vergleichende Darstellung des deutschen und ausländischen Strafrechts. Vorarbeiten zur deutschen Strafrechtsreform*, vol. 4, 81–470 (Berlin, 1908), 261.
54. Eduard Guckenheimer, *Der Begriff der ehrlosen Gesinnung im Strafrecht. Ein Beitrag zur strafrechtlichen Beurteilung politischer Verbrecher* (Hamburg: Gente, 1921), 18.
55. Consider also the following quote by a legal scholar: "Dishonorable are ways of thinking incited by low and selfish passions that dispense with the qualities of a better character"; Ludwig Fuld, "Das Motiv im deutschen Strafgesetzbuch," *GAS* 31 (1883): 321–25. In a similar vein, one could find the following phrase in August Köhler's handbook on criminal law: "The dishonorable disposition means the moral contempt that one's character traits bring about." August Köhler, *Deutsches Strafrecht. Allgemeiner Teil* (Leipzig, 1917), 593. Cf. Calker, *Ethische Werte im Strafrecht*, 37–38.
56. Helmut Klaere, *Die Entstehung der Schwurgerichte im 19. Jahrhundert*, http://jesz.ajk.elte.hu/klaere3.html (last accessed 29 March 2022).
57. Blasius, *Geschichte der politischen Kriminalität*, 56–57.
58. On the founding of the political police, see Albrecht Funk, *Polizei Und Rechtsstaat: Die Entwicklung des staatlichen Gewaltmonopols in Preussen 1848–1918* (Frankfurt a.M.: Campus, 1986), 257–60.
59. "Gesetz gegen die gemeingefährlichen Bestrebungen der Sozialdemokratie," *Deutsches Reichsgesetzblatt*, vol. 34, 351–58 (Berlin, 1878).
60. One such instance can be found in Wilhelm Kulemann, *Die Sozialdemokratie und deren Bekämpfung. Eine Studie zur Reform des Sozialistengesetzes* (Berlin: Heymann, 1890), 204–5.
61. Vernon L. Lidtke, *Outlawed Party. Social Democracy in Germany* (Princeton, NJ: Princeton University Press, 1966), 78–80; Annelies Laschitza, *Die Liebknechts. Karl und Sophie—Politik und Familie* (Berlin: Aufbau-Verl., 2009), 28–29.
62. Jonathan Sperber, "The Social Democratic Electorate in Imperial Germany," in *Between Reform and Revolution. German Socialism and Communism from 1840 to 1990*, ed. David E. Barclay and Eric D. Weitz, 167–94 (New York: Berghahn Books, 2002), 171–73; James Retallack, *Red Saxony. Election Battles and the Spectre of Democracy in Germany, 1860–1918* (Oxford: Oxford University Press, 2017), 133–35.
63. Kai Müller, *Der Hüter des Rechts. Die Stellung des Reichsgerichts im Deutschen Kaiserreich 1879–1918* (Baden-Baden: Nomos, 1997).
64. E. Künzel, *Der erste Hochverratsprozess vor dem Deutschen Reichsgericht* (Leipzig: Hesse, 1881), 67–73; cf. Heinz-Gerhard Haupt, "Gewalt als Praxis und Herrschaftsmittel. Das deutsche Kaiserreich und die Dritte Republik in Frankreich im Vergleich," in *Das Deutsche Kaiserreich in der Kontroverse*, ed. Sven-Oliver Müller and Cornelius Torp, 154–64 (Göttingen, Vandenhoeck & Ruprecht, 2009), 160–61.
65. Cf. Malte Wilke, *Staatsanwälte als Anwälte des Staates?: Die Strafverfolgungspraxis von Reichsanwaltschaft und Bundesanwaltschaft vom Kaiserreich bis in die frühe Bundesrepublik* (Göttingen: Vandenhoeck & Ruprecht, 2016), 51–54; Joachim Wagner, *Politischer Terrorismus und Strafrecht im Deutschen Kaiserreich von 1871* (Heidelberg: v. Decker, 1981), 332–38. These two

studies give a more complete overview of the grounds on which they were accused and discuss the problems of finding evidence against this group based on §86. The question about the kind of punishment, however, is only marginally addressed in these works.
66. Wagner, *Politischer Terrorismus*, 334.
67. Karl Braun, "Die beiden großen Hochverratsprozesse vor dem RG," *Das Tribunal. Zeitschrift für praktische Strafrechtspflege* 1 (1885): 65–97, 96–97.
68. Künzel, *Der erste Hochverratsprozess*, 71.
69. For a description of the criminologists' ideas of criminal gangs as a *counterworld* to normal society, see Becker, *Verderbnis und Entartung*, 177–254.
70. Gustav Otto, *Die Verbrecherwelt von Berlin* (Berlin: J. Guttentag, 1886), 85.
71. Andreas Fleiter, "Strafen auf dem Weg zum Sozialismus. Sozialistische Standpunkte zu Kriminalität und Strafe vor dem Ersten Weltkrieg," *Mitteilungsblatt des Instituts für soziale Bewegungen* 26 (2001): 105–38, 117.
72. *Verhandlungen des Parteitags der deutschen Sozialdemokratie St. Gallen* (Zürich, 1888), 40.
73. See, for example, Wilhelm Liebknecht, *Hochverrath und Revolution* (Zürich: Verlag der Volksbuchhandlung, 1887), v. Cf. August Bebel, *Attentate und Sozialdemokratie* (Berlin: Vorwärts, 1905).
74. The Kingdom of Belgium was still one of these sanctuaries at that time.
75. Braun, "Die beiden großen Hochverratsprozesse," 164.
76. Ibid.
77. Carl Stooss, *Die Grundzüge des schweizerischen Strafrechts* (Basel: Georg, 1892), 407.
78. Guckenheimer, *Begriff der ehrlosen Gesinnung*, 61–62.
79. Ibid., 62.
80. The outcome of this trial was also debated in the Reichstag, and the use of the statements by the *agent provocateur* Mr. Horsch, especially, provoked controversy. The issue was whether this witness was indeed an *agent provocateur* and how much his statements influenced the judges' verdict. Even the conservative authorities, however, seemed to agree that the use of *agents provocateurs* was illegitimate. As the Prussian Minister Robert von Puttkammer stated, only secret agents were worthy of and necessary for state action, and he believed Rumpf made legitimate use only of these; *Stenographische Berichte über die Verhandlungen des Reichstages*, vol. 66 (Berlin, 1882), 317ff.
81. August Bebel, *Aus meinem Leben*, vol. 3 (Stuttgart: Dietz, 1914), 220.
82. Wagner, *Politischer Terrorismus*, 329.
83. See the files of the office of the highest public prosecutor at the Reichsgericht: BA-BL, R 3003.
84. "Gesetz gegen den verbrecherischen und gemeingefährlichen Gebrauch von Sprengstoffen," *Deutsches Reichsgesetzblatt* (1884): 61–64.
85. Sepp Oerter, *Acht Jahre Zuchthaus. Lebenserinnerungen* (Berlin: Verlag der Tribüne, 1908).
86. Hartmut Wiedner, "Soldatenmißhandlungen Im Wilhelminischen Kaiserreich (1890–1914)," *Archiv Für Sozialgeschichte* 22 (1982): 159–99.
87. BA-BL, R. 3003 C3/07, Karl Liebknecht, "Rekrutenabschied," *Die Junge Garde*, 22 September 1906.
88. Cited by Bebel: *Stenographische Berichte über die Verhandlungen des Reichstages*, vol. 148 (Berlin, 1897), 4692.
89. Ibid., 4691–701.
90. The influential progressive prison reformer Carl Krohne, for instance, also warned of *heeresfeindliche agitation* among the youth in a memorandum for the penal reform of 1909. See BA-BL 3001/5909, "Freiheitsstrafen und sichernde Maßnahmen des Vorentwurfs."
91. Cited in *Lübecker Volksboten*, 3 March 1908.
92. Olshausen, *Kommentar zu den Strafgesetzen des Deutschen Reiches*, vol. 1. See also the Introduction.
93. *Der Hochverratsprozeß gegen Karl Liebknecht* (Berlin: Dietz, 1907), 47.

94. Ibid., 79.
95. Laschitza, *Die Liebknechts*, 61.
96. Cited in "Das rettende Zuchthaus," *Volksstimme*, 29 February 1908.
97. Rudolf Oestreich, *Wegen Hochverrats im Zuchthaus* (Berlin: Verlag der Tribüne, 1913), 10. Cf. Ulrich Linse, *Organisierter Anarchismus im Deutschen Kaiserreich von 1871* (Berlin: Duncker & Humblot, 1969), 36–40.
98. Oestreich, *Wegen Hochverrats im Zuchthaus*, 9.
99. *Stenographische Berichte über die Verhandlungen des Reichstages*, vol. 232 (Berlin, 1908), 4469.
100. Karl Liebknecht, "Kritische Betrachtungen," in *Gesammelte Reden und Schriften*, vol. 2 (Berlin: Dietz, 1985), 29.
101. *Statistik des Deutschen Reichs*, vol. 257 (Berlin, 1911).
102. George Otto Kent, *Arnim and Bismarck* (Oxford: Clarendon Press, 1968), 89–95; Otto Pflanze, *Bismarck and the Development of Germany*, vol. 2 (Princeton, NJ: Princeton University Press, 1990), 230–33.
103. Kent, *Arnim and Bismarck*, 144–75.
104. Franz von Holtzendorff, *Rechtsgutachten erstattet zum Process des Grafen H. v. Arnim* (Munich: Oldenbourg, 1875).
105. Harry von Arnim, *Pro Nihilo! Vorgeschichte des Arnim'schen Processes* (Zürich, 1876).
106. *Der Proceß Arnim. Dargestellt von einem alten Juristen* (Heidelberg: Bassermann, 1877).
107. Hall, "By Other Means," 369–70.
108. Kirchheimer defined this as the "derivative political trial" in his *Political Justice*, 46.
109. Ignaz Auer, *Nach zehn Jahren*, 224–32. Wilhelm, *Das Deutsche Kaiserreich*, 288.
110. Wilhelm Gustav Karl Starke, *Verbrechen und Verbrecher in Preußen 1854–1878. Eine kulturgeschichtliche Studie* (Berlin: Enslin, 1884), 84. There are more examples of crime statisticians defending this thesis, such as in a law student's book on the origins of crime from 1899: "In the numerous class of laborers, more generally than heretofore class and power consciousness have awoken, which often drives them to raw violent acts." Heinrich Wilhelm Müller, *Untersuchungen über die Bewegung der Criminalität in ihrem Zusammenhang mit den wirtschaftlichen Verhältnissen* (Halle a.S.: Kaemmerer & Co., 1899), 56. This thesis was fiercely disputed by Marxist criminologist Willem Adriaan Bonger in his "Verbrechen und Sozialismus," *Die Neue Zeit* 30 (1912): 801–67.
111. Starke, *Verbrechen und Verbrecher*.
112. Karl Frohme, *Politische Polizei und Justiz im monarchischen Deutschland. Erinnerungen* (Hamburg: Auer, 1926), 117–41.
113. Hans Blum, *Die Lügen unserer Sozialdemokratie. Nach amtlichen Quellen enthüllt und widerlegt* (Wismar: Hinstorff, 1891), 385. Cited in Frohme, *Politische Polizei*, 128.
114. Antonius Romen, *Meineid und Socialdemokratie. Ein Beitrag zu einer brennenden Tagesfrage* (Berlin, 1892).
115. Frohme, *Politische Polizei*, 122–24.
116. Ibid., 129–32.
117. Frome cites many critics of these practices, not all of whom were affiliated with the SPD, such as liberal politician Eugen Richter: ibid., 134.
118. For more details about Ludwig Schröder and his role as the delegate to the emperor, see Hans Georg Kirchhoff, *Die staatliche Sozialpolitik im Ruhrbergbau 1871–1914* (Cologne: Westdeutsche Verlag, 1958), 56–59.
119. Franz Lütgenau, *Der Essener Meineids-Prozeß vom 14. bis 17. August 1895. Geschichte und Glossen* (Berlin: Vorwärts, 1895), 3–6.
120. Hall, "By Other Means," 382. Cf. Lütgenau, *Essener Meineids-Prozeß*, 30–33.
121. Lütgenau, *Essener Meineids-Prozeß*, 16.

122. Ibid.; cf. *Berliner Volkszeitung*, 19 August 1895.
123. Ignaz Jastrow, "Die Lehre des Essener Meineidsprozesses," *Das freie Wort* 10, no. 23 (1911): 892–901, 900.
124. Hall, "By Other Means," 384.
125. For a discussion of the legal debate about this question, see Carl Legien, *Das Koalitionsrecht der deutschen Arbeiter in Theorie und Praxis*. *Denkschrift der Generalkommission der Gewerkschaften Deutschlands* (Hamburg: Verlag der Generalkommission der Gewerkschaften Deutschlands, 1899), 33–75.
126. This case was extensively narrated in Hugo Friedländer, *Interessante kriminal-prozesse von kulturhistorischer Bedeutung*, vol. 8 (Berlin, 1913), 104–75. Cf. *Adolf Stöcker und die Angriffe seiner Gegner im Lichte der Wahrheit* (Berlin: Warneck, 1901).
127. Norman Domeier, *Der Eulenburg-Skandal. Eine politische Kulturgeschichte des Kaiserreichs* (Frankfurt a.M., 2010), 269–326.
128. Lèse-majesté was not a form of high treason, so it was tried in lower-level courts.
129. Wilhelm, *Das Deutsche Kaiserreich*, 335. Cf. Kirchheimer, *Political Justice*, 35.
130. Hall, "By Other Means."
131. Goldberg, *Honor, Politics, and the Law*, 101.
132. Andrea Hartmann, *Majestätsbeleidigung und Verunglimpfung des Staatsoberhauptes* (Berlin: Berliner Wissenschafts-Verlag, 2006), 165–66. The architect Ludwig Feuth expressed very strong criticism of the use of pretrial detention in the German Empire. See Ludwig Feuth, *Humanität und Strafverfolgung im XX. Jahrhundert* (Berlin, 1908).
133. Cf. Wilhelm, *Das Deutsche Kaiserreich*, 386–93.
134. Gary D. Stark, *Banned in Berlin: Literary Censorship in Imperial Germany 1871–1918* (New York: Berghahn, 2009), 91–92; Hartmann, *Majestätsbeleidigung*, 136.
135. The verdict was published in the *Volkszeitung*, 5 November 1898.
136. "Die Krücken der Ehrfurcht," *Hamburger Anzeiger*, 8 November 1898.
137. Thomas Vormbaum, *Einführung in die moderne Strafrechtsgeschichte* (Berlin: Springer, 2011), 84.
138. Rainer Schröder, "Die strafrechtliche Bewältigung der Streiks durch Obergerichtliche Rechtssprechung zwischen 1870 und 1914," *Archiv für Sozialgeschichte* 31 (1991): 85–102, 91.
139. Gerhard A. Ritter, *Arbeiterbewegung, Parteien und Parlamentarismus* (Göttingen: Vandenhoeck & Ruprecht, 1976), 71–73.
140. Klaus Saul, "Der Staat und die 'Mächte des Umsturzes.' Ein Beitrag zu den Methoden antisozialistischer Repression und Agitation vom Scheitern des Sozialistengesetzes bis zur Jahrhundertwende," *Archiv für Sozialgeschichte* 12 (1972): 293–350.
141. Ibid.
142. Advocatus, "Der Umsturz des Strafrechts," *Die Neue Zeit* 13 (1895): 780–87, 780.
143. Cf. Margaret Lavinia Anderson, *Practicing Democracy: Elections and Political Culture in Imperial Germany* (Princeton, NJ: Princeton University Press, 2000), 246–49.
144. Cf. Nipperdey, *Machtstaat vor der Demokratie*, 714. The official title of the bill was "Gesetz zum Schutze des gewerblichen Arbeitsverhältnisses" (Law for the Protection of Commercial Employment).
145. Ernst Johann, *Reden des Kaisers* (Munich: Dtv-Verlag, 1977), 79–81.
146. John C. G. Röhl, *Wilhelm II.: The Kaiser's Personal Monarchy, 1888–1900* (Cambridge: Cambridge University Press, 2015), 873–83.
147. "Denkschrift, betreffend die Ausschreitungen bei den Arbeitskämpfen der letzten Jahre," in *Stenographische Berichte über die Verhandlungen des Reichstages*, vol. 174 (Berlin, 1899), 2248–98.

148. An example of the phrases used in the memorandum translates as follows: "Repeatedly, the terrorism of the non-residents has repeatedly been directed against the relatives of workers willing to work," ibid., 2263.
149. Legien, *Das Koalitionsrecht*.
150. Support of the moral entitlement of workers to protest their contract was also found in scholarly works on contract law, most notably in Philipp Lotmar, *Der unmoralische Vertrag. Insbesondere nach gemeinem Recht* (Leipzig: Duncker & Humblot, 1896); Philipp Lotmar, *Der Arbeitsvertrag nach dem Privatrecht des Deutschen Reiches*, vol. 1 (Leipzig: Duncker & Humblot, 1902), 116–19; Emil Steinbach, *Die Moral als Schranke des Rechtserwerbs und der Rechtsausübung* (Vienna: Manz, 1898), 73.
151. Max Weber noted this in his review of Lotmar's book: "Rezension von: Lotmar, Philipp, Der Arbeitsvertrag," in Max Weber, *Gesamtausgabe*, vol. 8, 37–61 (Tübingen: Mohr Siebeck, 2005), 51.
152. A collection of the reactions of the press can be found in BA-BL R 1501/106846.
153. BA-BL R 1501/106846, *Vorwärts*, 2 February 1899.
154. BA-BL R 1501/106846. *Vorwärts*, 8 February 1899, and 13 February 1899.
155. Wolfgang J. Mommsen, *Max Weber und die deutsche Politik, 1890–1920* (Tübingen: Mohr Siebeck, 2004), 122.
156. Wilhelm, *Das Deutsche Kaiserreich*, 386–93; Gerd Linnemann, *Klassenjustiz und Weltfremdheit, Deutsche Justizkritik 1890–1914* (Kiel, 1989), 134–35.
157. BA-BL, R. 3001/6035, "Der Vorentwurf zum neuen Strafgesetzbuch," *Vorwärts*, 12 September 1909.
158. Raphael, *Recht und Ordnung*, 141–44.
159. *Protokoll über die Verhandlungen des Parteitages der Sozialdemokratischen Partei Deutschlands abgehalten zu Halle a.S. vom 12. bis 18. Oktober 1890* (Berlin, 1890), 5.
160. "Die Hamburger Accordmaurer vor dem Parteigericht," *Sozialistische Monatshefte* 5 (1901): 728–30. See also Eduard Bernstein, *Die Geschichte der Berliner Arbeiter-Bewegung* 3 (Berlin: Vorwärts, 1910), 147.
161. *Protokoll über die Verhandlungen des Parteitages der Sozialdemokratischen Partei Deutschlands abgehalten zu Lübeck vom 22. bis 28. September 1901* (Berlin, 1901), 218.
162. Ibid.
163. An example was H. Schadebach, "Der Ehrbegriff der Arbeiterschaft," *Vorwärts*, 14 September 1901.
164. "Die Hamburger Akkordmaurer und der Parteitag," *Lübecker Volksbote*, 28 August 1901.
165. See Andreas Fleiter, "Strafen auf dem Weg zum Sozialismus. Sozialistische Standpunkte zu Kriminalität und Strafe vor dem Ersten Weltkrieg," *Mitteilungsblatt des Instituts für soziale Bewegungen* 26 (2001): 105–38, 118.
166. Cf. August Bebel, "Die Gewerbeordnungs-Novelle," *Die Neue Zeit* 9 (1891): 364–74, 406–15, 406–7.
167. Ernst Francke, "Das deutsche Auswanderungsgesetz," *Archiv für Sozialwissenschaft und Sozialpolitik* 11 (1897): 181–214, 187–89.
168. Frevert, *Men of Honor*, 136–49.
169. Reprinted in *Lübecker Volksboten* (supplement), 9 March 1908. In a way, these remarks are quite similar to the critique of the dueling aristocracy mentioned in chapter 1. In this case, however, these remarks were not as saturated with anti-statism as the criticism of these commentators was.
170. Paul Albers, "Der Ehrverlust," *Berliner Tageblatt*, 15 December 1907; cf. De Groot, "Politieke Misdadigers of Eerloze Criminelen?," 40–43.

Chapter 4

"THE CHAIN OF DISHONOR"
Petitioning for Rehabilitation in Imperial Germany

Peter J.¹ was an auctioneer and judicial consultant of Wegberg who was convicted of embezzlement and forgery in 1888. In 1891, he sent a sixteen-page petition to Kaiser Wilhelm II asking for the restoration of his civil privileges. Peter J. was clearly sensitive about his reputation, and the suspension of his civil privileges vitally undermined his good name, he felt:

> I feel it is a source of endless unhappiness to have lost my civil privileges. Since my release, I have been living reclusively and quietly, I do not interact with people at all, because I have such a mind and such a character that I am ashamed to go out because I think that the people will see my status as an ex-convict written on my forehead.²

In a different passage, he described experiencing this secondary punishment (*Nachstrafe*) as the harshest part of his conviction and claimed that the shame of it forced him to lead a sequestered life. A district commissioner (*Landrat*) confirmed Peter J.'s genuine sense of shame, stating that Peter J. had in fact retreated from public life.³ When his wife became dependent on the poor relief system—something he had hoped to avoid at all costs—he felt further disgraced. In his experience, the stigma associated with poor relief was significantly worse than being dependent on the support of relatives.

Peter J.'s beliefs about his civil position contributed to his sensitivity to the effects of his conviction. In his petition, he explained that people in the town knew him for his honesty and his professional competence. He had taken on an "honorary post" as a lawyer in Aachen, which meant he did not receive any financial compensation for it. He also emphasized his constant deference (*Ehrfurcht*) and regard (*Ansehen*) for the court in all his conduct. He expressed his loyalty and obedience to and reverence for the kaiser, along with his pride in having been

---

Notes from this chapter begin on page 146.

mercifully released from prison on the birthday of Wilhelm II's grandfather, the "glorious hero kaiser (*Heldenkaiser*), Wilhelm, the Victorious."[4]

Peter J.'s petition demonstrates the intimate connection between policies of stigmatization and mercy in the penal system of the German Empire. Disenfranchisement and the stigma of imprisonment could only be lifted by a special act of sovereign grace. Therefore, people like Peter J. were eager to demonstrate their loyalty and obedience to the kaiser in the hope that they would be officially rehabilitated. At the same time, these two core components of the felony disenfranchisement policy, stigmatization and mercy, came under pressure, became contested, and were then reinvented during the time of the German Empire. Several changes in German society, such as urbanization and the increased mobility of citizens, together with the expanding bureaucratic administration of the German nation-state, had significant effects on the functioning of stigmas and the possibility of being rehabilitated. Meanwhile, disenfranchised felons increasingly discarded the traditional vocabulary of mercy and started to deploy different rhetoric. The goal of this chapter, therefore, is to describe how disenfranchisement affected the lives of individual ex-offenders in the German Empire and the efforts they undertook to try and get rehabilitated.

Anxiety about "Dishonored Felons" Passing as Normal Citizens

Without a doubt, stigmatization was key to the punishment of disenfranchisement. After all, disenfranchisement had an expressive, public function, entailing a full-fledged revocation of one's citizenship rights. It was therefore crucial for fellow citizens to be aware of an offender's stigma. However, even though the word "stigma" originally signified visible marks like tattoos and brands used to identify people who had committed crimes or otherwise deviated from the norm, the stigma attached to dishonored ex-convicts in German society was generally invisible.[5] The notion of "stigma," therefore, is closely related to that of "passing." In Ervin Goffman's famous theory of stigma, its very invisibility is critical because its bearer can then choose freely whether to reveal it. Stigmatized individuals can either try to pass as "normal" by adjusting their conduct to general behavioral norms or accept the stigma as part of their identity. Goffman called this "stigma management."[6]

Prior to 1870, imprisonment, stigmatization, and disenfranchisement were intertwined in the penal policy of the German states as the stigma of disenfranchisement was closely connected to the offender's place of residence. Because the German states had no overseas colonies, no legal punishment could compare to deportation, as practiced in the British, French, and Russian empires.[7] All prison sentences were carried out within the borders of the German states. A guiding idea behind the penal policies was that felons would be reintegrated into their former lives after their incarceration. This meant that offenders were often incarcerated far away from their hometowns and returned to their communities afterward.

In 1797, in order to prevent discharged prisoners from roaming the towns where penal institutions were located, the Prussian government decreed that discharged prisoners had to settle in the town they had resided in before their conviction.[8] In fact, a compulsory passport (*Zwangspaß*) often forced discharged prisoners to move back to their pre-conviction town.[9] Berlin municipal authorities, in particular, coerced discharged prisoners to reunite with their families in their hometowns outside of Berlin to prevent them from staying in the city.[10] In addition, some prisoners were visibly marked: before their release, their hair would be shaven off, forcing them to carry a demeaning symbol of incarceration into the outside world.[11] Such regulations and practices made it nearly impossible for a criminal conviction to be hidden from the community. Moreover, after prisoners returned to their hometowns (*Heimat* or *Heimatsort*), the people there were responsible for helping them in their future endeavors; in most cases, they would be handed over to poor relief.[12] These practices made the local community a centerpiece of punishment and rehabilitation in the first half of the nineteenth century. The connection between imprisonment and the convicts' return to their local communities undergirded the stigma they experienced.

This practice also suggests that incarcerating criminals, that is, putting them beyond the public gaze, was not motivated by growing concerns about their "privacy." Pieter Spierenburg famously argued that the need for imprisonment arose when bourgeois citizens of various western European states started to experience shame about the "spectacle" of punishment.[13] That workhouses, which were mainly used in the political struggle against poverty and vagrancy during the early modern period, were now remodeled as places for the execution of various punishments (*Straf-Anstalte*), including corporal punishments and the death penalty, supports Spierenburg's view.[14] Consequently, even though the 1794 General State Laws for the Prussian States (Allgemeines Landrecht für die Preußischen Staaten) had already replaced most of the punishments of public display with imprisonment, the Brandenburg House of Representatives still agreed, in 1843, to the policy of carrying out corporal punishment on people from the working classes (including women) inside penitentiaries.[15] Spierenburg sees this long-term evolution toward hiding the administration of punishment as evidence of Norbert Elias's idea of the civilization process: the repression of violent impulses and the internalization of norms of polite behavior were clearly reflected in the public's growing aversion to viewing the execution of punishments.[16]

By the mid-nineteenth century, imprisonment had therefore largely replaced "the spectacle of punishment" inherited from the *Ancien Régime*.[17] Yet, some people who were involved in early nineteenth-century penal policy argued that some offenders' reputations were so damaged by their incarceration that they could not possibly lead a "normal" life in their hometowns. Many authorities therefore felt that it was in prisoners' best interest not to return to their hometowns after their release. Even though deportation was not common in the German Empire, sentences were nevertheless often reduced in exchange for voluntary emigration.[18] The extent to which this emigration was truly "voluntary" probably differed from case to case, but the authorities did not view it as a penal measure. The number of people who migrated under these circumstances is not clear, but it was surely substantial.[19] Along with the general wave of transatlantic migration, this practice started with the abolition of the redemption system in the United States in the 1820s.[20] For example, approximately three thousand ex-convicts migrated from the Kingdom of Hanover to the United States between 1832 and 1866.[21] Some convicted felons also went to South America, as, for example, in the case of a group of discharged prisoners from Mecklenburg who emigrated to Brazil after their release.[22] An influential prison official defended this practice as a two-edged measure since the ex-convicts were able to start a new life without the burden of their stigma, on the one hand, while local officials reduced the risk of recidivism, on the other.[23]

Indeed, voluntary exile had a strong connection with disenfranchisement. People deprived of their civil privileges often found it very difficult to reintegrate into their communities, either because their reputations were too tarnished or because they simply could no longer exercise their professions. In fact, judges sometimes suggested voluntary exile as an alternative to incarceration when they believed a penitentiary conviction and its consequences would be too harmful.[24] Thus, certain offenders enjoyed the class privilege of being able to choose emigration over incarceration. The most famous example of this was perhaps Friedrich List, the public official from the Kingdom of Württemberg who migrated to the United States after he was convicted of publishing and distributing a highly critical petition about the malfunctioning of the Württemberg bureaucracy in 1821.[25]

This practice—known as "transportation" rather than deportation—came to an end in the early 1860s, although its use had been diminishing since the late 1840s.[26] This decrease was not due to stricter border control or restrictions on immigration in countries like the United States. Rather, other "regular" migrants, concerned that (ex-)convicts could undermine the reputation of migrants in general, agitated to abolish this practice. They increasingly lamented the dangers such offenders posed to other migrants during their travels west. Consequently, migrant societies wanted to restrict access to the ships sailing west and asked the consul in Hamburg to prevent prison governors from sending inmates for transportation, and they were successful.[27] This meant that disenfranchised felons lost the option of transportation as an alternative to incarceration in the German Empire, so that they had to reintegrate into society on German soil.

At the same time, the measures taken to prevent the movement of ex-convicts in the early nineteenth century largely aligned with the German states' policies on geographic mobility. Citizens of various German states did not have the unconditional right to settle in different communities until the Freedom of Movement Act of 1867 was implemented, guaranteeing free travel and settlement for German citizens within the borders of the North German Confederation.[28] This new regulation actually also included ex-convicts, unless a court explicitly ruled that they needed to be under police surveillance,[29] so that ex-convicts could more easily escape their stigma, albeit on German soil. As a result, the Freedom of Movement Act, along with the related phenomena of a rural exodus (*Landflucht*) and urbanization, deeply impacted disenfranchisement. The essential connection between imprisonment, stigma, and the ex-convict's local community no longer existed.

Arguably, this undermined the effectiveness of disenfranchisement as a stigmatizing punishment, or at least rendered the "invisibility" of the stigma much more pertinent. In 1878, these developments led Guido von Held, the governor of the penitentiary in Spandau, to conclude that released prisoners in the German Empire were not branded as they had been before but had to deal with an invisible or internal stigma (*innerliche Brandmarkung*).[30] Many citizens were preoccupied by the notion that criminals could "pass" as normal citizens, especially given the living circumstances in the metropolises: in a big city (like Berlin), people could blend in much more easily without worrying that their "true identity" might be uncovered.[31] Fear of the growing cities and the complexity, obscurity, and anonymity of life in the metropolis thus generated anxieties about criminality.[32] Public prosecutor Gustav Otto brilliantly captured this anxiety in his book *Berlin's Criminal World*, which he filled with descriptions of criminals blending into society while imitating the behavior of "normal" citizens:

> The clueless citizen or visitor in Berlin who walks around, goes to restaurants and looks at the sights doesn't realize that a large number of the people he comes into contact with who offer him their services or who actually serve him are really subjects with a lengthy criminal record. . . . The Berlin criminal . . . is generally polite and humble and has the urbane sensibilities that life in a big city impresses even upon its lower-class residents. His appearance is not unkempt and filthy. Rather, he is, as long as he can afford it, well-kempt and well-dressed, even elegant, and he goes further in ensuring a fine appearance by keeping his skin clean and taking good care of his hair and beard.[33]

The anxiety Otto expressed about criminals' "passing" was ubiquitous in discussions on crime and punishment at the time.[34] This anxiety persisted into the twentieth century, as evidenced by the 1906 affair that came to be known as the "Köpenickiade," in which discharged prisoner Friedrich Wilhelm Voigt tricked Prussian soldiers into believing he was a superior officer to steal money from the city treasury.[35] The same anxiety about passing also affected public debate about the efficacy of felony disenfranchisement. For instance, a public prosecutor from

Ulm named Elwert complained in the journal *Das Recht* that disenfranchisement was "not a form of public branding," much to his regret. Since dishonored criminals were no longer recognizable as such, he advocated that these sentences at least be published somewhere: "the traitor to his country, the perjurer, the pimp, the marriage imposter, the dealer in stolen goods . . . all these people should be subject to public censure by having their sentences published alongside their names."[36]

Keeping Track of Offenders in the Criminal Registry

If disenfranchisement's invisibility rendered the stigma of the punishment ineffective, why would people still be interested in legal rehabilitation? Was it even something disenfranchised felons pursued? In fact, many influential scholars believed that most offenders were not interested in getting their rights restored. In the second half of the nineteenth century, several international circles of legal scholars, lawyers, and prison directors debated such topics. The most famous of these was the Internationale Kriminalistische Vereinigung (IKV, the International Criminal Law Assocation), which the legal scholars Franz von Liszt (German), Adolphe Prins (Belgian), and Gerard van Hamel (Dutch) founded in 1889. The IKV's members were mostly left-liberal legal scholars, criminologists, and lawyers who were strongly associated with the "modern" approach to criminal law. The society served as a platform for those who wished to reform the penal system, both in Germany and in other parts of Europe.[37]

Ernst Delaquis's presentation on the topic of rehabilitation in different countries during an IKV meeting in 1906 sparked debate among scholars regarding criminals' interest in their civil privileges. Delaquis was a Swiss-German lecturer at Berlin University, Lizst's right-hand man between 1907 and 1914, and had been collecting material on the topic of rehabilitation for his *Habilitation*.[38] He was a staunch advocate of granting offenders the chance to have their rights restored. The director of the Moabit penitentiary, Karl Finkelnburg, however, argued that most offenders did not attach much value to their civil privileges: "Most people don't even think about this loss. They leave the prison and are just happy that they don't have to deal with any administration anymore."[39] He based this judgment on his personal experience, claiming that he had only once ever encountered a former inmate who wished to have his rights restored: a construction foreman whose subordinates refused to work under him. In this meeting, the Dutch society founder Van Hamel, like Finkelnburg, rejected the idea that a formal procedure for petitioning for rehabilitation was needed, arguing that most Dutch criminals did not value honor much anyway.[40]

Yet many more people petitioned for the restoration of their civil privileges than Finkelnburg suggested at the assembly. The files of the governmental offices of the districts of Aachen and Düsseldorf, where the authorities dealt with petitions like Peter J.'s much more frequently than Finkelnburg led his colleagues to believe, confirm this.[41] Ex-offenders actively sought ways to be rehabilitated as normal citizens, relying on the legal and administrative possibilities available in the German Empire at the time. Any and every request made to reverse disenfranchisement undermined claims that disenfranchised felons did not care about their civil privileges. Thus, despite objections to generating a procedure for it, rehabilitation was a real possibility for disfranchised felons in the German Empire. Legal scholars' long neglect of rehabilitation is no reason to assume felons did not seek it.[42]

Most rehabilitation seekers handwrote their petitions themselves. A general petition typically contained a statement of the nature of the punishment, an elaboration of the difficulties the punishment had wrought in the petitioner's daily life, and an appeal to the mercy of the authorities. In some instances, petitioners also elaborated on the details of their offense to explain why they had committed the crime. The petitioners could draw on examples from several practical guides on communication between citizens and the authorities that were available at that time: the so-called *Briefsteller*.[43] In a few cases, the petitioners did not write the petitions themselves, as was clear from the signature not matching the handwriting of the letter. Unfortunately, it is unclear whether a family member, the clerk of the local police office (*Revierschreiber*), or someone else wrote these petitions. Nonetheless, given Germany's high literacy rate at that time, it is not surprising that many petitioners wrote on their own behalf.[44]

Peter J.'s case initially seems to confirm that disenfranchisement only had a stigmatizing effect in small communities. His community of Wegberg was certainly small enough that fellow townspeople would have known about his conviction. This also explains his feeling as if the conviction were written on his forehead. Yet, Peter J. also claimed that people knew about his conviction even before meeting him. For instance, he found it very difficult to find a job, even though he often kept silent about his criminal conviction. He suggested that potential employers in the entire Rhine region somehow had this information and rejected him on account of it. He also accused people of exploiting him by offering him a low salary because of his standing as a "dishonored citizen." In fact, he argued that the disenfranchisement held him back the most since many employers accepted ex-offenders in their businesses, "but only if they were still in possession of their civil privileges." This suggests that whether convicts had been given a "regular" prison sentence or had lost their civil privileges really made a difference.

As noted in chapter 2, disenfranchisement was about more than just losing the right to vote. The punishment affected one's entire functioning in German society. Private organizations, like workers' unions, depended on disenfranchisement as a means of controlling their membership. It was similar with insurance funds.

Thus, disenfranchisement was interwoven with the emerging German social state in many ways. Indeed, Julius S., a mine worker from Bochum, convicted for perjury, was a victim of this policy. His criminal conviction and disenfranchisement resulted in him losing his "first-class" membership in an insurance fund, causing him to eventually lose his right to a worker's pension. He petitioned in 1892 to get his rights restored so he would once again be eligible for first-class membership.[45] Some additional consequences of disenfranchisement did not follow directly from the law but were nevertheless highly restrictive. For example, being without the civil privileges made it more difficult to find housing, to obtain credit, or to find a job as many institutions required a *polizeiliche Führungszeugnis* (a certificate of good conduct from the police), and the police declined requests from those not in possession of their civil privileges.[46] This highlights a second reason ex-cons sought rehabilitation in the German Empire: there was a nationally coordinated criminal registry.[47]

During the 1880s, the uniform, decentralized criminal registry enabled officials to more effectively keep track of criminal records across multiple institutions within the empire.[48] It was undeniably a technology of bureaucratic surveillance as any interested authorities could reconstruct people's "criminal careers."[49] As many historians have argued, the creation of technologies of surveillance like the criminal registry was entangled with questions of security.[50] Many European countries developed criminal registries in the second half of the nineteenth century due to the intense international discussion and collaboration that characterized the emerging field of criminological science. Numerous international conferences allowed leading scholars to exchange ideas about criminal sciences and policy. During the 1876 International Conference on Criminology in Budapest, criminal registries were a central point of debate, and it was unanimously decided there that they were key to determining rates of recidivism.[51]

Germany implemented the criminal registry several years after other countries in Europe had done so. In 1882, the German Empire had decentralized the administration of the registry, which meant that criminal histories were collected and registered in convicts' places of birth. As a result, the information pertaining to a single person was kept in one place instead of being scattered throughout the entire country, even if that person had been sentenced by different courts in different towns.[52] In general, the records were kept at a special office under the governance of the state prosecutor in the local municipality. This decentralized system contrasted with centralized systems featuring a single storage site for all information about criminal convictions. Furthermore, the constituent states, not the imperial government, set the regulations for how the criminal registry was to be managed.

This way of organizing the criminal registry meant that the courts of the German Empire and the local offices of the state prosecutors had to be in active communication. The protocols dictated that court officials were to request information from the criminal registry, and then state prosecutors were to send the information on a form specially designed for the purpose, known as the "excerpt" from the criminal registry. Consequently, local authorities often had to deal with petitions from people who now lived far away. Josef S., for example, lived and worked in Liberec (Bohemia) but was afraid that his employer would find out about his disenfranchisement by a court in Düsseldorf. In his petition of December 1896, he claimed that nobody in Liberec knew about his conviction, but his anxiety about being exposed was so strong that it remained even after he moved.[53] It is impossible to assess whether his anxieties were justified, but the implementation of the criminal registry did facilitate communication across borders about prior convictions.[54]

Of course, military officials were also interested in the emergence of the criminal registry and attached great value to the information it contained. The German Imperial Admiralty Staff, for example, utilized it to assess young men who voluntarily joined the navy and applied to become sea captains. In 1907, the staff complained that many had positive references from the local authorities but turned out to have lengthy criminal records, so it demanded that civil adminis-

Figure 4.1. Cartoonist Thomas Theodor Heine mocks German officials' preoccupation with a criminal record. "Throw him out, the guy was in prison once," a police officer says about an individual who is about to enter heaven. Thomas Theodor Heine, "Zur Fürsorge für entlassene Sträflinge," *Simplicissimus* 11, no. 41 (1906): 658. Courtesy Klassik Stiftung Weimar.

trations mention whether an applicant had a criminal record in their letters of recommendation. Only then could they determine whether the applicants had "the necessary moral dignity" to join the navy.[55] The Minister of the Interior supported them in this, writing a circular to the local authorities demanding that they follow this directive. This directive combined with the public's strong interest in the previous convictions of citizens to give the criminal registry an important place in German society.[56]

"The Whole or Partial Recovery of the Decrease in Moral and Legal Honor"

The implementation and development of the criminal registry greatly impacted rehabilitation. Expungement now became an integral part of legal rehabilitation—as is apparent in various studies and articles on this topic. In the earliest encyclopedic entries on rehabilitation, the notion was defined in a legally positivistic way. Karl Buchner defined it in Welcker and Rotteck's 1865 *Staatslexicon* as: "The cancellation of legal incapacities resulting from a sentence."[57] While Buchner primarily focused on the "legal incapacities" (loss of civil privileges) that followed from a punishment, later scholars included non-legal elements of rehabilitation in their definitions as well. In a 1913 book on rehabilitation, law student Georg Lindemeyer developed a very different definition: it was "the whole or partial recovery of the decrease in moral and legal honor that had been caused by the crime and punishment."[58]

Lindemeyer's more widely applicable definition demonstrated two distinct dimensions of the concept of rehabilitation. In contrast to Buchner, Lindemeyer distinguished between the legal and moral (*sittliche*) consequences of a criminal conviction. Moreover, his definition included a notion that was remarkably absent from Buchner's: honor. Erwin Bumke, a former president of the Reichsgericht, defined rehabilitation in the *Concise Dictionary of Jurisprudence* of 1928 in a similar vein, calling it "the restoration of reputation that has been lost as the consequence of a punishment."[59] Interestingly, this definition replaced the notion of honor with "reputation" (*Ansehen*) and disregarded the legal consequences of punishment. It seemed that legal scholars had gradually become more interested in the subjective question of "honor" and "reputation" than in the legal consequences of rehabilitation.

Once the criminal registry was introduced, formal rehabilitation came to mean two things: 1) reversal of the punishment of disenfranchisement, and 2) expungement of the punishment from one's criminal record. Legal scholars and local authorities often struggled to keep the two things separate. The biggest issue in discussions about rehabilitation was not its definition but rather how the restoration of one's civil privileges was related to the rule of law. To wit, was it a legal right guaranteed by the law, or was it of a different nature? In the end, this question guided much of the discussion about rehabilitation in the German Empire. Legal discussions of rehabilitation and how it should be incorporated into the laws truly began in Germany in the early 1900s on the initiative of Ernst Delaquis. In books and articles that he started publishing around 1905, he identified a crucial difference between pardons granted as favors of the monarch and those issued via a bureaucratic procedure. At the same time, he remarked that the latter were gradually coming to dominate pardoning practices.[60]

In his books and articles, Delaquis drew important distinctions between three understandings of rehabilitation that he derived from the French context: gracious rehabilitation (*rehabilitation gracieuse*), the restoration of civil privileges granted as a favor by the monarch; judicial rehabilitation (*rehabilitation judiciaire*), a pardon granted by the judge or state prosecutor as the outcome of a legal procedure; and legal rehabilitation (*rehabilitation de droit*), with the criteria for rehabilitation codified in penal law. In judicial rehabilitation, supplicants had to meet certain court-set standards, such as providing proof of good conduct, before their rights could be restored; the designated official had to decide whether supplicants had met these standards. In legal rehabilitation, rehabilitation was considered a right offenders could claim after a certain time.

In drawing these distinctions, Delaquis argued that the system of rehabilitation had undergone historical development, passing in most countries from gracious to judicial and finally to legal rehabilitation.[61] He illustrated this by highlighting developments in nineteenth-century France. The Napoleonic *Code Pénal* of 1810 stipulated that only the kaiser could grant a pardon. With the second Berenger Law of 1891, the power shifted to the judicial parties.[62] Afterward, laws increasingly regulated the procedure. Thus, alongside the analytical distinction between different kinds of rehabilitation, Delaquis also developed a theory of legal history that moved away from mercy to a system of rights. Delaquis himself, however, strongly favored a system of judicial rehabilitation because it centered on offenders' efforts and ensured that people whose rights were restored were truly eligible for this because the public recognized that they had conducted themselves "with honor."[63]

"His Majesty Alone . . ."

Even though Delaquis advocated for judicial rehabilitation, the German Empire's system remained, in theory, one of gracious rehabilitation: administratively, ex-convicts' petitions to have their civil privileges restored were categorized as requests for clemency (*Gnadengesuche*). Thus, this structure strongly suggested that rehabilitation was part of the system of mercy and had to be considered a formal pardon. This perspective is also evident in the wording of these petitions.

Ferdinand L.—a former post officer from the town of Soest who had been sentenced for professional misconduct by a court in Aachen—closed his petition of 1871 with a typical expression of subservience to the monarch:

> All merciful kaiser and king! His majesty alone is able to save me from my wretched state. One word of mercy and I will have my civil privileges returned to me and can ... then live the rest of my life with regret but without wretchedness. I throw myself at his majesty's feet and beg him to speak a word of mercy for your majesty's most obliging subject.[64]

Ferdinand L.'s most immediate concern in writing this petition was to secure his pension because disenfranchisement also caused him, as a civil servant, to lose his claim to a state pension. Until the late 1880s, most people who sought clemency were (former) state servants, which is perhaps not surprising given their direct interest in civil privileges. Post officers, in particular, were well represented in this group, predominantly charged with professional misconduct, which included any form of deceit. A book on the development of the German postal services in 1893 highlighted the honesty required of post officers: "The extremely high level of trust placed in the postal services justifiably requires impeccable honesty (*makellose Ehrenhaftigkeit*) of its officials."[65] Hence, these servants of the state appealed personally to the individual mercy of the king.

Ferdinand L.'s loyalty to the monarch aligned with the idea of mercy as the sovereign's prerogative. Indeed, there is a great deal of evidence to support this historical link between the granting of mercy and the monarchy—not least the coronation of Elector Friedrich III as the first king of Prussia in 1701. During this ceremony, the new king issued a general pardon to many imprisoned offenders deliberately to symbolize his power.[66] The event remained unique since his successors dispensed with a coronation ritual, but the power to grant pardons was clearly associated with the king and considered one of his prerogatives. In light of this history, American philosopher Kathleen Moore described the pardon as historically understood as "a gift freely given from a God-like monarch to a subject."[67] In fact, Kaiser Wilhelm II also granted annual amnesties to many imprisoned subjects on his birthday.[68]

The case of Albrecht Stein, a journalist with a doctorate in law, provides further evidence of this link as he pinned his hopes on such a birthday amnesty. Stein had been convicted of serious forgery and disenfranchised for twenty years, resulting in the permanent loss of his right to use his doctor's title. In the petition he wrote to the emperor in 1897, he lamented that no newspaper would accept his articles or hire him as an editor as long as he was unable to sign his articles as "Dr. Stein." He had in fact been charged with unlawfully using his doctor title on multiple occasions, so the Düsseldorf court of justice ruled that he was permanently stripped of this public rank due to his conviction. In his petition protesting against this punishment, he stressed that, unlike his father, who was the

Silesian democratic politician Julius Stein, he was a member of the Conservative Party and a loyal subordinate to the kaiser. He hoped that the amnesty granted on the one-hundredth birthday of Kaiser Wilhelm I, the grandfather of the presiding German emperor, in 1897 would reverse this part of his sentence.[69] Albrecht Stein's petition demonstrates that the idea of civil privileges as a gift granted by the sovereign also implied that people placed their hope on the monarch's personal discretion to get their rights restored.

The Female Consciousness

Frequently, wives wrote petitions on behalf of their convicted husbands. For instance, the wife of Arnold H., a cheesemonger from Krefeld, wrote a petition to the kaiser in 1891, a few days after Arnold H. had sent one himself. He had been convicted of fraud and sentenced to nine months in the penitentiary and three years of loss of honor. The two petitions were similar. Both argued that Arnold H. needed to have his trade license back, which he had been refused due to the suspension of his civil privileges. The only extra information Arnold H. added to his own request was that his fraud offense was his first and only lapse (*Fehltritt*) and that he had served his country well as a soldier before becoming a cheesemonger.[70] The theme of being a one-time offender often arose in petitions, but in Arnold H.'s case, the district president firmly contradicted this claim: Arnold H. had been arrested more than thirty times, mainly for disturbance of the peace and Sunday rest, as well as for trade offenses and insulting the public prosecutor, so he viewed Arnold H. as a troublemaker.

Arnold H.'s wife's petition was much longer. First, she dismissed his other offenses as small misdemeanors (*kleine Vergehen*) and focused on the circumstances in which the couple lived. She referred to the "severe" industrial crisis and the rising cost of food, which made their lives more difficult. Indeed, even though this was the time of high industrialization in Germany, many regions were struggling with economic crises between 1873 and 1896. The early 1890s, in particular, saw low economic growth.[71] Secondly, she addressed the kaiser more elaborately. For instance, she effusively praised his enormous heart (*großmächtiges Herz*), as evident in his role in bringing about the positive reforms in social security in the early 1890s: "With the labor laws, the kaiser truly manifested himself in a humane way."[72] With this, she alluded to Wilhelm II's curated image as the friend of laborers (*Arbeiterfreund*).[73]

One reason women may have written petitions on behalf of their husbands was that these requests had a more "apolitical" meaning, appealing more to the power of mercy. In different historical contexts, historians have argued that petitions were frequently seen as requests without any partisan interests and as direct expressions of people's desires. The ruling classes saw women as particularly suited to writing such requests as "pure" messengers of their beliefs.[74] This aligns with the fact that these petitions were letters seeking pardons and not supplications, petitions often used in early modern Germany to voice political complaints.[75]

At the end of her petition, Arnold H.'s wife emphasized that she was making her request on behalf of herself and her young children. In this, her petition was typical of such letters, which were often presented as pleas coming from the entire family. Johann H.'s wife wrote in a similar vein, but her plea, signed by her and her children, was even more remarkable because her husband had been sentenced by the court of Düsseldorf for a sex offense, apparently against his teenage daughter. That is, he had been sentenced for violating §173 and §176 of the penal code, which outlawed incest and sexual abuse. Nonetheless, his wife still petitioned for the restoration of his rights and signed the petition as "wife of Johann H. together with children." This case was also remarkable because Johann H. was 63 years old and terminally ill when his wife wrote the petition. He was hospitalized, and there seemed to be no immediate practical reason to seek the restoration of his rights. She only mentioned that "it would be very painful for me, and for my children, to see my husband pass away without his civil privileges."[76] Clearly, she attached great value to her husband's honor since she believed it reflected on the entire family.

Such petitions from wives often appealed to the kaiser's "humane character." Johann H.'s wife repeatedly appealed to "the humane sentiments" of the kaiser and even added a religious dimension to her request in writing that she would "press her lips" and send to the heavens a prayer of thanksgiving and praise "that also extended to the heart of the kaiser." Such phrases, focusing on generosity, big-heartedness, and merciful favors, avoided potential political conflict by leaving out notions such as rights and duties. This register of emotional language seemed to be more readily available to women than to men.

Women's greater access to emotionality also played a role in beliefs about their potential for rehabilitation when they themselves were criminals. In fact, in criminological works it was widely thought that they were less likely to be able to have their honor restored than men. Delaquis, in particular, argued that "criminal women" were often considered more degenerate than convicted men, and that, although they were less likely to turn to crime, once they had, it was harder for them to return to a "normal" life. Contemporary literature on the female conscience supported this view: "Female conscience is more led by feelings and, where it truly speaks, less compromised and more insistent," theologian and moral philosopher Wilhelm Gass argued in 1869 in his *Lehre vom Gewissen*.[77] Crucially, women's emotionality, Gass and others believed, also made them more persevering. This was the reason Delaquis, too, believed that it was harder for women to have their honor restored.[78]

Indeed, in other realms of Wilhelmine culture, women had more difficulty appealing to their honor. A woman's honor mostly consisted in chastity and otherwise she was an indirect "carrier" of honor, serving the honor of her husband, as Ute Frevert has shown.[79] Consequently, proving one's honor was principally seen as a male affair in the judicial system. Delaquis therefore also felt that the rehabilitation of female offenders was a marginal issue because it was only relevant to women working in "honorable" professions, which he argued was not the case for most female offenders.[80] Delaquis' argument again reinforces the close relationship between work and honor in the judicial mindset of the era.

Even so, women petitioned for the restoration of their own rights in exceptional cases. After all, they could be deprived of their civil privileges just like men, despite not being the principal bearers thereof. One such case was that of Anna R., a midwife from the town of Düren sentenced for perjury and incitement to commit perjury. In her petition, she used a style similar to that of civil servants like Peter J. For instance, she wrote extensively about her professional career and declared that she had "earned much trust" from her clientele and was widely respected in her town.[81] However, she did not go into too much detail about the reasons behind her offense but rather emphasized the "honorable" character of her husband: a member of the volunteer fire department, he had been injured while battling a fire in the local hospital, during which he had rescued the patients.

There is an interesting paradox in Anna R.'s request. She seemed unaware that civil privileges did not apply to her situation, yet she believed that official rehabilitation was of great value to her. Accordingly, the burgomaster of Düren replied to her puzzling request with an extensive statement. He first contradicted her assertion that she enjoyed a good reputation and pointed out how misguided her attempt was. After all, Anna R. believed she would be able to practice her profession again the moment she was rehabilitated, but he explained that before she could work as a midwife again she would need to renew her certificate, for which he did not believe she would be eligible. Nonetheless, he declared that Anna R. deserved special consideration. Anna R.'s case shows that both the authorities and petitioners believed that "honor" could be as important to women as it was to men, even though the civil privileges, in theory, only applied to men.

In Search of "Special Circumstances"

Delaquis objected to gracious rehabilitation because pardons from the monarch seemed arbitrary. As early as the eighteenth century, many famous Enlightenment philosophers from various European countries had criticized pardons for this reason, and enlightened thinkers soon came to share this critical view. Most commonly, it was argued that pardons were incompatible with a republican form of government. French Enlightenment philosopher Montesquieu, for instance, emphasized the purely monarchical character of the pardon, although he was not necessarily opposed to its use in a monarchical state.[82] The fiercest opposition to the practice came from the Italian philosopher Gaetano Filangieri. In his *Science of Legislation*, he highlighted many arbitrary and unjust decisions that had been made in the name of mercy.[83]

These Enlightenment criticisms often equated monarchical rule with arbitrary rule. If monarchs could soften the consequences of the law with pardons, this only meant that the laws themselves were poor and imperfect; there was no genuine rule of law. Motivated by the idea of the perfectibility of laws, these thinkers argued that pardons should, ideally, not be necessary. In an essay on criminal justice (cited also in chapter 1), Globig and Huster contended that every pardon issued by a ruler breached the social contract that legitimated his authority.[84] A few decades later, the prominent philosopher of law Karl Salomo Zachariae called the pardon an injustice against the community in which it was exercised, arguing that the pardon was "a call to commit crimes because it increases the hope that one can sin without being punished."[85]

Yet, despite these serious criticisms, many scholars still defended the pardon in the nineteenth century. After all, the constitutional monarchy was still seen as the ideal model of state government, and pardons worked well with this mode of government.[86] As Sylvia Kesper-Biermann has pointed out, legal scholars at that time used three basic arguments to justify pardons. The first was based on justice: clemency could restore justice by correcting possible failures and weaknesses in the law. The second pertained to questions of social policy: too many prisoners generated dangers for the state, so pardons could help restore the balance to prevent the decomposition of society. The third claimed that pardons served to express the benevolence of the ruler. This final argument was often considered to be the most controversial since it reinforced the sovereign's arbitrary power.[87]

Paul Laband, an influential professor of constitutional law in the German Empire, supported the widespread understanding of mercy as the prerogative of the sovereign; he also believed that mercy was of considerable importance in society in general, "permeat[ing] every part of the life of the state," a "constant companion of public law," softening its harshness.[88] This claim that they mitigated the severity of the law was a classic defense of pardons. Moreover, Laband argued that the notion of mercy (as the bestowal of a benefit without any legal obligations) only applied to cases in which there was a relationship between a ruler and a subject (*Herrschaftsverhältnis*):

> Mercy is something granted without legal obligation. It is only used when there is a relationship between sovereign and subject; granting mercy is a prerogative of the sovereign and being "merciful" is his attribute.[89]

At the same time, under the influence of the "modern" criminological school, the notion that pardons were beneficial to the system of criminal justice experienced a sort of renaissance in the second half of the nineteenth century. Echoing phrases by legal philosopher Rudolf Jhering, Franz Liszt, for instance, argued in his handbook of criminal justice that pardons could be a "safety valve" for the criminal justice system.[90] The fact that Delaquis was a pupil of Liszt seems contradictory. Yet, it makes sense knowing that Liszt had a certain type of pardon in mind. Such "modern" scholars were particularly supportive of parole: as this kind of pardon was conditional on the conduct of a released prisoner in society, the pardon came with incentives for the offender's reform. Thus, they did not view pardons as a correction of the laws but as a tool for helping social policy makers prevent the disintegration of society. This was very much in line with the "purpose"-oriented approach of the modern school.[91] This is the context in which one must understand Delaquis's preference for "judicial rehabilitation" because it granted ex-convicts the possibility of rehabilitation as a reward for good conduct.

Interestingly, the real procedure for rehabilitation in the German Empire, although it took the form of "gracious rehabilitation," was often closer to what Delaquis advocated in his work. He held that rehabilitation should ideally be awarded only after determining through extensive interviews with important individuals from the local community that it is warranted.[92] And although ex-convicts wrote petitions of clemency to the kaiser in the system of gracious rehabilitation, the local authorities actually made the decisions along these lines. The district president (*Regierungspräsident*) played the most important role in this because a ministerial decree of 1853 had made this community figure responsible for making the decision for or against clemency, emphasizing that it could only be granted in "exceptional" cases.[93] The same decree stated that district presidents had to consult with other local authorities before making a decision, most importantly the judiciary and especially the local state prosecutor.[94] Other frequently consulted authorities included the local burgomaster and the district commissioner (*Landrat*). However, these figures could only advise the district president. So, even though it has been argued that district commissioners held the real power in Prussia, the district presidents had more authority in clemency decisions, given their function as the heads of the police departments.[95]

Local authorities usually followed this procedure precisely. Petitions addressed to the kaiser usually ended up in the office of the Minister of the Interior, who forwarded them to the district president of the town where the petitioner resided. In almost all cases, the Minister of the Interior advised the district president to decline the request unless there were extraordinary circumstances. The district president would then make a decision based on information he had compiled and inform the petitioner. Local authorities' reactions to the petitions, however, differed from case to case. The burgomaster and state prosecutor, for instance, displayed great sympathy for Peter J. and Ferdinand L., seeming to truly regret that they could not find special circumstances for granting these former civil servants a pardon. Not even Ferdinand L.'s loss of entitlement to his pension was reason enough for the district president to support his request.

However, when Düsseldorf post officer Gottfried T. deployed similar arguments in his petition, the local authorities reacted dismissively. Gottfried T. had been sentenced for embezzlement in 1894 and, like Peter J. and Ferdinand L., he made loyalty to his office the leitmotif of his petition. He claimed he was honored to have been entrusted with the office and repeatedly expressed his remorse for the breach in confidence he had caused—a "most ignominious" (*schnödeste*) offense. He also addressed the kaiser in a subservient tone and claimed that he was unworthy of his mercy. Of course, he was simply trying to convince the kaiser that he had an essentially moral character and finally asked him for his "undeserved grace."[96] His rhetoric fit perfectly with the image of the loyal servant asking for sovereign grace. Yet, the burgomaster was not moved. Set on proving that Gottfried T. was a recidivist with an egoistic character, he described Gottfried T. as living a loose life, maltreating his wife and children, and neglecting his family since his conviction. In addition, and very importantly, the burgomaster emphasized that Gottfried T. was only interested in enriching himself.[97] Furthermore, the burgomaster mentioned Gottfried T.'s attempted escape from the Krefeld prison in the company of a "band of robbers" (an event that was also discussed in the local newspapers) as additional evidence of his reprehensible character.[98] Gottfried T.'s request was therefore denied without any further ado. The evidence amassed by the burgomaster illustrates the effort authorities put into processing cases, even if they generally rejected them.

Local community members also dedicated efforts to rehabilitation proceedings. Some of these people were less directly concerned with the ex-convicts' well-being than they were with the ex-convicts' immediate relatives. In 1897, the local citizens' association (*Bürgerverein*) of Rupelrath near Solingen tried to help two residents convicted of manslaughter who had been sentenced to eight to ten years in the penitentiary. Two men, both named Karl S., 21 and 26 at the time of the crime, had stabbed a day laborer to death. The citizens' association, just like Albrecht Stein, hoped that Kaiser Wilhelm I's hundredth birthday celebration would be a suitable occasion to plead for clemency in their case.[99] Both the burgomaster and the district commissioner of Solingen, however, remained steadfast in their judgments. They claimed that the extreme brutality of the crime disqualified the applicants from having their rights restored.[100] Such statements confirmed the repulsion local members of the bourgeoisie felt toward acts of brutal violence.[101]

The planned penal law reform of 1909 included a proposal to further codify this communal aspect of rehabilitation. In the first decade of the twentieth century, the German government had decided that, after more than thirty years, the Reich Penal Code needed to be significantly revised, which gave many experts an occasion to voice their ideas about the legal aspects of rehabilitation. The massive scholarly work, the *Vergleichende Darstellung*, which systematically compared penal systems across the world, preceded the draft reform. In §50 of the draft, it was stipulated that the rights of disenfranchised offenders could be restored if local courts decided that they had conducted themselves "honorably" for a certain period of time.[102] This plan would be more in keeping with Delaquis's idea of "judicial rehabilitation," demonstrating that penal experts broadly supported this concept. Interestingly, however, this draft was largely based on the ideas of the "classical" school and only marginally adopted ideas from the "moderns."[103] Commentators envisioned some problems with the practical implementation of this plan. Increased mobility in the German Empire, for instance, made it difficult to determine who should decide on rehabilitation: the authorities in the ex-convicts' place of residence, or those in their place of conviction?[104] In the end, though, these reforms were never ratified or implemented, so the authorities continued to handle rehabilitation as described above.

A New Vocabulary of Entitlement

Feelings of honor and shame often had a material side too. Manfred Hettling argued that a central value of the German bourgeoisie was independence.[105] And, indeed, many petitioners referred to independence as a key aim. Increasingly, independence became associated with honor, as well as the possession of material resources and ideas about masculinity. In other words, as many historians have pointed out, the notion of honor had by this period become deeply entangled with economic independence.[106] Since the loss of civil privileges often undermined ex-convicts' ability to find work, the material consequences of the punishment were often considered to be integral to the dishonoring component of the conviction. The greatest dishonor lay in being dependent on the support of others. Almost always, a loss of independence was seen as disgraceful because a dependent life was undesirable in itself, never mind that it prevented people from fulfilling their material needs. Thus, ex-convicts were motivated to ask for the restoration of their honor not only by the prospect of job opportunities and financial means but also in order to maintain their independence.

Heinrich N., for instance, worked as a retailer in Duisburg and was convicted of perjury in 1883. His inability to find an occupation—or at least one equivalent to his previous one—created a "an oppressive feeling of unfreedom," he wrote in his petition to the kaiser. It went beyond his lack of work in that the punishment itself also had a direct emotional effect: "my current state makes being around people difficult and makes me anxious." He believed that this feeling would go away the moment these obstacles were removed: "my old joy in working would come back to me if I could again freely move among my fellow citizens."[107] Heinrich N.'s description of his feelings strongly suggests that he valued independence for intrinsic reasons and considered his current lack of freedom deeply dishonorable. One could argue, moreover, that his petition testified to a certain emotionalization of his future prospects as he hoped to experience a new "joy" in being a productive citizen (*Schaffensfreudigkeit*).

Ex-convicts expressed their desire for independence nowhere more forcefully than in their wish not to have to appeal to the poor relief system, as many of the previous cases have already shown. The stigma associated with the poor relief system caused people to view taking recourse to it as a serious disgrace related to their experience of dependence. As we saw with Peter J. above, people preferred to get help from their families over utilizing the poor relief system. Another petitioner who feared the stigma of poor relief was Friedrich S. from Sterkrade. Convicted to one year in the penitentiary for pimping, he petitioned primarily out of a desire to no longer be a burden on the poor relief system.[108] Indeed, many petitioners voiced concerns about being "a burden" to the community; their state of dependence provoked the dishonor they felt and motivated them to seek rehabilitation.

In his petition, Friedrich S. also mentioned that he was old and very ill. This shows that the value ex-convicts ascribed to their civil privileges and to the state of being independent was not necessarily associated with their age. That is, older people also had material reasons to seek the restoration of their rights. Jacob S. from Barmen, for instance, who was sentenced for helping someone have an abortion, is a case in point: he was forty-five years old and was hoping to be admitted to a local burial fund. The burial funds, however, only admitted people up to age forty-five who were in possession of their civil privileges. Jacob S.'s material concerns cannot be isolated from his ideas about his reputation. Securing the financial means for his burial was clearly intrinsically valuable to him: "I view it as my duty to ensure that in the case of my death means for a burial will be there."[109]

These petitions did not focus on the convicts' former life conduct or the nature of their crimes. In fact, more petitions started emphasizing the difficulties of life after conviction to appeal directly to the kaiser's empathy. This was, for instance, the case in Heinrich K.'s petition of 1896. A bailiff from Beeck (Wegberg), he was convicted of embezzlement by the court of Aachen in 1894. After listing the problems his disenfranchisement caused in his daily life (three positions had already been denied to him), he concluded by appealing to the kaiser's empathy:

> Your Highness, please consider how difficult this punishment has made it for me to return to civil society, how difficult it has made it for me and my family to make a living, when my loss of honor remains in place, no institution, no business will take me, I thus stand before you, cast out with bound hands, and face an uncertain future.[110]

Heinrich K.'s differed from most in that he directly asked the kaiser to put himself in his shoes, whereas others usually just listed their hardships. Furthermore, Heinrich K. placed much less emphasis on his biography and his former conduct as a civil servant. In this, it illustrates the shift in petitions' focus to life after prison and future prospects.

Johann Josef J. used rhetoric similar to that of Heinrich K.'s in a petition he sent fifteen years later, in 1911, to appeal to the kaiser's empathy. Johann Josef J. was a businessman from Aachen who had been sentenced to three years in the penitentiary for fraud in 1907. However, his approach differed in that he tried to generate awareness of ex-convicts' general experience of being dishonored in Germany. His petition was completely dedicated to the difficulties his conviction created in his daily life and did not mention the offense he had been sentenced for. Clearly, he did not consider this important in the context of his request.

What is striking in Johann Josef J.'s style is that he constantly shifted between a first-person and a third-person perspective. He referred to himself in the third person as "the convict," and even as "the miserable one" (*der Unglückliche*). In this way, he connected his personal experience with the general condition of other dishonored ex-convicts and created a sense of collective identity. He started his personal account by highlighting the shared experience—"I share in the general miserable fate of all released convicts"—and continued in this generalizing mode:

> I cannot describe how difficult it is to forge a good life as a citizen for those unlucky ones who, in the isolation of their sentences, have come to see things differently and now only want to survive in life but are forced to drag along the chain of dishonor behind them.[111]

The petition leaves the reader with the impression that Johann Josef J. was pursuing a higher political cause in his request for the restoration of his civil privileges. In a sense, he truly identified himself with the social group of dishonored felons.

One can clearly see the two different discursive strategies when comparing Johann Josef J.'s petition to Peter J.'s. Peter J. and other former civil servants prided themselves on being law-abiding citizens, presenting their professional conduct as an extension of state power and downplaying their offenses as momentary lapses. Johann Josef J., on the other hand, described his misery as an experience he shared with other ex-convicts. Thus, he expressed a sense of collective identity and used a vocabulary of political protest. In a way, he tried to convince the kaiser that ex-convicts were citizens with rights too. Johann Josef J.'s letter therefore reads more as a complaint about the consequences of his sentence than as a request for the restoration of his rights.

Both Heinrich K.'s and Johann Josef J.'s requests were rejected. The authorities advised against clemency primarily because both Heinrich K. and Johann Josef J. had previous sentences before their rights were stripped. In fact, Johann Josef J. had been sentenced six times.[112] Heinrich K. had even been sentenced to an additional honor punishment by a different court. The authorities therefore categorized them as "habitual offenders," referring to them as such in internal communications.

Over time, it became clear that people petitioning for the restoration of their rights came from various backgrounds. There were civil servants, businessmen, artisans, street vendors, and even day laborers who were interested enough in their civil privileges to seek their restoration. Notably, the number of petitions sent in the districts of Aachen and Düsseldorf rose from the 1890s onwards, even though fewer people were deprived of their civil privileges.[113] Perhaps this is not surprising. After all, as fewer people were sentenced to honor punishments, those who were came to feel more isolated. One possible explanation is that ex-convicts had more trust in the rule of Wilhelm II.[114] Another explanation could be that the end of economic crises made people more optimistic about their future prospects, which, in turn, made them more eager to have their privileges restored.

Even though rehabilitation was formally an act of mercy, the discussion among local authorities increasingly revolved around prisoners' conduct after release, so, in practice, dealing with such cases bore many similarities to rehabilitation as a reward for good behavior. In their petitions, civil servants initially often elaborated on their honor in relation to their life conduct in office; in this context, they found the punishment most demeaning. If they used a vocabulary of entitlement, this entitlement was based on their biography. That is, they tried to utilize this "symbolic capital" to make their case.[115] Other petitioners, however, eventually started to stress other misfortunes related to their conviction, particularly that they had become a burden on the community and wanted this situation reversed. They hardly talked about their biography but emphasized their intention to become useful citizens in the future. In their experience, full citizenship was not just a privilege awarded for their honorable life conduct but something they were entitled to by virtue of their membership in a community—both the local community and the national community. Armed with this conception of citizenship, they sought to hold the state accountable and criticize what they perceived to be unjust practices in the penal system.

Notes

1. Parts of this chapter draw on a previously published article: Timon de Groot, "The Criminal Registry in the German Empire: The 'Cult of Previous Convictions' and the Offender's Right to Be Forgotten," *German History* 39, no. 3 (2021): 358–76.
2. LAV NRW R, BR 0005, no. 22776, petition from Peter J. addressed to Kaiser Wilhelm II, 17 August 1891.
3. Ibid., statement from the district commissioner on the case of Peter J., 28 September 1891.

4. Ibid.; Wilhelm I was often depicted as the *Heldenkaiser* as a consequence of the outcome of the wars of German unification between 1864 and 1871; cf. Wilhelm Oncken, ed., *Unser Heldenkaiser. Festschrift zum hundertjährigen Geburtstage Kaiser Wilhelms des Großen* (Berlin: Schall & Grund, 1897).
5. Cf. Erving Goffman, *Stigma: Notes on the Management of Spoiled Identity* (Englewood Cliffs, NJ: Prentice-Hall, 1965), 1–3, 48–51; Martha C. Nussbaum, *Hiding from Humanity: Disgust, Shame and the Law* (Princeton, NJ: Princeton University Press, 2004), 217–21.
6. Goffman, *Stigma*, 48–62.
7. Cf. Fitzpatrick, *Purging the Empire*, 19–39. See also Rosenblum, *Beyond the Prison Gates*, 75–78; Schauz, *Strafen als moralische Besserung*, 270.
8. Philipp Zeller, *Systematisches Lehrbuch der Polizeiwissenschaft nach preußischen Gesetzen, Edicten, Verordnungen und Ministerial-Rescripten*, vol. 1 (Quedlinburg: Basse, 1828), 58.
9. Wick, *Über Fürsorge für entlassene Sträflinge*, 38–40.
10. Hermann Friedrich Ortloff, *Das Zellengefängniß zu Moabit in Berlin* (Gotha: Perthes, 1861), 176.
11. Cf. Gustav Radbruch, "Der Ursprung des Strafrechts aus dem Stande der Unfreien," in *Elegantiae Juris Criminalis. Vierzehn Studien zur Geschichte des Strafrechts*, ed. Gustav Radbruch, 11–12 (Basel, 1950); Richard Braune, "Die Freiheitsstrafen einst und jetzt," *ZStW* 42, no. 1 (1922): 14–32, 18.
12. Wick, *Über Fürsorge für entlassene Sträflinge*, 39.
13. Pieter Spierenburg, "Geweld, repressie en schaamte. Enige historische gegevens," *Tijdschrift voor criminology* 20 (1978): 133–38. Spierenburg's take on the rise of the prison is different from Foucault's, of course. Yet, as Spierenburg also indicates, Foucault's thesis that the system of incarceration grew out of changing ideas about disciplining bodies and souls can easily be combined with the fact that sensitivities and mentalities regarding the execution of punishment had changed. Cf. Garland, *Punishment and Modern Society*, 159. Other works on the "spectacle of punishment" include Richard van Dülmen, *Theater des Schreckens. Gerichtspraxis und Strafrituale in der frühen Neuzeit* (Munich: C. H. Beck, 1987), 62–81; Foucault, *Surveiller et punir*, 53–59; Ute Frevert, "Empathy in the Theater of Horror, or Civilizing the Human Heart," in *Empathy and Its Limits*, ed. Aleida Assmann and Ines Detmers, 79–99 (Basingstoke: Palgrave Macmillan, 2015).
14. Bretschneider, *Gefangene Gesellschaft*, 271–305, 523–29; Nutz, *Strafanstalt als Besserungsmaschine*, 49–69.
15. Cf. Karl Adam, "Stände und Berufe in Preußen gegenüber der nationalen Erhebung des Jahres 1848," *PJ* 89 (1897): 285–308, 290; Ernst Feder, *Die Prügelstrafe* (Berlin: J. Guttentag, 1911), 17–18; cf. Ute Frevert, *Die Politik der Demütigung: Schauplätze von Macht und Ohnmacht* (Frankfurt a.M.: S. Fischer, 2017).
16. "Outbursts of cruelty did not exclude one from social life. They were not outlawed. The pleasure in killing and torturing others was great, and it was a socially permitted pleasure. To a certain extent, the social structure even pushed its members in this direction, making it seem necessary and practically advantageous to behave in this way." Norbert Elias, *The Civilizing Process: Sociogenetic and Psychogenetic Investigations*, trans. Eric Dunning (Oxford: Blackwell, 2000), 163.
17. Pieter Spierenburg, *The Spectacle of Suffering: Executions and the Evolution of Repression from a Preindustrial Metropolis to the European Experience* (Cambridge: Cambridge University Press, 1984). It is important to mention that Spierenburg sees this as a longer-term evolution and not as particular to the early nineteenth century. He argues that this process started with the erection of workhouses in the seventeenth-century cities of Amsterdam and Hansa. Nonetheless, the early nineteenth century still marked something of a new era since the prison idea spread significantly across Europe, more clearly taking on the function of a penal institution as opposed to a poor relief policy.

18. Günter Moltmann, "Die Transportation von Sträflingen im Rahmen der deutschen Amerikaauswanderung des 19. Jahrhunderts," in *Deutsche Amerikaauswanderung im 19. Jahrhundert. Sozialgeschichtliche Beiträge*, ed. Günter Moltmann (Stuttgart: Metzler, 1976), 147–96, 150.
19. Ibid.
20. Jürgen Osterhammel, *Die Verwandlung der Welt. Eine Geschichte des 19. Jahrhunderts* (Munich: Beck, 2009), 236–39.
21. Antonius Holtmann, "Auswanderungs- und Übersiedelungspolitik im Königreich Hannover 1832–1866," in *Schöne Neue Welt. Rheinländer Erobern Amerika*, ed. Kornelia Panek and Dieter Pesch, vol. 2 (Wiehl, 2001), 185–214, 194.
22. Matthias Manke, "Sträflingsmigration aus Mecklenburg-Schwerin vom Ende des 18. bis zur Mitte des 19. Jahrhunderts," *Jahrbuch für europäische Überseegeschichte* 9 (2009): 67–103, 78–81.
23. Wick, *Über Fürsorge für entlassene Sträflinge*, 42.
24. Moltmann, "Die Transportation," 149–50.
25. Wunder, *Geschichte der Bürokratie in Deutschland*, 7; Harald Focke, "Friedrich List und die südwestdeutsche Amerikaauswanderung 1817–1846," in *Deutsche Amerikaauswanderung*, ed. Moltmann, 63–95.
26. On a discussion of the concepts of transportation vs. deportation, see Manke, "Sträflingsmigration aus Mecklenburg-Schwerin," 68–70.
27. Moltmann, "Die Transportation," 178–81.
28. Bettina Hitzer, "Freizügigkeit als Reformergebnis und die Entwicklung von Arbeitsmärkten," in *Handbuch Staat und Migration in Deutschland seit dem 17. Jahrhundert*, ed. Jochen Oltmer (Berlin: De Gruyter, 2016), 245–90.
29. William Hesse, *Die Aufenthaltsbeschränkungen bestrafter Personen in Deutschland* (Lüneburg: König, 1905).
30. Cited in Richard Braune, "Wider die Polizeiaufsicht!," *ZStW* 9, no. 1 (1889): 807–32, 808. The lecture was held on 26 March 1878 at the general assembly of the Görlitzer Verein zur Fürsorge für aus Strafanstalten Entlassene. Cf. *BfG* 13 (1879): 315.
31. Consider the following remark by Peter Becker: "Above all, the crooks were considered experts of false appearances: they hid behind assumed names and professions in order to carry out their thefts unhindered and to evade the investigative activities of the police; they also used acting and rhetorical skills to deceive trusting citizens and peasants." Becker, *Verderbnis und Entartung*, 221.
32. Jürgen Reulecke, *Geschichte der Urbanisierung in Deutschland* (Frankfurt a.M.: Suhrkamp, 1985); Klaus Tenfelde, *Arbeiter, Bürger, Städte. zur Sozialgeschichte des 19. und 20. Jahrhundert* (Göttingen: Vandenhoeck & Ruprecht, 2012), 319; cf. Daniel Siemens, *Metropole und Verbrechen. Die Gerichtsreportage in Berlin, Paris und Chicago 1919–1933* (Stuttgart: Steiner, 2007).
33. Otto, *Die Verbrecherwelt von Berlin*, 86. Cited also in: Timon de Groot, "The Criminal Registry in the German Empire: The 'Cult of Previous Convictions' and the Offender's Right to Be Forgotten," *German History* 39.3 (2021): 358–76, 369.
34. Cf. de Groot, "The Criminal Registry in the German Empire," 369.
35. The controversy around the captain of Köpenick is discussed in great detail in Benjamin Carter Hett, *Death in the Tiergarten: Murder and Criminal Justice in the Kaiser's Berlin* (Cambridge, MA: Harvard University Press, 2004), 179–94; Rosenblum, *Beyond the Prison Gates*, 103–21; Müller, "'But We Will Always Have to Individualize.'"
36. Elwert, "Der Pranger," *Das Recht*, 628–29. Similar critique can be found in BA-BL 3001/6027, *Berliner Neueste Nachrichten*, 19 October 1913.
37. Sylvia Kesper-Biermann, "Die Internationale Kriminalistische Vereinigung. Zum Verhältnis von Wissenschaftsbeziehungen und Politik im Strafrecht 1889–1932," in *Die Internationalisierung von Strafrechtswissenschaft und Kriminalpolitik (1870–1930). Deutschland im Vergleich*,

ed. Sylvia Kesper-Biermann and Petra Overath, 85–107 (Berlin: Berliner Wissenschafts-Verlag, 2007); idem, "Wissenschaftlicher Ideenaustausch und 'kriminalpolitische Propaganda.' Die Internationale Kriminalistische Vereinigung (1889–1937) und der Strafvollzug," in *Verbrecher im Visier Der Experten. Kriminalpolitik. Zwischen Wissenschaft und Praxis im 19. und Frühen 20. Jahrhundert*, ed. Désirée Schauz and Sabine Freitag, 79–97 (Stuttgart: Steiner, 2007).

38. Eberhard Schmidt, "Ernst Delaquis zum Gedächtnis," *ZStW* 64, no. 1 (1952): 434–35, 434.
39. *Mitteilungen der Internationalen Kriminalistischen Vereinigung*, vol. 13 (Berlin: Guttentag, 1906), 578.
40. *Mitteilungen der Internationalen Kriminalistischen Vereinigung*, vol. 13, 572.
41. For various reasons, it is not possible to give a complete overview of the number of petitions that reached the offices of the districts of Aachen and Düsseldorf. One is that the Düsseldorf files (in contrast to those in Aachen) were not all saved. The Düsseldorf files only contain petitions from the period 1888–1902. Files for other periods were lost or not archived. However, the large number of petitions in the Düsseldorf files suggests that petitions were submitted more frequently in Düsseldorf than in Aachen. This makes sense because the district of Düsseldorf had a larger population. Another complication is that the files contain a summary of petitions in which it is difficult to determine the precise aims of the petitioners—whether they wanted their rights restored or sought, for instance, a termination of police supervision. I did not consider these petitions in this chapter but studied forty-nine petitions for the period of 1870–1914. The petitions associated with many cases mentioned in the files were not preserved. I left those out here.
42. Friedrich Oetker came to the same conclusion in his *Strafe und Lohn*.
43. Examples include Hermann Börner, *Der praktische Rathgeber für bürgerliche Kreise. Mit einer Auswahl von Muster-Formularen zur Abfassung von Anträgen, Bittschriften, Vorstellungen etc. in verschiedenen persönlichen Angelegenheiten* (Breslau: Freund, 1893); Matthias Übelacker, *Großer deutscher Muster-Briefsteller für die gesamte Privat- und Handels-Korrespondenz*, 10th edn. (Berlin: Euler, 1903); Franz Keller, *Allgemeiner Geschäfts- und Familien-Briefsteller*, 40th edn. (Berlin: A. Weichert, 1900).
44. Dieter Langewiesche, "Entwicklungsbedingungen im Kaiserreich," in *Geschichte des deutschen Buchhandels im 19. und 20. Jahrhundert*, ed. Georg Jäger, vol. 1, 42–86 (Berlin: De Gruyter, 2001), 63–69.
45. LAV NRW R, BR 0007, no. 30722, petition from Julius S. addressed to the state prosecutor of Düsseldorf, 11 February 1892.
46. Cf. Nikolaus Wachsmann, *Hitler's Prisons: Legal Terror in Nazi Germany* (New Haven, CT: Yale University Press, 2004), 52.
47. Cf. de Groot, "The Criminal Registry in the German Empire."
48. Several local police departments kept files on individual offenders during the first half of the nineteenth century, but there was no formal system. Cf. Becker, *Verderbnis und Entartung*, 64–74.
49. Alex R. Piquero, David P. Farrington, and Alfred Blumstein, "The Criminal Career Paradigm," *Crime and Justice* 30 (2003): 359–506; cf. De Groot, "The Criminal Registry in the German Empire," 360.
50. Sven Reichardt, "Einführung. Überwachungsgeschichte(n)," *Geschichte und Gesellschaft* 42, no. 1 (2016): 5–33, 9–10.
51. Franz von Holtzendorff, *Handbuch des Gefängnisswesens. In Einzelbeiträgen* (Hamburg: Richter, 1888), 571.
52. H. Marchand, *Das Strafregister in Deutschland* (Berlin: J. Guttentag, 1900); Josef Müller, *Vorstrafen und Strafregister* (Breslau: Schletter, 1908).
53. LAV NRW R, BR 0007, no. 30722, petition from Josef S. addressed to the state prosecutor of Düsseldorf, 1 December 1896.

54. The Reichsjustizamt (the Reich Justice Office) was responsible for international communication on criminal records: BA-BL, R 3001/5578.
55. LAV NRW R, BR 0005, no. 22834, circular from 7 July 1907.
56. De Groot, "The Criminal Registry in the German Empire."
57. Welcker and Rotteck, *Das Staats-Lexicon*, vol. 12, 423.
58. Georg Lindemeyer, *Die Wiedereinsetzung, Rehabilitation, Unter besonderer Berücksichtigung der §§50–52 des Vorentwurfs und der §§110–112 des Gegenentwurfs* (Berlin: A. W. Schade, 1913), 21.
59. Erwin Bumke, "Rehabilitation," in *Handwörterbuch der Rechtswissenschaft*, ed. Fritz Stier-Somlo and Alexander Nikolaus Elster, vol. 5, 774–76 (Berlin: De Gruyter, 1928).
60. Ernst Delaquis, *Die Rehabilitation Verurteilter* (Berlin: J. Guttentag, 1906); idem, *Die Rehabilitation im Strafrecht* (Berlin: J. Guttentag, 1907).
61. Delaquis, *Die Rehabilitation im Strafrecht*, 107.
62. Cf. Robert Badinter, *La Prison Républicaine (1871–1914)* (Paris: Fayard, 1992), 247–50.
63. Delaquis, *Die Rehabilitation im Strafrecht*, 121.
64. LAV NRW R, BR 0005, no. 22776, petition from Ferdinand L. addressed to Kaiser Wilhelm I, 12 July 1871.
65. J. Jung, *Entwickelung des deutschen Post- und Telegraphenwesens in den letzten 25 Jahren* (Leipzig: Duncker & Humblot, 1893), 172.
66. Christopher Clark, *Iron Kingdom: The Rise and Downfall of Prussia, 1600–1947* (London: Penguin Books, 2007), 68.
67. Kathleen D. Moore, *Pardons: Justice, Mercy, and the Public Interest* (New York: Oxford University Press, 1997), 8–9.
68. Monika Wienfort, "Zurschaustellung der Monarchie. Huldigungen und Thronjubiläen in Preußen-Deutschland und Großbritannien im 19. Jahrhundert," in *Symbolische Macht und inszenierte Staatlichkeit. 'Verfassungskultur' als Element der Verfassungsgeschichte*, ed. Peter Brandt, Arthur Schlegelmilch, and Reinhard Wendt, 81–100 (Bonn: Dietz, 2005), 96–97.
69. GStA PK, 1. HA Rep. 77 tit. 1001 Bd.4, Petition of Albrecht Stein, 10 February 1897.
70. LAV NRW R, BR 0007, no. 30722, petition from Arnold H. addressed to Kaiser Wilhelm II, 17 July 1891, 38–39.
71. Hans Rosenberg, *Grosse Depression und Bismarckzeit. Wirtschaftsablauf, Gesellschaft und Politik in Mitteleuropa* (Berlin: de Gruyter, 1967), 41; Hans-Ulrich Wehler, *Das deutsche Kaiserreich, 1871–1918* (Göttingen: Vandenhoeck & Ruprecht, 1973), 43.
72. LAV NRW R, BR 0007, no. 30722, petition from Arnold H.'s wife (name unknown) addressed to Kaiser Wilhelm II, 1891, 44–45.
73. Victor Böhmert, "Kaiser Wilhelm und Kaiser Friedrich als Arbeiterfreunde," *Der Arbeiterfreund* 26 (1888): 1–10; "Kaiser Wilhelm, der Arbeiterfreund," *Germania*, 6 February 1890.
74. Cf. Susan Zaeske, *Signatures of Citizenship: Petitioning, Antislavery, and Women's Political Identity* (Chapel Hill: University of North Carolina Press, 2003), 9–10, 17–18. Other historians called the belief that women were considered more suited to conveying a sensitive message a "politics of sense and sensibility." See Wendy Gunther-Canada, "The Politics of Sense and Sensibility: Mary Wollstonecraft and Catharine Macaulay Graham on Edmund Burke's 'Reflections on the Revolution in France,'" in *Women Writers and the Early Modern British Political Tradition*, ed. Hilda L. Smith, 126–47 (Cambridge: Cambridge University Press, 1998). One could also argue that women's voices could more easily be ignored by the authorities because the voices themselves lacked a certain political quality in the opinion of the ruling classes. Cf. G. R. Searle, *Morality and the Market in Victorian Britain* (Oxford: Clarendon Press, 1998), 157–58.
75. Andreas Würgler, "Voices from among the 'Silent Masses'. Humble Petitions and Social Conflicts in Early Modern Central Europe," *International Review of Social History* 46, no. 9 (2001): 11–34.

76. LAV NRW R, BR 0007, no. 30722, petition from Johann H.'s wife (name unknown) addressed to Kaiser Wilhelm II, 8 January 1901, 281.
77. Wilhelm Gass, *Die Lehre vom Gewissen. Ein Beitrag zur Ethik* (Berlin: Reimer, 1869), 152.
78. Delaquis, *Die Rehabilitation im Strafrecht*, 127.
79. Frevert, "Ehre—männlich/weiblich," 39–41; Ute Frevert, *Emotions in History: Lost and Found* (Budapest: Central European University Press, 2011), 73.
80. Ibid.
81. LAV NRW R, BR 0005, no. 22776, petition from Anna R. addressed to Kaiser Wilhelm II, 22 December 1892.
82. Charles de Secondat Baron de Montesquieu, *De l'esprit des lois* (1748), book 6, chapter 21.
83. Cited in: Louis Günther, "Die Strafrechtsreform im Aufklärungszeitalter," *AKK* 28 (1907): 112–92, 225–91, 170.
84. Globig and Huster, *Abhandlung von der Criminalgesetzgebung*, 157.
85. Zachariae, *Vierzig Bücher vom Staate*, vol. 3, 315.
86. Cf. Dieter Langewiesche, *Die Monarchie im Jahrhundert Europas. Selbstbehauptung durch Wandel im 19. Jahrhundert* (Heidelberg: Winter, 2013); Frank Lorenz Müller, *Royal Heirs in Imperial Germany: The Future of Monarchy in Nineteenth-Century Bavaria, Saxony and Württemberg* (London: Palgrave, 2017), 7–8.
87. Kesper-Biermann, "Gerechtigkeit, Politik und Güte," 26–28.
88. Paul Laband, "Das Gnadenrecht in Finanzsachen nach preußischem Recht," *Archiv für öffentliches Recht* 7, no. 2 (1892): 169–211, 172.
89. Ibid., 169–70.
90. Liszt, *Lehrbuch des deutschen Strafrechts*, 268.
91. Wetzell, *Inventing the Criminal*, 34; Arndt Meyer-Reil, *Strafaussetzung zur Bewährung. Reformdiskussion und Gesetzgebung seit dem Ausgang des 19. Jahrhunderts* (Münster: Lit, 2006), 13–16.
92. Delaquis, *Rehabilitation im Strafrecht*, 142.
93. LAV NRW R, BR 0005, no. 22781.
94. Hugo von Marck and Alfred Kloss, *Die Staatsanwaltschaft bei den Land- und Amtsgerichten in Preussen* (Berlin: Heymann, 1903), 553.
95. Lysbeth W. Muncy, "The Prussian 'Landräte' in the Last Years of the Monarchy: A Case Study of Pomerania and the Rhineland 1890-1918," *Central European History* 6, no. 4 (1973): 299–338.
96. LAV NRW R, BR 0007, no. 30722, petition from Gottfried T. addressed to Kaiser Wilhelm II, 9 February 1896, 207.
97. Ibid., statement from the burgomaster of Düsseldorf on the case of Gottfried T., 28 September 1891, 206.
98. Ibid., *Crefelder Zeit*, 7 March 1894.
99. Ibid., 259–62.
100. Ibid., 26–24.
101. Ralph Jessen, "Gewaltkriminalität im Ruhrgebiet zwischen bürgerlicher Panik und proletarischer Subkultur (1870–1900)," in *Arbeitskultur im Ruhrgebiet zwischen Kommerz und Kontrolle (1850–1974)*, ed. D. Kift, 226–55 (Paderborn: Schöningh, 1992).
102. *Vorentwurf zu einem Deutschen Strafgesetzbuch* (Berlin, 1909), 175–77; Hermann Lucas, "Das Strafrecht," in *Deutschland unter Kaiser Wilhelm II.*, ed. Siegfried Körte, vol. 3, 28–44 (Berlin: Reimar Hobbing, 1914).
103. BA-BL, R 3001/6035, Karl Birkmeyer, "Strafrechtsreform," *Münchner Neueste Nachrichten*, 9 November 1909.
104. BA-BL, R 3001/6036, *Heidelberger Tageblatt*, 7 August 1910.
105. Manfred Hettling, "Die persönliche Selbständigkeit. Der archimedische Punkt bürgerlicher Lebensführung," in *Der bürgerliche Wertehimmel. Innenansichten des 19. Jahrhunderts*, ed.

Manfred Hettling and Stefan-Ludwig Hoffmann, 57–78 (Göttingen: Vandenhoeck & Ruprecht, 2000).
106. Spierenburg, *Violence and Punishment.*
107. LAV NRW R, BR 0007, no. 30722, petition from Heinrich Heinrich N. addressed to Kaiser Wilhelm II, 18 May 1891, 33–34.
108. Ibid., petition from Friedrich S. addressed to Kaiser Wilhelm II, 12 February 1896, 217–18.
109. Ibid., Petition from Jacob S. addressed to Kaiser Wilhelm II, 20 January 1889, 2.
110. LAV NRW R, BR 0005, no. 22776, petition from Heinrich K. addressed to Kaiser Wilhelm II, 20 July 1896.
111. Ibid., petition from Johann Josef J. addressed to Kaiser Wilhelm II, 21 November 1911.
112. Ibid., statement of the public prosecutor on the case of Johann Josef Johann Josef J., 29 December 1911.
113. See chapter 3.
114. This partially contradicts Sylvia Kesper-Biermann's claim that ex-convicts were not especially interested in having their honor restored. See Sylvia Kesper-Biermann, "Gerechtigkeit, Politik und Güte. Gnade im Deutschland des 19. Jahrhunderts," *Jahrbuch der Juristischen Zeitgeschichte* 13, no. 1 (2012): 21–47.
115. Bourdieu, *Outline of a Theory of Practice*, 10–30.

Chapter 5

"THE BLESSING OF THE WAR"
World War I as a Chance for Rehabilitation

Disenfranchised felons used the formal rehabilitation process to negotiate how they could "pay for their crimes," deploying various rhetorical strategies in doing so. They either pointed out their upstanding character or stressed their deep sense of remorse. Meanwhile, the authorities could also express their sympathy in relation to a request, for instance, if an ex-convict enjoyed a good reputation locally. In their deliberations about rehabilitation cases, the local authorities assessed both the seriousness of the crimes and the character of the felons, weighing them against one another, as well as various social interests. Most often, they found enough reasons to deny a request, with many stressing the need for a legal penalty to be carried out in full and for felons to "serve their time." Yet, others were convinced that social cohesion was important and that disenfranchisement could disrupt the sense of local community. Generally, there was a contrast between the stance of the local and national authorities. Whereas the local authorities were more open to different social interests, the national authorities were more adamant about denying rehabilitation requests out of respect for the penal code. This suggests that the clash between modern scholars' focus on resocialization and moral improvement and lawmakers' emphasis on justice and retribution was more trenchant on the national level than on the local one.

The outbreak of World War I seriously impacted these deliberations. Both prison officials and ex-convicts increasingly conceptualized alternative ways of "paying for a crime," and reconsidered the local and national interests of excluding or including ex-convicts in the army. Interestingly, welfare agents also started to assist disenfranchised felons get enlisted in the army for the sake of both the national community and the individual offenders. Historian Warren Rosenblum has previously argued that World War I "hastened the assimilation of the penal question into the social question."[1] One example was the pardon policy, which

---

Notes from this chapter begin on page 168.

was implemented to support the mobilization for total war and also helped to produce new welfare support initiatives for ex-convicts. Yet, while I, in part, draw on sources similar to those Rosenblum consulted for his study, I wish to highlight in this chapter how much disenfranchised felons, even at the height of war, were still treated as exceptional offenders with no entitlement to enlistment.

In this chapter, I will analyze the attempts of formerly incarcerated and disenfranchised citizens to join the ranks in the early war years, as well as the attempts of policymakers to convince people that the war could help to rehabilitate them. I will demonstrate that these attempts largely failed; the national authorities could not be convinced that these offenders could join the military. This illustrates that the national authorities adhered tenaciously to the principle of excluding "dishonored felons" from the army. I will conclude the chapter by showing that only in the final year of the war did the national authorities gradually set aside this "fundamental" principle, even though local authorities had already long been suggesting this change.

Remorse for a Momentary Lapse

Before World War I began, local authorities decided individual rehabilitation cases based on the nature of the offense and the character of the offender, debating each time which of these was more important. Sometimes the local authorities would even have completely diverging opinions about this. Carl H. from Werden, for instance, was sentenced in 1880 to six years in the penitentiary for a sex offense and was deprived of his civil privileges for ten years. His case was peculiar in that he had no trouble finding employment after his release: he was immediately employed at a factory in his hometown. Nonetheless, he petitioned for the restoration of civil privileges, focusing predominantly on the notion of remorse:

> I do not want to expound on how much I regret my misstep, how deeply it hurts me every day, how I still suffer from the deprivation of my civil privileges, how much I wish that His Majesty's mercy would restore them to me . . . So long as this [punishment] still afflicts me, it will be impossible for me to improve my situation, and yet, my large family necessitates that I do so.[2]

In response to this petition, the burgomaster of Werden highlighted Carl H.'s good character, noting his respectability in his community.[3] The state prosecutor, however, found the character of the offender irrelevant and emphasized the reprehensible nature of Carl H.'s crime, even adding, "Considering the case, the punishment even seems mild."[4]

Remorse was a key notion in the image of the "typical criminal" that criminologists (*Kriminalisten*) had in the first half of the nineteenth century.[5] They regarded criminals as human beings who had originally possessed a moral sense but turned to crime when they failed to obey the voice of their conscience. Since criminologists believed that this fall from grace was self-imposed, they also held that criminals' return to a "normal" life should be an autonomous choice resulting from genuine remorse. Accordingly, many ex-convicts tried to cast their crimes as momentary lapses and to express their remorse in their petitions. They hoped this would convince the authorities of their character as respectable citizens and make them eligible for rehabilitation.

Carl H. repeatedly used the notion of remorse (*Reue*) in his petition to show that his crime was not a sign of anti-authoritarian sentiment. His expression of remorse, in fact, signaled loyalty to the state. Peter J., an offender mentioned in chapter 4, similarly argued in his petition that his offense did not arise from any form of rebellion against the state and its institutions. Rather, his offense resulted from his wretched circumstances, which he even called a "stroke of fate" (*Schicksalsschlag*). Like Carl H., Peter J. also repeatedly expressed his remorse.[6] All in all, most of the civil servants who petitioned for the restoration of their rights downplayed their offenses, portraying them as unique events or momentary lapses that did not truly reflect their character. The concept of remorse (*Reue*) comes up frequently in these requests to indicate that a person's moral conscience was stronger than his status as a one-time offender.

Peter J. also compared himself to other offenders in his petition: "I believe that I have been treated worse than a robber or murderer because at least they do not lose their civil privileges."[7] This raises the question of why this man was sentenced to the penitentiary in the first place. As his petition detailed, he was dealing with a lot of money in his job and also loaned money to various people. In the end, he loaned more money than was readily available and was eventually arrested and convicted of fraud. Even though he considered his punishment just, he emphasized that he had never pursued any form of "pecuniary advantage." Evidently, Peter J. knew that this was crucial because "pursuit of profit" (*Gewinnsucht*) was a fundamental legal category that judges used to determine whether a crime was dishonorable.

Peter J. instead tried to convince the kaiser that he had committed his crime not for himself but for the benefit of others. Interestingly, Peter J. argued that he used the money to good ends and that he believed that his punishment was deserved. In other words, he did not try to downplay the seriousness of his offense but rather sought to change the perception of how it reflected on his character. He considered his actions a crime and a breach of the trust bestowed on him, by which he showed that he had internalized the norms of professional conduct and compliance, but considered his actions permissible as he believed he had acted for the good of others.

In reflecting on their crimes, ex-convicts used the fact that their offenses had not caused harm as ammunition. Albrecht Stein, the journalist no longer allowed to use his doctor's title (see chapter 4), averred that there were no excuses for forgery and that he deeply regretted his crime. Yet, he also noted in passing that it had harmed no one (except himself), which he believed softened its seriousness. All in all, his petition displays a tension between his loyal remorse and his own judgment about his crime.

Judgment of both character and the crime were important. Some ex-convicts were able to count on a great deal of sympathy because their character was valued. Adolf M., for instance, was a civil servant employed in the municipal government of Müllheim as a bookkeeper for the public gas and waterworks. In 1891, he was convicted of embezzlement and sentenced to two years and nine months in the penitentiary, combined with a three-year suspension of his civil privileges. Attenuating Adolf M.'s crime, Müllheim's burgomaster remarked that he liked "to live briskly" (*flott*) and simply could not resist appropriating some of the money he had to manage for his work. He thus seemingly suggested that Adolf M.'s offense was excusable and added that Adolf M. had always been an outstanding civil servant for the municipality. In fact, the burgomaster was very involved in the case: he had assisted Adolf M. after his release from the penitentiary and was also trying to help him find good employment. Yet, because this seemed nearly impossible, the burgomaster advised Adolf M. to petition for the restoration of his civil privileges.[8] In general, the local governments seemed to place more emphasis on an offender's character, whereas the state prosecutors gave more weight to the nature of the crime. Therefore, as was also visible in the case of Carl H., Adolf M. found it difficult to get his sentence reduced. Even though he was clearly a valued member of his community, embezzlement was too serious a crime to be pardoned.

Nevertheless, local authorities also often used the accused's character to highlight the reprehensible character of certain offenses. This became clear, for instance, in the case of Johann C. from the town of Crefeld, who was convicted of manslaughter. Crefeld's burgomaster wrote a lengthy statement reflecting on Johann C.'s general character. Johann C. had conducted himself very well after his release, he believed, but he still considered his crime unforgivable and exacerbated by Johann C.'s violent temperament. Moreover, he believed that Johann C. was more interested in getting his trade license back than in his civil privileges per se—a fact he felt spoke against the granting of Johann C.'s request. In other words, the burgomaster concluded that his strong interest in material matters was not a sign of good character.

War Pedagogy

Despite the prevalence of the notion of remorse in these petitions, some scholars expressed doubt about its function in criminal reform. At the end of the eighteenth century, penologists had already voiced such doubt, but around the turn of the twentieth century, such arguments resurfaced in academic journals.[9] For instance, Moritz Liepmann, a proponent of the "modern school," argued in a 1902 essay for the *Zeitschrift für die gesamte Strafrechtswissenschaft* that emphasis on remorse in writings on solitary confinement and moral reform in the first half of the nineteenth century had been counterproductive: it had paved the way for hypocrisy since many convicts faked remorse and it was impossible to prove whether they were being "authentic."[10] Because many penal experts tried to deal with this problem of hypocrisy, however, Liepmann focused on arguing that the premises of these former administrators had been wrong.[11] What society needed, he held, was not people continuously reflecting on their past decisions and thus experiencing constant conflict (*friedlos*) but people who could do their jobs normally and enjoy a peaceful life.[12] With this societal need in mind, penal administrators should approach offenders they considered capable of reform. His line of reasoning aligned well with the modern school's distinction between "corrigible" and "incorrigible" offenders.[13]

Interestingly, the outbreak of World War I prompted many people involved in the penal system to reconsider the importance of atonement and remorse and to find alternative ways for offenders to "pay" for their crimes. The war even revived Schmölder and Küppers's idea of putting (former) penitentiary inmates in the army.[14] These suggestions arose in the context of more general debates about the war's pedagogical effects and the opportunities it generated to reform the educational system.

Inspired by the enthusiasm in the early months of the war, many renowned German pedagogues regarded the conflict as having the potential, as a source of moral education, to boost the spirit of the people.[15] One such pedagogue was philosopher Rudolf Eucken. In a lecture at the University of Jena in 1914, he addressed the idea of the war's "moral powers" (*sittliche Kräfte*), suggesting that it could destroy the "selfish inclinations" of people who participated in it by creating a much-needed sense of mutual fellowship among the German people.[16] The famous drafter of the "Ten Commandments of Wartime Pedagogy," Theobald Ziegler, expressed similar thoughts in a lecture in the war's early months, referring to the war as an "educator" of the people.[17] Although he conceived of the war as an unwelcome event, he held that the war could create a stronger sense of comradeship,[18] bolstering this argument with a comparison to the war of 1870. The experiences of the soldiers during the German wars of unification and the Franco-Prussian War were crucial to generating a sense of mutual citizenship in the German Empire. In his words, this war created a set of "extraordinary Germans" that could thereafter serve the German nation.[19]

Thus, an important question of the so-called "War Pedagogy" was whether the experience at the front had a function in the moral education of German citizens.[20] Earlier, Ziegler had expressed more nuanced beliefs about warfare. In his influential book *Das Gefühl*, a book on people's sentiments in general, he painted a diverse picture of the influence of war on the moral senses of its participants. He argued in two directions: on the one hand, war could disrupt people's feelings of selfishness and could create enthusiasm for the common good, but, on the other hand, the experience of war made people blunt, "one-sided, narrow, rough and cruel."[21] At the outbreak of the war, Ziegler left out this second aspect, but other commentators did argue for a more diverse understanding of the effects of war on the participants. Based on his own experiences with warfare, the German art critic Erich Everth, for instance, wrote that war always had "polar" effects on its participants; it had the potential to strengthen the strong and weaken the weak.[22]

This debate about the war's impact on the sentiments of the people figured particularly prominently in the question of convicts. Some penal experts adopted Ziegler's and Eucken's wartime views about the conflict's positive effects and applied it to questions of criminal justice. They believed that the war would not only make "normal" citizens better people but also ex-convicts. Enlistment could thus truly become a "school" for degenerate citizens. A governor from Zwickau suggested, remarkably, that convicted felons be sent off to the front immediately, even before they were incarcerated.[23] Yet, in this debate, as in others, the distinctions between types of offenders proved crucial. For instance, this governor only wished to apply his suggestion to offenders who had acted out of "youthful naiveté," not to serious habitual offenders.

Many people who worked with convicts and ex-convicts were also convinced that the war could positively impact them. The German prison societies, like the Berlin-based Society for the Reformation of Convicts (Verein zur Besserung der Strafgefangenen) or the Prison Society of the Rhineland and Westphalia (Rheinisch-Westfälische Gefängnisgesellschaft), supported ex-convicts seeking rehabilitation. In fact, as the president of the Hamburg Prison Society, Heinrich Seyfarth, argued in 1915, it was the key priority of these societies to help annul the secondary sentences of formerly incarcerated individuals.[24] Consequently, prison societies actively contributed to the increase in rates of petitions seeking the restoration of people's right to join the army. The annual account of the Society for the Reformation of Convicts from 1914 indicated that a large population of ex-convicts utilized the same rhetoric about military service in the hopes of getting rehabilitated: "Many ex-convicts turned to us to help them be allowed to join the army. One can say with certainty that most were less inspired by financial distress than by patriotism and the fiery desire to rehabilitate themselves in the war."[25]

The members of the society were very supportive of ex-convicts' efforts to join the army. They even stated that these individuals' "brave conduct" on the front indicated that prison societies' assistance had succeeded, thus endorsing the quality of their work. Moreover, they presented this success as an argument for their professional point of view—that the best way to combat crime was to release ex-convicts into society, with participation in the army being one component of active involvement in society. Just like the Berlin Society for the Reformation of Convicts, the West-Prussian Prison Society estimated that most of these petitioners aimed to get rehabilitated in the war because they saw the war as an opportunity to pay for their offense in another way.

"From the Military Perspective"

Even though penal experts actively sought to convince officials that ex-convicts were both enthusiastic about joining the war and could contribute meaningfully to it, it remained unconventional to integrate penal policy and army discipline in the conflict's early years. Army officials still insisted that recruiting such individuals would threaten the "honor of the army," and the amnesties granted in the first months of the war did little to change their stance. The first of wave of amnesties in Germany on 4 August 1914 immediately pardoned German citizens convicted of acts of resistance against the state power and attempts to create public disorder, among others, and dropped ongoing legal proceedings for the same crimes. As a result, numerous Social Democrats convicted for public disturbance or insulting the authorities were released. This amnesty was partly due to the outbreak of the war, as part of the politics of the so-called *Burgfrieden*: partisan rivalries were set aside to support the government in its war aims.[26] The kaiser's official text accompanying the decree noted that the amnesty would encourage Germans' patriotism, promoting their willingness to make sacrifices for the greater cause.[27]

This large-scale amnesty was not unique to Germany but was also granted in other countries during the war, mainly to reduce labor shortages and to mobilize additional soldiers.[28] Nonetheless, the kaiser's granting of amnesty raised questions. Could participation in the war actually serve to rehabilitate the offenders? Also, what would happen to the charges that had been dropped after the war had ended? A prominent Augsburg lawyer, Joseph Fischer, asked precisely this in an article in the *Berliner Tageblatt*. After all, the decree had not made it clear whether this amnesty constituted a permanent acquittal or just a postponement of prosecution. Fischer argued that it would be fair for the accused not to have to stand trial after the war, essentially recommending that war participation function as a form of legal rehabilitation for these offenders.[29]

It is important to stress that this amnesty did not address the possible reversal of convicts' stripped rights, so a significant group of ex-offenders remained excluded. Soon after the first amnesty had been granted, it became clear that the authorities were firmly adhering to their principle of excluding such "serious" offenders. In fact, when the Minister of the Interior learned that many disenfranchised felons were sending petitions for the restoration of their rights, he sent a circular to local state attorneys urging them not to treat the amnesty as an occasion to rehabilitate former penitentiary inmates or other people deprived of their civil privileges. He considered it extremely important that the local authorities maintain this rule because rehabilitation "from the military perspective . . . is fundamentally unwanted."[30]

"Even the Social Democrats!"

Nonetheless, local state attorneys also had to think about the potential added value of ex-convicts in relation to their wartime ambitions. Each petition for a disenfranchised felon that reached the office of the district president in Aachen prompted the state attorney to individually assess the ex-convict and, when rehabilitation was not granted, to provide a detailed explanation. One case was that of Wilhelm A., a factory worker from Aachen. Having been sentenced at least twelve times for petty theft and other offenses, he was denied rehabilitation in December 1915 even though his petition mentioned that he was eager to join his brothers, who had been decorated with the Iron Cross for their service, in fighting the war. He even added that the only place he really felt happy was at the front.[31] The state attorney of Aachen denied Jacob H.'s request on the grounds that he repeatedly made unfounded criminal reports, was involved in many "dubious" lawsuits, and regularly engaged in legal proceedings to insult his fellow citizens: "Jacob H. is a malicious, spiteful and ruthless human being, who enjoys upsetting his opponents with denunciations and such things."[32]

In rejecting these requests, the state attorneys supported the idea that the enlistment of such individuals would endanger the army's honor. In denying Jakob P.'s request, the state attorney even made this point explicitly: "it is in the interest of the army and the reputation of Germany that convicts and people like them are forbidden from becoming soldiers."[33] These examples show that the local authorities actively appropriated the notion of exclusion of ex-convicts in their day-to-day deliberations because they felt that the army (and thus the reputation of the German Empire in general) needed to be safeguarded from their influence.

The amnesty, however, was important to many ex-convicts as it prompted reflection on their own situation. One such ex-convict was Karl H., a resident of Roelsdorf, who wrote a petition for his right to join the army to be restored on 1 August, the very day Germany declared war on France. A 32-year-old former soldier convicted of embezzlement, he had been deprived of his civil privileges (including the right to join the army) for a period of five years by a local court in 1912. He strongly opposed his exclusion from joining the troops: "I have atoned a lot for my actions, and have borne much discrimination, but the expulsion from the army is too much. I was always a good soldier and want to be one today. I give and sacrifice my life for your majesty."[34] Karl H.'s tone in his petition to the kaiser was both very patriotic and desperate.

After Karl H. heard about the amnesty, and when the authorities failed to react quickly, he continued to write petitions, not only addressed to the kaiser but also to his wife Augusta Victoria and his children. In the end, he wrote four petitions, underscoring his desperation. In his second letter, Karl H. directly commented on the imperial amnesty of 4 August, specifically comparing his own offenses to the types of charges the amnesty had caused to be dropped. In his mind, embezzlement was not worse than many political offenders' crimes (public disturbance, lèse majesté). The release of "Social Democrats" was particularly hard for him to bear (". . . even the Social Democrats!"). His own offense had solely harmed a "private individual," he argued—harm he felt he was capable of repairing—whereas Social Democrats had harmed the entire nation.[35]

On 21 August, he wrote another petition, this time addressed to the eldest son of Wilhelm II (Crown Prince Wilhelm). With the inclusion of the following remark, he left no doubt that the war was his main motivation for writing: "In this difficult time, when the motherland is under attack by its enemies to such a degree and everything depends on the kaiser's call to sacrifice our comforts and our blood, I am unhappy not to be worthy to take up arms with the others."[36] When this third petition failed, he wrote the Duchess of Braunschweig, the kaiser's youngest daughter, making nearly the same request.[37] In these four petitions, Karl H. sought to renegotiate the seriousness with which his crime was perceived compared to others and believed one should distinguish between crimes that harmed the interests of the nation and those that only hurt other individuals.

In many other petitions for the restoration of rights, petitioners expressed a clear desire to fight for the nation, particularly out of solidarity with other war participants (often friends and family members). In addition, they infused their statements with a sense of strong masculinity and an emphasis on their physical characteristics, which gave their requests a bodily dimension.[38] For example, Joseph S., a 38-year-old former coachman from Aachen, wrote in his petition: "As a young and strong single man, my heart bleeds in my body as I sit by and watch my comrades march into the battlefield and I have to stay behind."[39] Many also brought up past experience in the army to underscore their competence and their added value to the cause. Jacob H., for instance, a former non-commissioned officer deprived of his civil privileges for a period of five years, focused in his petition on his inability to fulfill (what he believed to be) his "duty" to fight for Germany's honor.[40]

Quirin P. echoed ex-convicts' wish to join the war in order to pay for their offenses in his petition from 1921, several years after the conflict was over. Although his immediate cause for petitioning was to obtain a trade license (*Freihandelserlaubnis*), which he could not do without the restoration of his rights, the war played an important role in his narrative. He had been convicted for assisting a married couple to obtain an abortion in 1912. He stated that his crime had not been motivated by profit, but that he did it out of "genuine human charity," since the woman was threatening to attempt suicide if he refused to help. Quirin P. used the oft-repeated argument that his offense was a one-time lapse to convince the authorities that he was a law-abiding citizen. He underscored this by referring to his offense as a misdemeanor (*Vergehen*), although it was unequivocally regarded as a felony (*Verbrechen*) in the legal vocabulary of that time.[41]

As noted, Quirin P.'s petition of 1921 focused on the war. The history of his case helps clarify why. When his offense became public knowledge, Quirin P. fled the country, but he returned to Aachen when the war began in 1914 and enlisted voluntarily. In his 1921 petition, he recalled that he had wanted to fight in the war "shoulder to shoulder" with his sons, and concluded that he could pay for his crime with his military service: "I preferred a heroic death over a ticket to the penitentiary as atonement for my offense."[42] Although he returned injured from the battlefield in 1915, he was convicted and sentenced to two years in the penitentiary and ten years without civil privileges. Quirin P.'s hope for rehabilitation as a citizen through military service was a false one since he was nonetheless sentenced for his crime. Quirin P.'s case is interesting since it demonstrates how ex-offenders, even so many years after the war, still entertained and expressed their own ideas about "paying" for a crime in battle.

During the war, some experts in academic journals complained about dishonored ex-convicts' "phantasm" of paying for their offenses in this way. "Even though they believe that they have their duty to fulfill," Ernst Kleeman, a prison minister from Leipzig, commented in the *Archiv für Kriminalanthropologie*, "they stand under extra scrutiny and will be immediately eliminated if they enlist."[43] Nonetheless, petitioners continued to draw on the idea that the war could be viewed in various ways as a chance for rehabilitation. The petitioners either evoked their interest in joining the army as proof of their good and honorable intentions, or they argued that the front allowed them to atone for their sins by being useful to the nation. In another sense, the war experience itself was supposed to be seen as a form of atonement. These ideas, in fact, constituted an alternative idea of punishment and rehabilitation that both former prisoners and welfare workers set against the traditional idea of remorse and atonement as possible grounds for rehabilitation.

Able Bodies in Search of Rehabilitation

Although the idea of paying for their crimes in alternative ways motivated some convicts to petition to join the army during World War I, some cited other reasons as well. One reason addressed in the petitions was that enlistment could provide a decent living. Nonetheless, members of prison societies favored the atonement argument for wartime participation. Therefore, they were eager to present evidence that war participation had a positive effect on people who had previously chosen a path of crime.

But what constituted such evidence? Although crime statistics were occasionally brought up to support the benefits of war participation on criminals, they were seriously flawed.[44] Nevertheless, this did not stop some from utilizing these statistics well after the war to argue that war enthusiasm had led to decreasing crime rates.[45] One salient development in the statistics was the tremendous decline in the German prison population. Of course, this was largely due to the broad amnesties the kaiser granted on several occasions. The amnesty from August 1914 was one of three in the first month of World War I, and many more followed.[46] In light of the large numbers of freed prisoners and charges dropped, commentators like Joseph Fischer justifiably raised the question of what would happen to these ex-convicts who had enlisted once the war ended.

Ernst Kleeman, by contrast, feared that the prison exodus was only temporary and that prisons would fill up immediately after hostilities ceased.[47] In other words, he believed the war would not seriously impact the morality of most German convicts in the long term. Once crime rates, especially youth crime rates, started to rise again in the second half of the war, many people warned in the national and local media that the prison exodus presented a frightening scenario.[48] Criminologist Robert Heindl, for instance, in the *Leipziger Neueste Nachrichten*, wrote that criminals should be detained even more securely during the war rather than set free because they could cause more trouble. He also feared their biological impact: setting criminals free, he argued, meant providing them with the opportunity to procreate. Thus, he even proposed to organize concentration camps to prevent them from procreating while free.[49] Many of these commentators likewise found it reprehensible that (ex-)prisoners could be recruited for the war. For instance, urging policymakers to dismiss this idea immediately, a journalist for the *Leipziger Neueste Nachrichten* actively contrasted the German "purity" regulations in conscription policy to the enlistment policies in France, where the French army had enlisted a regiment of Zwawa Berbers (Zouaves). Although the Zouaves were not a group of ex-convicts, they were "aliens," highlighting France's less protective policies. In essence, this journalist equated ex-convicts with foreigners. The German army, by contrast, protected its honorable nature by excluding ex-convicts from the ranks: "We want to leave Zouave regiments to the French."[50]

Welfare agents and prison officials, on the other hand, based their counterargument initially on the war enthusiasm they claimed to have observed in the German prisons during the first months of the war. A pastor employed at the penitentiary in Insterburg in Eastern Prussia, for instance, recalled that the mobilization of August 1914 had seriously improved the general mood among the inmates:

> At this moment, one thought touched the hearts of all: that the sounds of mobilization, which tore so many sons of the fatherland loose from their normal environment and occupation, would also bring fundamental changes for prisoners, in other words,

that it would mean freedom for them. After all, there is a large portion of the 450 inmates who had worn the royal army uniform in honor (or dishonor) and who on the battlefield hope to restore their human dignity for their fatherland.[51]

According to this prison pastor, the *Augusterlebnis* that so many people recalled from the first month of the war was not only experienced on the streets of bigger cities in Germany but could also be found in the country's institutions of confinement.[52] Of course, we should be careful not to conclude from these remarks that all prisoners were eager to join the army; they are better understood as the pastor's way of arguing for the importance of the pedagogical principles of criminal policy. If prisoners were so enthused by the war, he reasoned, perhaps they could even become useful in the war and join the troops to fight for "the honor of the German nation."

Prison governors and welfare society members frequently used this "enthusiasm" to argue that the war brought out human beings' better sentiments, even among detained criminals. Rudolf Franz, a pastor in the women's prison in Voigtsberg, spoke in this context of "the blessing of the war" for convicts.[53] Franz, however, did find that the situation was somewhat different among female inmates. In his view, immediate war enthusiasm was clearly a masculine reaction, whereas women were more inclined to react with fear and anxiety. Gradually, though, female prisoners also showed their willingness to support the war, he argued. Through this contrast, he could also emphasize the strong masculinity one could still find in the male prisoners. Yet the question remained whether the prisoners' enthusiasm constituted mere opportunism or a genuine manifestation of moral improvement.

Following Ziegler and Eucken's pedagogical principles, experience on the front was the most significant aspect of the war that people believed could stimulate goodness in people. The ultimate proof of this, however, had to be found in the personal accounts of former inmates who had joined the fight. Some prison officials possessed letters from former prisoners who had fought on the front and used them as testimonials to persuade people that war had a pedagogical effect on ex-convicts and that they did not undermine the army's honor.

Similarly, presidents of welfare societies for prisoners were eager to demonstrate the honorable intentions of many of their clients. The annual account of the Prison Society of the Rhineland and Westphalia, for example, referred to a letter it had received from a man the society had assisted in his efforts to join the ranks. The former convict had expressed his gratitude to the welfare society but also shared his belief that he had now truly atoned for his crime(s) after fighting for his nation in the war.[54] Welfare societies for ex-convicts enthusiastically welcomed testimonials like these.

Heinrich Seyfarth, a key figure in the German welfare organizations for discharged prisoners, also used such testimonials to make a similar point in a 1916 article for the *Blätter für Gefängniskunde*.[55] He was a strong advocate of the idea that prisoners should be enlisted in the war, even those deprived of their civil privileges and those still in prison, since fighting for the nation helped them become better human beings more effectively than incarceration. Furthermore, he argued, many former prisoners wished to participate in the war: "even among the offenders with lengthy criminal records are people who have a burning desire to rehabilitate themselves in the war."[56]

To underscore prisoners' wish to serve in the war, Seyfarth elaborated on a correspondence he had with one of the former convicts he had represented, Hugo B. from Hamburg. Convicted of multiple crimes, such as embezzlement, theft, and causing mayhem, Hugo B. still had the right to enlist, so he voluntarily joined a regiment in Bavaria the moment the war broke out. Though injured repeatedly during battle, he remained at the front to fight for the German nation, even receiving the Iron Cross for the courage he demonstrated. Seyfarth cited a letter Hugo B.'s captain had sent to the ex-convict's mother, who spoke of the "courage and intrepidity" her son had displayed during the war. Seyfarth also mentioned that he had personally met with Hugo B. after a serious injury had forced him to return from the front and that Hugo B. had proudly showed him his decorations.[57] Seyfarth used this story, one of many he claimed to know, to demonstrate the positive contribution formerly incarcerated individuals could make to the war cause.

In an article published the previous year, Seyfarth had already mentioned that he had personally helped fifteen former prisoners from Hamburg join the ranks, none of whom had had a damaging effect on the morale of the troops, and eight of whom had even received the Iron Cross for their courage at the front.[58] Seyfarth reinforced the positive effects the war had on them by referring to some of the letters they had sent him. Seyfarth also contrasted these stories with examples of excluded ex-convicts and prisoners deprived of the right to join the army. One, for instance, had become seriously depressed and mentally unstable.[59]

The question of whether the use of (former) prisoners in the war was advantageous to the military or the prisoners themselves was not a real dilemma for the people involved in this debate. In fact, most saw it as mutually beneficial: what was good for the war was also good for these ex-convicts and vice versa. However, the ex-convicts' physical constitution was of primary importance to many, making their usefulness to the army a key concern. Hence, many of the prison officials, including Seyfarth, often resorted to talking about the "bodies" that could be made useful in the war.

Thus, the welfare agents combined two rhetorical strategies in their effort to convince officials to accept ex-convicts into the ranks. On the one hand, they argued that the prisoners' moral disposition was not as bad as was often believed, and that participation in the war could only improve their disposition. On the other hand, they shifted attention away from prisoners' moral disposition to their physical strength, maintaining that manpower needs outweighed concerns about the honor of the army. Seyfarth, as one representative of this group, even believed that forty thousand or even fifty thousand extra men could be recruited for the war if the government followed his recommendations.[60] Sometimes, again stressing prisoners' bodily strength, welfare agents even argued that they could be used in labor units if they were still not considered fit to fight at the front.[61] Thus, even this kind of labor, indirectly supporting the war effort, could be conceived of as a form of atonement.

A Legal Breakthrough

All in all, the war prompted many ex-convicts to try and change their situation, with many welfare agents and prison officials supporting them in their efforts. On the national political level, however, the authorities only gradually shifted their perspective. The high number of ex-convicts in German society was a frequent topic during the war, but some commentators argued that this crisis only arose out of the circumstances of the war, whereas others believed that the war, in fact, presented an opportunity for long-needed reforms. Ernst Mamroth, a lawyer of good reputation from Breslau, for instance, wrote an open letter to the *Berliner Tageblatt* in August 1915, a year after the war broke out, arguing that the government could finally revise the general system of civil privileges and their possible suspension as it was untenable in wartime.[62] Many German academics, too, echoed this idea that the war constituted an opportunity to reform the legal system; one of their "wartime ambitions" was to find a solution to the problem of citizens being legally excluded from war participation.[63]

In the second half of 1916, after Field Marshal Paul von Hindenburg and General Erich Ludendorff assumed command of the German forces, the situation for disenfranchised offenders started to change. In a renewed attempt to win the war, these commanders put more emphasis on extracting manpower for it.[64] In December of that year, a true break with the prior policy occurred—one clearly motivated by this growing need for manpower: the High Command pushed the kaiser to issue a new decree; this time, however, the decree did not grant amnesty, like the ones before it, but enabled "dishonored" ex-convicts to regain their eligibility to join the army. Delaquis emphasized the decree's significance by highlighting its reversal of the "sacred and inviolable" legal measure of excluding dishonored citizens.[65]

After the decree of December 1916, local authorities were asked to actively search for people sentenced with the loss of honor. In May 1917 in the district of Aachen, fourteen people whose civil rights had been suspended were found and voluntarily enlisted; the public prosecutor considered them eligible for the restoration of their right to join the army. These people had been sentenced for various offenses, including robbery, trespassing, begging, and smuggling. One of them, Josef S., was sentenced for pimping in combination with physical abuse.[66] It is striking that someone with these offenses on his record was included in the public prosecutor's list of potential recruits as pimping was often explicitly mentioned by legal scholars as a primary example of a dishonorable offense. That such an individual was deemed eligible to join the army shows that the mentality regarding exclusion had truly changed within a short period of time.

Nonetheless, the authorities were likewise repeatedly asked to be consider "dishonored" ex-convicts' eligibility for the war very carefully. The decree presented an obvious conflict to some conservative leaders. Although many were still attached to the idea of exclusion, they also saw prisoners' potential usefulness for the war. The *de facto* commander-in-chief Erich Ludendorff was one such conservative. In a letter to Chancellor Georg von Hertling in December 1917, he tried to raise awareness of the "social evil" ex-convicts who were not active in the army generated in Germany. Ludendorff expressed his belief that the policy of excluding ex-offenders, combined with the wartime circumstances, created a social and economic problem and wasted a great deal of potential manpower.

At the same time, he did not wish to dispense with the idea of dishonoring a certain class of ex-convicts. Thus, Ludendorff tried to persuade Hertling to make a change in policy that could fulfill the ideas of punishment, retribution, and rehabilitation, but likewise address German people's "rightful discontent." This discontent derived from ex-convicts being employed in other sections of the German economy, receiving considerable money for little output, while soldiers at the front endured tremendous "stresses and strains" (*Strapazen*) for less payment. Clearly, Ludendorff felt that this discontent was "rightful" as it conflicted sharply with his own ideas about the moral economy of the German Empire, wherein "dishonored" convicts should not be better off than soldiers: "Former penitentiary inmates enjoy the protection of the fatherland just as much as any other person. I do not see why they could not be made useful for the fatherland with the same pay as the soldier."[67]

Consequently, Ludendorff urged Hertling to find a way to make "dishonored" ex-convicts useful for the war while upholding their demeaned status. His own suggestion was to employ them in the army but "without any honorable appearance" (meaning without a uniform and with less pay). Ludendorff clearly disagreed that serving in the war could morally improve offenders but still tried to utilize their manpower in a way that aligned with traditional ideas of punishment, retribution, and rehabilitation by creating several new distinctions within the army. In other words, unlike welfare agents who advocated that former prisoners could restore their honor in the war by joining the ranks, Ludendorff tried to mobilize their labor while retaining their "dishonored" status with the argument that this would help repay their "normal" debt to society.

Despite Ludendorff's (and others') wishes to the contrary, most of the "dishonored" ex-convicts were called to join the troops at the front in the final year of the war. The Ministry of Justice estimated that approximately 1,500 (ex-)convicts availed of this opportunity.[68] Although this recruitment (probably) did not change the course of the war, it did mark a crucial change in ideas about punishment and rehabilitation in the German Empire. The war challenged many of the seemingly entrenched ideas about crime and punishment, paying off one's debt to society, and the possibility of moral improvement. Various people involved in the penal system or conscription policy reinterpreted these ideas, dramatically revising the fundamental separation between the army and penitentiary inmates that had marked the moral economy of punishment, retribution, and rehabilitation before the outbreak of World War I. Yet, this was only possible in an alternative moral economy that either defined "honor" and "rehabilitation" in different moral terms or conceived of paying off one's debts in a new way.

The historiographical debates about the practices of inclusion and exclusion in the German army during World War I have been dominated by questions of age and citizenship. Yet, the question of including ex-convicts in the army was just as important to the historical actors deciding on matters of military conscription during this period.[69] Initially, the official policy concerning disenfranchised felons remained clear: they were to be excluded from joining the army—regardless of any possible reformatory effects army service might have had. The granting of several waves of amnesty during the first months of war did not change anything about this situation. Only in the final one and a half years of the war did perspectives begin to shift. The amnesty of December 1916 clearly played an important role in this change as it encouraged people to justify the temporary lifting of legal rules in ways that aligned with their beliefs about punishment and rehabilitation. Nonetheless, this did not mean that the legal constellation at the end of the war was completely new. The amnesty had temporarily raised hopes that ex-convicts could be rehabilitated after the war in accordance with official legal procedures, but no such "right to rehabilitation" was introduced. Even so, the changing understanding of the moral economy did make it easier for people to argue in favor of such legal reform in the postwar period.

Notes

1. Rosenblum, *Beyond the Prison Gates*, 121.
2. LAV NRW R, BR 0007, no. 30722, 62–63.
3. Ibid., 64.
4. Ibid., 65.
5. Peter Becker, *Verderbnis und Entartung*, 35–74. Becker distinguishes *Kriminalisten* (criminologists) from the first half of the nineteenth century, whose focus was on the model of "biogra-

phy," from those from the turn of the twentieth century, who focused more on the model of "genealogy."
6. LAV NRW R, BR 0005, no. 22776, petition from Peter J. addressed to Kaiser Wilhelm II, 17 August 1891.
7. Ibid.
8. LAV NRW R, BR 0007, no. 30722, statement from the burgomaster of Mülheim on the request of Adolf M., 12 February 1895.
9. Nutz, *Strafanstalt*, 59–61.
10. Moritz Liepmann, "Die Reue vom kriminalistischen Standpunkt," *ZStW* 22, no. 1 (1902): 72–98, 81.
11. On combating hypocrisy in prisons, see Schauz, *Strafen als moralische Besserung*, 184–86.
12. Liepmann, "Die Reue."
13. Wetzell, *Inventing the Criminal*, 36; Müller, *Verbrechensbekämpfung im Anstaltsstaat*, 131.
14. See chapter 2.
15. Fritz K. Ringer, *The Decline of the German Mandarins* (Cambridge, MA: Harvard University Press, 1969).
16. Rudolf Eucken, *Die sittlichen Kräfte des Krieges* (Leipzig: Gräfe, 1914).
17. Andrew Donson, *Youth in the Fatherless Land: War Pedagogy, Nationalism, and Authority in Germany, 1914–1918* (Cambridge, MA: Harvard University Press, 2010), 243–44.
18. Theobald Ziegler, *Der Krieg als Erzieher* (Frankfurt a.M: Knauer, 1914).
19. Ibid., 8.
20. Donson, *Youth in the Fatherless Land*, 59–67.
21. Theobald Ziegler, *Das Gefühl. Eine psychologische Untersuchung*, 5th edn. (Berlin: Göschen, 1912), 321.
22. Erich Everth, *Von der Seele des Soldaten im Felde. Bemerkungen eines Kriegsteilnehmers* (Jena: Diederichs, 1915), 45.
23. Freund, "Strafvollzug und Krieg," *BfG* 49 (1915): 167–71, 168.
24. Heinrich Seyfarth, "12. Jahresbericht des Deutschen Hilfsvereins für entlassene Gefangene in Hamburg für das Jahr 1915," *BfG* 50 (1915): 93.
25. *Bericht über die Wirksamkeit des Vereins zur Besserung der Strafgefangenen* (Berlin, 1914), 9.
26. Jeffrey Verhey, *The Spirit of 1914: Militarism, Myth, and Mobilization in Germany* (Cambridge: Cambridge University Press, 2000), 52–57.
27. Cited in *Berliner Börsen-Zeitung*, 5 August 1914.
28. Andrew Novak, *Comparative Executive Clemency: The Constitutional Pardon Power and the Prerogative of Mercy in Global Perspective* (London: Routlege, 2016), 10.
29. *Berliner Tageblatt*, 12 December 1914.
30. LAV NRW R, BR 0005, no. 22781, circular from the Minister of the Interior, 4 November 1914.
31. Ibid., petition from Wilhelm A. addressed to Kaiser Wilhelm II, 25 December 1915.
32. LAV NRW R, BR 0005, no. 22777, statement from the public prosecutor on the case of Jacob H., 19 October 1914.
33. Ibid., statement from the public prosecutor on the case of Jakob P. A similar phrase was used by the public prosecutor in the case of Joseph S.
34. LAV NRW R, BR 0005, no. 22777, petition from Karl H. addressed to Kaiser Wilhelm II, 1 August 1914.
35. The full quotation in translation reads as follows: "His Majesty the German Kaiser has heartily forgiven even the Social Democrats, who have done a lot of evil to his Majesty, and so I can expect that I will also receive forgiveness since I only inflicted something on a private man, which I can still make good in my life." Ibid., petition from Karl H. addressed to Victoria Augusta, 5 August 1914.

36. Ibid., petition from Karl H. addressed to Crown Prince Wilhelm, 21 August 1914.
37. Ibid., petition from Karl H. addressed to Victoria Louise, the Duchess of Braunschweig, 24 August 1914.
38. On strenuous masculinity, see Donson, *Youth in the Fatherless Land*, 229–30.
39. LAV NRW R, BR 0005, no. 22777, petition from Joseph S. addressed to Kaiser Wilhelm II, 1 October 1915.
40. Ibid., petition from Jacob H. addressed to Kaiser Wilhelm II, 3 August 1914. See also the petition of Jakob P., who was a reservist who felt it was his "duty" to fight for Germany. Ibid., petition from Jakob P. addressed to Kaiser Wilhelm II, 4 July 1915.
41. LAV NRW R, BR 0005, no. 22779, petition from Quirin P. to the Minister of the Interior, 26 August 1921.
42. Ibid.
43. Ernst Kleeman, "Kriegserfahrungen im Gefängnis," *AfK* 67, no. 1 (1915): 1–24, 3.
44. Hugo Hoegel, "Die Kriminalstatistik," *Deutsche Strafrechtszeitung* 3 (1916): 3–10; Ernst Delaquis, "Strafrechtliche Kriegsziele," *ZStW* 39, no. 1 (1918): 276–99, 283.
45. See, for example, Franz Exner, *Krieg und Kriminalität* (Leipzig: Wiegandt, 1926), 3. Wetzell, *Inventing the Criminal*, 109–15.
46. Cf. Carl Falck, "Der Krieg und die Staatsanwaltschaft," *DJZ* 20 (1915): 374–75; idem, "Die Gnadenerlasse vom 27. Januar 1916," *DJZ* 21 (1916): 36–39.
47. Ernst Kleeman, "Kriegserfahrungen im Gefängnis," *AKK* 67 (1915): 1–24, 5.
48. Cf. Donson, *Youth in the Fatherless Land*, 162–66.
49. Cited in "Eine gute Zeit für Zuchthäusler," *Leipziger Neueste Nachrichten*, 21 October 1916.
50. Ibid.
51. Pastor Lenkeit, "Kriegserinnerungen aus dem Zuchthaus," in *Kriegserlebnisse Ostpreussischer Pfarrer*, ed. Karl Moszeik, 169–78 (Berlin: Runge, 1915), 169. Cf. Freund, "Strafvollzug und Krieg."
52. On the question of whether the *Augusterlebnis* was reality or a myth created after the war for propaganda purposes, see Verhey, *The Spirit of 1914*.
53. Rudolf Franz, "Der Segen des Krieges für die Strafgefangenen," *BfG*, 49, no. 2 (1915): 221–25.
54. *Jahresbericht der Rheinisch Westfällischen Gefängnisgesellschaft* (Düsseldorf, 1915), 5.
55. Rosenblum, *Beyond the Prison Gates*, 133–35.
56. Heinrich Seyfarth, "Aus den Akten des deutschen Hilfsvereins für entlassene Gefangene Hamburg," *BfG* 50 (1916): 71–74.
57. Ibid.
58. Heinrich Seyfarth, "Strafvollzug und Kriegsdienst," *BfG* 49 (1915): 185–202, 192.
59. Ibid., 186–89.
60. Ibid., 197.
61. Schwandner, "Heeresdienst und Strafvollzug mit besonderer Berücksichtigung der Zuchthausstrafe," *BfG* 49 (1915): 198–200.
62. Ernst Mamroth, "Die bürgerlichen Ehrenrechte in der Kriegszeit," *Berliner Tageblatt*, 28 August 1915.
63. Cf. Karl Meyer, "Gesetzgebung und Krieg," *DJZ* 19, no. 21 (1914): 1229–32. An interesting example of such a "wartime ambition" was the introduction of a unified Central-European Penal Code for Germany and the Habsburg Monarchy: Franz von Liszt, "Einheitliches mitteleuropäisches Strafrecht," *ZStW* 38 (1917): 1–20. Cf. Kubiciel, "Einheitliches europäisches Strafrecht und vergleichende Darstellung seiner Grundlagen." These legal scholars' war ambitions have not yet received much scholarly attention, as Kesper-Biermann has also noted: Sylvia Kesper-Biermann, "Die Internationale Kriminalistische Vereinigung. zum Verhältnis von Wissenschaftsbeziehungen und Politik im Strafrecht 1889–1932," in *Die Internationalisierung von Strafrechtswissenschaft und Kriminalpolitik (1870–1930). Deutschland im Vergleich*, ed. Syl-

via Kesper-Biermann and Petra Overath (Berlin: BWV, Berliner Wiss.-Verl., 2007), 85–107, 98.
64. Martin Kitchen, *The Silent Dictatorship: The Politics of the German High Command under Hindenburg and Ludendorff, 1916–1918* (New York: Holmes & Meier Publishers, 1976), 56.
65. Delaquis, "Strafrechtliche Kriegsziele," 298.
66. LAV NRW R, BR 0005, no. 22777, register of ex-convicts residing in Aachen who had voluntarily enlisted in the army, 9 May 1917.
67. LAV BW, S: M 1/7 Bü 29, copy of letter from Erich Ludendorff to Georg von Hertling, 28 December 1917, 29, 66.
68. Ernst von Wrisberg, *Heer und Heimat 1914–1918* (Leipzig: Koehler, 1921), 96–97.
69. Gosewinkel, *Schutz und Freiheit*, 98–134.

Chapter 6

"Your Honor Is Not My Honor"
Disenfranchisement and Rehabilitation as a Political Battleground from the War to the End of the Weimar Republic

This chapter describes the critique of felony disenfranchisement that erupted in the Weimar Republic. From the mid-nineteenth century, felony disenfranchisement had been criticized by some scholars as a severe hindrance to ex-convicts' reintegration and moral improvement, but during and after World War I, it increasingly came to be viewed as an "uncivilized" punishment—a relic that needed to be abolished. In the first months after the war, opposition to disenfranchisement clearly grew in scholarly circles. Plans to abolish the punishment suddenly became very serious and were actively debated in the circles of the Internationale Kriminalistische Vereinigung (IKV). This debate was novel in that it did not focus on judges' verdicts but on felony disenfranchisement itself, along with the fundamental distinction between "dishonorable" actions and morally permissible offenses.

This chapter also shows that, even though the debate was mostly confined to scholarly circles, the general public had likewise begun to feel that felony disenfranchisement served no purpose. Indeed, in the early Weimar Republic, critics of felony disenfranchisement were ascendant. The Reichstag was close to abolishing the punishment from the penal code, but in the mid-1920s, the mood shifted in favor of the punishment's advocates. The assassination of the influential politician Walther Rathenau and the subsequent introduction of the Republikschutzgesetz (Law for the Protection of the Republic) can be seen as a turning point. Following these events, influential scholars started to reevaluate felony disenfranchisement as a means of producing solidarity. The reform of penal law, which by that time was well underway and included the abolition of felony disenfranchisement, was put on hold in 1922. The idea that felony disenfranchisement enhanced a sense

---

Notes from this chapter begin on page 200.

of community spread to several political parties, becoming part of their agendas. In the end, the Nazi Party also highlighted it in its agenda, but it importantly subordinated the notion of honor to that of the *Volk*. This would not have happened, however, had the notion of "dishonorable disposition" not already become a battleground in efforts to persecute revolutionaries after the war.

The Revolutionary Postwar Era

The immediate postwar era was a time of great political turmoil. In November 1918, Socialist Party members proclaimed the republic after the leader of the Majority Social Democratic Party of Germany (MSPD), Friedrich Ebert, had been appointed Reich Chancellor and Kaiser Wilhelm II had abdicated the Prussian and German crown. In the period that followed, Germany witnessed numerous violent confrontations between left-wing revolutionaries and right-wing paramilitary groups. In the midst of these, in January 1919, the government formally in charge announced that there would be elections for the "National Constitutional Assembly" (Verfassunggebende Deutsche Nationalversammlung). The National Assembly (afterward known as the Weimar Assembly) functioned as the provisional German parliament.

Holding elections for this assembly was, in many ways, a historical achievement in itself; for instance, they introduced women's suffrage, resulting in the voting procedure being ahead of its time from an international perspective.[1] Meanwhile, in the Prussian voting system, the MSPD had managed to abolish the *Dreiklassenwahlrecht* (see discussion in chapter 2), making the elections in Prussia more equal, too. Thus, in a short time, German politicians had achieved a great deal on the level of electoral policy. In the Social-Democratic press, the German electoral system was, indeed, often celebrated as the most liberal voting procedure in the world (*das freieste Wahlrecht der Welt*).[2]

What was innovative about the Weimar Constitution, which the National Assembly passed in August 1919, was that it explicitly listed the individual rights of all German citizens for the first time. As discussed in chapter 1, up until that time the civil privileges had been defined in the penal code. However, since the penal code remained unaltered in 1919, this created a peculiar parallel system: the civil privileges (*bürgerliche Ehrenrechte*) defined in penal law coexisted with the civil rights (*staatsbürgerliche Rechte*) defined in the constitution.[3] This explains why, in the case of franchise rights, for instance, the constitution did not guarantee an unconditional right to vote but relegated this to the voting law. Thus, despite its progressivism, the Weimar constitution had no real significance for the provisions on felony disenfranchisement. Consequently, it remained a harsh reality in many ways after the war: a wave of crime in the final year of the war led to many people having their rights suspended.

In fact, there were still initiatives to instrumentalize felony disenfranchisement for various political ideologies, for example the socialist ideology. In April 1919, during the second Reichsrätekongress, Arthur Crispien, at that time an influential member of the Independent Social Democratic Party of Germany (USPD), suggested that felony disenfranchisement be included in the voting policy for works councils, which emerged all across Germany in the aftermath of Word War I. Crispien argued that people who had acted dishonorably "from a socialist perspective" should be excluded from the voting procedure for the works councils; that is, those whose "socialist rights of honor" (*sozialistische Ehrenrechte*) had been suspended by a socialist court should be excluded from the franchise.[4] Although it is not clear what Crispien meant by "socialist rights of honor," the example shows that felony disenfranchisement was still a vivid element of political discourse in the postwar years, even in left-wing political circles.

Yet, the punishment's future was uncertain in the early Weimar Republic. In fact, social engineers who believed that "society" and "community" could be planned with tools from the applied sciences increasingly influenced Weimar politics between 1919 and 1924.[5] The sudden end of the war created an experience of a rupture, which numerous politicians welcomed as presenting a possibility of social and cultural renewal.[6] Many citizens perceived this time as a so-called *Traumland* (dreamland) phase—a period of free-floating utopian ideas about the organization of society.[7] The notion of a welfare state (*Sozialstaat*) was writ large in the Weimar Republic's constitution, prompting a large expansion of welfare policies that had already been introduced in the German Empire.[8] In the midst of politicians' and social engineers' attempts to build a new society from the ground up, the future of felony disenfranchisement was also debated, with more people feeling that felony disenfranchisement was incongruent with the idea of moral improvement.

Other historians of penal policy in the Weimar Republic have demonstrated the focus on welfare policy in the penal system of that time. Rosenblum, for instance, argues that there was a widespread consensus about the social function of penal policy in this era. The ideas of social engineers dominated the landscape of Germany's interwar criminal justice system. This was most visible in the institution of welfare assistance to courts, and the implementation of the "stages system," a system that prepared inmates for life in freedom by granting them gradual benefits inside the facility.[9] With the penal system so aligned with the philosophy of the social welfare state, the punishment of felony disenfranchisement was hotly debated. Two fundamentally opposed visions of its function and place in Weimar society existed in scholarly circles. One group was deeply critical of it and wanted to abolish it, while the other maintained that the punishment could benefit German society by boosting the morale of the people. Both sides, however, were motivated by the same objective: to create a stronger sense of community in the new republic.

Thus, advocates of felony disenfranchisement, whose opinions will be discussed further on in this chapter, believed that the punishment was indispensable to creating a much-needed sense of community in the deeply divided nation. Indeed, supporters of the republican form of government in the "improvised democracy" of Weimar tirelessly pursued a common narrative with a view to creating a sense of togetherness.[10] In this context, these advocates felt that "dishonoring" felons would unite Germans in their aversion to these common enemies and create a sense of national belonging. Indeed, several historians have emphasized Weimar leaders' efforts to create a collective sense of national community and to affirm the cultural authority of the republic.[11] Critics of felony disenfranchisement, however, believed that disenfranchisement undermined the sense of community as it generated disparities in society and frustrated the resocialization programs that were so central to many of Weimar's reform initiatives.

These two opposing ideas about the function of disenfranchisement, however, cannot simply be reduced to the disparity between the "classic" and the "modern" legal scholars. Even though advocates of felony disenfranchisement generally belonged to the circles of the "classics," the most vocal people on both sides were actually members of the progressive IKV, sharing its "modern" take on penal policy. Some strong advocates were just as convinced as the critics that welfare assistance and resocialization programs were crucial, above all, in helping "corrigible" convicts to reform themselves into productive citizens.

Among liberal scholars, there were two main arguments for abolishing the punishment: the first was informed by the broader ideology about the purpose of punishment and its connection to welfare policies; within this ideology, the stigmatization of disenfranchisement was seen as a hindrance to offenders' resocialization. The second pertained to more immediate concerns converging around the "politicization" of the punishment in the immediate aftermath of the war. In this context, liberal scholars believed that the notion of the "dishonorable disposition" had become too much of a battleground in courtrooms and in the media.

Liebknecht's Penitentiary Status as a Badge of Honor

As argued in previous chapters, a "dishonorable disposition" was crucial to disenfranchisement sentences. Yet, immediately after World War I, this notion came to be contested as never before. Many revolutionaries sought to renegotiate what was considered honorable even more emphatically, while the judiciary's application of the punishment seemed ever more arbitrary. All in all, this increased the politicization of the punishment.

An important moment in this politicization was the trial against Karl Liebknecht during World War I. In 1917, Liebknecht was tried for high treason for a second time; the first trial had taken place in 1907 (see chapter 3) and ended in him being sentenced to open custody.[12] This time, he was charged with high treason after organizing a large demonstration to protest the war spending in June 1916. This famous trial ended differently than the 1907 trial as Liebknecht was sentenced with the very harsh punishments of penitentiary confinement and disenfranchisement. The large group of followers that had gathered around Liebknecht and Rosa Luxemburg was outraged,[13] seeing the sentence as a clear sign that the judges had instrumentalized the war to legitimate this excessive punishment in order to silence political protest. After the trial and his criminal conviction, Liebknecht insisted that the exact wording of the plea he made before the high court in Leipzig after hearing the verdict be included in the records. It read:

> You and I, we belong to two different worlds and speak two different languages. . . . "Penitentiary!" "Loss of civil privileges!" Yes, yes! Your honor is not my honor! But I can assure you that no general ever wore his uniform with as much honor as I will wear the penitentiary outfit.[14]

This statement became a banner for the political movement that had splintered from the SPD because of heightened frictions within the party about the level of support for the military spending, the issuing of war bonds and the so-called *Burgfrieden*. Like many Social Democrats before him, Liebknecht drew on typical criticisms of judges, accusing them of a lack of worldliness. However, apart from that, Liebknecht's way of protesting was novel: critics before him had always implicitly supported the "dishonoring" component of these sentences, but he instead called the punishment an "honor." By regarding the penitentiary sentence as honorable, he reversed the logic of the "honor punishment" of disenfranchisement.

Of course, the verdict against Liebknecht had one very practical consequence: he was no longer eligible to be a member of the Prussian House of Representatives or the Reichstag. This effect was also clear for his fellow party member, Rosa Luxemburg, who argued that this consequence had, in fact, motivated the punishment. In a pamphlet, she accused the authorities of politically instrumentalizing it: "Liebknecht certainly had to be sent to the penitentiary since the deprivation of his civil privileges is connected with this punishment, and he thus lost his seat in the Reichstag and Landtag!"[15] Independent Social Democratic Party founder Arthur Stadthagen likewise argued in the Reichstag that the sentence was clearly motivated by a desire to make Liebknecht ineligible for parliament, adding that this political instrumentalization reminded him of the reactionary era of the 1850s, when political offenders also received harsh sentences.[16] Even the board of the MSPD (despite Liebknecht's radical break from it) shared Luxemburg's and Stadthagen's criticism of the sentence—not because they felt that Liebknecht should not be punished but because they believed that disenfranchisement was not the appropriate way to go about punishing him.[17]

After the trial, Liebknecht's sympathizers, who demonstrated against the sentence under the threat of being detained themselves (sometimes even in front of the penitentiary where he was incarcerated), distributed numerous pamphlets with slogans such as "Long live the penitentiary convict Liebknecht!"[18] Liebknecht's followers thus turned his status as a penitentiary convict into a kind of praise and honor, as Luxemburg clearly underscored in one of the pamphlets: "Liebknecht's penitentiary uniform is the best testament to his honor and the fact that he served the people and their true interests and fought for the future of socialism."[19] Liebknecht's writings and actions surely contributed to making disenfranchisement a battleground after World War I, particularly since he openly inveighed against the existence of such punishments in his famous treatise *Gegen die Freiheitsstrafe*, which he wrote in 1918 after his release from prison.[20] Luxemburg and Liebknecht had actively sought to redefine the fundamental assumptions of the criminal justice system. Their movement purposefully appropriated the old symbols of some felons' morally reprehensible character, like penitentiary outfits and disenfranchisement, as badges of honor.

The "Dishonorable Disposition" Contested

The immediate postwar years witnessed several groundbreaking revolutionary moments: the Kiel Mutiny in November 1918, initiated by German Navy members protesting the planned mission against the British Navy, the proclamation of the republic that same month by Social Democrat Philipp Scheidemann, the Spartacist uprising in January 1919 culminating in the assassination of Liebknecht and Luxemburg by the paramilitary Free Corps, and several other separatist revolts across the German territory. In this time of social unrest, the contested nature of the notion of "dishonorable disposition" was apparent in a wave of high treason trials following the revolution of 1918/19. The judiciary's treatment of the political offenders in these events increasingly came under attack in several areas of the German Empire.[21]

The press and commentators interested in the question of political justice directed most of their attention to the situation in Bavaria. In November 1918, the Wittelsbach dynasty was forced to abdicate, which resulted in the founding of the People's State of Bavaria, which was led by the Independent Social Democrat Kurt Eisner. After Eisner was assassinated in February 1919, Munich saw a new wave of revolutionary activities leading up to the founding of the short-lived Bavarian Council Republic in April 1919.[22] The establishment and dismantling of the Bavarian Council Republic and the subsequent high treason trials against many of its leaders put a spotlight on this question of political justice.

The trials against people involved in the Bavarian Council Republic had all come to an end by late 1919. The most prominent people charged with high treason—whose verdicts were the most discussed in the press—were the leaders of the Council Republic: Ernst Toller, Erich Mühsam, Otto Neurath, Tobias Axelrod, Arnold Wadler, and Eugen Leviné. Many observers considered these trials to be a "test" of the criminal justice system. Emil Gumbel's important critical treatise on political justice in the Weimar Republic, published by the Deutsche Liga für Menschenrechten (German League for Human Rights) in 1922, listed all the verdicts in these cases.[23] In each individual case, the judges had to assess whether the accused had acted out of an "honorable" or "dishonorable" disposition, but none of the trials clarified what these terms meant.

In the trial against Toller, for instance, the public prosecutor demanded that he be sentenced to open custody because the trial had proved to him that Toller had not acted out of a dishonorable disposition. Toller was lucky because many notable intellectuals had vouched for his honorable character during the trial. Karl Hauptmann, Thomas Mann, Romain Rolland, and Max Weber—all high-profile intellectuals from Munich—had testified to his good character. Thomas Mann and other artists, for instance, had stated that his poetry expressed a laudable ethos that could not possibly come from a person with a "dishonorable disposition."[24] Interestingly, Max Weber, taking a rather different tack, had remarked that Toller was "ignorant" about politics and "worldly affairs" and that his ideas were of a free-floating kind.[25] Thus, Weber tried to demonstrate that Toller had no dishonorable intentions not by pointing out his political idealism but by underscoring his youthful naiveté.

Whereas Toller received the kind of privileged treatment befitting political offenders, things looked quite different for the others. Tobias Axelrod and Arnold Wadler (other leaders of the Council Republic) were sentenced to the penitentiary and had their civil privileges suspended. The treatment of Eugen Leviné, who had been sent by the communist KPD in March of that year to reorganize the republic, generated the most controversy.[26] As the judiciary considered him most responsible for the radicalization of the Council Republic, he was sentenced to death and had his civil privileges suspended. Various media expressed outrage at the differences between these verdicts, mostly noting the marked contrast between the treatment of Neurath, Mühsam, and Toller, on the one hand, and that of Leviné, Axelrod, and Wadler on the other. Advocates for the abolition of the death penalty were also upset about Leviné being sentenced to death.[27] In the end, most commentators attributed the disparity to the right-wing stance of the judges in Munich, drawing attention to the often-arbitrary way in which they had applied the notion of the dishonorable disposition.

These verdicts would perhaps not have come under such fire if not for another trial that occurred in the aftermath of the Bavarian Council Republic—against the right-wing assassin of Kurt Eisner, the Minister-President of the People's State of Bavaria that preceded the Council Republic, Anton Graf von Arco auf Valley (Arco-Valley). Arco-Valley was a member of the *völkisch* Thule Society and saw

Eisner as the principal instigator of the revolution against the old monarchy. However, Arco-Valley claimed that he had acted alone out of his "hatred" for Eisner resulting from Eisner's treason to the "king and fatherland."[28] Tried a year after the assassination, he was initially sentenced to death but was not deprived of his civil privileges, meaning that it was, unlike Leviné's, an "honorable" death sentence.

In his defense, Arco-Valley argued that the assassination was "a matter of honor" and that he felt no remorse for committing it: "[Eisner] had made our so respected people ridiculous through childish political maneuvers in the German Reich and abroad. This is a matter of honor!"[29] Arco-Valley only expressed remorse for the "crafty" (*hinterlistig*) way in which he had assassinated Eisner. Interestingly, he stated that it conflicted with the demands of his own code of honor:

> I regret that I had to commit such an insidious attack, but I believed that I could cleanse the dishonor of this insidious attack with my blood. In general, I regret every human life lost, I regret that I shot some Englishmen, but they were sincere and honorable opponents. Eisner, however, was an insidious traitor and I could only counter him with insidiousness.[30]

By demonstrating his regret for his insidiousness, he tried to appeal to the judge's understanding of honorable conduct and further underscore his own attachment to his personal code of honor. Moreover, since he considered Eisner's actions to have been just as low, he thought that his methods were justified and that the harms were balanced out. Apparently, Acro-Valley's honor rhetoric persuaded the judge. Adding to the controversy of the initial verdict, the Bavarian Ministry of Justice turned Arco-Valley's sentence from death to open custody by an act of sovereign grace.

Socialist writers denounced the disparity between Arco-Valley's punishment and those of Leviné and Axelrod. But critics did not necessarily complain that Arco-Valley's sentence was too mild. Editors of the communist *Schlesische Arbeiter-Zeitung*, for instance, agreed with the "milder" sentence given to this political opponent of theirs because they stood by their opinion that political offenders should not be treated as "common criminals." However, they contended that people like Leviné and Axelrod should have been treated similarly, rather than being locked up like "common criminals" and not as privileged political offenders.[31]

Another important case that invited comparison with these verdicts was that of Alois Lindner, the man who had tried to assassinate the MSPD politician Erhard Auer the day Eisner was killed. This was presumably an act of vengeance as Lindner believed that Auer had ordered Eisner's assassination.[32] In contrast to Arco-Valley, Lindner was sentenced with lengthy penitentiary incarceration and deprived of his civil privileges. Opinions differed, though, about what sentence was just for this attempted assassin. A writer for the Social Democratic newpaper

Volksstimme, for instance, argued that assassination was never permissible and that the MSPD had always been against it. In his eyes, Lindner's attempt to assassinate Auer was not a truly Social Democratic act, and not even an act of political conviction, but resulted from a feeble-minded individual (*Schwachsinniger*) acting out of ignorance (*Unwissenheit*).[33] By applying the "No true Scotsman" fallacy to this case, he sought to disassociate the SPD from all political assassins by asserting that no true Social Democrat had ever tried to commit murder for political ends.

Overall, the diverging outcomes of such trials against political activists—which were most prominent in Bavaria but occurred all over Germany—turned the notion of the "honorable disposition" into a battleground. Against the backdrop of these verdicts' asymmetry, as Gumbel called it,[34] people increasingly accused the judges of abusing their discretion to determine whether an offender had acted out of an honorable or dishonorable disposition for political ends.[35] That judges had the privilege of tenure, meaning they could not be removed from office, only sharpened the criticism against them. This privilege, as Karl Dietrich Bracher has argued, enabled the judiciary to remain an important authoritarian element in the Weimar Republic.[36] It was not uncommon in the following years of the Weimar Republic for judges to be accused of constituting some kind of fifth column within the state.[37] At the same time, a new type of "political barrister" who often pursued a partisan ideological agenda emerged in this era, contributing to the more confrontational character of the Weimar system of justice.[38]

Fellow Travelers

As a result of the revolutionary moment after the war, the prison population of the Weimar Republic had entirely changed. Ever more people were sentenced for contributing to political protest. "Political crime," it seemed, had become a mass phenomenon, making the question of disenfranchisement more pressing. In March 1920, in many towns across Germany, people had participated in violent uprisings in opposition to or in support of the Kapp–Lüttwitz Putsch and the Ruhr uprising. The Kapp–Lüttwitz Putsch was the failed attempt of former general Walther von Lüttwitz, an ardent monarchist and commander of the Freikorps in Berlin, to launch a coup d'état with the assistance of the Prussian high civil servant Wolfgang Kapp. The Ruhr uprising grew out of large strikes initiated by the labor movement and was largely organized in reaction to the Kapp–Lüttwitz Putsch. The leaders of the Kapp–Lüttwitz Putsch received remarkably mild sentences while some striking workers received incredibly harsh sentences, often including disenfranchisement.[39]

Since many people were taken into custody after these events, they could not vote in prison. This immediately put the first Reichstag elections in 1920 under serious tension. The records of the debate in the National Constitutional Assembly on the voting regulations for the Reichstag demonstrate the extent to which politicians tried to adjust disenfranchisement rules for their own political gain. Considering the mixture of offenders, from army members who had participated in a coup d'état to laborers who protested in reaction to it, the question had become whether this kind of mass disenfranchisement benefited one or the other political party too greatly.[40] Members of the USPD, who saw many party members stripped of their right to vote, vigorously attacked the system of felony disenfranchisement. But they simultaneously wanted to "depoliticize" the army by excluding army members from the right to vote. The franchise itself thus became a battleground, and felony disenfranchisement factored into its contested status.

Complicating matters, as many commentators reflected after the Kapp–Lüttwitz Putsch and the Rhine Strike, was the fact that so many people were now being punished for politically motivated crimes. This made it more problematic to distinguish between "political offenders" and "common criminals." Friedrich Kitzinger, a prominent legal commentator of the Weimar Republic, used these cases to openly criticize the underlying ideas of the penal code and to specifically address the unprecedented number of political offenders. In fact, he believed that there was a large middle group of "troublemakers" who were neither "serious criminals" nor selfless idealistic offenders but were, rather, psychologically triggered to commit these offenses by a mixture of political idealism and personal egotism. He described them as "recruited and voluntary fellow travelers; confluent latecomers; a motley crew with various motives: a lust for trouble making, naïveté, seduction and herd reflex, a combination of political conviction, personal egotism and opportunism."[41] It was novel, Kitzinger maintained, that so many people were committing political offenses—this had never occurred in the time of the German Empire. Furthermore, as one could not know the exact psychological state of all in these masses, he considered it absurd that there were only two kinds of punishments for such "political" offenders, and that these were at the extreme ends of the penal system: penitentiary with disenfranchisement or open custody without any loss of civil status. Kitzinger was therefore one of many scholars then recommending that the prescriptions in the penal code be changed to the effect that such "fellow travelers" could be sentenced with the "middle" kind of incarceration: regular prison.

Some commentators considered the addition of this middle category an insult to political offenders and a way of denying them their privileged treatment. Gustav Klingelhöfer, a journalist and active politician for the MSPD and USPD, for instance, responded to Kitzinger's suggestion by accusing him of doing exactly what many judicial authorities in the German Empire had tried to do: redefine "political" acts as "criminal" ones to deny political offenders their privileged status.[42] In doing so, Klingelhöfer presented himself as a fierce supporter of privileged punishments but argued that they were only possible if the authorities upheld a clear distinction between "criminal" actions—motivated by personal and financial gain—and idealistic, political ones.⁴³

Hans von Hentig, a young and promising criminologist who had made a name for himself with his refutation of the application of natural selection theories to the question of criminality, also tackled the problem of "pseudo-political" offenders.⁴⁴ He commented on this issue in response to the amnesty many participants had received, often due to a simple lack of judicial capacity. In the summer of 1920, after the Kapp–Lüttwitz Putsch had ended, the judicial system was too overburdened to deal with all the people charged with high treason. They could not be put on trial, and the prisons were overcrowded.⁴⁵ The government

Figure 6.1. Cartoonist Thomas Theodor Heine depicts the political fellow traveler as a chameleon crawling out of a dilapidated house: "Which way is the wind blowing today?" Thomas Theodor Heine, "Der Mitläufer," *Simplicissimus* 24, no. 9 (1919): 117. Courtesy Klassik Stiftung Weimar.

therefore announced a broad amnesty affecting large groups of people, dropping charges against them and releasing them from prison. In fact, it had already issued the first amnesty in late 1918 for some participants of the November revolutions. It issued a much broader amnesty in August 1920 for participants of the Kapp–Lüttwitz Putsch and the Ruhr uprising.

Hentig, who had also participated in the Bavarian Council Republic, argued that these amnesties were, from a criminological standpoint, fully unwarranted measures since the authorities had no idea how to justify distinctions between "real political offenders" and "pseudo-political" ones. According to Hentig, many of the political offenders who, for instance, supported the Kapp–Lüttwitz Putsch had acted out of nothing more than selfish motives: "Just as there are ascetics who act out of self-interest, so there are not seldom criminals who act on an extreme political idea and do things like harm people for the revolution, while at the same time acting to their own personal advantage."[46]

With so many more people incarcerated for political crimes, the question of disfranchisement took on greater political significance. Even Fritz von Calker, a scholar who had always strongly supported the privileged treatment of political offenders (see chapter 3), agreed with Kitzinger and recommended sending most "political offenders" to a regular prison to avoid judges having to choose between harsh sentences for "common criminals" and mild ones for "political offenders."[47] Meanwhile, the authorities could keep these "fellow travelers" in custody so that they would not pose a serious threat to the new republic, as Hentig feared.[48] The notion of the "fellow traveler" was therefore a convenient instrument enabling legal authorities to both level up people labeled as "serious criminals" and to downgrade supposedly "political offenders."

The IKV

The trials against members of the Bavarian Council Republic and the mass nature of political crime became important fodder for discussion for penal justice experts. The work of one young legal scholar, in particular, proved crucial: Eduard Guckenheimer. In 1921, he finished a legal dissertation under the auspices of Moritz Liepmann on the "dishonorable disposition," in which he studied the trials against members of the Bavarian Council Republic, using them as a litmus test for the usefulness of the notion of the "dishonorable disposition" in criminal policy. In short, he concluded that the outcome of these trials demonstrated how empty and meaningless the notion had become.

In his assessment, Guckenheimer contrasted the use of the notion in his present time to its use in the German Empire. In the authoritative hierarchical state (*Obrigkeitsstaat*) of the Wilhelmine era, the "dishonorable disposition" had been useful, he maintained, as there was some consensus about what constituted "common criminal behavior" and what made up a political offense. Such a consensus about the concept was fundamentally missing in the early Weimar Republic, however. The disparities in the trials' verdicts bolstered his and others' suspicions that judges decided whether the accused had acted "dishonorably" on the basis of their political convictions. Disenfranchisement, he argued, was designed for peaceful times, but in heated political moments, humans lacked the cognitive ability to make neutral decisions about an offender's disposition.[49] In this sense, Guckenheimer framed the problem as one of descriptive psychology and judges' ability to make such decisions. His advisor Moritz Liepmann, by that time a prominent legal authority, felt that Guckenheimer's book persuasively demonstrated the shortcomings of the category of the "dishonorable disposition," particularly in the context of political crimes. Thus, Liepmann continued, Guckenheimer had provided the ultimate arguments for abolishing this notion from the penal code, and, by extension, the punishment of disenfranchisement, as well.[50]

In 1921, the IKV conference in Jena placed the issue of disenfranchisement high on the agenda. The political context of this punishment was hard to dismiss. After the war, the IKV had largely lost its international character because Germany's invasion of Belgium created a strong rift between the founders of the society, Franz von Liszt (who died shortly after the war) and Adolphe Prins.[51] Nonetheless, German IKV members still met annually. Furthermore, as many of them were active MSPD or liberal DVP members—that is, in parties that were prominent in the governments of the early years of the Weimar Republic—the IKV was able to influence criminal law reform significantly. During the conference in Jena, modern scholars seemed to fully agree that felony disenfranchisement was a flawed legal notion. Not since the Reich Penal Code was introduced had there been so much agreement about this punishment.

As mentioned in chapter 1, the Hessian judge Friedrich Noellner had argued as early as 1846 that felony disenfranchisement sabotaged the process of moral reform.[52] Even though several critics shared Noellner's appraisal of the system, most legal scholars of Imperial Germany supported disenfranchisement. At the first international conference on crime and crime prevention held in Rome in 1885, for instance, the (mostly progressive) scholars present unanimously agreed that felony disenfranchisement was well suited to penal purposes of modern nation states.[53] Only gradually did scholars grow worried about how the punishment's execution reflected on the civilization they lived in.

At the 1921 assembly in Jena, Moritz Liepmann was the most explicit critic of the punishment. He argued that felony disenfranchisement was a relic from medieval times that merely stigmatized offenders:

> Law should not distinguish between two categories of prisoners, between those with honorable and those with dishonorable dispositions. Rather, all prisoners remain

humans who are more or less capable of or in need of improvement. Prisoners should only be treated in this way.[54]

His rejection of disenfranchisement was closely linked to his own suggestions for reforming the prison system as he vociferously advocated the "stages system" that aimed to help ease ex-convicts' transition from incarceration to freedom.[55] This system was based entirely on the idea there were two categories of inmates: "incorrigible" and "corrigible" ones; long supported by the "modern" criminological school, this distinction became important in the penal and policing systems of the Weimar Republic.[56] Independent of the reforms, many prisons introduced reforms to their internal regimes during the Weimar Republic, with the implementation of the stages system being the most dramatic of these. Nonetheless, the different facilities in Germany varied tremendously according to the ideas of the respective prison wardens.[57]

Liepmann, however, had come to believe that the distinction between "corrigible" and "incorrigible" could not be made compatible with the distinction between honorable and dishonorable offenders. He noted that many dishonored felons were, in fact, quite "corrigible," while many "habitual" criminals were indifferent to their privileges. In the end, he felt, the destructive effects of disenfranchisement merely demoralized corrigible offenders.

Liepmann's comments received almost universal approval and lots of applause. Prominent scholars like Siegfried Löwenstein, Robert Von Hippel, and Hermann Kantorowicz held similar views and pushed even harder for the abolition of disenfranchisement during this assembly. Kantorowicz, in particular, argued that the punishment undermined the morality of the people as a whole (*Volksmoral*).[58] Similar to arguments for the abolition of the death penalty, he held that the punishment brought about uncivilized inclinations in the punishers and had a negative overall effect on society.[59] Interestingly, all these scholars and Liepmann referenced the "medieval" character of this punishment; thus, the punishment often ridiculed for its insignificance in the time of the German Empire ironically became the primary example of cruel and "medieval" barbarism.[60]

Radbruch's Reform Plans

The critique of felony disenfranchisement voiced at the Jena conference found its way into important attempts at legislative reform. Gustav Radbruch, a prominent member of the IKV and one of Liszt's students, played a major role in this. As early as 1910, he was making influential comments on the reform proposals for criminal law.[61] During the Weimar Republic, he became an authority on legal matters and frequently contributed at IKV meetings, but he was also a salient member of the MSPD. Radbruch became Minister of Justice for the MSPD in the second Wirth cabinet (1921–22) and remained in this post in the Stresemann cabinets (1923). One of his first actions as Minister of Justice in 1921 was to grant amnesty to a large group of people who were on death row and sentenced to the penitentiary, and whom he explicitly mentioned, were regarded predominantly as "fellow travelers" rather than serious criminals.[62] Radbruch famously argued that amnesties were "milestones on the path to revolution."[63] At the same time, he was reluctant to grant amnesty to a large group of prisoners on hunger strike, which prompted criticism from the extreme left.[64]

As Minister of Justice, Radbruch was predominantly tasked with coming up with a new proposal for thorough reform of the penal code—the first comprehensive attempt to reform the penal code since the failed attempts of 1909/10.[65] As Minister of Justice, Radbruch presented his draft plan, which included the abolition of the punishment of disenfranchisement from the penal code. The controversy concerning the category of the "dishonorable disposition," as well as the renewed emphasis on properly reintegrating offenders into society, informed his program for this. Radbruch first presented his plan in 1922, the year he commissioned an official draft of a reformed penal code, stating that the abolition of disenfranchisement would do away with the "distrust" (*Mißtrauen*) of and "enmity" (*Übelwollen*) toward convicted citizens. The new penal code, by contrast, would no longer hinder convicts' reintegration into society through disenfranchisement.[66]

Radbruch was aware that disenfranchisement could not be abolished in isolation but that its abolition had to be part of a more overarching reform of the penal system. He therefore proposed to make former penitentiary inmates eligible to join the army. This would mean that penitentiary inmates would no longer be branded with the stigma of "dishonor."[67] Yet, even Radbruch was reluctant to eliminate all the penal system's means of exclusion. For instance, he adhered to the idea of preventing former penitentiary inmates from holding public office, though he added that this should not be understood as a punishment. Instead, he maintained that these convicts should be denied this privilege because they could not be fully trusted. Many commentators were puzzled as to how this differed from the former regulations. Conservative legal scholar Alexander Graf zu Dohna, for one, noted that the "lack of trust" had always been the basic reason for depriving ex-convicts of their privileges. In his view, Radbruch was merely putting old wine in new bottles without making any serious reforms.[68]

Following the publication of the draft reforms, the dominant progressive legal journals spearheaded a campaign to support Radbruch's plans. The most important advocates were two of Liszt's students: Max Grünhut and Eberhard Schmidt. In the articles in these journals, too, the main argument for the abolition of disenfranchisement was that the punishment was "uncivilized" and that the notion of the "dishonorable disposition" had become politically contested. According to Schmidt, the stigma associated with the loss of honorary rights led to forms of "moral lynch mob justice."[69] Along the lines of the draft, both Schmidt and Grünhut argued that the punishment directly contradicted the aim of modern penal justice to reintegrate offenders into society as it interfered with the moral reformation of "corrigible" offenders. In Grünhut's words, "demeaning punishments conflict with the reformation of deviants and are an impetus for wrongdoing."[70] In Weimar society, he held, the existence of the punishment precipitated a kind of *Gesinnungsstrafrecht* in that the explicit connection between disenfranchisement and a convict's "dishonorable disposition" implied that convictions rather than actions were put on trial.[71]

As Radbruch translated the growing criticism of disenfranchisement into actual law, some advocates of "modern" ideas in criminal law found fault with these endeavors. Wilhelm Kahl, the president of the *Juristentag* and long-time member of the IKV, was one such skeptic, who chided Radbruch's plans for abolishing disenfranchisement when he presented them at the national assembly of the MSPD in Augsburg in 1922. Kahl, himself a member of Stresemann's German People's Party (DVP), regarded the repeal of the laws on felony disenfranchisement as a partisan issue and felt that it would not be beneficial to the entire nation.[72] In his view, the call for abolition was just a way for the MSPD to gain more votes.

Kahl's criticism has to be viewed in light of the debate on the "mass character" of political offenses: members of left-wing parties complained that their sympathizers were deprived of their civil privileges more often than right-wing sympathizers. Since they also believed this influenced the outcome of the elections, they saw disenfranchisement as a political tool that was being used by the right-wing parties. Iwan Katz, a member of the Communist Party, vehemently made this same argument in 1924, charging that the system of criminal justice (which he called *Schandjustiz, Klassenjustiz, Justizhure*) deliberately disenfranchised left-wing sympathizers for political gain:

> Have you ever heard of a profiteer or usurer losing his civil privileges? That has never happened. But almost every day, proletarian fighters, honest workers who struggle against the capitalist system, are punished with long sentences in the penitentiary and prison and stripped of their civil privileges. . . . Capitalists and fascists go unpunished and honest men, proletarians, are punished in the most brutal fashion and declared dishonorable.[73]

In contrast to these left-wing critics of disenfranchisement, however, Kahl argued that this punishment could have an important function for the success of the Weimar Republic: its prudent use could help generate support for the democratic constitution of the Weimar Republic. His argument boiled down to the idea that a clearly identifiable class of "dishonored" felons would forge a sense of unity among the German people, who would wish to distance themselves from them.[74]

Kahl and other politicians felt that such a sense of unity was urgently needed and, in this respect, Radbruch and Kahl were no opponents. They both stressed the importance of a sense of community among the citizens of the Weimar Republic. In his public lectures, Radbruch fiercely defended the republic's constitution, representing a kind of militant republicanism.[75] Yet, by the mid-1920s, the legitimacy of the Weimar Republic was increasingly called into question, sometimes with explicit reference to the idea that it had its origins in "dishonorable" crimes. In 1924, the Archbishop of Munich, Cardinal Faulhaber, for instance, claimed that the constitution of the Weimar Republic was founded in acts of perjury and treason.[76] Indeed, this statement came to define much of the Center Party's approach to the constitution after 1924; around this time, the party changed its stance toward the existence of the republic from mildly positive to more critical.

For politicians like Kahl, however, such arguments made the need to affirm the legitimacy of the Weimar Republic and to dissociate it from any "dishonorable crime" all the more pressing. In this context, the punishment of disenfranchisement could help distance "irreproachable" Weimar citizens from "real criminals" and strengthen ideas of the unity of the German people beyond partisan contestation.[77] Kahl thus wanted to restore the idea, so prevalent in Imperial Germany, that "dishonored" felons stood for everything model German citizens considered unworthy.[78]

Even though Kahl was considered a "modern" scholar, the long-time proponent of the "classical" school Friedrich Oetker defended the existence of disenfranchisement with similar arguments in an article for the *Juristische Wochenschrift*. In response to Schmidt's and Grünhut's articles, Oetker emphasized that, in his view, disenfranchisement was not a form of *Gesinnungsstrafrecht* since it was not directed at someone's disposition. The category of the "dishonorable disposition" was merely used to determine the measure of a punishment.[79] More importantly, however, he argued, along the same lines as Kahl, that disenfranchisement was one of the clearest expressions of the people's conscience (*Volksbewusstsein*): if "the German people" considered someone dishonorable, he should be punished accordingly.[80] This idea of the people's conscience would become more salient in the following years when the Nazi Party would appropriate it, along with the notions of honor and *Volk*. Overall, one can say that both the advocates and opponents of felony disenfranchisement shared the same ideal—the unity of the German people—but they differed in the role they saw disenfranchisement playing in forging or undermining that unity.

The Community Appeal of Disenfranchised Felons

As noted earlier, the Weimar years have often been depicted as a state of permanent crisis—economic, political, and cultural.[81] In the wake of the events of 1918/19, various crisis narratives dominated contemporary commentaries.[82] After World War I, many German citizens experienced hunger, inflation, and unemployment, but there was also a crisis in the concept of masculinity. Many men had initially envisioned fighting in the war as a grand "duel of honor," but the reality was rather different.[83] Fighting men's negative experience of trench warfare, therefore, fueled a fundamental reappraisal of the notion of honor in German society. The outbreak of street violence after the war—particularly in the "second phase" of the revolution of 1918/19, during which many returned soldiers engaged in brutal acts of face-to-face violence—has been attributed to this crisis of masculinity.[84] The postwar years, however, also engendered a culture of self-reliance in which citizens often felt that unlawful action was their only reasonable option.[85] These circumstances, among others, prompted disenfranchised citizens to protest the nature of their sentence.

As argued in chapter 4, the mentality of disenfranchised felons had gradually changed in the first decades of the twentieth century. Many started to experience a sense of collective injustice and believed that they had similar concerns to each other. They also developed a new sense of entitlement, along with the idea that they could "pay" for their crimes by participating in society. At the same time, disenfranchised citizens felt that "society" had to help enable them to do this. In other words, what they (and society) had previously regarded as a purely individual affair between an offender and the law they now saw as an affair between ex-convicts and the community. They grew angry—less at the punishment, as such, than at society for not treating them like full citizens.

The postwar experience of crisis also generated a new awareness among German citizens that they possessed fundamental democratic rights.[86] German women's experience of subjecthood is an example of this. After many women had managed a significant amount of production in the wartime economy, women in general had not only gained the right to vote for parliament in 1919 but, more importantly, had also acquired a deeper understanding of citizenship as subjects, as Kathleen Canning argues.[87] This experience of subjecthood is evident in the arguments of disenfranchised ex-convict Maria M. from Dühren. In her 1930 petition for rehabilitation, she articulated the pride she felt in having always exercised her right to vote after she was granted this right, and felt it was an important duty in times of political turmoil. Consequently, she wished to have her voting right restored: "As a German woman with unquestioning loyalty to the constitution, I wish not to be excluded from the vote," she wrote, adding that she would vote for a "state-supportive" party.[88] Thus, Maria M., like many other petitioners in this period, combined a sense of loyalty to the state with a call for ex-convicts to be granted a better social and political position within it.

Does that mean that Weimar-era petitioners had a greater political consciousness than those in the time of the German Empire? This depends on the definition of "political." People petitioning for the restoration of their rights certainly did not defend a particular political ideology, but they did "politicize" their arguments for rehabilitation. They truly viewed their punishment as an injustice not because they refused to accept the blame for their offense, but because they considered it disproportionate to the crime—that is, disenfranchisement seemed like an excessive payment.

Disenfranchised citizens' sense of entitlement clearly grew stronger in the postwar years. Influential thinkers and politicians propagated ideals of community to overcome the crisis of the postwar society, and these ideals fit well with disenfranchised felons' rhetoric of entitlement. The felons connected their desire for rehabilitation with the crisis in German society. Consider, for instance, this statement by Leo V., an electrical engineer from the city of Aachen:

> To subject a family father, a citizen of the city and a diligent worker—with an impeccable reputation—apart from the sentence caused by unfortunate times and family relations—to such difficulties is not in line with the sense of national community so needed today. The city council should be aware of the fact that the economic crisis already threatens enough lives and creates massive unemployment, and that it is unnecessary to hinder those willing and able to work with bureaucratic conniving and red tape.[89]

Leo V. wrote this in a letter to the district president of Aachen, who had previously refused to grant his request for rehabilitation. In his original request, he had explained that he wanted his rights restored to be able to establish a business as an independent electrician in 1925. As he had already been trained as an electrician by a certified master craftsman and had passed the examination for the master craftsman's diploma (*Meisterbrief*), the only thing he still needed was a permit from the city council—anybody who established an electrical plant needed one to connect it to the city network. To obtain this permit, Leo V. needed a certificate of good conduct, but he could not get one due to his conviction for trading in stolen goods in 1922. The criminal court of Aachen had given him a harsh sentence for this crime.

In Leo V.'s personal account of his offense, the postwar crisis played a large role. He maintained that he had been living in abject poverty due to the war and through no fault of his own. His wife, he explained, had "hung around" (*herumtreiben*) with French people while he fought at the front. She wasted their money, drove their children out of their house, and sold the house. Although they divorced during the war, she reported him afterward to the French authorities and he became a prisoner of war. In Leo V.'s words, these were the "unbelievable strokes of fate" (*unglaubliche Schicksalsschläge*) that preceded his offense.[90]

The story Leo V. told about his wartime conduct may seem irrelevant to his request since the sentence he wished to have expunged had been imposed four years after the end of the war. But for Leo V., this wartime affair was both proof of his loyalty to the nation (*treudeutsche Gesinnung*) and an ameliorating circumstance of his offense. Thus, he emphasized the postwar culture of self-reliance and argued that a lack of community forced him to commit the crime. Furthermore, he hoped to underscore this by contrasting his own "masculine" patriotism with the behavior of "feminine" deserters. He supplemented his petition with letters of recommendation proving his loyalty to the German cause. These letters were written by people he had met during his wartime captivity. One of them, Otto P., was a high-ranking civil servant in the district government, who backed up Leo V.'s claim that he was completely without blame:

> In prison he always gave me the impression of being an honest and sincere human being. I am therefore convinced that the loose life of his ex-wife, her anti-German behavior, and the ruin of their family life are to blame for the applicant's lapse.[91]

Leo V.'s arguments—and the testimonials to support them—influenced the position of the district president of Aachen toward his case. In his letter to the Prussian minister, the district president noted that he had been unaware of Leo V.'s wartime story when he initially refused to support Leo V.'s request. Now that he knew the background, he fully supported Leo V.'s request.[92]

Even so, Leo V.'s depiction of his problems (as being with the local bureaucracy) contrasted sharply with the national authorities' view of his case. The office of the Minister of the Interior responded that this request should absolutely be rejected, above all because it concerned a very serious offense that had not been "atoned for in the way the judge considered necessary."[93] This demonstrates a disparity between local officials, who were willing to consider the circumstances behind the case, and the national authorities, who focused on the nature of the crime.

Clearly angry with the city authorities after this rejection, Leo V. then repeatedly referred to his identity as a citizen of Aachen while protesting the bureaucratic hindrances faced by people like him: people with the intention of transforming themselves into useful citizens who were working hard to find a secure place in society. The polemic Leo V. unleashed after this rejection highlighted the distinction between "public" and "private" affairs, which he felt the city council used to its own ends. It was the members of the city council who refused to grant him the permission to work as an independent electrician, and they had told him that his problem was of "private," and not "public," concern, using the label "private" as an easy way out. As the city authorities ruled by virtue of the trust the local population gave them, he argued, they should take not shirk responsibility in such a matter:

> The city administration, with the mayor and city council at its top, have the trust of the electorate. The city owes its municipal welfare institutions to the tax-paying citizen. And yet, irrespective of this, it treats the well-being of a family father who is struggling for his existence in such a way.[94]

When local authorities frustrated citizens' attempts to improve their standing with such "bureaucratic conniving," Leo V. continued, they fundamentally disrupted the bond of mutual dependency between the citizens and themselves. This statement underscores Leo V.'s conviction that the mutual dependency of citizens and authorities was fundamental to the thriving of the community as such. For him, German citizenship came down to one's personal development within the local or national community. Disenfranchisement was not just a personal problem but an "obstacle" for the community as it frustrated the free development of a citizen so punished.

Leo V. was not the only person to contend that disenfranchisement contradicted the fundamental entitlement of membership in a community. This idea was associated with a belief that the authorities had certain duties vis-à-vis the members of their community. Thus, it became common for disenfranchised felons to utilize the strategy of stressing their membership in a community and highlighting the duties and responsibilities they shared with its other members. In the period of "relative stability" in Weimar, between 1924 and 1927, most offenders turned to the authorities in the hope of profiting from the community.[95] Franz von D., who had been sentenced for robbery by a criminal court in Aachen (which he, like Leo V., had committed during the final months of the war) cast his request for rehabilitation as a duty shared by him and the local authorities: "It is not just my duty to make a useful human being out of myself; it is also that of the responsible authorities."[96] He supported this appeal with another appeal to the empathy of the reader. That is, he urged the reader to place himself in his shoes:

> Only a person who has been in the same situation as I can measure how difficult it has been for me and how frequently I was weakened. The strength needed to lead an orderly life as a discharged prisoner, to find a job without references, and to start a sincere existence from the ruins exceeds the power of even those with the best intentions.[97]

Indeed, notions of "suffering, entitlement, and victimization" were typical for subjects in the expanding welfare system of the Weimar period, as Greg Eghigian argues.[98] Appeals to the "duty" of the administration, as seen in Franz von D.'s petition, were never present in petitions written before 1914. The feelings of remorse and atonement so central to petitions in the time of the German Empire had given way to an emphasis on the common interests and duties of the entire community. These petitioners clearly expected more from the authorities. Furthermore, they did not rely on their biographies to support their honorable character (unless they were talking about military service during World War I), nor did they not talk about the honor of their profession or their class. Even Aloys R., a former police officer from Aachen, was not interested in the restoration of his former status as a civil servant and expressed no attachment to the notion of honor. He merely wanted to meet the necessary requirements to get a visa and be able to move to southwest Africa and work on a farm.[99] Ideas about the honor of his former position were clearly not as central to his beliefs about his future life conduct as they had been to ex-convicts in the earlier era. These Weimar ex-convicts were concerned not with restoring a specific status but with a desire to be recognized as individuals with the potential for a productive future.

At the same time, many disenfranchised felons felt that the punishment had no purpose and lamented being transformed into "useless" subjects in the community. This sense of purposelessness echoed the appraisal of legal scholar Oswald Freisler, who, in 1921, pointed out how ridiculous disenfranchisement was: it created a whole charade of repealing a punishment that was redundant to begin with.[100] Eventually, petitioners themselves even started to ridicule the sentence. Jacob W., a day laborer from Eschweiler, for instance, wrote the local government in 1925 to ask whether his ten-year disenfranchisement also exempted him from paying taxes. Other people had suggested this possibility to him. He even added his salary of the previous months and the amount of income tax he had paid so that the authorities would know how much to refund him.[101] In his entirely serious answer, the district president indicated that he was not aware of such a regulation and referred him to the tax authorities. Whether Jacob W.'s question was serious, or whether he was playfully provoking the authorities, remains unclear, but his petition nonetheless illustrates the changing attitudes and the rising expectations disenfranchised ex-convicts had of the local authorities.

The Moralizing Framework of the Local Authorities

Ironically, disenfranchised felons' increased tendency to explicitly express their desire to be included as members of the community could also be seen as supporting the communal function of disenfranchisement (see Kahl's arguments above). If the punishment caused the disenfranchised to desire feelings of community more frequently than before, then it had achieved its intended goal of creating a sense of national unity. That is, it could be called a successful form of "reintegrative shaming."[102] In fact, despite petitioners' changing attitudes, the authorities were often more reluctant to offer petitioners the possibility of reintegration into the community than they had been before, stressing instead the importance of exclusion. Rehabilitation remained a matter of mercy.

Although the Expungement Law of 1920 allowed for "normal offenses" to be expunged, this changed nothing for disenfranchised citizens.[103] In most cases, therefore, petitioners' arguments stood in sharp contrast to the reactions of the authorities. Whereas the disenfranchised ex-convicts increasingly protested their treatment and fashioned themselves as members of a *Volksgemeinschaft*, or people's community, the authorities emphasized the need for moral atonement more than ever before. This also demonstrates that legislative reforms did not necessarily align with the stance authorities took toward these ex-convicts. The introduction of the Expungement Law, one could even argue, strengthened their idea that disenfranchised felons were a special set of offenders whose punishment needed to be more severe to facilitate proper atonement.

For instance, the authorities' dismissiveness was quite evident in their rejection of Karl S.'s request for rehabilitation in November 1921. Sentenced to five years' loss of honor for pimping for prostitution, he explained that he had been naïve and never considered it "a real profession" (*Gewerbe*).[104] Karl S. felt that characterizing his crime as a "profession" would clearly make it dishonorable because that would imply that he had been motivated by financial profit (*gewinnsüchtige Absicht*). The district president took this case very seriously and stressed the importance of old dictums about the exclusion of dishonored ex-convicts. In his letter to the Minister of the Interior, he not only opposed Karl S.'s request but also added that a proven procurer like Karl S. should have to endure the full sentence. He wished to see the sentence upheld as a deterrent to other potential offenders (*zur Abschreckung anderer*).[105] Unaffected by the experiences of the war, the district president applied a discourse of exclusion to this case. Whereas others who had committed similar crimes during the war had been eligible to join the army, Karl S. was denied rehabilitation based solely on the nature of his offense. Moreover, the district president emphasized the emotional impact of the punishment on Karl S., using its deterrent effects to justify his decision: he added that refusal was especially to be recommended if the offender personally experienced his dishonoring as the most severe part of his sentence. In fact, the district president considered such statements by dishonored criminals to be proof of the punishment's effectiveness. Karl S.'s case shows that local authorities could justify their decisions based on their personal views of the purpose of punishment.

Joseph H.'s request for rehabilitation was rejected for similar reasons. He had been sentenced to three months in prison and five years' loss of honor for attempted manslaughter and violating game law. The loss of honor was added to his sentence because he had apparently shot at a fleeing man. The state prosecutor had two reasons to reject his request: Joseph H.'s dishonorable disposition was evident in his shooting at a fleeing man, and he did not understand how the loss of honor frustrated Joseph H. in his profession as a pavior.[106] Although Joseph H. repeatedly stressed his good conduct in his petition, the prosecutor hardly mentioned this. For him, it was important that dishonored criminals serve their full sentences.

Exceptions only seemed to be made for people with mental disorders. Andreas B., a mine worker from Aachen, for instance, was convicted of rape, but the public prosecutor restored his rights because he determined that he had a mental disorder. Andreas B. had also been intoxicated while committing the offense, and the public prosecutor felt that the two factors indicated that the criminal did not have an "immoral character" but should be labeled "insane."[107] This case thus provides an interesting example of how ingrained the belief still was that "honor" was a moral category based on the free will of rational subjects and should not be applied to "degenerate" people. Other "recidivist" petitioners, by contrast, like Wilhelm S. and Wilhelm P., both of whom the authorities described as "recidivist thieves," received responses similar to those of "dishonored" offenders. In Wilhelm P.'s case, the public prosecutor even argued that he did not like to work and parasitized his wife's income.[108] This clearly did not testify to an "honorable" character for a self-sufficient man in this era. In rejecting petitions, authorities also held that offenders were more concerned about their public reputation than about genuinely reforming their moral character. The state prosecutor wrote exactly that in rejecting the petition of arsonist Josef H.: "It creates the impression that it is not the illegal act (the crime) that causes his mental pains, but that it is the embarrassing effects (of the punishment) in public life."[109]

In the end, local authorities, in their assessments of individual cases, drew upon various reasons to oppose rehabilitation, but judging an offender's moral character as lacking was the most important one. This demonstrates that, at least on this level of bureaucratic decision-making in the penal justice system, there was no evidence of criminal policy becoming "medicalized" or penal welfare taking precedence. On the contrary, authorities aimed to prevent such "degraded" citizens from developing a genuine collective identity by stressing the idea of individual guilt. They were not punished as political opponents, the authorities averred, but as individual felons guilty of egoistic and insidious crimes, and they had breached the trust put in them as citizens.

The Rise of Nazism

To return now to the level of political decision-making, it was politics that prevented the reformed penal code Radbruch presented in 1922 from ever being ratified. In fact, Radbruch found himself, after the murder of Foreign Minister Walther Rathenau in June 1922, forced to introduce a law that contradicted his own opinions on crime and punishment and the treatment of political offenders: the Law for the Protection of the Republic (*Republikschutzgesetz*).[110] This law prescribed penitentiary confinement and death penalty sentences for political offenders, particularly people who had joined an organization that aimed to assassinate politicians. In his academic texts, Radbruch would later argue that political offenders were people with different views (*Andersdenkenden*) of the legitimacy of social norms who did not, however, break those norms for egoistic ends, as "common criminals" did.[111] By calling these political offenders *Überzeugungsverbrecher*, or criminals out of conviction, Radbruch tried to make the case that a neutral democratic state cannot argue about the moral legitimacy of such criminals' convictions.

Yet, despite Radbruch's own opinions, he complied with the wishes of the Reichstag and introduced the Law for the Protection of the Republic. Many politicians afterward claimed and acknowledged that the law was biased against right-wing offenders. Historian Gotthard Jasper argues that it was more a measure to guarantee the safety of the authorities than to safeguard the Weimar constitution as such.[112] That is, it did not entail a definitive idea of just punishments for political offenders but was rather a temporary deterrence measure. Ironically, although there were numerous debates on criminal law reform in the first half of the twentieth century, serious reforms, such as the abolition of felony disenfranchisement, were hardly ever ratified. The penal code of 1870 remained largely unchanged over a longer period. Even under Nazi rule, the old penal code continued to apply.

The Law for the Protection of the Republic did nothing to eliminate the "asymmetry" in verdicts against political offenders. Consequently, legal scholars continued to debate the purpose of disenfranchisement and the use of the notion of "dishonorable disposition" in judicial verdicts. The notorious trial against Felix Fechenbach, held at the Bavarian "People's Court" in 1924, provided ample fodder for such debates. In the final years of World War I, Fechenbach had sold confidential information from the Bavarian state administration to a foreign news agency. The judge ruled that he clearly displayed a "dishonorable disposition" as he acted purely out of financial interest. This verdict (combined with the question of the legitimacy of the People's Court) prompted a great deal of debate. Prominent lawyers, even Radbruch himself, protested the reference to Fechenbach's "dishonorable disposition" because they believed he had acted out of a desire to put pressure on the peace negotiations. In other words, his motive was clearly political rather than financial.[113]

After the 1930 elections six years later, when the NSDAP had become one of the largest parties in the Reichstag, the chances that disenfranchisement would be removed from the penal code were even smaller. National Socialists focused heavily on the proper use of disenfranchisement and the question of political offenders in their discussions of penal law. In fact, they believed that this part of penal law, in particular, would enable the Nazi regime to show what it meant to be a genuinely "authoritarian" state.[114] The ideological support for felony disenfranchisement in the service of the Nazi Party program first became evident in 1930, when its members promoted a bill in the Reichstag called Law for the Protection of the German Nation (*Gesetz zum Schutz der deutschen Nation*). This bill aimed to punish people guilty of "miscegenation" (*Rassenverrat*) with long-term penitentiary sentences combined with the deprivation of their civil privileges.[115] Such dishonoring essentially sought to equate people who committed miscegenation with the lowest kind of untrustworthy criminals. The 1930 proposal already

Figure 6.2. Cartoonist Thomas Theodor Heine deliberately deprives the political assassin of the status as an "honorable" political offender by depicting him as a sneaky robber after the murder of Walther Rathenau. Thomas Theodor Heine, "Der politische Mord," *Simplicissimus* 27, no. 16 (1922): 229. Courtesy Klassik Stiftung Weimar.

hints at the way the Nazi Party started to tamper with an important principle of disenfranchisement, namely, that loss of privileges constituted part of criminals' payment for their offenses within the norms of citizenship. The Nazi Party, by contrast, disconnected the punishment from the norms of citizenship, aligning it instead with the notions of *Volk* and race.

From the moment National Socialists became a prominent political force in Germany, legal scholars who supported the Nazi Party engaged extensively with the question of how criminal law could be made to conform to Nazi ideology. Such scholars deemed this necessary since the Nazi Party up until that time had said little about penal law apart from the fact that they advocated the use of the death penalty (§18) against "*gemeine Volksverbrecher*" (vulgar criminals against the people).[116] The notions of *Volk* (the people) and race took center stage in these debates, fully subordinating the notion of an individual's honor in these scholars' philosophy of penal law.[117] Nazi legal scholars and officials increasingly referred to "the honor of the German *Volk*," introducing the notion of "social honor" for this purpose. This was partially inspired by the works of one of the most prominent Nazi ideologists, Alfred Rosenberg, who completely subordinated the notion of honor to that of race in his book *Der Mythus des 20. Jahrhunderts* (The Myth of the Twentieth Century).[118] Later, some pieces of Nazi legislation actively endorsed the idea of "social honor." The Work Order Act of 1934, for instance, which aimed to protect the "Aryan" working classes from capitalist employers, did so most prominently in invoking the "social honor" of labor.[119]

After the Nazi Party came to power in 1933, with the so-called Reichstag Fire Decree of 28 February suspending many of the civil rights stipulated in the Weimar constitution, Nazi party ideologues and legal scholars who sympathized with the party immediately started working on reforming criminal law according to the party's principles. In their writings, these legal scholars made no fundamental distinctions between law and morality.[120] They held that the state derived its power to punish from the moral judgments of the *Volk*, so it exerted its authoritarian rule on behalf of the *Volk*, not against it.[121] In their view, this implied a thorough "moralization" (*Ethisierung*) of penal law.[122] In other words, they contended that National Socialism was founded on a "moral idea," so any person acting against this idea should, by definition, be deemed immoral and should thereby have no civil privileges. Indeed, they repeatedly claimed that a clear and indisputable idea about "moral rights and moral wrongs" finally held sway in German society.[123]

Georg Dahm and Friedrich Schaffstein, both prominent theoreticians of the National Socialist philosophy of criminal law, for example, asserted that the "neutrality" of political offenders implied in the "liberal" philosophy of felony disenfranchisement was a typical symptom of the "pale" (*blass*) and "empty" ideology of the liberal state. In this context, Radbruch's idea of *Überzeugungsverbrecher*—which urged jurists to refrain from making any *moral* judgments about political offenders' actions—constituted the epitome of this liberal philosophy of criminal justice.[124]

This alignment of law and morality did not, in the end, precipitate the annulment of distinctions between different kinds of incarceration. Rather, it prompted the Nazi state to think of a dual system of punishment based on two different kinds of offenders: those who committed their crimes in the service of the *Volk*, and those who acted against the *Volk*. This system transformed the "asymmetry" in verdicts into a cornerstone of Nazi criminal policy. Consequently, the commission responsible for redesigning the penal system under Nazi rule, headed by scholar Franz Gürtner, retained the distinction between "dishonoring" and non-dishonoring sentences.

In fact, this Nazi Party stance had already become apparent in 1932 in the context of the notorious "Potempa murders." Under the auspices of the (second) Law for the Protection of the Republic, the SA stormtroopers who brutally murdered a communist worker and his family were sentenced to a "dishonorable" death.[125] Hitler himself immediately declared that these men should not be sentenced as "dishonorable" murderers and openly praised them for their actions. Moreover, party ideologue Rosenberg explicitly endorsed a dual system of criminal sentences in relation to this sentence: "This judgment of the court contradicts the elementary sense of national self-preservation of the nation . . . For us one soul is not like another; one human is not like another."[126]

This shift in perspective, irrespective of any change in criminal legislation, revealed the Nazis' goals for felony disenfranchisement. By applying a logic similar to Kahl's, they sought to use it to generate an image of people who acted against the interests of the national society. Yet, their replacement of the notion of "citizenship" with that of the "*Volk*" shows that it was not their aim to use the penal law to disenfranchise people who did not belong to the *Volk*. After all, once the Nazi Party had seized power, Nazi officials immediately drafted laws that disenfranchised—or, even better, denaturalized—citizens on racial grounds. These eventually culminated in the Nuremberg Laws, which were drafted separately from the debates about penal reform. Penal law played no role in this process.[127]

In short, the Nazi state aimed to denaturalize people who did not belong to the *Volk* by depriving them of their citizenship status altogether, while felony disenfranchisement remained a punishment for members of the *Volk* who acted against its interests. A new penal code was not introduced under the National Socialists, but they did increasingly use disenfranchisement in ways that aligned with their ideology of race and *Volk*. For example, the Blood Protection Law (*Blutschutzgesetz*), when it was introduced, arranged for disenfranchisement to be imposed, in principle, primarily on people guilty of miscegenation.[128]

The revocation of people's civil rights based on their race, which the Reich Citizens Act effected as part of the Nuremberg Laws in 1935, narrowed the application of disenfranchisement. The Nuremberg Laws effectively took away both Jewish citizens' rights and their entitlement to "civil honor" because the punishment only applied to people who had "honor" to begin with. Even so, the 1871 penal code remained principally in place during the Nazi regime, and criminal courts could still strip Jewish citizens of their civil honor. These practices did not correspond with the ideological intention of National Socialism, which explains Himmler's discomfort with disenfranchising sentences against Jewish citizens, discussed in the introduction of this book. From the start, the Nazi Party aimed to denaturalize Jewish people based on their race, ultimately ending in the program to annihilate European Jewry. The punishment of disenfranchisement, however, only remained in place for people who were entitled to civil honor but acted against the basic interests of the German *Volk*.

In the early years of the Weimar Republic, disenfranchisement came to be hotly debated. Liberal scholars and social engineers claimed that it undermined a sense of community, generated disparities in society, and frustrated resocialization programs for released prisoners. The arbitrariness many perceived in relation to the "dishonoring" sentences reinforced modern scholars' complaints about the punishment. Above all, disenfranchisement conflicted with liberal tendencies that emphasized prisoners' basic rights. These negative appraisals of felony disenfranchisement found their way into important attempts at legislative reform. However, ideas about ex-convicts' rights did not resonate with local authorities, who showed little inclination to think of reforming or resocializing ex-convicts. The moral categories of honor, culpability, and atonement still dominated their assessment of rehabilitation petitions, even though ex-convicts appealed ever more often to the idea of community and community members' mutual dependence.

Once it came to power, the Nazi Party, like other political parties before it, instrumentalized felony disenfranchisement for its political agenda. The National Socialists were able to combine two elements associated with disenfranchised felons in this instrumentalization: the moral vocabulary of the authorities and the community-centered appeals of petitioners. On the one hand, Nazi ideologues promoted the moralization of penal law by reasserting the importance of categories such as honor and moral accountability. On the other hand, though, they simultaneously subordinated these notions to the *Volk* and introduced the notion of "social honor" to underscore honor's dependence on community.

Notes

1. Kathleen Canning, "Das Geschlecht der Revolution. Stimmrecht und Staatsbürgertum 1918/19," in *Die vergessene Revolution von 1918/19*, ed. Alexander Gallus, 84–116 (Göttingen: Vandenhoeck & Ruprecht, 2010).
2. *Freiheit*, 2 January 1919; *Vorwärts*, 14 January 1919; *Vorwärts*, 19 March 1919.
3. Fritz Stier-Somlo, *Die Verfassung des Deutschen Reichs vom 11. August 1919. Ein systematischer Überblick* (Bonn: Marcus & Weber, 1925), 135–36.
4. Arthur Crispien, "Das Rätewahlrecht," *Freiheit*, 2 June 1919.
5. Thomas Etzemüller, *Die Ordnung der Moderne. Social Engineering im 20. Jahrhundert* (Bielefeld: Transcript, 2015), 1–39.

6. Peter Fritzsche, "Landscape of Danger, Landscape of Design: Crisis and Modernism in Weimar Germany," in *Dancing on the Volcano: Essays on the Culture of the Weimar Republic*, ed. Thomas W. Kniesche and Stephen Brockmann, 24–46 (Columbia, SC: Camden House, 1994).
7. Wolfgang Schivelbusch, *Die Kultur der Niederlage: Der amerikanische Süden 1865 –Frankreich 1871—Deutschland 1918* (Berlin: Rowohlt, 2012).
8. Gerhard A. Ritter, *Der Sozialstaat: Entstehung und Entwicklung im internationalen Vergleich* (Munich: Oldenbourg, 1989), 115–16.
9. Rosenblum, *Beyond the Prison Gates*; idem, "Welfare and Justice"; Wachsmann, "Between Reform and Repression."
10. he notion of improvised democracy comes from Theodor Eschenburg, *Die improvisierte Demokratie* (Munich: Piper, 1963).
11. Anthony McElligott, *Rethinking the Weimar Republic: Authority and Authoritarianism, 1916–1936* (London: Bloomsbury, 2014), 133; Nadine Rossol, "Repräsentationskultur und Verfassungsfeiern der Weimarer Republik," in *Demokratiekultur in Europa, Politische Repräsentation im 19. und 20. Jahrhundert*, ed. Detlef Lehnert, 261–80 (Cologne: Böhlau, 2011).
12. For more on Liebknecht's first trial, see chapter 3.
13. Emil Barth, *Aus der Werkstatt der deutschen Revolution* (Berlin: Hoffman, 1920), 17. Carl E. Schorske, *German Social Democracy, 1905–1917: The Development of the Great Schism* (Cambridge, MA: Harvard University Press, 1955), 296–312; Hans-Ulrich Wehler, *Deutsche Gesellschaftsgeschichte*, Vol. 4: *Vom Beginn des Ersten Weltkriegs bis zur Gründung der beiden deutschen Staaten 1914–1949* (Munich: Beck, 2003), 205–15.
14. *Das Zuchthausurteil gegen Karl Liebknecht. Wörtliche Wiedergabe der Prozeßakten, Urteile und Eingaben Liebknechts* (Leipzig: Frankes Verlag, 1919), 108.
15. Rosa Luxemburg, "Was ist mit Liebknecht? (1916)," https://www.marxists.org (last accessed 4 April 2017).
16. *Stenographische Berichte Verhandlungen des Reichstages*, vol. 308 (Berlin, 1916), 1844–48.
17. *Protokoll der Reichskonferenz der Sozialdemokratie Deutschlands* (Berlin: Vorwärts, 1916).
18. "Flugblatt mit Aufruf zum Protestreik gegen die Verurteilung Karl Liebknechts," *Deutsches Historisches Museum, Berlin*, Do 56/2197.1.
19. Rosa Luxemburg, "Wofür kämpfte Liebknecht, und weshalb wurde er zu Zuchthaus verurteilt?" (1916).
20. Karl Liebknecht, "Gegen die Freiheitsstrafe," in *Gesammelte Reden und Schriften*, 3rd edn., vol. 9, 391–96 (Berlin: Dietz, 1974).
21. Reinhard Baumann, ed., *Die Revolution von 1918/1919 in der Provinz* (Konstanz: Universitäts Verlag Konstanz, 1996).
22. Allan Mitchell, *Revolution in Bavaria, 1918–1919: The Eisner Regime and the Soviet Republic* (Princeton, NJ: Princeton University Press, 1965).
23. Emil Julius Gumbel, *Vier Jahre politischer Mord* (Berlin: Verlag der neuen Gesellschaft, 1922).
24. Stefan Grossmann, *Der Hochverräter Ernst Toller. Die Geschichte eines Prozesses* (Berlin: Rowohlt, 1919), 23.
25. Max Weber, "Zeugenaussage im Prozeß gegen Ernst Toller," in *Gesamtausgabe*, vol. 16, 485–91 (Tübingen: Mohr Siebeck, 1988).
26. Martin H. Geyer, *Verkehrte Welt. Revolution, Inflation und Moderne. München 1914–1924* (Göttingen: Vandenhoeck & Ruprecht, 1998), 82–83.
27. Evans, *Rituals of Retribution*, 489.
28. Hans von Pranckh, *Der Prozeß gegen den Grafen Anton Arco-Valley, der den bayer. Ministerpräsidenten Kurt Eisner erschossen hat* (Munich: J. F. Lehmann, 1920), 8.
29. Ibid., 10.
30. Ibid., 12.
31. *Schlesische Arbeiter-Zeitung*, 20 January 1920.

32. Norman Dankerl, *Alois Lindner. Das Leben des bayerischen Abenteurers und Revolutionärs* (Viechtach: Lichtung, 2007), 86ff.
33. "Der Mörder Eisners," *Volksstimme*, 18 January 1920.
34. Gumbel, *Vier Jahre politischer Mord*.
35. Heinrich Hannover, Elisabeth Hannover-Drück, and Karl Dietrich Bracher, *Politische Justiz 1918–1933* (Frankfurt a.M.: Fischer, 1966).
36. Karl Dietrich Bracher, "Vorwort," in Hannover, Hannover-Drück, and Bracher, *Politische Justiz*, 12–21.
37. Anthony McElligott, *Rethinking the Weimar Republic: Authority and Authoritarianism, 1916–1936* (London: Bloomsbury, 2014), 111.
38. Henning Grunwald, *Courtroom to Revolutionary Stage: Performance and Ideology in Weimar Political Trials* (Oxford: Oxford University Pres, 2012), 48–51.
39. Gotthard Jasper, "Justiz und Politik in der Weimarer Republik," *Vierteljahrshefte für Zeitgeschichte* 30, no. 2 (1982): 167–205, 172–73; cf. Dirk Schumann, *Political Violence in the Weimar Republic, 1918–1933. Fight for the Streets and Fear of Civil War*, trans. Thomas Dunlap (New York: Berghahn Books, 2009), 35–41.
40. See the debate in *Verhandlungen der Verfassunggebenden Deutschen Nationalversammlung*, vol. 333 (Berlin 1919), 5330–40.
41. BA-BL, R 3001/6028, Friedrich Kitzinger, "Die Bestrafung der politischen Verbrechen," *Frankfurter Zeitung*, 4 September 1920.
42. Gustav Klingelhöfer, "Politische Verbrecher," *Die Zukunft*, no. 111 (1920): 42–48.
43. Klingelhöfer wrote this response from the fortress in Niederschönenfeld, where he was incarcerated for his participation in the Bavarian Council Republic and served his time alongside other prominent members thereof, such as Toller and Mühsam.
44. Hans von Hentig, *Strafrecht und Auslese. Eine Anwendung des Kausalgesetzes auf den rechtbrechenden Menschen* (Berlin: Springer, 1914).
45. Jürgen Christoph, *Die politischen Reichsamnestien, 1918–1933* (Frankfurt a.M.: Lang, 1988), 65.
46. Hans von Hentig, "Politische Verbrechen der Gegenwart," *Deutsche Strafrechtszeitung*, no. 6 (1919): 218–22.
47. BA-BL, R 3001/6028, "Festung oder Zuchthaus für politische Verbrecher?," *Kölnische Zeitung*, 19 October 1920.
48. Cf. Hans von Hentig, *Aufsätze zur Deutschen Revolution* (Berlin: Springer, 1919), 8.
49. Guckenheimer, *Begriff der ehrlosen Gesinnung*, 78.
50. Moritz Liepmann, *Die Reform des deutschen Strafrechts. Kritische Bemerkungen zu dem "Strafgesetzentwurf"* (Hamburg: Gente, 1921), 123.
51. D. Simons, "Franz von Liszt," *Tijdschrift voor Strafrecht* 30 (1919): 333–36.
52. See chapter 1.
53. Paul Köhne, "Die Arbeiten des internationalen Kongresses für Gefängniswesen in Rom, 1885," *ZStW* 8, no. 3 (1888): 439–64.
54. *Mitteilungen der Internationalen Kriminalistischen Vereinigung* 22 (Berlin, 1924), 22.
55. Nikolaus Wachsmann, "Between Reform and Repression. Imprisonment in Weimar Germany," in *Crime and Criminal Justice in Modern Germany*, ed. Richard F. Wetzell, 115–36 (New York: Berghahn Books, 2014); Schauz, *Strafen als moralische Besserung*, 333–43.
56. Schauz, *Strafen als moralische Besserung*, 388; Patrick Wagner, *Volksgemeinschaft ohne Verbrecher. Konzeptionen und Praxis der Kriminalpolizei in der Zeit der Weimarer Republik und des Nationalsozialismus* (Hamburg: Christians, 1996), 20.
57. Wachsmann, "Between Reform and Repression," 123–24.
58. *Mitteilungen der Internationalen Kriminalistischen Vereinigung* 22: 30–32.
59. Evans, *Rituals of Retribution*, 515.

60. The Nazi legal scholar Greinert also mentioned this in his notes on the "Nebenstrafen und Nebenfolgen an der Ehre" that he drafted for the penal reform commission of the National Socialist Party; BA-BL R 3001/20933.
61. Gustav Radbruch, "Das System der Freiheitsstrafen im Vorentwurf," *MKS* 7, no. 4 (1910): 207–12.
62. Christoph, *Reichsamnestien*, 118.
63. Cited in ibid., 75.
64. Friederike Goltsche, *Der Entwurf eines Allgemeinen Deutschen Strafgesetzbuches von 1922 (Entwurf Radbruch)* (Berlin: De Gruyter, 2010), 45.
65. Ibid.; Ulfried Neumann, "Gustav Radbruchs Beitrag zur Strafrechtsreform," in *Gustav Radbruch als Reichsjustizminister (1921–1923)*, ed. Irina Mohr, 49–62 (Berlin: Mohr, 2004).
66. *Entwürfe zu einem Strafgesetzbuch (1919, 1922, 1924/25 und 1927)*, ed. Werner Schubert (Berlin, 1995), 191, 284.
67. At the meeting of the IKV in Hamburg in 1924, Liepmann noted the following about the treatment of prisoners in ideal circumstances: "In their treatment, which should be serious, just, but above all humane, their sense of honor should be preserved and strengthened," *Mitteilungen der Internationalen Kriminalistischen Vereinigung*, 22, 35.
68. Alexander Graf zu Dohna, "Der innere Konnex von Freiheitsstrafen und Ehrenstrafen," *MKS* 17 (1926): 352–59, 353. See chapter 1 on the importance of trust in the justification of felony disenfranchisement.
69. Eberhard Schmidt, "Die Gestaltung der Ehrenstrafen im künftigen Strafrecht," *ZStW* 45 (1925): 10–43, 28. Cf. James Q. Whitman, "What Is Wrong with Inflicting Shame Sanctions?," *Yale Law Journal* 107, no. 4 (1998): 1055–92.
70. Grünhut, "Die Abschaffung der Ehrenstrafen," 261.
71. Ibid., 265. On the notion of *Gesinnungsstrafrecht*, see chapter 2.
72. *Stenographische Berichte über die Verhandlungen des Reichstages*, vol. 358 (Berlin, 1923), 9652.
73. GStA PK, I. HA Rep. 84a Nr. 7870, 177. Landestag in Preussen, 03.04.1924.
74. Wilhelm Kahl, "Ehrenstrafen," *DJZ* 28 (1923): 507–12.
75. Nicole Rossol, "Weltkrieg und Verfassung als Gründungserzählung der Republik," *Aus Politik und Zeitgeschichte* 50–51 (2008): 13–18.
76. Thomas Ruster, *Die verlorene Nützlichkeit der Religion. Katholizismus und Moderne in der Weimarer Republik* (Paderborn: Schöningh, 1994), 74. This was, in fact, one of Adolf Hitler's favorite quotes, which he used in several of his speeches: cf. Paul Hoser, "Hitler und die katholische Kirche," *Vierteljahrshefte für Zeitgeschichte* 42 (1994): 473–92, 490.
77. Kahl, "Ehrenstrafen." Cf. Weinrich, *Statusmindernde Nebenfolgen als Ehrenstrafen*, 120.
78. Compare this to the notion of the "counter-world" of criminal groups; Becker, *Verderbnis und Entartung*.
79. Friedrich Oetker, "Die Ehrenstrafen nach dem Entwurf von 1919," *Juristische Wochenschrift* 55, no. 5 (1924): 254–60, 255.
80. Ibid.
81. Horst Möller, *Die Weimarer Republik. Demokratie in der Krise* (Munich: Piper, 2018); Peukert, *Die Weimarer Republik*.
82. Moritz Föllmer and Rüdiger Graf, eds., *Die "Krise" der Weimarer Republik: Zur Kritik eines Deutungsmusters* (Frankfurt a.M.: Campus Verlag, 2005).
83. Ute Frevert, "Die Ehre der Bürger im Spiegel ihrer Duelle," *Historische Zeitschrift* 249, no. 1 (1989): 545–82, 579; Ute Planert, "Kulturkritik und Geschlechterverhältnis. Zur Krise der Geschlechterordnung zwischen Jahrhundertwende und drittem Reich," in *Ordnungen in der Krise. Zur politischen Kulturgeschichte der Zwischenkriegszeit*, ed. Wolfgang Hardtwig, 191–214 (Munich: Oldenbourg, 2007).

84. A pro argument can be found in Mark Jones and Karl Heinz Siber, *Am Anfang war Gewalt: Die deutsche Revolution 1918/19 und der Beginn der Weimarer Republik* (Bonn: Bundeszentrale für politische Bildung, 2017); George L. Mosse, *Fallen Soldiers: Reshaping the Memory of the World Wars* (New York: Oxford University Press, 1990), 156. An argument against can be found in Schumann, *Political Violence in the Weimar Republic*.
85. Geyer, *Verkehrte Welt*.
86. Föllmer and Graf, eds., *Die "Krise" der Weimarer Republik*.
87. Kathleen Canning, "Das Geschlecht der Revolution. Stimmrecht und Staatsbürgertum 1918/19," in *Die vergessene Revolution von 1918/19*, ed. Alexander Gallus, 84–116 (Göttingen: Vandenhoeck & Ruprecht, 2010).
88. LAV NRW R, BR 0007, no. 22780, petition from Maria M. to the Reichspresident, 23.08.1930.
89. LAV NRW R, BR 0007, no. 22779, letter from Leo V. to the District President of Aachen, 14.06.1926.
90. Ibid., petition from Leo V. to the Minister of the Interior, 12.12.1925.
91. Ibid., statement from Otto P. on the case of Leo Leo V., 22.01.1926.
92. Ibid., letter from the District President of Aachen to the Minister of the Interior, 21.01.1926.
93. Ibid., letter from the Ministry of the Interior to the District President of Aachen, 30.03.1926.
94. Ibid., letter from Leo V. to the District President of Aachen, 14.06.1926.
95. Eberhard Kolb, *Deutschland 1918–1933: Eine Geschichte der Weimarer Republik* (Berlin: De Gruyter, 2012), 109.
96. LAV NRW R, BR 0007, no. 22779, petition from Franz von D. addressed to the Minister of the Interior, 14.09.1926.
97. Ibid.
98. Greg Eghigian, "Pain, Entitlement, and Social Citizenship in Modern Germany," in *Pain and Prosperity: Reconsidering Twentieth-Century German History*, ed. Paul Betts and Greg Eghigian, 16–34 (Stanford, CA: Stanford University Press, 2003).
99. LAV NRW R, BR 0005, no. 22779, petition from Aloys R. to the District President, 26.03.1926; ibid., petition from Aloys R. to the Minister of the Interior, 24.09.1926.
100. Friesler called it "complicated legislation on rehabilitation, which today offers us the spectacle of revoking inappropriate punishments after a certain period of time as inappropriate, which would have been better left unacknowledged [to begin with]." Oswald Freisler, "Die Ehrenstrafen und ihre Berechtigung," *ZStW* 4, no. 1 (1921): 438–42, 442.
101. Ibid., letter from Jakob W. to the District President of Aachen, 25.08.1925.
102. John Braithwaite, *Crime, Shame, and Reintegration* (Cambridge: Cambridge University Press, 1989).
103. Timon de Groot, "The Criminal Registry in the German Empire: The 'Cult of Previous Convictions' and the Offender's Right to Be Forgotten," *German History* 39, no. 3 (2021): 358–76.
104. LAV NRW R, BR 0005, no. 22778, petition from Karl S. to the District President, 24.11.1921.
105. Ibid., letter from the District President to the Minister of the Interior, 06.03.1922.
106. LAV NRW R, BR 0005, no. 22780, statement from the public prosecutor on the case of Joseph H., 14.12.1927.
107. Ibid., documents from the state prosecutor: request from Andreas B., 11.10.1929.
108. Ibid., documents from the state prosecutor: requests from 4.12.1927 and 18.04.1928.
109. Ibid., documents from the state prosecutor: request from Josef H., 29.01.1929.
110. Günter Spendel, "Gustav Radbruchs politischer Weg," in *Gustav Radbruch als Reichsjustizminister (1921–1923)*, ed. Irina Mohr, 24–34 (Berlin: Mohr, 2004), 32.

111. Gustav Radbruch, "Der Überzeugungsverbrecher," *ZStW* 44 (1924): 34–38. Cf. *Verhandlungen des 34. Deutschen Juristentages* (1926), 353ff.
112. Gotthard Jasper, *Der Schutz der Republik. Studien zur staatlichen Sicherung der Demokratie in der Weimarer Republik, 1922–1930* (Tübingen: Mohr Siebeck, 1963); Martin Sabrow, *Der Rathenaumord. Rekonstruktion einer Verschwörung gegen die Republik von Weimar* (Munich: Oldenbourg, 1994), 200–5.
113. Max Hirschberg and Friedrich Thimme, eds., *Der Fall Fechenbach. Juristische Gutachten* (Tübingen: Mohr, 1924).
114. Georg Dahm and Friedrich Schaffstein, *Liberales oder autoritäres Strafrecht?* (Hamburg: Hanseatische Verlagsanstalt, 1933).
115. Lothar Gruchmann, "'Blutschutzgesetz' und Justiz," *Vierteljahrshefte für Zeitgeschichte* 31 (1983): 418–42, 418.
116. Alfred Rosenberg, *Wesen, Grundsätze und Ziele der Nationalsozialistischen Deutschen Arbeiterpartei. Das Programm der Bewegung* (Munich: Boepple, 1930).
117. Helmut Nicolai, *Rasse und Recht* (Berlin: Hobbing, 1933).
118. Alfred Rosenberg, *Der Mythus des 20. Jahrhunderts. Eine Wertung der seelisch-geistigen Gestaltenkämpfe unserer Zeit*, 4th ed. (Munich: Hoheneichen, 1934). Cf. Arnold Zingerle, "Die 'Systemehre'. Stellung und Funktion von 'Ehre' in der NS-Ideologie," in *Ehre. Archaische Momente in der Moderne*, ed. Ludgera Vogt and Arnold Zingerle, 96–117 (1994), 103ff.
119. Alfred Hueck, Hans Carl Nipperdey, and Rolf Dietz, *Gesetz zur Ordnung der nationalen Arbeit. Kommentar* (Munich: Beck, 1934). Cf. James Q. Whitman, "On Nazi 'Honor' and the New European 'Dignity,'" in *Darker Legacies of Law in Europe: The Shadow of National Socialism and Fascism over Europe and Its Legal Traditions*, ed. Christian Joerges and Navraj Singh Ghaleigh, 243–66 (London: Bloomsbury, 2003), 252.
120. Helmut Nicolai, "Nationalsozialismus und Erneuerung des Deutschen Strafrechts," *Deutsches Recht. Zentralorgan des National-Sozialistischen Rechtswahrerbundes* 3 (1933): 5.
121. Wilhelm Sauer, "Aufgaben und Gefahren der Strafrechtsreform," *Deutsches Recht. Zentralorgan des National-Sozialistischen Rechtswahrerbundes* 3 (1933): 176–215, 177.
122. Hans Dieter von Gemmingen, *Strafrecht im Geiste Adolf Hitlers* (Heidelberg: Winter, 1933), 25; Alfred Balzer, *Die ehrlose Gesinnung im geltenden und zukünftigen Strafrecht* (Coburg: Tageblatt-Haus, 1934), 29–32.
123. Cf. Pamela E. Swett, "Political Violence, Gesinnung, and the Courts in Late Weimar Berlin," in *Conflict, Catastrophe and Continuity: Essays on Modern German History*, ed. Frank Biess, Mark Roseman, and Hanna Schissler, 60–79 (New York: Berghahn Books, 2007), 73–74.
124. Dahm and Schaffstein, *Liberales oder autoritäres Strafrecht?*, 26.
125. Dirk Blasius, *Weimars Ende: Bürgerkrieg und Politik 1930–1933* (Göttingen: Vandenhoeck & Ruprecht, 2005), 89–95.
126. Cited in Paul Kluke, "Der Fall Potempa," *Vierteljahrshefte für Zeitgeschichte* 5 (1957): 279–97, 285.
127. Gruchmann, "'Blutschutzgesetz' und Justiz," 418–20.
128. Alexandra Przyrembel, *"Rassenschande". Reinheitsmythos und Vernichtungslegitimation im Nationalsozialismus* (Göttingen: Vandenhoeck & Ruprecht, 2003), 399–409. Przyrembel, however, also notes that these sentences were not imposed that frequently. Meanwhile, non-legal actions such as public shaming were indeed very common in the early years of the Nazi era. Cf. ibid., 64.

Conclusion

This book aimed to elucidate the significance of the punishment of felony disenfranchisement in nineteenth- and early twentieth-century Germany. It did so by analyzing the lawmakers' views of the intended purpose of the punishment; the commentaries of judicial experts; the ways in which the execution of the punishment was sometimes challenged and contested by several subgroups in German society; and how the authorities instrumentalized the punishment to turn a certain group into "dishonorable" felons. In the process, one of my key considerations was that observers regarded the punishment as significant not only because of its emotional effects on the person so sentenced but also because they believed it reinforced collective sentiments about the proper use of the notion of honor. A wrongful execution of the punishment, by contrast, harmed the community's understanding of honor.

In the early nineteenth century, the authorities designed felony disenfranchisement in principle as an instrument for promoting a notion of honor that related to state institutions, trustworthy citizenship, and compliance with the law. Their aim was to make this "civil" concept of honor hegemonic and to thus discard feudal, estate-based notions of honor. The provisional character of rights of political participation was key to nineteenth-century states' efforts to create a moral order among their citizens. By maintaining the power to withhold civil privileges, they aimed to safeguard the institutions based on them. Lawmakers designed felony disenfranchisement to contribute to forging respect for the rule of law and to give the penal system the sole authority to determine what was honorable or dishonorable. Although the German higher classes strongly opposed this development, the notion of honor did indeed come to be increasingly equated with citizenship in nineteenth-century Germany. "Irreproachable" and "law-abiding" became core characteristics of honorable conduct. Actions in the legal sphere especially, such as telling the truth before the court, were crucial examples of the norms of modern citizenship. All of this was part of a broader attempt to make people subjects of the state first and foremost, with the state functioning as the only arbiter in questions of honor and dishonor.

In the early decades of the nineteenth century—a period still characterized by the ongoing process of state formation, the codification of criminal law, and the development of the system of civil privileges—some influential scholars criticized the punishment, either for harming offenders' process of reintegration and robbing too many citizens of their right to participate in state affairs, or for putting too much emphasis on the "civil" notion of honor. These criticisms, however, largely faded away when the codification of the punishment reached its final stage in the period of the German Empire. Hardly any commentator in Imperial Germany openly expressed doubts about the existence of this punishment. In fact, representatives of several subgroups of Wilhelmine society defended it in their pleas to have membership in certain institutions be opened up to a broader group of people. Meanwhile, time and time again, the authorities emphatically underscored the need to exclude "dishonored" felons from important state institutions.

The preoccupation with the notion of honor in the context of felony disenfranchisement apparent among Imperial Germany's authorities and citizens should certainly not be seen as a sign of legal backwardness, or as a way of protecting the interests of feudal elites. In fact, the notion of honor was highly intertwined with the idea of the rule of law. Thus, even though Imperial Germany's criminal justice system has often been described as authoritarian and biased, citizens' relation to felony disenfranchisement, as well as their engagement with it, also points to certain liberalizing features in the system that existed alongside these authoritarian elements. People's civil privileges, and by extension their "civil honor," could only be suspended as a consequence of legal punishment, and that principle was actively defended. The existence of felony disenfranchisement thus appeared to protect the rights and honor of citizens who had not been in contact with the law. In other words, it allowed "law-abiding" citizens to claim their rights and their entitlement to a certain kind of honor, thereby also limiting state power within certain bounds.

Felony disenfranchisement was an undisputed element of Imperial Germany's penal policy. Almost nobody challenged its existence; only its proper execution was a topic of debate, largely related to people's inclusion in or exclusion from certain, usually imperial, institutions. Although there was pressure for institutions to become more inclusive, several politicians, political commentators, and social activists instrumentalized felony disenfranchisement in the public debate to stress the need for some exclusion to defend the honor of these institutions. Even the workers' movement—a bastion of opposition against state-imposed ideas—applied the notion of honor in similar ways and emphasized the need to exclude "dishonored" felons. Thus, the notion of "civil honor" was prominent in several layers of German society.

The consensus about the intended purpose of felony disenfranchisement in Imperial Germany increasingly led to an association between honor and the possession of a certain moral and political conviction. If someone had acted out of political or moral conviction, that person was considered honorable. This was based on the premise that individuals always expressed their political opposition against state authorities overtly. The punishment was thus crucial in criminal procedures against political offenders that occurred during the time of the German Empire. The "dishonorable disposition"—a key notion in the execution of felony disenfranchisement—helped define the lines between morally permissible political offenses and serious crimes. According to the most authoritative interpretations of the Reich Penal Code, the punishment of felony disenfranchisement was only to be imposed if the criminal act had resulted from the defendant's "dishonorable disposition." In other words, it was not supposed to be used "politically" or to punish people who had acted out of an "honorable" political conviction. This consensus about the appropriate use of disenfranchisement went beyond partisan divisions, which was why disenfranchising sentences against "political offenders" sparked so much controversy in the German Empire. The magnitude of these protests showed that this consensus limited the state's power to use this punishment for political ends.

However, political agents more often instrumentalized the subjective, individual aspect of the notion of honor to recover their honor against the claims of their opponents. The more this happened, the more difficult it became to find common ground in the use of the notion of honor: everybody could claim to have acted out of a certain political conviction. At the same time, the judiciary came to suspect that some criminals instrumentalized political ideology to cover up their real motives for base criminal actions, making it hard to distinguish between "real political convictions" and criminal intentions. Consequently, the authorities actively tried to undermine certain offenders' claims that they had acted "politically," arguing instead that they had acted in a secretive manner rather than in an overtly honorable way. Indeed, most legal scholars of Imperial Germany seemed to agree that honorable and dishonorable dispositions marked the difference between overt, "real" idealism and sly selfishness.

Without a doubt, stigmatization was a decisive aspect of disenfranchisement, giving it a communicative, public function. Consistent with Durkheim's theory of punishment, this communicative function was not just directed at the person being punished but at the community as a whole, with the aim of reinforcing what was considered honorable conduct. Even though the stigma was invisible to direct observers, as it was not imprinted on the offenders' body, its effects worked in many ways in the bureaucratic state of the German Empire. For an extended period, disenfranchisement found support in circles of penal experts and politicians if it fulfilled two important criteria: it had to be applied apolitically, that is, only to people who had committed an offense clearly identifiable as "dishonorable"; and it had to be applied to all citizens equally. Imposing this punishment, after all, implied that those subject to it had, in principle, been entitled to the honor of citizenship before they were stripped of it.

Even though the prison reform movement grew during the time of the German Empire, and even though many prominent progressive legal and criminological experts started to argue that ex-convicts could experience moral improvement, supporters of these movements did not immediately fully reject felony disenfranchisement. Scholars and activists from the "modern approach" to criminal policy increasingly emphasized that offenders had the potential to reform themselves and that penal measures only designed to exclude citizens could thwart offenders' resocialization process. However, they hardly objected to the existence of felony disenfranchisement. Instead, they continued to try to appropriate the vocabulary of honor and exclusion by integrating felony disenfranchisement into their own reform agendas for a long time thereafter. This appropriation revealed that felony disenfranchisement was, in fact, a pliable and adaptable punishment that could fulfill various functions. The important emotional impact of felony disenfranchisement—that it appealed to German citizens' sense of honor—could reinforce its function within a comprehensive, modern penal policy.

Meanwhile, in contrast to modern scholars' emphasis on the resocialization of offenders, the authorities often vehemently extolled the notion of retribution and "just deserts" and emphasized the need to exclude those convicted of serious offenses as a way for them to atone for their crimes. World War I proved how entrenched official government policy concerning disenfranchised felons was—particularly concerning inclusion in the army. Disenfranchised felons were excluded from the army, regardless of any ideas about the reformatory effects of the army on ex-convicts. Although amnesty was extended to many in the first months of war, this did not fundamentally change this circumstance for disenfranchised felons but rather confirmed their exceptional status. Whereas other historians have focused on the questions of age and citizenship as basic categories determining the inclusion of citizens in the German army during World War I, I have argued in this book that a citizen's status as an ex-convict was equally important to the authorities in deciding on suitability for military conscription. Only in the second phase of the war, when politicians increasingly perceived the need for more manpower, did the army command reconsider this fundamental principle. Disenfranchised felons could finally be enlisted, but their character was still seriously scrutinized and their entrance to the army was treated with much suspicion.

Furthermore, over the course of World War I, the German criminal justice system increasingly failed to meet the standards of neutrality and equality. Actions that had previously been considered political offenses committed by "honorable" individuals now often led to felony disenfranchisement. This happened even more often after the war as the punishment became highly politicized. In the Weimar Republic, the argument about "neutrality" was more contested than it ever had been in the time of the German Empire. Revolutionary upheavals, political assassinations, coup d'états, the trials that followed, and the government's use of amnesty all contributed to the increasing politicization of this punishment. Moreover, the unprecedented mass character of political action and protest made it more difficult to draw clear distinctions between the political and the nonpolitical, as well as between honorable and dishonorable offenders. Protests against judges thought to be abusing this punishment swelled as they were alleged to be using it to silence political protest. In the Weimar Republic, however, such protest resulted in a fundamental questioning of the idea that "neutrality" was even possible.

This politicization continued after the Nazi Party rose to power. The Blutschutzgesetz was the Nazis' first way of instrumentalizing the punishment for their ideology. However, by declaring that people who did not belong to the German *Volk* could not have this sentence imposed on them, they also purposefully rejected the idea of inclusiveness. By no longer imposing this sentence on Jewish and Polish individuals, Nazi officials explicitly denied them the basic honor that came with German citizenship. The idea of equality—that all citizens were in principle entitled to a certain honor—was thus eliminated for certain individuals who were fundamentally denied the right to even be considered trustworthy on racial grounds. The politicization and instrumentalization of the punishment in relation to the notion of the *Volk* are the most important reasons that the punishment lost its utility as a part of penal law after World War II.

In the end, it is hard to argue that the punishment was abolished after World War II due to penal reformers' efforts to ensure that ex-offenders were granted a fair chance at reintegration. Plans to reform the criminal justice system in Weimar Germany often remained on the level of good intentions—this was particularly true for legislative change and the abolishment of felony disenfranchisement. What happened instead was that this legal punishment, long considered a self-evident part of the penal system, gradually fell out of favor due to an intensely contested and politicized understanding of the sentiments that the punishment was supposed to communicate and protect.

Even so, the punishment's increasing politicization was surely not all that characterized its development in the first half of the twentieth century. Dishonored felons also began to experience a sense of collective political concern in consequence of changing ideas about punishment, resocialization, and entitlement. Around 1900, the frustration expressed by disenfranchised felons about the impacts of this punishment took on a new quality. Formerly, disenfranchised felons who had petitioned to have their rights restored had appealed to their biographies and their former honorable conduct as reasons why they should be entitled to citizens' privileges. Now, many more ex-convicts began instead to stress their wish to become useful citizens in the future. In their experience, full citizenship was not just a privilege awarded for honorable life conduct but something one was entitled to by virtue of membership in a community—both local and national. Armed with this conception of citizenship and entitlement, they sought to hold the state accountable for their misery and criticized what they perceived to be an entirely unjust penal system.

In the traditional nineteenth-century idea of rehabilitation and entitlement, lawmakers' focus was on atonement and remorse. If one believed that one could "pay" for transgressions against the norms of citizenship, one implicitly signaled agreement with the idea behind the punishment. For instance, when ex-convicts appealed to their honorable, upstanding biography, they showed that they had effectively internalized the norms of moral and honorable citizenship. Expressions of shame and remorse crucially belonged within this rhetorical framework. In other words, as long as people believed that convicts deserved disenfranchisement for having transgressed the norms of moral citizenship, the effects of the punishment were consistent with lawmakers' intentions. Within this view of rehabilitation and entitlement, it was inconceivable that something like service to the community could pay for one's "dishonorable" crimes. In being disenfranchised, offenders were not paying for the damage they had done to others or to society at large but for the moral duty they had neglected, as well as for the harm they had caused to "collective sentiments" surrounding the notion of honor, to put it in Durkheim's terms.

The alternative to this traditional idea of rehabilitation and entitlement revolved around the notion that one could "pay" for one's crime by participating meaningfully in society. People who supported this notion started to argue that army service, for instance, could allow offenders to atone for their crimes. This new attitude toward punishment and entitlement enabled ex-convicts to protest their disenfranchisement without trying to deflect blame for their crimes or giving up on the notion of having to "pay" for them. Consequently, ex-convicts increasingly measured the seriousness of their crimes in terms of the harm they had caused rather than the norms they had failed to obey. Even "dishonored" felons demanded that their time be spent in a way that was useful to the nation; they expressed much less remorse and much more anger at the unjust penal system, increasingly regarding the punishment as disproportionate to the crime.

In light of these trends, I have tried to demonstrate in this book how the history of felony disenfranchisement in Germany informs us of the history of ideas and norms of citizenship there. In the Weimar Republic, ex-convicts' changing attitudes seemed to collide with those of the local authorities: the authorities still supported most of the traditional ideas of atonement and remorse, whereas many ex-convicts entertained new ideas of entitlement. The negotiations between ex-convicts and authorities about the justness of the punishment and the possibility of rehabilitation thereby show how controversial the penal system had become, and how much space there was for historical agents in this contested sphere to argue for their own interpretation of "just deserts."

In this book, I have argued that felony disenfranchisement was a significant part of the German penal policy, but I have also aimed to urge political historians to take the actual form and execution of punishments seriously in their research. The crucial differences between certain kinds of punishment and their impact on citizens are often not thematized in political history; researchers most often only focus on the fact that political agents are punished, and not *how* they are punished. Meanwhile, detailed analyses of different forms of punishment and rehabilitation are often treated as a subdiscipline of social history. The actual form of a punishment, however, could have political consequences, as I have aimed to show here. The execution of felony disenfranchisement over time certainly demonstrates this. The execution of this particular punishment had an emotional impact, and contemporary observers really cared a great deal about whether felons were deprived of their civil privileges.

BIBLIOGRAPHY

Archival Entries

Brandenburgisches Landeshauptarchiv
  2A I Pol 1, Regierung Potsdam
Bundesarchiv Berlin-Lichterfelde
  R 55, Reichsministerium für Volksaufklärung und Propaganda
  R 1501, Reichsministerium des Innern
  R 3001, Reichsjustizministerium
  R 3003, Oberreichsanwalt beim Reichsgericht
Geheimes Staatsarchiv Preußischer Kulturbesitz
  I. HA Rep. 77, Ministerium des Innern
  I. HA Rep. 84, Justizministerium
  I. HA Rep. 89, Geheimes Zivilkabinett
Landesarchiv Baden Württemberg—Hauptstaatsarchiv Stuttgart
  M 1/7, Kriegsministerium Justiz-Abteilung
Landesarchiv Nordrhein-Westfalen, Abteilung Rheinland
  Br 0005, Regierung Aachen
  Br 0007, Regierung Düsseldorf

Newspapers and Magazines

Berliner Börsen-Zeitung
Berliner Tageblatt
Berliner Volkszeitung
Die Volksstimme
Fliegende Blätter
Frankfurter Zeitung
Freiheit
Hamburger Anzeiger
Kölnische Volkszeitung
Lübecker Volksbote
Schlesische Arbeiter-Zeitung
Simplicissimus
Vorwärts
Vossische Zeitung
Wiener Zeitung
Wahre Jacob

Minutes and Statistics

Ministerial-Blatt für die gesammte innere Verwaltung in den Königlich Preußischen Staaten. Berlin: Starcke.
Mitteilungen der Internationalen Kriminalistischen Vereinigung. Berlin: J. Guttentag, 1889–.
Protokoll der Verhandlungen des Parteitages der Sozialdemokratischen Partei Deutschlands. Berlin: Vorwärts, 1890–.
Protokoll der Reichskonferenz der Sozialdemokratie Deutschlands. Berlin: Vorwärts, 1916.
Protokoll über die Verhandlungen des Parteitages der Sozialdemokratischen Partei Deutschlands abgehalten zu Lübeck vom 22. bis 28. September 1901. Berlin: Vorwärts, 1901.
Statistik des deutschen Reichs. Berlin: Statistisches Reichsamt, 1873–1919.
Stenographische Berichte über die Verhandlungen des Reichstages. Berlin: Sittenfeld, 1871–1919.
Stenographische Berichte über die Verhandlungen des Reichstages des Norddeutschen Bundes. Berlin: Sittenfeld, 1869–70.
Stenographischer Bericht über die Verhandlungen der Deutschen Constituirenden Nationalversammlung zu Frankfurt am Main, ed. Franz Wigard. Frankfurt a.M.: Sauerländer, 1849.
Verhandlungen der Verfassunggebenden Deutschen Nationalversammlung. Berlin: Sittenfeld, 1919–20.
Verhandlungen des deutschen Juristentages. Berlin: J. Guttentag, 1860–.
Verhandlungen des Preußischen Hauses der Abgeordneten. Berlin: Moeser, 1848–.

Laws and Statutes

Das Strafgesetzbuch und die Strafproceßordnung für das Königreich Sachsen. Leipzig: Voigt & Günther, 1855.
"Die Grundsätze welche bei dem Vollzuge gerichtlich erkannter Freiheitsstrafen bis zu weiterer gemeinsamer Regelung zur Anwendung kommen." *Central-Blatt für das Deutsche Reich* 25 (1897): 308–13.
Die Reichsgewerbeordnung in ihrer neuesten Gestalt nebst Ausführungsvorschriften. Berlin: Siemenroth & Worms, 1892.
Entwurf eines Strafgesetzbuches für den Norddeutschen Bund. Berlin: Decker, 1869.
Motive zum Entwurf des Strafgesetzbuchs für die Preussischen Staaten. Berlin: Enslin, 1851.
Reichsgesetz über die Wahlen der abgeordneten zum Volkshause. Frankfurt a.M.: Krebs-Schmitt, 1849.
Strafgesetzbuch für den Norddeutschen Bund. Berlin: Decker, 1870.
Strafgesetzbuch für die Preußischen Staaten. Berlin: Nauck, 1851.
Vorentwurf zu einem Deutschen Strafgesetzbuch. Berlin: Guttentag, 1909.

Printed Sources

Abegg, Julius Friedrich Heinrich. *System Der Criminal-Rechts-Wissenschaft Mit einer Vorrede über Die Wissenschaftliche Behandlung des Criminalrecht.* Königsberg: Unzer, 1826.
Adam, Karl. "Stände und Berufe in Preußen Gegenüber Der Nationalen Erhebung des Jahres 1848." *PJ* 89 (1897): 285–308.

Ammon, Otto. *Die Gesellschaftsordnung und ihre natürlichen Grundlagen: Entwurf einer sozialanthropologie zum Gebrauch für alle Gebildeten, die sich mit sozialen Fragen befassen.* Jena: G. Fischer, 1895.
Arndt, Adolf. *Bergbau und Bergbaupolitik.* Leipzig: Hirschfeld, 1894.
Arnim, Harry von. *Pro Nihilo! Vorgeschichte des Arnim'schen Processes.* Zürich, 1876.
Aschrott, Paul Felix, and Franz von Liszt. *Die Reform des Reichsstrafgesetzbuchs.* Berlin: Guttentag, 1910.
Balzer, Alfred. *Die ehrlose Gesinnung im geltenden und zukünftigen Strafrecht.* Coburg: Tageblatt-haus, 1934.
Bar, Ludwig von. *Geschichte des deutschen Strafrechts und der Strafrechtstheorien.* Vol. 1. Berlin: Weidmann, 1882.
Bauer, Bernhard. *Der Eid. Eine Studie.* Heidelberg: Winter, 1884.
Bebel, August. *Attentate und Sozialdemokratie.* Berlin: Vorwärts, 1905.
———. *Aus meinem Leben.* Vol. 1. Stuttgart: Dietz, 1910.
———. *Aus meinem Leben.* Vol. 3. Stuttgart: Dietz, 1914.
Behrendt, Friedrich. *Die Ehrenstrafen und ihre Weiterbildung.* Heidelberg: Rößler & Herbert, 1914.
Bernstein, Eduard. *Die Geschichte der Berliner Arbeiter-Bewegung.* Vol. 3. Berlin: Vorwärts, 1910.
Biedermann, Karl. "Der Polenprozeß in Berlin." *Unsre Gegenwart und Zukunft* 9 (1847): 205–53.
Binding, Karl. *Der Entwurf eines Strafgesetzbuchs für den norddeutschen Bund in seinen Grundsätzen.* Leipzig: Engelmann, 1869.
———. *Die Ehre und ihre Verletzbarkeit.* Leipzig: Duncker & Humblot, 1892.
———. *Grundriß des deutschen Strafrechts. Allgemeiner Teil.* 6th edn. Leipzig: Engelmann, 1902.
Blau, Bruno. *Die Kriminalität der deutschen Juden.* Berlin: Lamm, 1906.
Blum, Hans. *Die Lügen unserer Sozialdemokratie. Nach amtlichen Quellen enthüllt und widerlegt.* Wismar: Hinstorff, 1891.
Bonger, Willem Adriaan. "Verbrechen und Sozialismus." *Die Neue Zeit* 30 (1912): 801–67.
Börner, Hermann. *Der praktische Rathgeber für bürgerliche Kreise. Mit einer Auswahl von Muster-Formularen zur Abfassung van Anträgen, Bittschriften, Vorstellungen etc. in verschiedenen persönlichen Angelegenheiten.* Breslau: Freund, 1893.
Brauer, Wilhelm von. "Ueber Die Rehabilitation Verutheilter." *Der Gerichtssaal* 11 (1857): 321–39.
Bumke, Erwin. "Rehabilitation." In *Handwörterbuch Der Rechtswissenschaft*, ed. Fritz Stier-Somlo and Alexander Nikolaus Elster, vol. 5, 774–76. Berlin: De Gruyter, 1928.
Burlage, Eduard. *Die Entschädigung der unschuldig Verhafteten und der unschuldig Bestraften.* Berlin: Liebmann, 1905.
Calker, Fritz van. *Strafrecht und Ethik.* Leipzig: Duncker & Humblot, 1897.
Dahm, Georg, and Friedrich Schaffstein. *Liberales oder autoritäres Strafrecht?* Hamburg: Hanseatische Verlagsanstalt, 1933.
Das Zuchthausurteil gegen Karl Liebknecht. Wörtliche Wiedergabe der Prozeßakten, Urteile und Eingaben Liebknechts. Leipzig: Frankes Verlag, 1919.
Delaquis, Ernst. *Die Rehabilitation im Strafrecht.* Berlin: J. Guttentag, 1907.
———. *Die Rehabilitation Verurteilter.* Berlin: J. Guttentag, 1906.

———. "Strafrechtliche Kriegsziele." *ZStW* 39, no. 1 (1918): 276–99.

"Die Ehrenstrafen nach dem neuen Preußischen Strafgesetzbuche beleuchtet von einem Practischen Juristen." *Hitzig's Annalen der Deutschen und Ausländischen Criminal-Rechtspflege* 27 (1851): 1–23.

"Die Eidesnot." *Die Grenzboten* 53 (1894): 256–61.

Dietz, Heinrich. "Keine Wehrpflicht der Verbrecher!" *GAS* 53, no. 4 (1906): 225–35.

Eucken, Rudolf. *Die Sittlichen Kräfte des Krieges*. Leipzig: Gräfe, 1914.

Everth, Erich. *Von der Seele des Soldaten im Felde. Bemerkungen eines Kriegsteilnehmers*. Jena: Diederichs, 1915.

Exner, Franz. *Krieg und Kriminalität*. Leipzig: Wiegandt, 1926.

Falck, Carl. "Der Krieg und Die Staatsanwaltschaft." *DJZ* 20 (1915): 374–75.

———. "Die Gnadenerlasse vom 27. Januar 1916." *DJZ* 21 (1916): 36–39.

Feder, Ernst. *Die Prügelstrafe*. Berlin: J. Guttentag, 1911.

Fichte, Johann Gottlieb. *Grundlage des Naturrechts nach Principien der Wissenschaftslehre*. Vol. 2. Jena: Gabler, 1797.

Franz, Rudolf. "Der Segen des Krieges für die Strafgefangenen." *BfG* 49, no. 2 (1915): 221–25.

Freisler, Oswald. "Die Ehrenstrafen und Ihre Berechtigung." *Zeitschrift für die Gesamte Strafrechtswissenschaft* 42, no. 1 (1921): 438–42.

Freisler, Roland. "Das deutsche Polenstrafrecht." *Deutsche Justiz* 103 (1941): 1139–42.

Frohme, Karl. *Politische Polizei und Justiz im monarchischen Deutschland. Erinnerungen*. Hamburg: Auer, 1926.

Gass, Wilhelm. *Die Lehre vom Gewissen. Ein Beitrag zur Ethik*. Berlin: Reimer, 1869.

Gemmingen, Hans Dieter von. *Strafrecht im Geiste Adolf Hitlers*. Heidelberg: Winter, 1933.

Gerlach, Hellmut von. *Die Geschichte des preussischen Wahlrechts*. Berlin: Buchverlag der "Hilfe," 1908.

Gierke, Otto von. *Deutsches Privatrecht*. Vol. 1. Leipzig: Duncker & Humblot, 1895.

Globig, Hans Ernst von, and Johann Georg Huster. *Abhandlung von der Criminalgesetzgebung. Eine von der ökonomischen Gesellschaft in Bern gekrönte Preisschrift*. Zürich: Füessly, 1783.

Goldschmidt, James. "Zur Mitteleuropäischen Strafrechtsvereinheitlichung." *ZStW* 38, no. 1 (1917): 417–36.

Graf zu Dohna, Alexander. "Der Innere Konnex von Freiheitsstrafen und Ehrenstrafen." *MKS* 17 (1926): 352–59.

Grossmann, Stephan. *Der Hochverräter Ernst Toller. Die Geschichte eines Prozesses*. Berlin: Rowohlt, 1919.

Grünhut, Max. "Die Abschaffung der Ehrenstrafen." *ZStW* 46 (1925): 260–78.

Guckenheimer, Eduard. *Der Begriff der ehrlosen Gesinnung im Strafrecht. Ein Beitrag zur strafrechtlichen Beurteilung politischer Verbrecher*. Hamburg: Gente, 1921.

Günther, Louis. "Die Strafrechtsreform im Aufklärungszeitalter." *AKK* 28 (1907): 112–92, 225–91.

Hamm, Oskar. "Der Entwurf Eines Gesetzes Betreffend Die Entschädigung für Unschuldig Erlittene Untersuchungshaft." *DJZ* 9, no. 4 (1904): 177–85.

Hegel, Georg Wilhelm Friedrich. *Vorlesungen über die Aesthetik*. Vol. 2. Berlin, 1843.

Heine, W. *Die Besserung als Strafzweck und das Aufsichts-Personal der Strafanstalten*. Leipzig: Barth, 1866.

Hentig, Hans von. *Aufsätze zur Deutschen Revolution*. Berlin: Springer, 1919.

———. "Politische Verbrechen Der Gegenwart." *Deutsche Strafrechtszeitung* 6 (1919): 218–22.

———. *Strafrecht und Auslese. Eine Anwendung des Kausalgesetzes auf den rechtbrechenden Menschen*. Berlin: Springer, 1914.

Hepp, Ferdinand Carl Theodor. *Das Strafen-System des neuen Entwurfs eines Strafgesetzbuches für das Königreich Württemberg vom Jahr 1835. In Vergleichung mit dem gemeinen Rechte, dem Strafedicte und neueren Legislationen*. Heidelberg: Mohr, 1836.

———. *Die politischen und unpolitischen Staats-Verbrechen und Vergehen nebst angränzenden Amtsverbrechen und Polizei-Uebertretungen*. Tübingen: Zu-Guttenberg, 1846.

Hesse, William. *Die Aufenthaltsbeschränkungen bestrafter Personen in Deutschland*. Lüneburg: König, 1905.

Hirschberg, Max, and Friedrich Thimme. *Der Fall Fechenbach. Juristische Gutachten*. Tübingen: Mohr, 1924.

Hoenig, Fritz. *Mein Ehrenhandel mit dem Oberst und Flügeladjutant v. Schwartzkoppen und dem Oberst und Abteilungschef im Generalstabe von Bernhardi*. Berlin: H. Walther, 1902.

Holtzendorff, Franz von. *Handbuch des deutschen Strafrechts. In Einzelbeiträgen*. Berlin: Habel, 1871.

———. *Handbuch des Gefängnisswesens. In Einzelbeiträgen*. Hamburg: Richter, 1888.

———. *Rechtsgutachten erstattet zum Process des Grafen H. v. Arnim*. Munich: Oldenbourg, 1875.

Holtzendorff, Franz von, and Felix Stoerk. "Das Deutsche Verfassungsrecht." In *Encyklopädie Der Rechtswissenschaft in systematischer und alphabetischer Bearbeitung*, ed. Franz von Holtzendorff, 5th edn., 1041–153. Leipzig, 1890.

Hueck, Alfred, Hans Carl Nipperdey, and Rolf Dietz. *Gesetz zur Ordnung der nationalen Arbeit. Kommentar*. Munich: Beck, 1934.

Humboldt, Wilhelm von. *Ideen zu einem Versuch, die Gränzen der Wirksamkeit des Staats zu bestimmen*. Breslau: Trewendt, 1851.

Iphofen, Ernst Friedrich. "Ueber Politische Ehrenrechte." *Zeitschrift für Rechtspflege und Verwaltung* 24 (1863): 299–342.

———. "Ueber Politische Ehrenrechte II." *Zeitschrift für Rechtspflege und Verwaltung* 25 (1864): 314–48.

Jacoby, Johann. *Vier Fragen beantwortet von einem Ostpreußen*. Leipzig: Hoff, 1863.

Jagemann, Ludwig Hugo Franz von. "Die Bürgerliche Ehre im Verhältnisse zum Strafgesetze." *Archiv des Criminalrechts* 4 (1838): 248–72.

Jastrow, Ignaz. "Die Lehre Des Essener Meineidsprozesses." *Das Freie Wort* 10, no. 23 (1911): 892–901.

John, Richard Eduard. *Entwurf mit Motiven zu einem Strafgesetzbuche für den Norddeutschen Bund*. Berlin: Guttentag, 1868.

Jung, J. *Entwickelung des deutschen Post- und Telegraphenwesens in den letzten 25 Jahren*. Leipzig: Duncker & Humblot, 1893.

Kahl, Wilhelm. "Ehrenstrafen." *Deutsche Juristenzeitung* 28 (1923): 507–12.

Keller, Franz. *Allgemeiner Geschäfts- und Familien-Briefsteller*. 40th edn. Berlin: A. Weichert, 1900.

Kießlich, Hermann-Victor. *Die Ehrenstrafen*. Berlin: Siemenroth, 1911.

Kirchmann, Julius Hermann von. *Die Grundbegriffe des Rechts und der Moral als Einleitung in das Studium rechtsphilosophischer Werke*. Berlin: Heimann, 1869.

Kleeman, Ernst. "Kriegserfahrungen im Gefängnis." *Archiv für Kriminal-Anthropologie und Kriminalistik* 67 (1915): 1–24.

Kleinschrod, Gallus Aloys. *Systematische Entwicklung der Grundbegriffe und Grundwahrheiten des peinlichen Rechts nach der Natur der Sache und der positiven Gesetzgebung*. Erlangen: Johann Jakob Palm, 1799.

Klingelhöfer, Gustav. "Politische Verbrecher." *Die Zukunft* 111 (1920): 42–48.

Köhne, Paul. "Die Arbeiten des Internationalen Kongresses für Gefängniswesen in Rom, 1885." *ZStW* 8, no. 3 (1888): 439–64.

Krafft, Rudolf. *Glänzendes Elend*. Stuttgart: Lutz, 1895.

Kraus, Josef. *Das Rechtsgut der Ehre vom kulturgeschichtlichen und legislativ-politischen Standpunkte dargestellt*. Vienna: Manz, 1905.

Krävel, Rudolf von. *Entwurf nebst Gründen zu dem allgemeinen Theile eines für ganz Deutschland geltenden Straf-Gesetzbuchs unter besonderer Berücksichtigung der geltenden deutschen Straf-Gesetzbücher, sowie des baierischen und Lübeck'schen Entwurfs*. Halle: Waisenhaus, 1862.

Kriegsmann, Hermann. *Einführung in die Gefängniskunde*. Heidelberg: Winter, 1912.

Krug, August Otto. *Ideen zu einer gemeinsamen Strafgesetzgebung für Deutschland*. Erlangen: Enke, 1857.

Kulemann, Wilhelm. *Die Eidesfrage*. Eisenach: Thüringische Verlagsanstalt, 1904.

———. *Die Sozialdemokratie und deren Bekämpfung. Eine Studie zur Reform des Sozialistengesetzes*. Berlin: Heymann, 1890.

Künzel, E. *Der erste Hochverratsprozess vor dem Deutschen Reichsgericht*. Leipzig: Hesse, 1881.

Küppers, Alexis. "Die Unfähigkeit der zu Zuchthaus Verurteilten, in das deutsche Heer und die kaiserliche Marine einzutreten." *MKS* 8 (1912): 630–36.

Lenkeit, Pastor. "Kriegserinnerungen aus dem Zuchthaus." In *Kriegserlebnisse Ostpreussischer Pfarrer*, ed. Karl Moszeik, 169–78. Berlin: Runge, 1915.

Leser, Guido. *Untersuchungen über das Wahlprüfungsrecht des deutschen Reichstags*. Duncker & Humblot, 1908.

Liebknecht, Wilhelm. *Hochverrath und Revolution*. Zürich: Verlag der Volksbuchhandlung, 1887.

Liepmann, Moritz. *Die Reform des deutschen Strafrechts. Kritische Bemerkungen zu dem "Strafgesetzentwurf."* Hamburg: Gente, 1921.

———. "Die Reue vom kriminalistischen Standpunkt." *Zeitschrift für Die Gesamte Strafrechtswissenschaft* 22, no. 1 (1902): 72–98.

Lindemeyer, Georg. *Die Wiedereinsetzung, Rehabilitation, unter besonderer Berücksichtigung der §§ 50–52 des Vorentwurfs und der §§ 110–112 des Gegenentwurfs*. Berlin: A. W. Schade, 1913.

Liszt, Franz von. *Das Problem der Kriminalität der Juden*. Giessen: Töpelmann, 1907.

———. *Die Gefängnisarbeit*. Berlin: Guttentag, 1900.

———. "Die psychologischen Grundlagen der Kriminalpolitik." *ZStW* 16 (1896): 477–517.

———. "Einheitliches mitteleuropäisches Strafrecht." *ZStW* 38 (1917): 1–20.

———. "Kriminalpolitische Aufgaben." *Zeitschrift für Die Gesamte Strafrechtswissenschaft* 10 (1890): 51–83.

———. *Lehrbuch des deutschen Strafrechts*. 10th edn. Berlin: De Gruyter, 1900.

———. *Lehrbuch des Deutschen Strafrechts*, ed. Eberhard Schmidt, 26th edn. Berlin: de Gruyter, 1932.

———. *Meineid und falsches Zeugnis. Eine strafrechts-geschichtliche Studie*. Vienna: Manz, 1876.

———."Preussen, Königreich Sachsen und die übrigen Norddeutschen Staaten." In *Handbuch des Gefängnißwesens*, ed. Franz von Holtzendorff, 161–84. Hamburg: Richter, 1888.

Lotmar, Philipp. *Der Arbeitsvertrag nach dem Privatrecht des Deutschen Reiches*. Vol. 1. Leipzig: Duncker & Humblot, 1902.

———. *Der unmoralische Vertrag. Insbesondere nach gemeinem Recht.* Leipzig: Duncker & Humblot, 1896.

Lucas, Hermann. *Anleitung zur strafrechtlichen Praxis. Ein Beitrag zur Ausbildung unserer jungen Juristen und ein Ratgeber für jüngere Praktiker.* Berlin: Liebmann, 1905.

———. "Das Strafrecht." In *Deutschland unter Kaiser Wilhelm II.*, ed. Siegfried Körte, vol. 3, 28–44. Berlin: Reimar Hobbing, 1914.

Luden, Heinrich. *Handbuch des teutschen gemeinen und particularen Strafrechtes.* Jena, 1847.

Lütgenau, Franz. *Der Essener Meineids-Prozeß vom 14. bis 17. August 1895. Geschichte und Glossen.* Berlin: Vorwärts, 1895.

Mahler, Karl. *Die Programme der politischen Parteien in Deutschland.* Leipzig: Gracklauer, 1909.

Marchand, H. *Das Strafregister in Deutschland.* Berlin: J. Guttentag, 1900.

Marck, Hugo von, and Alfred Kloss. *Die Staatsanwaltschaft bei den Land- und Amtsgerichten in Preussen.* Berlin: Heymann, 1903.

Marcuse, Oswald. *Die Ehrenstrafe. Eine rechtsvergleichende Darstellung nebst Kritik unter besonderer Berücksichtigung des geltenden Deutschen Strafrechts.* Breslau: Schletter, 1899.

Maurer, Konrad. "Ehre." In *Deutsches Staats-Wörterbuch*, ed. Johann Caspar Bluntschli and Karl Brater, 226–87. Stuttgart; Leipzig: Expedition des Staats-Wörterbuchs, 1858.

Mayr, Georg von. *Statistik und Gesellschaftslehre*. Vol. 3. Tübingen: Mohr, 1917.

Medem, Rudolf. "Strafzumessung und Strafvollzug." *ZStW* 7 (1887): 135–74.

Merkel, Julius. "Ueber Verlust der bürgerlichen Ehrenrechte und über Wiederherstellung derselben." *Allgemeine Gerichtszeitung für Das Königreich Sachsen* 7 (1863): 1–24.

Mittelstädt, Otto. "Die Reform des deutschen Gefängniswesens." *PJ* 40 (1877): 425–35 and 487–99.

———. *Gegen die Freiheitsstrafen. Ein Beitrag zur Kritik des heutigen Strafensystems.* Leipzig: Hirzel, 1879.

———. "Kulturgeschichte und Kriminalstatistik." *ZStW* 4 (1884): 391–414.

Mittermaier, Carl Josef Anton. "Die entehrenden Strafen." *Allgemeine deutsche Strafrechtszeitung* 1, no. 12 (1861): 177–82.

———. *Die Strafgesetzgebung in ihrer Fortbildung. Geprüft nach den Forderungen der Wissenschaft und nach den Erfahrungen über den Werth neuer Gesetzgebungen, und über die Schwierigkeiten der Codifikation.* Heidelberg: Winter, 1841.

———. "Strafarten." In *Staats-Lexikon*, ed. Carl von Rotteck and Carl Welcker, vol. 15, 184–215. Altona: Hammerich, 1843.

———. "Ueber den Meineid nach dem Gemeinen Rechte und den Bestimmungen Der Neuesten Strafgesetzbücher." *Neues Archiv des Criminalrechts* 2 (1818): 85–120.

Müller, Heinrich Wilhelm. *Untersuchungen über die Bewegung der Criminalität in ihrem Zusammenhang mit den wirtschaftlichen Verhältnissen.* Halle a.S.: Kaemmerer & Co., 1899.

Müller, Josef. *Vorstrafen und Strafregister.* Breslau: Schletter, 1908.

Müller, Otto. *Die lex Heinze.* Freiburg: Lehmann, 1900.

Nicolai, Helmut. "Nationalsozialismus und Erneuerung des Deutschen Strafrechts." *Deutsches Recht. Zentralorgan des National-Sozialistischen Rechtswahrerbundes* 3 (1933).

———. *Rasse und Recht.* Berlin: Hobbing, 1933.

Noellner, Friedrich. *Das Verhältniss der Strafgesetzgebung zur Ehre der Staatsbürger. Ein Beitrag zur Reform der deutschen Strafsysteme, vom philosophischen, legislativen und praktischen Standpunkte.* Frankfurt a.M.: Bayrhoffer, 1846.

Oba, Shigema. *Unverbesserliche Verbrecher und ihre Behandlung.* Berlin: Bahr, 1908.

Oerter, Sepp. *Acht Jahre Zuchthaus. Lebenserinnerungen.* Berlin: Verlag der Tribüne, 1908.

Oestreich, Rudolf. *Wegen Hochverrats im Zuchthaus.* Berlin: Verlag der Tribüne, 1913.

Oetker, Friedrich. "Die Ehrenstrafen nach dem Entwurf von 1919." *Juristische Wochenschrift* 55, no. 5 (1924): 254–60.

———. *Strafe und Lohn.* Würzburg, 1907.

Olshausen, Justus von. *Kommentar zu den Strafgesetzen des Deutschen Reiches.* 4th edn. Vol. 1. Berlin: Vahlen, 1892.

Oncken, Wilhelm, and W. Röse. *Unser Heldenkaiser. Festschrift zum hundertjährigen Geburtstage Kaiser Wilhelms des Großen.* Berlin: Schall & Grund, 1898.

Ortloff, Hermann Friedrich. *Das Zellengefängniß zu Moabit in Berlin.* Gotha: Perthes, 1861.

Öttingen, Alexander von. *Die Moralstatistik. Inductiver Nachweis der Gesetzmässigkeit sittlicher Lebensbewegung im Organismus d. Menschheit.* Erlangen: Deichert, 1868.

———. "Über Die Methodische Erhebung und Beurteilung Kriminalstatistischer Daten." *ZStW* 1 (1881): 414–38.

Otto, Gustav [pseudonym: Σ.Ω.]. *Die Verbrecherwelt von Berlin.* Berlin: J. Guttentag, 1886.

Paulsen, Friedrich. *System der Ethik mit einem Umriss der Staats- und Gesellschaftslehre.* Vol. 2 Berlin: Hertz, 1900.

Pranckh, Hans von. *Der Prozeß gegen den Grafen Anton Arco-Valley, der den Bayer. Ministerpräsidenten Kurt Eisner erschossen hat.* Munich: J. F. Lehmann, 1920.

Radbruch, Gustav. "Das System der Freiheitsstrafen im Vorentwurf." *MKS* 7, no. 4 (1910): 207–12.

———. "Der Überzeugungsverbrecher." *Zeitschrift für Die Gesamte Strafrechtswissenschaft* 44 (1924): 34–38.

———. "Der Ursprung des Strafrechts aus dem Stande der Unfreien." In *Elegantiae Juris Criminalis. Vierzehn Studien zur Geschichte des Strafrechts*, ed. Gustav Radbruch, 1–11. Basel: Verlag für Recht und Gesellschaft, 1950.

———. *Einführung in die Rechtswissenschaft.* Leipzig: Quelle & Meyer, 1910.

Rannacher, Helmut. *Der Ehrenschutz in der Geschichte des deutschen Strafrechts von der Carolina bis zum Reichsstrafgesetzbuch von 1871 (Mit Berücksichtigung der Ehrenstrafen und des Zweikampfes).* Breslau Neukirch: Alfred Kurtze, 1938.

Rethwisch, Ernst. *Ueber den Werth Der Ehrenstrafen. Juristischer Essay.* Berlin: Puttkammer & Mühlbrecht, 1876.

Rosenberg, Alfred. *Der Mythus des 20. Jahrhunderts. Eine Wertung der seelisch-geistigen Gestaltenkämpfe unserer Zeit.* 4th edn. Munich: Hoheneichen-Verlag, 1934.

———. *Wesen, Grundsätze und Ziele der Nationalsozialistischen Deutschen Arbeiterpartei. Das Programm der Bewegung.* Munich: Boepple, 1930.

Romen, Anton. *Meineid und Socialdemokratie. Ein Beitrag zu einer brennenden Tagesfrage; auf Grund authentischer Quellen.* Berlin: Wilhelmi, 1892.

Roßhirt, Konrad Franz. *Geschichte und System des deutschen Strafrechts.* Vol. 3. Stuttgart: Schweizerbart, 1839.

Sauer, Wilhelm. "Aufgaben und Gefahren Der Strafrechtsreform." *Deutsches Recht. Zentralorgan des National-Sozialistischen Rechtswahrerbundes* 3 (1933): 176–215.

Schmidt, Eberhard. "Die Gestaltung der Ehrenstrafen im künftigen Strafrecht." *ZStW* 45 (1925): 10–43.

———. "Ernst Delaquis zum Gedächtnis." *ZStW* 64, no. 1 (1952): 434–35.

Schmölder, Robert. "Die Alte und Die Neue Kriminalistenschule und der Strafvollzug." *PJ* 115, no. 9 (1904): 489–96.

———. "Die Wehrpflicht Der Verbrecher." *DJZ* 10, no. 21 (1905): 982–85.

Schwandner. "Heeresdienst und Strafvollzug Mit Besonderer Berücksichtigung Der Zuchthausstrafe." *BfG* 49 (1915): 198–200.

Seuffert, Hermann. *Die Bewegung im Strafrechte während der letzten dreißig Jahre*. Dresden: Zahn & Jaensch, 1901.

Seutter, Leonore. *Die Gefängnisarbeit in Deutschland mit besonderer Berücksichtigung der Frauen-Gefängnisse*. Tübingen: Laupp, 1912.

Seyfarth, Heinrich. "12. Jahresbericht des Deutschen Hilfsvereins für Entlassene Gefangene in Hamburg für Das Jahr 1915." *BfG* 50 (1916): 92–94.

———. "Aus den Akten des Deutschen Hilfsvereins für Entlassene Gefangene Hamburg." *BfG* 50 (1916): 71–74.

———. "Strafvollzug und Kriegsdienst." *BfG* 49 (1915): 185–202.

Siegert, Emil. *Die im Vollbürgerthum enthaltenen bürgerlichen Ehrenrechte nach deutschem Reichsrecht*. Greifswald: F. W. Kunike, 1895.

Simmel, Georg. *Soziologie. Untersuchungen über die Formen der Vergesellschaftung*. Leipzig: Duncker & Humblot, 1908.

Simon, Hermann. *Ein Beitrag zur Kenntniss der Militärpsychosen*. Saargemünd: Völcker, 1898.

Sohnrey, Heinrich. *Der Meineid im deutschen Volksbewußtsein*. Leipzig: Werther, 1894.

Sontag, Karl Richard. *Die Festungshaft*. Leipzig, 1872.

Starke, Wilhelm Gustav Karl. *Verbrechen und Verbrecher in Preußen 1854–1878. Eine kulturgeschichtliche Studie*. Berlin: Enslin, 1884.

Steinbach, Emil. *Die Moral als Schranke des Rechtserwerbs und der Rechtsausübung*. Vienna: Manz, 1898.

Stier, Ewald. "Die Wehrpflicht der Verbrecher." *Monatsschrift für Kriminalpsychologie und Strafrechtsreform* 9 (1913): 272–77.

———. *Fahnenflucht und unerlaubte Entfernung. Eine psychologische, psychiatrische und militärrechtliche Studie*. Halle: Marhold, 1905.

Stier-Somlo, Fritz. *Die verfassung des Deutschen Reichs vom 11. August 1919: ein systematischer Überblick*. 3rd edn. Bonn: A. Marcus & E. Weber, 1925.

Stillich, Oscar. *Die Lage der weiblichen Dienstboten in Berlin*. Berlin: Akademie Verlag, 1902.

Stooss, Carl. *Die Grundzüge des schweizerischen Strafrechts*. Basel: Georg, 1892.

Tönnies, Ferdinand. "Das Reichstagswahlrecht für Preussen." *Das freie Wort* 7 (1907): 492–97.

Max Treu, *Der Bankrott des modernen Strafvollzuges und seine Reform*. Stuttgart: R. Lutz, 1904.

———. "Vorbestraft." *Der Türmer* 6, no. 9 (1904): 290–97.

Verein zur Abwehr des Antisemitismus (Berlin). *Die Wirtschaftliche Lage, soziale Gliederung und die Kriminalstatistik der Juden*. Berlin: Das Verein, 1912.

Wach, Adolf. *Die kriminalistischen Schulen und die Strafrechtsreform*. Leipzig: Duncker & Humblot, 1902.

Wassermann, Rudolf. *Beruf, Konfession und Verbrechen. Eine Studie über die Kriminalität der Juden in Vergangenheit und Gegenwart*. Munich: Reinhardt, 1906.

Welcker, Carl Theodor, and Carl von Rotteck. *Das Staats-Lexicon. Encyklopädie der sämmtlichen Staatswissenschaften für alle Stände in Verbindung mit vielen der angesehensten Publicisten Deutschlands*. 3rd edn. Vol. 12. Leipzig: Brockhaus, 1865.

Wick, Adolf von. *Über Ehrenstrafen und Ehrenfolgen der Verbrechen und Strafen. Eine Abhandlung aus dem Gebiete der Strafgesetzgebung*. Rostock: Stiller, 1845.

———. "Zur Gesetzgebung über die Ehrenfolgen der Verbrechen." *Archiv des Criminalrechts* 32, no. 1 (1851): 1–39.

Wick, Friedrich von. *Über Fürsorge für entlassene Sträflinge, insbesondere über Organisirung einer kirchlichen Fürsorge für dieselben*. Rostock: Hirsch, 1856.

Wrisberg, Ernst von. *Heer und Heimat 1914–1918*. Leipzig: Koehler, 1921.

Wulffen, Erich. *Psychologie des Verbrechers*. Vol. 2. Berlin: Langenscheidt, 1908.

Zachariae, Karl Salomo. *Vierzig Bücher vom Staate*. Vol. 6. Heidelberg: Winter, 1842.

Zeller, Philipp. *Systematisches Lehrbuch der Polizeiwissenschaft nach preußischen Gesetzen, Edicten, Verordnungen und Ministerial-Rescripten*. Vol. 1. Quedlinburg: Basse, 1828.

Ziegler, Theobald. *Das Gefühl. Eine psychologische Untersuchung*. 5th edn. Berlin: Göschen, 1912.

———. *Der Krieg als Erzieher*. Frankfurt a.M: Knauer, 1914.

Secondary Literature

Anderson, Margaret Lavinia. *Practicing Democracy. Elections and Political Culture in Imperial Germany*. Princeton, NJ: Princeton University Press, 2000.

Aschmann, Birgit. "Ehre—Das verletzte Gefühl als Grund für den Krieg." In *Gefühl und Kalkül—Der Einfluss von Emotionen auf die Politik des 19. und 20. Jahrhunderts*, 151–74. Stuttgart: Steiner, 2005.

———. *Preußens Ruhm und Deutschlands Ehre. zum nationalen Ehrdiskurs im Vorfeld der preußisch-französischen Kriege des 19. Jahrhunderts*. Munich: Oldenbourg, 2013.

Badinter, Robert. *La Prison Républicaine (1871–1914)*. Paris: Fayard, 1992.

Balibar, Étienne. *Equaliberty*, trans. James Ingram. Durham, NC: Duke University Press, 2014.

Barclay, David E., and Eric D. Weitz. *Between Reform and Revolution: German Socialism and Communism from 1840 to 1990*. New York: Berghahn Books, 2002.

Berger, Peter. "On the Obsolescence of the Concept of Honour." *Archives Européennes de Sociologie* 11 (1970): 339–47.

Blackbourn, David. *The Long Nineteenth Century. A History of Germany, 1780–1918*. Oxford: Oxford University Press 1998.

Blasius, Dirk. *Geschichte der politischen Kriminalität in Deutschland, 1800–1980*. Frankfurt a.M.: Suhrkamp, 1983.

Born, Karl Erich, Peter Rassow, and Florian Tennstedt. *Quellensammlung zur Geschichte der deutschen Sozialpolitik: 1867 bis 1914*. Vol. 6. Stuttgart: Fischer, 2002.

Bourdieu, Pierre. *Outline of a Theory of Practice*, trans. Richard Nice. Cambridge: Cambridge University Press, 1977.

Braithwaite, John. *Crime, Shame, and Reintegration*. Cambridge: Cambridge University Press, 1989.

Brakensiek, Stefan. *Fürstendiener, Staatsbeamte, Bürger. Amtsführung und Lebenswelt der Ortsbeamten in niederhessischen Kleinstädten (1750–1830)*. Göttingen: Vandenhoeck & Ruprecht, 1999.
Bretschneider, Falk. *Gefangene Gesellschaft. Eine Geschichte der Einsperrung in Sachsen im 18. und 19. Jahrhundert*. Konstanz: Universitätsverlag Konstanz, 2008.
Brubaker, Rogers. *Citizenship and Nationhood in France and Germany*. Cambridge, MA: Harvard University Press, 1992.
Canning, Kathleen. "Das Geschlecht der Revolution. Stimmrecht und Staatsbürgertum 1918/19." In *Die vergessene Revolution von 1918/19*, ed. Alexander Gallus, 84–116. Göttingen: Vandenhoeck & Ruprecht, 2010.
Christoph, Jürgen. *Die politischen Reichsamnestien, 1918–1933*. Frankfurt a.M.: Lang, 1988.
Clark, Christopher. *Iron Kingdom: The Rise and Downfall of Prussia, 1600–1947*. London: Penguin Books, 2007.
Collin, Peter. "Ehrengerichtliche Rechtsprechung im Kaiserreich und der Weimarer Republik. Multinormativität in einer Mononormativen Rechtsordnung?" *Rechtsgeschichte—Legal History* 25 (2017): 138–50.
Comaroff, Jean, and John L. Comaroff. *The Truth about Crime. Sovereignty, Knowledge, Social Order*. Chicago: The University of Chicago Press, 2016.
Craig, Gordon A. *The Politics of the Prussian Army, 1640–1945*. Oxford: Clarendon Press, 1955.
Dickinson, Edward Ross. *Sex, Freedom, and Power in Imperial Germany, 1880–1914*. New York: Cambridge University Press, 2014.
Dinges, Martin. "Die Ehre als Thema der historischen Anthropologie. Bemerkungen zur Wissenschaftsgeschichte und zur Konzeptualisierung." In *Verletzte Ehre. Ehrkonflikte in Gesellschaften des Mittelalters und der Frühen Neuzeit*, ed. Klaus Schreiner and Gerd Schwerhoff, 29–62. Cologne: Böhlau: 1995.
Donson, Andrew. *Youth in the Fatherless Land. War Pedagogy, Nationalism, and Authority in Germany, 1914–1918*. Cambridge, MA: Harvard University Press, 2010.
Drentje, Jan. *Thorbecke. Een filosoof in de politiek*. Amsterdam: Boom, 2004.
Dubber, Markus D. "Theories of Crime and Punishment in German Criminal Law." *American Journal of Comparative Law* 53 (2006): 679–707.
Durkheim, Émile. *The Division of Labour in Society*, trans. W. D. Halls. London: Macmillan, 1984.
Dülmen, Richard van. *Der Ehrlose Mensch. Unehrlichkeit und soziale Ausgrenzung in der Frühen Neuzeit*. Cologne: Böhlau, 1999.
———. *Theater des Schreckens. Gerichtspraxis und Strafrituale in der frühen Neuzeit*. Munich: C. H. Beck, 1987.
Eghigian, Greg. *Making Security Social Disability, Insurance, and the Birth of the Social Entitlement State in Germany*. Ann Arbor: University of Michigan Press, 2000.
———. "Pain, Entitlement, and Social Citizenship in Modern Germany." In *Pain and Prosperity: Reconsidering Twentieth-Century German History*, ed. Paul Betts and Greg Eghigian, 16–34. Stanford, CA: Stanford University Press, 2003.
Esser, Albert. *Die Ehrenstrafe*. Stuttgart: Kohlhammer, 1956.
Etzemüller, Thomas. *Die Ordnung der Moderne Social Engineering im 20. Jahrhundert*. Bielefeld: Transcript, 2015.

Evans, Richard J. *Rituals of Retribution. Capital Punishment in Germany 1600–1987*. Oxford: Oxford University Press, 1996.

Fahrmeir, Andreas. *Citizens and Aliens: Foreigners and the Law in Britain and the German States, 1789–1870*. New York: Berghahn Books, 2000.

———. *Citizenship. The Rise and Fall of a Modern Concept*. New Haven, CT: Yale University Press, 2007.

———. "Nineteenth Century German Citizenships. A Reconsideration." *The Historical Journal* 40, no. 33 (1997): 721–52.

Feinberg, Joel. "The Expressive Function of Punishment." In *Doing and Deserving. Essays in the Theory of Responsibility*, ed. idem, 95–118. Princeton, NJ: Princeton University Press, 1970.

Finzsch, Norbert, and Robert Jütte (eds.). *Institutions of Confinement: Hospitals, Asylums, and Prisons in Western Europe and North America, 1500–1950*. Cambridge: Cambridge University Press, 2003.

Fitzpatrick, Matthew P. *Purging the Empire. Mass Expulsions in Germany, 1871–1914*. Oxford: Oxford University Press, 2015.

Fleiter, Andreas. "Strafen auf dem weg zum Sozialismus. Sozialistische Standpunkte zu Kriminalität und Strafe vor dem Ersten Weltkrieg." *Mitteilungsblatt des Instituts für Soziale Bewegungen* 26 (2001): 105–38.

Föllmer, Moritz. *Die "Krise" der Weimarer Republik: zur Kritik eines Deutungsmusters*. Frankfurt a.M.: Campus, 2005.

Foucault, Michel. *On the Punitive Society. Lectures at the Collège de France 1972–1973*, ed. Bernard E. Harcourt. London, 2015.

———. *Surveiller et punir. Naissance de la prison*. Paris: Gallimard, 1975.

Franke, Peter. "Stadt und Bürgerrechtsentwicklungen im 19. Jahrhundert. Das Beispiel Preußen." In *Agrarische Verfassung und politische Struktur. Studien zur Gesellschaftsgeschichte Preußens 1700–1918*, ed. Wolfgang Neugebauer and Ralf Pröve, 123–43. Berlin: Spitz, 1998.

Frevert, Ute. *A Nation in Barracks. Conscription, Military Service and Civil Society in Modern Germany*. Oxford: Berg, 2004.

———. "Das jakobinische Modell. Allgemeine Wehrpflicht und Nationsbildung in Preußen-Deutschland." In *Militär und Gesellschaft im 19. und 20. Jahrhundert*, 17–47. Stuttgart: Klett-Cotta, 1997.

———. "Das Militär als 'Schule der Männlichkeit.' Erwartungen, Angebote, Erfahrungen im 19. Jahrhundert." In *Militär und Gesellschaft im 19. und 20. Jahrhundert*, ed. Ute Frevert, 145–73. Stuttgart: Klett-Cotta, 1997.

———. "Die Ehre der Bürger im Spiegel ihrer Duelle." *Historische Zeitschrift* 249, no. 1 (1989): 545–82.

———. *Die Politik der Demütigung: Schauplätze von Macht und Ohnmacht*. Frankfurt a.M.: S. Fischer, 2017.

———. "Ehre—Männlich/Weiblich. Zu einem Identitätsbegriff des 19. Jahrhunderts." *Tel Aviver Jahrbuch für deutsche Geschichte* 21 (1992): 21–68.

———. *Emotions in History. Lost and Found*. The Natalie Zemon Davis Annual Lecture Series. Budapest: Central European University Press, 2011.

———. "Empathy in the Theater of Horror, or Civilizing the Human Heart." In *Empathy and Its Limits*, ed. Aleida Assmann and Ines Detmers, 79–99. Basingstoke: Palgrave Macmillan, 2015.

———. *Men of Honour. A Social and Cultural History of the Duel*. Cambridge: Polity Press, 1995.

———. "Vertrauen—eine historische Spurensuche." In *Vertrauen. Historische Annäherungen*, ed. idem, 7–66. Göttingen: Vandenhoeck & Ruprecht, 2003.

———. *Vertrauensfragen. Eine Obsession der Moderne*. Munich: Beck, 2013.

Fritzsche, Peter. "Landscape of Danger, Landscape of Design. Crisis and Modernism in Weimar Germany." In *Dancing on the Volcano: Essays on the Culture of the Weimar Republic*, ed. Thomas W. Kniesche and Stephen Brockmann, 24–46. Columbia, SC: Camden House, 1994.

Fröhling, Mareike. *Der moderne Pranger. Von den Ehrenstrafen des Mittelalters bis zur Prangerwirkung der medialen Berichterstattung im heutigen Strafverfahren*. Marburg: Tectum Verlag, 2014.

Frommel, Monika. *Präventionsmodelle in der deutschen Strafzweck-Diskussion*. Berlin: Duncker & Humblot, 1987.

Funk, Albrecht. *Polizei und Rechtsstaat. Die Entwicklung des staatlichen Gewaltmonopols in Preussen 1848–1918*. Frankfurt a.M.: Campus, 1986.

Galassi, Silviana. *Kriminologie im Deutschen Kaiserreich. Geschichte einer gebrochenen Verwissenschaftlichung*. Stuttgart: Steiner, 2004.

Geyer, Martin H. *Verkehrte Welt. Revolution, Inflation und Moderne. München 1914–1924*. Göttingen: Vandenhoeck & Ruprecht, 1998.

Goffman, Erving. *Stigma. Notes on the Management of Spoiled Identity*. Englewood Cliffs, NJ: Prentice-Hall, 1965.

Goldberg, Ann. *Honor, Politics, and the Law in Imperial Germany, 1871–1914*. Cambridge: Cambridge University Press, 2010.

Goltsche, Friederike. *Der Entwurf eines Allgemeinen Deutschen Strafgesetzbuches von 1922 (Entwurf Radbruch)*. Berlin: De Gruyter, 2010.

Gosewinkel, Dieter. *Einbürgern und Ausschließen: die Nationalisierung der Staatsangehörigkeit vom Deutschen Bund bis zur Bundesrepublik Deutschland*. Göttingen: Vandenhoeck & Ruprecht, 2001.

———. *Schutz und Freiheit? Staatsbürgerschaft in Europa im 20. und 21. Jahrhundert*. Berlin: Suhrkamp, 2016.

———. "Staatsbürgerschaft und Staatsangehörigkeit." *Geschichte und Gesellschaft* 21, no. 4 (1995): 533–56.

Greenhouse, Carol J. "Solidarity and Objectivity. Re-Reading Durkheim." In *Crime's Power. Anthropologists and the Ethnography of Crime*, ed. Philip C. Parnell and Stephanie C. Kane, 269–91. New York: Palgrave Macmillan, 2003.

Groot, Timon de. "The Criminal Registry in the German Empire. The Cult of Previous Convictions and the Right to Be Forgotten." *German History* (forthcoming).

———. "Politieke misdadigers of eerloze criminelen?" *Tijdschrift voor geschiedenis* 132, no. 1 (2019): 21–47.

Gruchmann, Lothar. "'Blutschutzgesetz' und Justiz." *Vierteljahrshefte für Zeitgeschichte* 31 (1983): 418–42.

Grunwald, Henning. *Courtroom to Revolutionary Stage: Performance and Ideology in Weimar Political Trials*. Oxford: Oxford University Press, 2012.

Guinnane, Timothy W., and Jochen Streb. "Moral Hazard in a Mutual Health Insurance System: German Knappschaften, 1867–1914." *The Journal of Economic History* 71, no. 1 (2011): 70–104.

Gunther-Canada, Wendy. "The Politics of Sense and Sensibility. Mary Wollstonecraft and Catharine Macaulay Graham on Edmund Burke's 'Reflections on the Revolution in

France.'" In *Women Writers and the Early Modern British Political Tradition*, ed. Hilda L. Smith, 126–47. Cambridge: Cambridge University Press, 1998.

Habermas, Rebekka. *Diebe vor Gericht. Die Entstehung der modernen Rechtsordnung im 19. Jahrhundert*. Frankfurt a.M.: Campus, 2008.

———. "Von Anselm von Feuerbach Zu Jack the Ripper." *Rechtsgeschichte—Legal History* 3 (2003): 128–63.

Hall, Alex. "By Other Means. The Legal Struggle against the SPD in Wilhelmine Germany 1890–1900." *The Historical Journal* 17, no. 2 (2009): 365–86.

Hannover, Heinrich, Elisabeth Hannover-Drück, and Karl Dietrich Bracher. *Politische Justiz 1918–1933*. Frankfurt a.M.: Fischer, 1966.

Harcourt, Bernard E. *The Illusion of Free Markets. Punishment and the Myth of Natural Order*. Cambridge, MA: Harvard University Press, 2012.

Härter, Karl. "Security and 'Gute Policey' in Early Modern Europe. Concepts, Laws, and Instruments." *Historical Social Research* 35, no. 4 (2010): 41–65.

Hartmann, Andrea. *Majestätsbeleidigung und Verunglimpfung des Staatsoberhauptes*. Berlin: Berliner Wissenschafts-Verlag, 2006.

Hartwich, Esther. *Der Deutsche Juristentag von seiner Gründung 1860 bis zu den Reichsjustizgesetzen 1877 im Kontext von Nationsbildung und Rechtsvereinheitlichung*. Berlin: Berliner Wissenschafts-Verlag, 2008.

Hattenhauer, Hans. "Justizkarriere durch die Provinzen. Das Beispiel Otto Mittelstädt." In *Preußen in der Provinz*, ed. Peter Nitsche, 35–62. Frankfurt a.M.: Peter Lang, 1991.

Haupt, Heinz-Gerhard. "Gewalt als Praxis und Herrschaftsmittel. Das Deutsche Kaiserreich und die Dritte Republik in Frankreich im Vergleich." In *Das Deutsche Kaiserreich in der Kontroverse*, ed. Sven-Oliver Müller and Cornelius Torp, 154–64. Göttingen: Vandenhoeck & Ruprecht, 2009.

Hay, Douglas, et al. *Albion's Fatal Tree. Crime and Society and Eighteenth-Century England*. London: Allen Lane, 1975.

Henze, Martina. *Strafvollzugsreformen im 19. Jahrhundert. Gefängniskundlicher Diskurs und staatliche Praxis in Bayern und Hessen-Darmstadt*. Darmstadt: Hessischen historischen Kommission, 2003.

Hett, Benjamin Carter. *Death in the Tiergarten. Murder and Criminal Justice in the Kaiser's Berlin*. Cambridge, MA: Harvard University Press, 2004.

Hettling, Manfred. "Die persönliche Selbständigkeit. Der archimedische Punkt bürgerlicher Lebensführung." In *Der bürgerliche Wertehimmel. Innenansichten des 19. Jahrhunderts*, ed. Manfred Hettling and Stefan-Ludwig Hoffmann, 57–78. Göttingen: Vandenhoeck & Ruprecht, 2000.

Hitzer, Bettina. "Freizügigkeit als Reformergebnis und die Entwicklung von Arbeitsmärkten." In *Handbuch Staat und Migration in Deutschland Seit dem 17. Jahrhundert*, ed. Jochen Oltmer, 245–90. Berlin: De Gruyter, 2016.

Holloway, Pippa. *Living in Infamy: Felon Disfranchisement and the History of American Citizenship*. Oxford: Oxford University Press, 2014.

Holtmann, Antonius. "Auswanderungs- und Übersiedelungspolitik im Königreich Hannover 1832–1866." In *Schöne neue Welt. Rheinländer erobern Amerika*, ed. Kornelia Panek and Dieter Pesch, vol. 2, 185–214. Wiehl: Martina Galunder, 2001.

Hommen, Tanja. *Sittlichkeitsverbrechen. Sexuelle Gewalt im Kaiserreich*. Frankfurt a.M.: Campus, 1999.

Hoser, Paul. "Hitler und die Katholische Kirche." *Vierteljahrshefte für Zeitgeschichte* 42 (1994): 473–92.
Ingrao, Charles W. *The Habsburg Monarchy, 1618–1815*. Cambridge: Cambridge University Press, 2000.
Jasper, Gotthard. *Der Schutz der Republik. Studien zur staatlichen Sicherung der Demokratie in der Weimarer Republik, 1922–1930*. Tübingen: Mohr Siebeck, 1963.
———. "Justiz und Politik in Der Weimarer Republik." *Vierteljahrshefte für Zeitgeschichte* 30, no. 2 (1982): 167–205.
Jessen, Ralph. "Gewaltkriminalität im Ruhrgebiet zwischen bürgerlicher Panik und proletarischer Subkultur (1870–1900)." In *Arbeitskultur im Ruhrgebiet zwischen Kommerz und Kontrolle (1850–1974)*, ed. D. Kift, 226–55. Paderborn: Schöningh, 1992.
Joas, Hans. *The Genesis of Values*. Chicago: University of Chicago Press, 2000.
Johnson, Eric A. *Urbanization and Crime. Germany, 1871–1914*. Cambridge: Cambridge University Press, 1995.
Jones, Mark, and Karl Heinz Siber. *Am Anfang war Gewalt. Die deutsche Revolution 1918/19 und der Beginn der Weimarer Republik*. Bonn: Bundeszentrale für politische Bildung, 2017.
Kent, George Otto. *Arnim and Bismarck*. Oxford: Clarendon Press, 1968.
Kesper-Biermann, Sylvia. "Die Internationale Kriminalistische Vereinigung. zum Verhältnis von Wissenschaftsbeziehungen und Politik im Strafrecht 1889–1932." In *Die Internationalisierung von Strafrechtswissenschaft und Kriminalpolitik (1870–1930). Deutschland im Vergleich*, ed. Sylvia Kesper-Biermann and Petra Overath, 85–107. Berlin: Berliner Wissenschafts-Verlag, 2007.
———. *Einheit und Recht. Strafgesetzgebung und Kriminalrechtsexperten in Deutschland vom Beginn des 19. Jahrhunderts bis zum Reichsstrafgesetzbuch von 1871*. Frankfurt a.M.: Klostermann, 2009.
———. "Gerechtigkeit, Politik und Güte. Gnade im Deutschland des 19. Jahrhunderts." *Jahrbuch Der Juristischen Zeitgeschichte* 13, no. 1 (2012): 21–47.
———. "'Nothwendige Gleichheit der Strafen bey aller Verschiedenheit der Stände im Staat'? (Un)Gleichheit im Kriminalrecht der ersten Hälfte des 19. Jahrhunderts." *Geschichte und Gesellschaft* 35, no. 4 (2009): 603–28.
———. "Wissenschaftlicher Ideenaustausch und 'kriminalpolitische Propaganda'. Die Internationale Kriminalistische Vereinigung (1889–1937) und der Strafvollzug." In *Verbrecher im Visier der Experten. Kriminalpolitik zwischen Wissenschaft und Praxis im 19. und Frühen 20. Jahrhundert*, ed. Désirée Schauz and Sabine Freitag, 79–97. Stuttgart: Steiner, 2007.
———, ed. *Ehre und Recht. Ehrkonzepte, Ehrverletzungen und Ehrverteidigungen vom späten Mittelalter bis zur Moderne*. Magdeburg: Meine, 2011.
Kirchheimer, Otto. *Political Justice. The Use of Legal Procedure for Political Ends*. Princeton, NJ: Princeton University Press, 1961.
Kirchhoff, Hans Georg. *Die staatliche Sozialpolitik im Ruhrbergbau 1871–1914*. Cologne: Westdeutscher Verlag, 1958.
Kitchen, Martin. *The Silent Dictatorship: The Politics of the German High Command under Hindenburg and Ludendorff, 1916–1918*. New York: Holmes & Meier Publishers, 1976.
Klippel, Diethelm. "Das Privileg im deutschen Naturrecht des 18. und 19. Jahrhunderts." In *Das Privileg im europäischen Vergleich*, ed. Barbara Dölemeyer and Heinz Mohnhaupt, vol. 2, 329–45. Frankfurt a.M.: Klostermann, 1997.

Klippel, Diethelm, Martina Henze, and Sylvia Kesper-Biermann. "Ideen und Recht. Die Umsetzung Strafrechtlicher Ordnungsvorstellungen im Deutschland des 19. Jahrhunderts." In *Ideen als gesellschaftliche Gestaltungskraft im Europa der Neuzeit. Beiträge für eine erneuerte Geistesgeschichte*, ed. Lutz Raphael and Heinz-Elmar Tenorth, 372–94. Munich: Oldenbourg, 2006.

Kocka, Jürgen. *Arbeitsverhältnisse und Arbeiterexistenzen. Grundlagen der Klassenbildung im 19. Jahrhundert*. Bonn: Dietz, 1990.

Koselleck, Reinhart. *Preußen zwischen Reform und Revolution. Allgemeines Landrecht, Verwaltung und soziale Bewegung von 1791 bis 1848*. Stuttgart: Klett, 1967.

Kubiciel, Michael. "Einheitliches europäisches Strafrecht und vergleichende Darstellung seiner Grundlagen." *Juristenzeitung* 70, no. 2 (2015): 64–70.

Langewiesche, Dieter. *Die Monarchie im Jahrhundert Europas. Selbstbehauptung durch Wandel im 19. Jahrhundert*. Heidelberg: Winter, 2013.

———. "Entwicklungsbedingungen im Kaiserreich." In *Geschichte des Deutschen Buchhandels im 19. und 20. Jahrhundert*, ed. Georg Jäger, vol. 1, 42–86. Berlin: De Gruyter, 2001.

Laschitza, Annelies. *Die Liebknechts. Karl und Sophie—Politik und Familie*. Berlin: Aufbau-Verlag, 2009.

Ledford, Kenneth F. "Formalizing the Rule of Law in Prussia. The Supreme Administrative Law Court, 1876–1914." *Central European History* 37, no. 2 (2004): 203–24.

Leps, Marie-Christine. *Apprehending the Criminal. The Production of Deviance in Nineteenth-Century Discourse*. Durham, NC: Duke University Press, 1992.

Linden, Marcel van der. "San Precario: A New Inspiration for Labor Historians." *Labor. Studies in Working-Class History of the Americas* 10, no. 1 (2014): 9–21.

Linnemann, Gerd. *Klassenjustiz und Weltfremdheit, deutsche Justizkritik 1890–1914*. Kiel, 1989.

Linse, Ulrich. *Organisierter Anarchismus im deutschen Kaiserreich von 1871*. Berlin: Duncker & Humblot, 1969.

López-Guerra, Claudio. *Democracy and Disenfranchisement. The Morality of Electoral Exclusions*. Oxford: Oxford University Press, 2014.

Maehle, Andreas-Holger. *Doctors, Honour and the Law. Medical Ethics in Imperial Germany*. Basingstoke: Palgrave Macmillan, 2009.

Majer, Diemut. *"Fremdvölkische" im Dritten Reich: Ein Beitrag zur Nationalsozialistischen Rechtsetzung und Rechtspraxis in Verwaltung und Justiz unter besonderer Berücksichtigung der eingegliederten Ostgebiete und des Generalgouvernements*. Boppard am Rhein: Boldt, 1981.

Manke, Matthias. "Sträflingsmigration aus Mecklenburg-Schwerin vom Ende des 18. bis zur Mitte des 19. Jahrhunderts." *Jahrbuch für Europäische Überseegeschichte* 9 (2009): 67–103.

Manza, Jeff, and Christopher Uggen. *Locked out. Felon Disenfranchisement and American Democracy*. Oxford: Oxford University Press, 2006.

Marshall, T. H. "Citizenship and Social Class." In *Sociology at the Crossroads and Other Essays*, ed. T. H. Marshall, 67–127. London: Heinemann, 1963.

McAleer, Kevin. *Dueling. The Cult of Honor in Fin-de-Siècle Germany*. Princeton, NJ: Princeton University Press, 1994.

Meyer-Reil, Arndt. *Strafaussetzung zur Bewährung. Reformdiskussion und Gesetzgebung seit dem Ausgang des 19. Jahrhunderts*. Münster: Lit, 2006.

Mitchell, Allan. *Revolution in Bavaria, 1918–1919: The Eisner Regime and the Soviet Republic*. Princeton, NJ: Princeton University Press, 1965.

Mohr, Irina, ed. *Gustav Radbruch als Reichsjustizminister (1921–1923)*. Berlin: Mohr, 2004.
Möller, Horst. *Die Weimarer Republik. Demokratie in der Krise*. Munich: Piper, 2018.
Moltmann, Günter. "Die Transportation von Sträflingen im Rahmen der deutschen Amerikaauswanderung des 19. Jahrhunderts." In *Deutsche Amerikaauswanderung im 19. Jahrhundert. Sozialgeschichtliche Beiträge*, ed. Günter Moltmann, 147–96. Stuttgart: Metzler, 1976.
Mommsen, Wolfgang J. *Max Weber und die deutsche Politik, 1890–1920*. Tübingen: Mohr Siebeck, 2004.
Moore, Kathleen D. *Pardons. Justice, Mercy, and the Public Interest*. New York: Oxford University Press, 1997.
Mosse, George L. *Fallen Soldiers. Reshaping the Memory of the World Wars*. New York: Oxford University Press, 1990.
Müller, Christian. *Verbrechensbekämpfung im Anstaltsstaat: Psychiatrie, Kriminologie und Strafrechtsreform in Deutschland 1871–1933*. Göttingen: Vandenhoeck & Ruprecht, 2004.
Müller, Kai. *Der Hüter des Rechts. Die Stellung des Reichsgerichts im deutschen Kaiserreich 1879–1918*. Baden-Baden: Nomos-Verlag, 1997.
Müller, Sven Oliver, and Cornelius Torp, eds. *Das deutsche Kaiserreich in der Kontroverse*. Göttingen: Vandenhoeck & Ruprecht, 2009.
Nathans, Eli. *The Politics of Citizenship in Germany. Ethnicity, Utility and Nationalism*. Oxford: Berg, 2004.
Nipperdey, Thomas. *Deutsche Geschichte 1800–1866. Bürgerwelt und starker Staat*. Munich: Beck, 1983.
———. *Deutsche Geschichte 1866–1918. Machtstaat vor der Demokratie*. Munich: Beck, 1992.
Noriel, Gérard. "Der Staatsbürger." In *Der Mensch des 19. Jahrhunderts*, ed. Heinz-Gerhard Haupt and Ute Frevert, 201–27. Frankfurt a.M.: Campus, 1999.
Novak, Andrew. *Comparative Executive Clemency. The Constitutional Pardon Power and the Prerogative of Mercy in Global Perspective*. London: Routledge, 2016.
Nussbaum, Martha C. *Hiding from Humanity. Disgust, Shame and the Law*. Princeton, NJ: Princeton University Press, 2004.
———. *Upheavals of Thought. The Intelligence of Emotions*. Cambridge: Cambridge University Press, 2001.
Nutz, Thomas. *Strafanstalt als Besserungsmaschine. Reformdiskurs und Gefängniswissenschaft 1775–1848*. Munich: Oldenbourg, 2001.
———. "Strafrechtsphilosophie und Gefängniskunde. Strategien Diskursiver Legitimierung in Der Ersten Hälfte des 19. Jahrhunderts." *Zeitschrift für Neuere Rechtsgeschichte* 22 (2000): 95–110.
Offe, Claus. *Contradictions of the Welfare State*, trans. John Keane. London: Hutchinson, 1984.
Ortmann, Alexandra. "Jenseits von Klassenjustiz: Ein Blick in die ländliche Gesellschaft des deutschen Kaiserreichs." *Geschichte und Gesellschaft* 35, no. 4 (2009): 629–58.
———. *Machtvolle Verhandlungen. zur Kulturgeschichte der deutschen Strafjustiz 1879–1924*. Göttingen: Vandenhoeck & Ruprecht, 2014.
Osterhammel, Jürgen. *Die Verwandlung der Welt. Eine Geschichte des 19. Jahrhunderts*. Munich: Beck, 2009.
Peukert, Detlev. *Grenzen der Sozialdisziplinierung. Aufstieg und Krise der deutschen Jugendfürsorge von 1878 bis 1932*. Cologne: Bund-Verlag, 1986.
Piquero, Alex R., David P. Farrington, and Alfred Blumstein. "The Criminal Career Paradigm." *Crime and Justice* 30 (2003): 359–506.

Pflanze, Otto. *Bismarck and the Development of Germany*. Vol. 2. Princeton, NJ: Princeton University Press, 1990.

Planert, Ute. "Kulturkritik und Geschlechterverhältnis. zur Krise der Geschlechterordnung zwischen Jahrhundertwende und Drittem Reich." In *Ordnungen in der Krise. Zur politischen Kulturgeschichte der Zwischenkriegszeit*, ed. Wolfgang Hardtwig, 191–214. Munich: Oldenbourg, 2007.

Przyrembel, Alexandra. *"Rassenschande". Reinheitsmythos und Vernichtungslegitimation im Nationalsozialismus*. Göttingen: Vandenhoeck & Ruprecht, 2003.

Raphael, Lutz. *Recht und Ordnung. Herrschaft durch Verwaltung im 19. Jahrhundert*. Frankfurt a.M.: S. Fischer, 2000.

Reichardt, Sven. "Einführung. Überwachungsgeschichte(n)." *Geschichte und Gesellschaft* 42, no. 1 (2016): 5–33.

Reinalter, Helmut. "Aufgeklärter Absolutismus und Josephinismus." In *Der Josephinismus. Bedeutung, Einflüsse und Wirkungen*, ed. Helmut Reinalter, 11–21. Frankfurt a.M.: Peter Lang, 1993.

Retallack, James. *Red Saxony: Election Battles and the Spectre of Democracy in Germany, 1860–1918*. Oxford: Oxford University Press, 2017.

Reulecke, Jürgen. *Geschichte der Urbanisierung in Deutschland*. Frankfurt a.M.: Suhrkamp, 1985.

Reulecke, Martin. *Gleichheit und Strafrecht im deutschen Naturrecht des 18. und 19. Jahrhunderts*. Tübingen: Mohr Siebeck, 2007.

Ringer, Fritz K. *The Decline of the German Mandarins*. Cambridge, MA: Harvard University Press, 1969.

Richter, Hedwig. *Moderne Wahlen. Eine Geschichte der Demokratie in Preußen und den USA im 19. Jahrhundert*. Hamburg: Hamburger Edition, 2017.

Ritter, Gerhard A. *Arbeiterbewegung, Parteien und Parlamentarismus*. Göttingen: Vandenhoeck & Ruprecht, 1976.

———. *Der Sozialstaat. Entstehung und Entwicklung im internationalen Vergleich*. Munich: Oldenbourg, 1989.

———. *Sozialversicherung in Deutschland und England: Entstehung und Grundzüge im Vergleich*. Munich: Beck, 1983.

Röhl, John C. G. *Wilhelm II: The Kaiser's Personal Monarchy, 1888–1900*. Cambridge: Cambridge University Press, 2015.

Rosenberg, Hans. *Grosse Depression und Bismarckzeit. Wirtschaftsablauf, Gesellschaft und Politik in Mitteleuropa*. Berlin: De Gruyter, 1967.

Rosenblum, Warren. *Beyond the Prison Gates. Punishment & Welfare in Germany, 1850–1933*. Chapel Hill: University of North Carolina Press, 2008.

———. "Welfare and Justice." In *Crime and Criminal Justice in Modern Germany*, ed. Richard F. Wetzell, 158–81. New York: Berghahn Books, 2014.

Rosenwein, Barbara H. *Generations of Feeling: A History of Emotions, 600–1700*. Cambridge: Cambridge University Press, 2016.

Rossol, Nadine. "Repräsentationskultur und Verfassungsfeiern der Weimarer Republik." In *Demokratiekultur in Europa, Politische Repräsentation im 19. und 20. Jahrhundert*, ed. Detlef Lehnert, 261–80. Cologne: Böhlau, 2011.

———. "Weltkrieg und Verfassung als Gründungserzählung der Republik." *Aus Politik und Zeitgeschichte* 50–51 (2008): 13–18.

Rousseau, Jean-Jacques. *Discourse on Political Economy and the Social Contract*, trans. Christopher Betts. Oxford: Oxford University Press, 1999.
Rublack, Ulinka. "Interior States and Sexuality in Early Modern Germany." In *After the History of Sexuality: German Genealogies with and beyond Foucault*, ed. Scott Spector, Helmut Puff, and Dagmar Herzog, 43–62. New York: Berghahn Books, 2012.
Ruster, Thomas. *Die verlorene Nützlichkeit der Religion. Katholizismus und Moderne in der Weimarer Republik*. Paderborn: Schöningh, 1994.
Sabean, David Warren. *Power in the Blood*. Cambridge: Cambridge University Press, 1984.
Sabrow, Martin. *Der Rathenaumord. Rekonstruktion einer Verschwörung gegen die Republik von Weimar*. Munich: Oldenbourg, 1994.
Schauz, Désirée. *Strafen als moralische Besserung. Eine Geschichte der Straffälligenfürsorge 1777– 1933*. Munich: Oldenbourg, 2008.
Schenk, Christina. *Bestrebungen zur einheitlichen Regelung des Strafvollzugs in Deutschland von 1870 bis 1923. Mit einem Ausblick auf die Strafvollzugsgesetzentwürfe von 1927*. Frankfurt a.M.: Lang, 2001.
Schivelbusch, Wolfgang. *Die Kultur der Niederlage: Der amerikanische Süden 1865—Frankreich 1871—Deutschland 1918*. Berlin: Rowohlt, 2012.
Schorske, Carl E. *German Social Democracy, 1905–1917. The Development of the Great Schism*. Cambridge, MA: Harvard University Press, 1955.
Schröder, Rainer. "Die strafrechtliche Bewältigung der Streiks durch Obergerichtliche Rechtssprechung zwischen 1870 und 1914." *Archiv Für Sozialgeschichte* 31 (1991): 85–102.
Schubert, Werner. *Entstehung des Strafgesetzbuchs*. Vol. 1. Baden-Baden: Nomos Verlag, 2002.
Schumann, Dirk. *Political Violence in the Weimar Republic, 1918–1933. Fight for the Streets and Fear of Civil War*, trans. Thomas Dunlap. New York: Berghahn Books, 2009.
Schwab, Dieter. "Familie." In *Geschichtliche Grundbegriffe. Historisches Lexikon zur Politisch-Sozialen Sprache in Deutschland*, ed. Otto Brunner, Werner Conze, and Reinhart Koselleck, vol. 2, 253–301. Stuttgart: Klett-Cotta, 1975.
Searle, G. R. *Morality and the Market in Victorian Britain*. Oxford: Clarendon Press; Oxford University Press, 1998.
Siemann, Wolfram. *Die Deutsche Revolution von 1848/49*. Frankfurt a.M.: Suhrkamp, 1985.
Siemens, Daniel. *Metropole und Verbrechen. Die Gerichtsreportage in Berlin, Paris und Chicago 1919–1933*. Stuttgart: Steiner, 2007.
Spendel, Günter. "Gustav Radbruchs politischer Weg." In *Gustav Radbruch als Reichsjustizminister (1921–1923)*, ed. Irina Mohr, 24–34. Berlin: Mohr, 2004.
Spierenburg, Pieter. "Geweld, repressie en schaamte. Enige historische gegevens." *Tijdschrift voor criminology* 20 (1978): 133–38.
———. *The Prison Experience. Disciplinary Institutions and Their Inmates in Early Modern Europe*. Amsterdam: Amsterdam University Press: 2007.
———. *The Spectacle of Suffering. Executions and the Evolution of Repression from a Preindustrial Metropolis to the European Experience*. Cambridge: Cambridge University Press, 1984.
———. *Violence and Punishment. Civilizing the Body through Time*. Cambridge: Polity, 2013.
Stargardt, Nicholas. *The German Idea of Militarism. Radical and Socialist Critics, 1866–1914*. Cambridge: Cambridge University Press, 1994.
Stark, Gary D. *Banned in Berlin. Literary Censorship in Imperial Germany 1871–1918*. New York: Berghahn Books, 2009.

Stolleis, Michael. *Geschichte des öffentlichen Rechts in Deutschland*. Vol. 2. Staatsrechtslehre und Verwaltungswissenschaft: 1800–1914. Munich: Beck, 1992.

Stewart, Frank Henderson. *Honor*. Chicago: University of Chicago Press, 1994.

Swett, Pamela E. "Political Violence, Gesinnung, and the Courts in Late Weimar Berlin." In *Conflict, Catastrophe and Continuity. Essays on Modern German History*, ed. Frank Biess, Mark Roseman, and Hanna Schissler, 60–79. New York: Berghahn Books, 2007.

Tenfelde, Klaus. *Arbeiter, Bürger, Städte. zur Sozialgeschichte des 19. und 20. Jahrhundert*. Göttingen: Vandenhoeck & Ruprecht, 2012.

———. "Großstadtjugend in Deutschland vor 1914: Eine historisch-demographische Annäherung." *Vierteljahrschrift für Sozial- und Wirtschaftsgeschichte* 69, no. 2 (1982): 182–218.

Thompson, E. P. "The Moral Economy of the English Crowd in the Eighteenth Century." *Past & Present* 50 (1971): 76–136.

———. *Whigs and Hunters*. London: Allen Lane, 1975.

Tiedemann, Klaus. *Konkurs-Strafrecht*. Berlin: De Gruyter, 1985.

Tilly, Richard H. *Kapital, Staat und sozialer Protest in der deutschen Industrialisierung. Gesammelte Aufsätze*. Göttingen: Vandenhoeck & Ruprecht, 1980.

Ulbicht, Otto. "Supplikationen als Ego-Dokumente. Bittschriften von Leibeigenen aus der ersten Hälfte des 17. Jahrhunderts als Beispiel." In *Ego-Dokumente. Annäherung an den Menschen in der Geschichte*, ed. Winfried Schulze, 149–74. Berlin: Akademie Verlag, 1996.

Verhey, Jeffrey. *The Spirit of 1914. Militarism, Myth, and Mobilization in Germany*. Cambridge: Cambridge University Press, 2000.

Vogt, Ludgera, and Arnold Zingerle. *Ehre. Archaische Momente in der Moderne*. Frankfurt a.M.: Suhrkamp, 1994.

Vormbaum, Thomas. *Eid, Meineid und Falschaussage. Reformdiskussion und Gesetzgebung seit 1870*. Berlin: Duncker & Humblot, 1990.

———. *Einführung in die moderne Strafrechtsgeschichte*. Berlin: Springer, 2011.

———. *Politik und Gesinderecht im neunzehnten Jahrhundert vornehmlich in Preußen 1810–1918*. Berlin: Duncker & Humblot, 1980.

Wachsmann, Nikolaus. "Between Reform and Repression. Imprisonment in Weimar Germany." In *Crime and Criminal Justice in Modern Germany*, ed. Richard F. Wetzell, 115–36. New York: Berghahn Books, 2014.

———. *Hitler's Prisons: Legal Terror in Nazi Germany*. New Haven, CT: Yale University Press, 2004.

Wacquant, Loïc. *Punishing the Poor. The Neoliberal Government of Social Insecurity*. Durham, NC: Duke University Press, 2009.

Wagner, Joachim. *Politischer Terrorismus und Strafrecht im Deutschen Kaiserreich von 1871*. Heidelberg: v. Decker, 1981.

Wagner, Patrick. *Volksgemeinschaft ohne Verbrecher. Konzeptionen und Praxis der Kriminalpolizei in der Zeit der Weimarer Republik und des Nationalsozialismus*. Hamburg: Christians, 1996.

Weber, Max. "Zeugenaussage im Prozeß gegen Ernst Toller." In *Gesamtausgabe*, 16: 485–91. Tübingen: Mohr Siebeck, 1988.

Wehler, Hans-Ulrich. *Das Deutsche Kaiserreich, 1871–1918*. Göttingen: Vandenhoeck & Ruprecht, 1973.

———. *Deutsche Gesellschaftsgeschichte*. Vol. 1. vom Feudalismus des Alten Reiches bis zur defensiven Modernisierung der Reformära 1700–1815. Munich: Beck, 1987.

———. *Deutsche Gesellschaftsgeschichte*. Vol. 4. vom Beginn des Ersten Weltkriegs bis zur Gründung der beiden deutschen Staaten 1914–1949. Munich: Beck, 2003.

Whitman, James Q. *Harsh Justice. Criminal Punishment and the Widening Divide between America and Europe*. Oxford: Oxford University Press, 2005.

———. "On Nazi 'Honour' and the New European 'Dignity.'" In *Darker Legacies of Law in Europe. The Shadow of National Socialism and Fascism over Europe and Its Legal Traditions*, ed. Christian Joerges and Navraj Singh Ghaleigh, 243–66. London: Bloomsbury, 2003.

———. "What Is Wrong with Inflicting Shame Sanctions?" *Yale Law Journal* 107, no. 4 (1998): 1055–92.

Wiedner, Hartmut. "Soldatenmißhandlungen im Wilhelminischen Kaiserreich (1890–1914)." *Archiv Für Sozialgeschichte* 22 (1982): 159–99.

Wienfort, Monika. "Zurschaustellung der Monarchie. Huldigungen und Thronjubiläen in Preußen-Deutschland und Großbritannien im 19. Jahrhundert." In *Symbolische Macht und inszenierte Staatlichkeit. "Verfassungskultur" als Element der Verfassungsgeschichte*, ed. Peter Brandt, Arthur Schlegelmilch, and Reinhard Wendt, 81–100. Bonn: Dietz, 2005.

Wilde, Marc de. "Just Trust Us. A Short History of Emergency Powers and Constitutional Change." *Comparative Legal History* 3, no. 1 (2015): 110–30.

Wilke, Malte. *Staatsanwälte als Anwälte des Staates?. Die Strafverfolgungspraxis von Reichsanwaltschaft und Bundesanwaltschaft vom Kaiserreich bis in die frühe Bundesrepublik*. Beiträge zu Grundfragen des Rechts; Band 16. Göttingen: Vandenhoeck & Ruprecht, 2016.

Wunder, Bernd. "Die Reform Der Beamtenschaft in den Rheinbundstaaten." In *Reformen im Rheinbündischen Deutschland*, ed. E. Weis, 181–93. Munich: Oldenbourg, 1984.

———. *Geschichte der Bürokratie in Deutschland*. Frankfurt a.M.: Suhrkamp, 1991.

Würgler, Andreas. "Voices from among the 'Silent Masses.' Humble Petitions and Social Conflicts in Early Modern Central Europe." *International Review of Social History* 46, no. 9 (2001): 11–34.

Zaeske, Susan. *Signatures of Citizenship. Petitioning, Antislavery, and Women's Political Identity*. Chapel Hill: University of North Carolina Press, 2003.

Ziemann, Benjamin. "Sozialmilitarismus und Militärische Sozialisation im Deutschen Kaiserreich 1870–1914." *Geschichte in Wissenschaft und Unterricht* 53, no. 3 (2002): 148–64.

Zunkel, Friedrich. "Ehre, Reputation." In *Geschichtliche Grundbegriffe. Historisches Lexikon zur politisch-sozialen Sprache in Deutschland*, ed. Otto Brunner, Werner Conze, and Reinhart Koselleck, vol. 2, 1–63. Stuttgart: Klett-Cotta, 1975.

Index

anarchy, anarchism, 96–102, 111
  and Law on explosives (1884), 100
Anti-Socialist Laws (*Sozialistengesetze*), 84, 94–5, 100–03, 108
antisemitism, 87, 108
Arco-Valley, Anton Graf von, 178–79
army
  General Staff of the Prussian army, 55–61, 73
  honor and the army, 49–51, 56–61, 100–02, 158–68, 209–11
  labor divisions, 60, 167
  militarization, 50, 58, 100
  military courts of honor, 15, 73
  pedagogy, 50, 59, 74, 157, 164
  reserve officers, 72–3
  See also conscription
Arnim, Harry von, 103–04

Baader, Ottilie, 62
bankrupcy, 21, 72
Bavarian Council Republic, 174, 177–8, 183, 202
Bebel, August, 53, 94, 101, 104, 113, 115
Binding, Karl, 51, 59, 74, 92
Birkmeyer, Karl, 59
Bismarck, Otto von, 40, 54, 56, 94, 103–04
Blood Protection Law (*Blutschutzgesetz*), 199
bodies, bodily/physical characteristics of offenders, 6–7, 51, 57, 60, 161–5, 208
bureaucracy, bureaucratic reforms, 3, 10–11, 17, 21, 37, 126–8, 132, 190–95
Burgfrieden. *See* World War I

Calker, Fritz von, 91–92, 183
citizenship, 1, 7, 10–12, 20–25, 30–33, 38–41, 62–64, 74, 146, 157, 168, 192, 209–11
  female, 22, 62, 189

  irreproachableness (*Unbescholtenheit*) and, 38–40
  National Socialism on, 197, 199
  Prussian Municipal Ordinance (1808) on, 21–22, 188, 206
civil privileges/*bürgerliche Ehrenrechte*
  penal law, 22–23
  provisionality of, 20–25, 206
  restoration of, 35–38
civil servants, 21–22, 31, 103, 136, 139, 145–46, 155
class/social stratification, 3, 9, 27, 30–35, 39–40, 51–53, 98, 102–03, 113–14, 127–29, 198, 206
  bourgeoisie, 9–10, 39–40, 103, 127, 142–43
  Klassenjustiz, 108, 113, 187
  Lumpenproletariat, 115
Code of Criminal Procedure (1877), 95
Communist Party (KPD), 178–79, 187, 199
conscription, 22, 48–51, 57–61, 100, 153–54, 163–66, 168, 209
Constitutio Criminalis Theresiana, 27–8
constitution, 22, 25
  constitutional monarchy, 25, 140
  Prussian constitution, 22
  Weimar Constitution, 173–74, 187–89, 198
corporal punishment (*Prügelstrafe*), 5, 70, 127
crime
  counterfeiture, 27, 29, 82
  theft/robbery, 30–32, 35, 52, 84, 88, 98, 107, 117, 142, 148, 155, 160, 165, 167, 192, 197
  high treason, 90–96, 99–104, 123, 175–79, 182
  lèse majesté (*Majestätsbeleidigung*), 90, 108–09, 123, 161

perjury, 22, 26–29, 32, 34, 44, 84–88, 91, 104–08, 130, 132, 139, 143, 188
pursuit of profit (*Gewinnsucht*), 29–31, 88, 99, 155, 161, 187, 194
crime statistics, 49, 60, 84–89, 103, 118, 163
criminal registry, 130–34
criminal underworld, 97–98
criminology, 12–13, 27, 43, 48, 59, 97, 105, 132, 138–40, 155, 185, 209
  Schulenstreit between classical and modern scholars, 58–61, 70, 74, 91–92, 119, 143, 175, 188
Crispien, Artur, 174

Dave, Victor, 96, 98
Delaquis, Ernst, 130, 135, 138–143, 166
deportation, 126–28
Dietz, Heinrich, 49, 60
Durkheim, Emile, 7–8, 33–34, 38, 208, 211

early modern Europe/Ancien Regime, 9–10, 14, 27, 127
Ebert, Friedrich, 173
Eisner, Kurt, 177–79
emotions. *See also* honor
empathy, 144–47, 192
Enlightenment, 28, 38, 44, 139–40
entitlement, sense of, 25, 40, 143, 146, 154, 189–90, 192
Essen perjury trial (Essener Meineidsprozess), 106

Fechenbach, Felix, Trial, 196
fellow travelers, 180–83, 186
felony disenfranchisement, 2–14, 21–27, 31–40, 48–55, 59, 62, 74, 84, 126, 129, 172–175, 181, 184–88, 196, 199–200, 206–12
  in France, 9, 21
  and National Socialism, 1–2, 11, 196–200
  in the USA, 9
Fichte, Johann Gottlieb, 30–32
Finkelnburg, Karl, 130–31
Foucault, Michel, 6, 50, 70
Frankfurt Parliament, 52

Freedom of Movement Act 1967, 129
Friedberg, Heinrich von, 54, 57
Friedrich Wilhelm IV (King of Prussia), 90
Frohme, Karl, 80, 105–06

Gädke, Richard, 73
Garland, David, 6
Gauvain, Herrmann von, 39
Gesinnung (disposition), 26–27, 50, 55, 190
  dishonorable disposition (*ehrlose Gesinnung*), 30–32, 43, 68, 83–85, 90–104, 114–16, 173–88, 194–96, 208
Gesinnungsstrafrecht, 91–92, 102, 187–88
Gierke, Otto von, 39
Globig, Hans Ernst von, 28, 140
Guckenheimer, Eduard, 93, 99, 183–84

Harden, Maximilian, 109
Hegel, Georg Wilhelm Friedrich, 40
Hentig, Hans von, 182–83
Hepp, Carl, 24, 29
Himmler, Heinrich, 1, 2, 200
Hitler, Adolf, 199
Hoenig, Fritz, 73
Holtzendorff, Franz von, 104
honor
  Bourdieu on, 9
  civil, 13, 24, 38–40, 55, 74, 199–200, 207
  diffusion of honor concepts, 8–9, 39
  economic solidity/independence and, 30, 40, 143–44
  honor punishment (*Ehrenstrafe*), 2, 88, 176
  sense of, 5, 50, 67–70, 203, 209
  shame and, 5, 125, 127, 143, 211
  Simmel on, 9
  trust and, 7, 24–39, 43–44, 71, 84–85, 191
Humboldt, Wilhelm von, 40
Huster, Johann Georg, 28, 140
hygiene, 60

Ibsen, Karl, 104
imprisonment
  fortress confinement (*Festungshaft*), 55, 90, 93–94, 202

penitentiary (*Zuchthaus*), 3, 19, 24, 35–37, 49, 51, 53, 55–57, 59–60, 65–66, 69–71, 76, 88, 93–97, 99–113, 118, 128–130, 137, 142, 144–45, 154–63, 168, 175–81, 187, 190, 196
pretrial detention (*Untersuchungshaft*), 71
regular prison, 3, 65–70, 89, 95, 104, 109–10, 118, 131, 181–83
indemnity, 71
independence. *See* honor
Internationale Kriminalistische Vereinigung (IKV, the International Criminal Law Assocation), 130, 172, 175, 183–85, 187, 203

Jacobsen, Adolf, 72
Jacoby, Johann, 90
Jews
  crime statistics on, 87–88
  disenfranchisement and, 1–2, 199–200, 210
John, Richard, 91
Juristentag, 54, 187

Kaiser Wilhelm I, 126, 136–37, 142
Kaiser Wilhelm II, 125–26, 136–38, 141–45, 159–163, 166
Kant, Immanuel, 90
Kapp-Lüttwitz Putsch, 180–83
Kinkel, Gottfried, 116
Kirchheimer, Otto, 83
Kleinschrod, Gallus Aloys, 33
Krohne, Karl, 66
Kulturkampf, 87
Laband, Paul, 73, 140

labor
  precarious, 9
  in prisons, 65–69
Lasker, Eduard, 93
Laufkötter, Franz, 116
Law for the protection of the Republic (*Republikschutzgesetz*), 172, 195
Legien, Carl, 111, 114
Leuss, Hans, 108
Levine, Eugene, 178–79

Liebknecht, Karl, 100–02, 175–77
Liebknecht, Wilhelm, 94, 98, 100
Liszt, Franz von, 9–10, 28, 59, 61, 66, 69, 92–93, 130, 141, 184–86
Local autonomy, 21
Luxemburg, Rosa, 176–77

Manteuffel, Otto Theodor von, 36
masculinity, 10, 30, 50, 67, 143, 161, 164, 189, 191
Medem, Rudolf, 59
mercy/grace, 37, 126, 131, 135–37, 140–42, 146, 154, 193
  amnesty, 136–37, 159–61, 163, 166–68, 182–83, 186, 209–210
Merkel, Julius, 25
miscegenation, 196, 199
Mittermaier, Carl Joseph Anton, 29, 51–53, 65
Moltke, Helmut von, 56–58

National Socialism, *Volk*, National socialist take on, 173, 188, 197–200, 210
National Socialism, 1–2, 198–200
Noellner, Friedrich, 23, 184
North German Confederation, 51, 54–56, 65, 129
Nuremberg Laws, 199

Oerter, Sepp, 100
Oestreich, Rudolf, 101–02
Oetker, Friedrich, 59, 188
offenders (types of)
  corrigibles, 13, 48, 70, 74, 157, 185, 187
  habitual offenders, 146, 155, 185
Olshausen, Justus, 101
Öttingen, Alexander von, 86
Otto, Gustav, 97–98, 129

parliament
  National Constitutional assembly, 173
  Prussian House of Representatives, 176
  Reichstag, 3, 40, 57, 62, 71–72, 93–94, 101–06, 111, 172, 176, 180–81, 196, 198
Paulsen, Friedrich, 74
Pedagogy, 50, 156–57

penal law
  Code pénal, 135
  draft penal reform of 1909, 10, 70, 142, 186
  General State Laws for the Prussian States (*Allgemeines Landrecht für die Preußischen Staaten*) (1897), 35, 127
  Lex Heinze (1892/1900), 84
  Municipal Ordinance of the Kingdom of Saxony from 1837
  Prussian Penal Code (1851), 20, 22, 54–55, 76, 89
  Reich Penal Code, 2, 13, 29, 49, 53, 56, 58, 61, 66, 69, 72–74, 84, 88–95, 101, 109, 110, 119, 142, 184, 208
Penitentiary Bill (*Zuchthausvorlage*) (1899), 109–13
Petitions (*Gnadengesuche*), 12–14, 37, 125–46, 154–62, 189–95, 210
Polenprozess (1847), 32
Polenstrafrechtsverordnung, 1
Political crime, political offenders, 31–32, 52–53, 83–4, 90–116, 161, 176–183, 195–98
  political assasinations, 93–94, 99, 119, 172, 177–180, 195, 197, 210
Posadowsky-Wehner. Arthur von, 110–11
prison societies (*Gefängnisvereine*), 69, 158–59, 164
punishment. *See* imprisonment, corporal punishment, felony disenfranchisement

Radbruch, Gustav, 185–88, 195–98
Reich Commercial and Industrial Code (*Reichsgewerbeordnung*), 65, 115
Reichstag. *See* parliament
remorse, 31–32, 142, 153–157, 162
Rethwisch, Ernst, 39
revolutions of 1848/49, 24–25, 52–53, 116
Rhine Strike, 181
Romen, Anton, 105–06
Roon, Albrecht Theodor von, 56
Rumpf, Ludwig, 96, 99

satire, 3, 62
Sattelzeit, 21, 34

Schmölder, Robert, 49, 51, 58–61, 157
Sedition Bill (*Umsturzvorlage*), 110
serving classes (*Gesinde*), 34–35
Seyfarth, Heinrich, 158, 164–66
Simmel, Georg, 9
Social Democrats, social democracy, 62, 71, 94–95, 98, 100, 102, 105–116, 159–61, 169, 176–77, 180
  Independent Socialist Party (USPD), 174–77, 181
  Majority Social Democratic Party of Germany (MSPD), 173, 176, 179–181, 184–185, 187
  Social Democratic Party of Germany (SPD), 103–107, 111, 113–15, 176
Stadthagen, Arnold, 102, 176
Stahl, Julius Friedrich, 33
Starke, Wilhelm, 86, 105
Stein-Hardenberg Reforms, 21
Stein, Karl vom und zum, 21–22
Steinmetz, Karl von, 56–57
Stigma, stigmatization, 29, 104, 126, 131, 184, 208
  Ervin Goffman on stigma management, 126
strikes, 103, 109–14, 180–81
Stüve, Johann Carl Bertram, 33

terrorism, 103, 111
Toller, Ernst, 178
Tönnies, Ferdinand, 62
transportation. *See* deportation

unions, 64–65, 106–07, 111, 113–14, 131

Vormärz, 2, 21, 23, 35, 42
voting rights, 22, 62–64, 103, 173, 180, 187, 196
  Dreiklassenwahlrecht, 62, 173
  German Empire, 53
  Reichsgesetz über die Wahlen der abgeordneten zum Volkshause (1848), 52–53

Wahlberg, Emil, 54, 104
war enthusiasm, 157–59, 163–64
Weber, Max, 21, 113, 178

welfare
    insurance funds, 64–65, 74, 131–32
    and prisons, 6–7, 12, 153–54, 162–67
    social security, 64, 67
    Weimar welfare state, 174–75, 192, 195

Wick, Adolf von, 24–37
Wick, Friedrich von, 35
World War I, 8, 153–68

Zachariae, Karl Salomo, 22, 140

www.ingramcontent.com/pod-product-compliance
Lightning Source LLC
Chambersburg PA
CBHW051537020426
42333CB00016B/1967